Praise for *Frederick the Wise*

To his family, friends, peers, and subjects, Elector Frederick the Wise of Saxony was much more than simply Martin Luther's noble protector. Dr. Wellman's thoroughly researched and engaging biography paints a vivid image of the Saxon elector. It is sure to become a valuable resource for students of German history and the Reformation period. Interested readers will be introduced to a Christian prince whose humanity and integrity were rare for someone of his elite status within the German empire. They will also encounter political intrigue and scandalous behavior. Praiseworthy, yet not without his flaws, Frederick the Wise steps out from the pages as an exceptional and noteworthy man of his time.

—Paul M. Bacon, PhD
Adjunct Professor of Art History
Dominican University
River Forest, IL

Sam Wellman's telling of the story of the public and personal life of Luther's celebrated protector, Frederick the Wise, is a welcome addition to Reformation scholarship as we approach 2017. His careful research and well-crafted prose provide readers with insights into the risky yet resolute Christian prince who defended Luther even as he received the consolation of evangelical pastoral care from the Reformer. Aspects of the relationship between these two men often only alluded to in standard Luther biographies are developed with precision by Wellman. In this book we learn much about Frederick but a lot about Luther as well.

—John T. Pless, MDiv
Assistant Professor of Pastoral Ministry and Missions
Concordia Theological Seminary
Fort Wayne, IN

In a biography with the character development, twists and turns, and absorbing storyline of a novel, Sam Wellman recreates the life and times of the powerful and resourceful ruler who made the Reformation possible. Duke Frederick emerges as the adult in the room of squabbling princes and an inept emperor. A man of peace, a vigorous patron of the arts and education, and a skillful player in the byzantine mazes of late medieval politics, Frederick was also a man of moral and theological contradictions. But Frederick was a shrewd and stalwart defender of Martin Luther, who was not above criticizing his protector. This book brings the historical context of the Reformation to life.

—Gene Edward Veith, PhD
Professor of Literature
Patrick Henry College

Frederick the Wise typically plays a supporting role in histories of the Lutheran Reformation—important, but in the wings. Here he rightfully occupies center stage. Wellman's quick-moving treatment of Frederick's life is a delight to read and fills an important gap in English-language Reformation resources.

—Lawrence R. Rast Jr., PhD
President, Concordia Theological Seminary
Fort Wayne, IN

Sam Wellman has written a thorough biography of one of the most significant princes in late medieval Germany. While many recognize Frederick's important role in the early part of the Lutheran Reformation, Wellman's biography reveals Frederick's significance as an elector in the Holy Roman Empire of the German nation. This work also demonstrates Frederick's political sophistication as someone connected to the most powerful leaders of his own time. Simply put, if Luther's Reformation had never occurred, scholars would still find Frederick's life to be a compelling object of scholarship. However, the Lutheran Reformation did take place and Wellman's biography explains the political and social context of that pivotal event. Frederick's defense and support of Martin Luther in the early 1520s ensured that the Reformation did succeed as a social and political movement.

—Matthew Phillips, PhD
Associate Professor of History
Concordia University Nebraska

FREDERICK THE WISE

SEEN AND UNSEEN LIVES OF MARTIN LUTHER'S PROTECTOR

Sam Wellman

CONCORDIA PUBLISHING HOUSE • SAINT LOUIS

Published 2015 by Concordia Publishing House
3558 S. Jefferson Ave., St. Louis, MO 63118-3968
1-800-325-3040 • www.cph.org
Text © 2011 Sam Wellman

Scripture quotations from the ESV Bible® (The Holy Bible, English Standard Version®), copyright © 2001 by Crossway Bibles, a division of Good News Publishers. Used by permission. All rights reserved.

The quotations from Luther's Works in this publication are from *Luther's Works*, American Edition (56 vols.; St. Louis: Concordia Publishing House and Philadelphia: Fortress Press, 1955–86).

Quotations from Paul M. Bacon, "Mirror of a Christian Prince: Frederick the Wise and Art Patronage in Electoral Saxony," (PhD diss., University of Wisconsin-Madison, 2004) used by permission of author.

Quotations from *Here I Stand* by Roland Bainton ©1950, renewal 1977 Abingdon-Cokesbury Press. Used by permission.

Quotations from Susan Karant-Nunn, "Luther's Pastors: The Reformation in the Ernestine Countryside" in *Transactions of the American Philosophical Society* 69 (1979). Used by permission.

Manufactured in the United States of America

Library of Congress Cataloging-in-Publication Data

Wellman, Sam.

Frederick the Wise / Sam Wellman.

pages cm

Includes bibliographical references and index.

ISBN 978-0-7586-4917-1

1. Frederick III, Elector of Saxony, 1463-1525. 2. Saxony (Germany)--Kings and rulers--Biography. 3. Reformation--Biography. I. Title.

DD801.S382W45 2015

943'.21029092--dc23

[B]   2014038251

1 2 3 4 5 6 7 8 9 10   24 23 22 21 20 19 18 17 16 15

TABLE OF CONTENTS

ILLUSTRATIONS

CONTEMPORARIES RELEVANT
TO FREDERICK THE WISE

WETTIN FAMILY

Frederick the Meek (*der Sanftmütige*) [1412–64], Frederick's grandfather and Elector of Saxony (1428–64).

Ernst of Saxony [1441–86], Frederick's father and Elector of Saxony (1464–86).

Albrecht the Courageous (*der Beherzte*) [1443–1500], Frederick's uncle and ruling duke of Albertine Saxony; one of the imperial military leaders.

Ernst of Saxony [1464–1513], Frederick's irritating brother and archbishop of Magdeburg.

Albrecht of Saxony [1467–84], Frederick's brother and administrator of Mainz archbishopric.

Johann the Constant (*der Beständige*) [1468–1532], Frederick's brother and Elector of Saxony (1525–32).

Christine of Saxony [1461–1521], Frederick's sister and wife of King Johann I of Denmark, Norway, and Sweden; mother of King Christian II.

Margarete of Saxony [1469–1528], Frederick's sister and wife of Prince Heinrich of Braunschweig-Lüneburg.

Johann Friedrich the Magnanimous (*der Großmütige*) [1503–54], Frederick's nephew and ill-fated Elector of Saxony (1532–47).

George the Bearded [1471–1539], Frederick's troublesome cousin and ruling duke of Albertine Saxony.

Wilhelm III the Brave (*der Tapfere*) of Saxony [1425–82], Frederick's great uncle and Landgrave of Thuringia; fought Elector Frederick the Meek in the infamous "Brother War."

Elisabeth [1443–84], Frederick's mother; sister of Albrecht IV of Bavaria.

Margaretha [1416–86], Frederick's paternal grandmother; sister of Emperor Frederick.

Claus Narr [c. 1435–1515], Frederick's legendary jester.

"SECRET FAMILY"

Anna [?1480–1525+], Frederick's "God-given wife."

Sebastien [c. 1500–35], "Bastien"; Frederick's first son by Anna.

Friedrich [?1502–25+], "Fritz"; Frederick's second son by Anna.

CLERGY

Martin Luther [1483–1546], Augustinian professor of Bible in Wittenberg and religious reformer.

Johann von Staupitz [1460–1524], Augustinian general vicar and organizer of university in Wittenberg; longtime acquaintance of Frederick as well as Luther's mentor.

Andreas Karlstadt [1486–1541], professor and volatile religious reformer.

Thomas Müntzer [c. 1488–1525], religious reformer, violently radical; local leader in *Bauernkrieg*.

Jakob Vogt [?–1522], Frederick's longtime Franciscan father confessor.

Gabriel von Eyb [1455–1535], prince bishop of Eichstätt; one of Frederick's "favorites."

Friedrich IV, Margrave of Baden [1458–1517], bishop of Eutrecht; one of Frederick's "favorites."

Lorenz von Bibra [1459–1519], prince bishop of Würzburg; one of Frederick's "favorites."

IMPERIAL TERRITORIAL PRINCES

Philipp the Magnanimous (*der Großmütige*) [1504–67], Landgrave of Hesse (1518–67). His long regency was trouble for Frederick.

Ulrich, Duke of Württemberg [1487–1550]; ruthless, unpopular. In 1519 the Swabian League caused loss of his duchy for fifteen years.

Albrecht IV, Duke of Bavaria [1447–1508], Frederick's maternal uncle. Married Kunigunde, daughter of Emperor Frederick. Shining linguist.

ELECTORAL PRINCES

Richard von Greiffenklau [1467–1531], Trier archbishop (1511–31); one of Frederick's close and trusted acquaintances.

Berthold von Henneberg [1442–1504], Mainz archbishop (1484–1504); one of Frederick's "favorite colleagues." Firebrand imperial reformer.

Albrecht of Brandenburg [1490–1545], Mainz archbishop (1514–45); one of Frederick's milder foes.

Hermann IV of Hesse [1450–1508], Cologne archbishop (1480–1508); one of Frederick's "favorite colleagues."

Joachim I [1484–1535], Brandenburg elector (1499–1535); a mild foe of Frederick.

Johann Cicero [1455–99], Brandenburg elector (1486–99); one of Frederick's "favorite colleagues."

Philipp [1448–1508], Palatine elector (1476–1508); one of Frederick's "favorite colleagues." Lost heavily in the Bavarian Succession War.

Johann II, Margrave of Baden [1434–1503], Trier elector (1456–1503); one of Frederick's "favorite colleagues."

FOREIGN SOVEREIGNS

Ferdinand of Aragon [1452–1516]. As regent for daughter Joanna, he was virtual king of united Spain (1506–16); grandfather of emperors Karl V and Ferdinand I.

Christian II [1481–1559], king of Denmark (1513–23); Frederick's nephew.

Henry VIII [1491–1547], king of England (1509–47); in Frederick's lifetime not yet infamous.

Matthias Corvinus [1443–90], king of Hungary (1458–90) and part of Bohemia. Dangerous foe of the empire; occupied eastern Austria (1485–90).

Vladislaus II [1456–1516], son of the Polish king Casimir IV. King of Bohemia (1471–1516); king of Hungary (1490–1516). Weak but enduring sovereign.

Charles VIII [1470–98], king of France (1483–98); reviled (and underestimated) by Maximilian.

Louis XII [1462–1515], king of France (1498–1515); aggressive, effective sovereign.

Francois I [1494–1547], king of France (1515–47); Duke of Valois.

Charles the Bold, Duke of Burgundy [1433–77], father of Maria, wife of Maximilian and mother of Philipp the Fair and Margarethe of Austria.

Anne, Duchess of Brittany [1477–1514], queen of France for Charles VIII (1491–98), for Louis XII (1499–1514). Proxy marriage in 1490 to Maximilian I not consummated.

René II, Duke of Lorraine [1451–1508], Frederick's friend and fellow negotiator between Maximilian and the French court. In 1477 René defeated Charles the Bold at Nancy.

SAXON ELECTORAL OFFICIALS

George Spalatin [1484–1545], Frederick's secretary, pastor, and confidant; Luther's confidant as well.

Fabian von Feilitzsch [c. 1457–1520], highly regarded adviser in Frederick's court.

Hans von der Planitz [c. 1473–1535], very competent diplomat for Frederick's court.

Heinrich von Bünau [?1465–1507], trusted adviser, confidant, and "Renaissance man."

Dr. Martin Mellerstadt [c. 1450–1513], Frederick's physician and organizer of university in Wittenberg. Fair scholar and as volatile as Luther.

Degenhart von Pfeffinger [1471–1519], financial administrator, key adviser, and serious relic collector.

Gregory Brück [c. 1485–1557], chancellor beginning 1520. Jurist and key adviser in "Luther affair."

Hans Hundt von Wenkheim [?–1509], early keeper of the privy purse and "accountant."

Hans von Leimbach [1445–1513], main financial administrator prior to Degenhart Pfeffinger.

Dr. Alvensleve Pasca [?–1525+], Frederick's physician and caretaker of his daughter in Magdeburg.

Heinrich von Ende [?1455–1515], dominant administrator in Frederick's early court.

Johann Mogenhofer [?1460–1510], powerful chancellor in Frederick's court in the middle years.

Dr. Hieronymus Schurff [1481–1554], outstanding university jurist who often advised Luther.

POPES

Julius II [1443–1513], pope (1503–13). Warring and building pope, amassed huge debts.

Leo X [1475–1521], pope (1513–21). Princely lifestyle and papal debt left by Julius II led to widespread corruption to raise money.

HABSBURGS

Friedrich III [1415–93], king/emperor (1452–93) of the Holy Roman Empire.

Maximilian I [1459–1519], son of Frederick III. King/emperor (1493–1519) of the Holy Roman Empire. Charismatic, reckless adventurer.

Philip the Fair [1478–1506], son of Maximilian I; sovereign of Burgundy. By marriage to mentally ill Joanna of Castile, de facto ruler of Castile.

Margarethe of Austria [1480–1533], daughter of Maximilian I. Guardian of Philip's children and governor of Burgundy for Karl.

Karl V [1500–58], son of Philip the Fair. King of Spain (1506–56). King/emperor (1519–56) of the Holy Roman Empire.

Ferdinand I [1503–64], son of Philip the Fair. De facto ruler of much of the Germanic empire (1519–56). King/emperor (1556–64) of the Holy Roman Empire.

IMPERIAL OFFICIALS

Matthäus Lang [1469–1540], so-called "Swabian" and malicious chamber secretary in Maximilian's inner circle. Bishop of Gurk.

Count Heinrich VII von Fürstenberg [1464–99], so-called "Swabian" and Hofmarshall in Maximilian's inner circle.

Dr. Konrad Stürtzel [c. 1435–1509], so-called "Swabian" in Maximilian's inner circle. Chancellor and behind-the-scenes intriguer.

Jean Glapion [c. 1460–1522], chaplain and duplicitous negotiator in Karl V's inner circle.

SCHOLARS AND ARTISTS

Albrecht Dürer [1471–1528], Nuremberger. One of Frederick's favorite artists.

Jacopo de Barbari [c. 1440–c. 1516], Venetian artist in Frederick's court for a short time.

Lucas Cranach [1472–1553], artist in Frederick's court since 1505. Prolific and entrepreneurial.

Konrad Pflüger [?–c. 1505], Frederick's master builder since at least 1488.

Conrad Celtis [1459–1508], Humanist poet laureate of the empire, promoted by Frederick.

Desiderius Erasmus [1466–1536], Humanist scholar of renown.

WITTENBERGERS

Philip Melanchthon [1497–1560], Greek scholar and close colleague of Luther (and Spalatin). First systematic theologian of Evangelicals.

NUREMBERGERS

Anton Tucher [1458–1524], Patrician and longtime acquaintance of Frederick.

CHRONOLOGY OF EVENTS
RELEVANT TO FREDERICK THE WISE

1346

Wittenberg: Pope Clemens VI decreed the Castle Church a relic center subordinate only to the pope (thus, no local bishops).

1356

Golden Bull declared Saxon sovereign an elector and, in the emperor's absence, the imperial vicar of the eastern empire.

1398

Wittenberg: Pope Boniface IX granted the All Saints' Foundation of the Castle Church its own indulgence (Portiuncula-Ablaß) for All Saints' Day.

1423

Electoral rank gained for the Wettiners by Frederick's great grandfather, Frederick I the Warlike (*der Streitbare*) of Meissen.

1451

Frederick's grandfather Frederick II the Meek and his brother Wilhelm III the Brave ended the bloody six-year "Brother War."

1463

January 17 in Torgau: Frederick born to Elector Ernst and Elisabeth, sister of Bavaria's Duke Albrecht IV (the Wise).

1464

Frederick's father, Ernst, became Elector of Saxony.

1471

First great silver lode discovered in the Saxon Erzgebirge; many follow.

1473

Frederick began a rigorous, Latin-based education in Grimma.

1476

Uncle Albrecht the Courageous traveled to the Holy Land.

1480

Ernst traveled to Rome, gaining ecclesiastical plums for two sons and the Golden Rose for himself (but alienating his brother Albrecht).

1484

Frederick's brother Albrecht and mother Elisabeth died (probably both from the plague).

1485

Infamous division of Saxony in Leipzig (*Leipziger Teilung*).

1486

Reichstag in Frankfurt: possibly Frederick's first; Maximilian elected "king."

Father Ernst died from hunting accident; Frederick succeeded him as Elector Frederick III of Saxony.

Frederick worried about dangerous King Matthias Corvinus of Hungary who had conquered Vienna in 1485.

1487

Reichstag in Nuremberg: Frederick presented himself as a grand prince.

1488

Master builder Pflüger was already living in Wittenberg.

Frederick helped free Maximilian from captivity in Brussels.

Emperor Friedrich III rejuvenated military might of the Swabian League.

1489

Wittenberg: workers began not to renovate the old castle but to raze it.

1490

King Matthias Corvinus of Hungary died, ending threat from the East.

1493

Frederick expelled Jews from his electorate.

Frederick traveled to the Holy Land.

Emperor Friedrich III died, succeeded by son Maximilian.

1494

Frederick was retained as imperial councillor in Maximilian's court.

1495

Reichstag in Worms: "eternal peace" (*Ewiger Landfriede*) ended feud as way to resolve disputes.

1496

Frederick was first important patron of Albrecht Dürer, who painted his portrait as well as future altarpieces for Wittenberg Castle Church.

1497

Frederick resided in Austria to serve Maximilian.

1498

Frederick named imperial governor (*Reichsstatthalter*), next in authority to Maximilian.

Frederick abruptly cooled toward Maximilian and returned to Saxony.

1499

Approximate time when Frederick and "companion" Anna began their enduring relationship.

1500

Brother Johann married Sophie of Mecklenburg in a colossal wedding in Torgau.

Uncle Albrecht died. His son George, who succeeded him, was to prove unrelentingly antagonistic.

Maximilian appointed Frederick *Statthalter* of the newly created imperial governing council (*Reichsregiment*).

1502

The disingenuous imperial governing council (*Reichsregiment*) ended.

Wittenberg University founded; studies began October 18.

Near complete Wittenberg Castle Church consecrated by Cardinal Peraudi.

1503

Johann Friedrich, born to Johann and wife Sophie, became a legitimate heir to the electorate.

1504

Berthold, archbishop of Mainz, died.

Bavarian-Palatine succession war crushed the Palatine elector Philipp.

Wittenberg: Augustinian Hermits began building their cloister.

Lucas Cranach became Saxon electoral court painter (until he died in 1553).

1506

Frederick permanently broke with brother Ernst for sowing dissention among the Wettins and slurring his companion Anna.

Saxon electorate introduced inheritance books in the *Amts*.

1507

Reichstag in Constance: Pope Julius II appealed to the imperial estates to bequeath their relics to Frederick (who readied grand reliquaries).

1508

Martin Luther called to Wittenberg temporarily to teach Aristotle's ethics.

Spalatin joined the electoral court to tutor Johann's son.

Maximilian mandated an end to escalating disputes between Frederick and Cousin George.

1509

Taxing nine-year guardianship of Philipp, future Landgrave of Hesse, began.

Wittenberg: castle complex virtually completed.

Erfurt, semi-dependent on Saxony, began its bloody "Year of Madness."

The exceptional "Relic book" (*Heiltumbuch*) with woodcuts of Lucas Cranach printed.

1510

Gout and stones irreversibly ruined health of Frederick, who could rarely ride or hunt.

Frederick asked Spalatin to write the Saxon history and stock a relevant library.

1511

Luther called to Wittenberg to become professor of the Bible.

Albertine Saxon Frederick died, succeeded as *Hochmeister* of the Teutonic order by a Brandenburger. Saxons continued to decline as the Brandenburgers rose.

Pope prohibited concubines, much to chagrin of Frederick and "wife" Anna.

1512

Spalatin became university librarian with means to acquire books.

1513

Frederick suffered depression and poor eyesight as well as constant poor health.

Frederick's artists finally mastered a medallion for representation.

Brother Ernst, archbishop of Magdeburg, died of syphilis. Again a Brandenburger (Albrecht) succeeded a Saxon.

Frederick's relic collecting exploded; collection tripled in size in three years.

Frederick began a "Power Sharing" (*Mutschierung*) with Johann.

Frederick wrote letters to support the persecuted Hebrew scholar Reuchlin.

1514

Intensive building in Torgau at Hartenfels castle, Frederick's favorite residence.

Brandenburger (Albrecht) gained the highly desirable Mainz electorate.

Spalatin and Luther became friends, suggesting Frederick was also aware of Luther.

1516

Spalatin served only at the electoral court.

First known time Frederick took personal interest in Luther.

1517

October 31: Luther posted ninety-five theses against indulgences at Wittenberg Castle Church.

Albrecht of Mainz reported the "Luther affair" to Pope Leo X.

1518

Wittenberg: Melanchthon (Reuchlin's nephew) came as a Greek scholar.

Frederick allowed interrogation of Luther by Cardinal Cajetan in Augsburg.

1519

Maximilian died; Frederick was key to selecting the new emperor, abruptly changing the politics of Europe (including the pope).

Marriage contract between Johann Friedrich and Karl's sister Katharina was possible bribe for Frederick's vote.

Frederick rejected the crown himself and swung the election to Karl V.

Frederick conditioned Karl V's election on revival of the imperial governing council.

Luther's booklet "*Tessaradecas consolatoria pro laborantibus & onerantibus*" consoled Frederick during his worsening health.

1520

Wittenberg: university student unrest.

Frederick discussed Luther with Erasmus in Cologne.

Wittenberg: Luther burned the bull from the pope.

1521

Wittenberg: Castle Church displayed relics but offered no indulgences.

Karl V exempted the Wettin territory from extra-territorial courts.

Wittenberg: the university was reorganized.

Luther appeared before the emperor at the Worms *Reichstag*.

Frederick had Luther "kidnapped" and hidden at Wartburg castle.

Wittenberg: unrest triggered by Karlstadt and zealous reformers.

1522

Frederick appointed Spalatin court chaplain and preacher.

Luther returned to Wittenberg to restore order.

Frederick attended the revived imperial governing council in Nuremberg.

Frederick ended his acquisition of relics.

1523

Karl reneged on the marriage contract between Johann Friedrich and his sister.

King Christian II of Denmark sought refuge with his uncle Frederick.

Luther urged Frederick (unsuccessfully) to dissolve the century-old All Saints' Foundation.

1524

Wittenberg: Luther managed to stop the celebration of the Mass.

In Weimar, Johann and Johann Friedrich heard in alarm Thomas Müntzer's radical sermon; he disappeared, then resurfaced outside the territory.

1525

Spalatin urged Frederick (unsuccessfully) to reform all chapters, monasteries, and clergy.

Frederick's final will acknowledged "companion" Anna, two sons, and one daughter.

On his deathbed, Frederick took communion with both bread and wine.

May 5: Frederick died as countryfolk rebelled over much of the empire.

May 11: Frederick was buried in the Wittenberg Castle Church.

PREFACE

This work about Frederick the Wise drew from published sources, predominantly those in German and to a much lesser extent those in English. What it offers the curious who read only English is access to the German sources, which overwhelmingly dominate research on Frederick the Wise. The state archives in Weimar for Frederick the Wise and other Ernestine electors are famously "inexhaustible." Above all others, this work is indebted to Ingetraut Ludolphy and her biography *Friedrich der Weise* (1984). Her struggle to complete her *magnum opus* would be a book in itself. Dr. Ludolphy labored in the old German Democratic Republic (*Deutsche Demokratische Republik*; DDR) and was herself labeled a political "reactionary." Unable to publish her work in the DDR, she emigrated (perhaps illegally) as a "pensioner" to West Germany. Vandenhoeck & Ruprecht in Göttingen published her *Friedrich der Weise*. After reunification (*der Wende*), Dr. Ludolphy was able to return to Saxony. She turned ninety-three in 2014. She was kind enough in 2011 to read portions of this book and to offer numerous improvements. The mistakes that remain are solely my own.

This work owes much to librarians and library staffs in both Germany and the United States. Very helpful were those in Berlin (Staatbibliothek and Humboldt-Universitätbibliothek), Leipzig (Bibliothek Theologie at Universität Leipzig), and Lutherstadt Wittenberg (Bibliothek des Evangelischen Predigerseminars and the Stadtbibliothek). Equally supportive were libraries in Kansas (Newton Public Library and the Mennonite Library and Archives at Bethel College).

Numerous individuals helped. This work had a lightning start thanks to Dr. Martin Treu in Wittenberg summarizing (as of 2006) the research on the Ernestine Wettins, especially Frederick.

Special thanks are due to the support and advice of Rev. Paul T. McCain, editor Laura Lane, and others at Concordia Publishing House in St. Louis.

Particular thanks to my wife, Ruth, supportive throughout.

Figure 1: Frederick III of Saxony c. 1486 by Nuremberg Master (courtesy Städel Museum, Frankfurt am Main, and Artothek)

CHAPTER 1

THE BEGINNING

(1463–87)

> "If one wants to judge, then one should know
> the reason for matters from the beginning."
> —Proverb favored by Frederick the Wise[1]

WHEN A PRINCE DIES . . .

In late summer of 1486, couriers burst from Colditz, one of many castles serving the House of Wettin princes in Saxony. Over the next days messengers prompted more messengers in ever farther reaches. They urged their steeds through forests, past harvesting fields, on trails, along wagon furrows—all arteries into and out of cities and noble strongholds. Each courier surrendered his message at the destination to an official who, after judging its importance, rushed it to a superior. No one in the entire Holy Roman Empire dawdled over this message, for the news from Colditz was of imperial magnitude.

Ernst, the electoral prince of Saxony, was dead.

The great prince had died on the heels of hounds that chased that most noble prey, the red stag, in the most prime month of the hunt, August.[2] The prince collected spirited stallions like children collect baubles, and perhaps his mount that day was a new prize that stumbled and rolled its steely croup over his chest, breaking ribs and driving them into his lungs. No simple fall would kill a hard-muscled noble of forty-five who had ridden horses from his earliest memory and jousted ahorse before the first stiff hair on his chin appeared.[3]

Wife and parents buried, Ernst's death most affected his oldest son, Frederick. This twenty-three-year-old, as decreed by the Golden Bull of the Holy Roman Empire, would assume the seat of Saxon elector vacated by Ernst.[4] As a Nuremberg master had portrayed Frederick in those very days (fig. 1, page xxiv),[5] the Saxon exuded youth and sensitivity. To some observers he even revealed softness despite a beard, for it just fuzzed meekly along his jawline. His saucer-eyed, pink face was convex, open, and as defenseless as an egg, saved from appearing totally feckless by a firm jaw and the raptorish royal nose.[6] God help him if others saw in his great brown eyes the eyes of a rabbit.[7]

Was it the perception of frailty in this wide-eyed son Frederick that had led his father Ernst just the year before to insist on officially dividing mighty Saxony with Ernst's own brother Albrecht? After all, could the portrait's slope-shouldered Frederick with the delicate hands of a lutist defend his throne against battle-fisted Uncle Albrecht, a warrior so domineering, so fierce that he was one of the emperor's favorite field marshals?[8] For that matter, could Frederick someday defend himself against Albrecht's oldest son, George, already showing his teeth at fifteen? Whatever Ernst's motive before his demise, if he and his leading official Hugold von Schleinitz[9] had schemed shrewdly enough, Frederick could at least try to rule his half of Saxony and hope Uncle Albrecht was satisfied with his better half. For Albrecht had definitely already received the cream of Saxony.[10]

How had the rift between the brothers Ernst and Albrecht happened? They had exhibited an exceptionally healthy bond, even sharing for nearly twenty years a common household, though like most sovereigns of the day never in one permanent location.[11] Albrecht himself recalled the brothers' days of harmony when they "lived in the most friendly way in one castle, needed one table and one key, even received and disbursed all annuities, money, and income at the same time, and always were so brotherly and friendly that whichever one demanded from the other whatever goods that were to come to him or his children, the other was happy and ready to grant and bestow."[12]

Harmony became an illusion, exposed in full discord when Ernst traveled to Rome in 1480 to secure powerful ecclesiastical positions for two of his sons.[13] Pointedly, Elector Ernst did not leave Albrecht in sole charge of Saxony during his absence. Albrecht had but one voice in a coalition with Ernst's most trusted councillors.[14] At the head of the councillors was High Marshal von Schleinitz, who in particular annoyed and perhaps even slandered Albrecht. That offense together with the affront that Ernst openly showed he no longer trusted Albrecht was like poking a lion in both eyes. Albrecht remained with his family in the common household after Ernst's return from Rome and even in some ways helped reform Saxony, but finally in 1482 the smoldering lion departed. He set up his own residence in Torgau at the Hartenfels, a favorite castle perched on a rock prominent over the River Elbe.[15]

When their uncle Wilhelm (the Brave) died that same year of 1482, Albrecht asked to assume Wilhelm's rule of Thuringia.[16] Thuringia was expansive and prosperous, but no equal to what remained for Ernst. He refused. This refusal to placate Albrecht was only one of a succession of decisions by Ernst that seemed to defy understanding. Why would he further anger Albrecht? Had he forgotten the infamous Brother War (*Bruderkrieg*)[17] that erupted in 1445 between their father Frederick and their uncle Wilhelm? The sad truth was that the Brother War had erupted *after* their father Frederick had given Thuringia to younger brother Wilhelm. Influential councillor Apel Vitzthum kept Wilhelm unhappy enough with his share of property and power to fight his brother to the death.[18] The brothers had gathered their allies and fought each other year after year. Emperor Friedrich III himself relished the Saxons weakening their territory (his house of Habsburg's greatest rival). That the emperor's sister Margaretha was married to Elector Frederick no doubt forced the emperor finally to threaten to intercede[19] after six senseless years of lost lives and property.

Both Ernst and Albrecht had reason to remember the conflict well. At the ages of fourteen and twelve, the two boys had been kidnapped for a short time by a knight[20] who had ardently supported their father in the Brother War but felt uncompensated. The rescue of Ernst and Albrecht was celebrated in song at every Saxon festival, though the real heroes of the story—brave forest people, including one stalwart charcoaler— crumbled to dust. The young princes, especially Albrecht, evolved into the heroes. But now they, too, were at odds with each other.

In 1484, Albrecht negotiated an annual salary with Ernst and officially withdrew from any rule of Saxony for ten years. This action by Albrecht jolted Ernst.[21] The year 1484 had already been wrenching for Ernst. His wife, Elisabeth, died in March at only forty-one. Next his son Albrecht, placed so well by Ernst to become an elector, suddenly died in May at only seventeen. Although Ernst promoted another son for the open position, the pope awarded it almost immediately to Berthold von

Henneberg-Römhild. These tragic setbacks plus the estrangement from Albrecht seemed to change Ernst from a hard-driving optimist to a fearful pessimist.

The tactic of withdrawal by Albrecht in some eyes released him from any obligation to Ernst or to Ernst's wishes. Was this a prelude to another brutal "Brother War"? The threat was now genuine to Ernst and he was well aware he was no match for Albrecht in a fight. Ernst could further reflect that he was himself forty-three years old and his father had died at fifty-two. If Ernst died during the ten-year withdrawal, Albrecht could claim the electorate. Who could stop him? Ernst must have reasoned, therefore, that he needed to resolve the danger for his own heirs while he was still alive.

Ernst announced he intended to rip Saxony in two!

THE MUTILATION OF SAXONY

A division of this kind to resolve a family dispute was not rare for the time. In the division involving Ernst and Albrecht, however, the consequences were rare. Not only had their father forbidden any division in his last will in 1459,[22] not only did the Golden Bull forbid dividing an electorate, but consider also, as Saxons have done in all the centuries since, the enormity of that division by Ernst. Saxons from the first moment lamented the division officially acted upon in 1485 in Leipzig, thus known as the Leipzig Division (*Leipziger Teilung*). In the early 1470s, Saxony, one of the largest princely territories of the empire with many more than one million subjects, was beginning to discover lode after lode of silver, treasure that was making it even richer than its great size merited. Then in 1482 Thuringia once again was within the electoral territory. Saxony, controlled by the House of Wettin, was becoming the only territory that could challenge in wealth and power the House of Habsburg. The Habsburgs had controlled the empire since 1440. The difference between the two royal houses in the eyes of most imperial subjects was that the Habsburgs were suspiciously Austrian and now Burgundian, too, whereas the Saxons were German to the core.[23] Albrecht, clearly more oriented than Ernst to an imperial scale of thinking, protested the division for all the obvious reasons, denouncing High Marshal von Schleinitz in particular. Young Frederick may have protested the division as well.[24] This enormous potential for Saxony, this powerful nucleus for nation-building, Ernst was about to throw away. And this he did.[25]

Both brothers conceded that Ernst as the elector (*Kurfürst*) had to retain the original electoral land (*Kurlande*) to the north around Wittenberg. This one-eighth of their total territory was beloved by neither. For the rest, according to Saxon custom, Ernst as the elder brother would divide the territory and then Albrecht would pick the half he wanted.[26] Ernst assigned his advisers, led of course by the ubiquitous von Schleinitz, to divide the territory. The high marshal and his group purposely left the halves splintered, yet interconnected, on the premise that two such ugly halves would have to cooperate yet as a whole. The silver mines, because they were just developing, defied even this poor strategy, so they remained in common ownership along with coinage, the bishopric of Meissen[27] (considered the religious center of Saxony by all Wettiners[28]), and four large properties to the east outside Saxony proper. In truth, no one could have fairly appraised the territory because data on wealth and population were so lacking. In addition, elements such as feudal rights defied evaluation.

Nevertheless, how true rang the proverb "Whoever smells it, cringes from it."[29] The resulting division by Ernst and von Schleinitz smelled foul to the dullest nose (fig. 2, next page). The better half included the major part of the political entity Mark Meissen, as well as northern Thuringia. This half even included most of the precious silver works, though commonly owned, within its borders. It also had a major trade route from the southwest that passed through Leipzig to the eastern countries. Leipzig also boasted special trade fair privileges as well as the only university in Saxony. The poorer half created by Ernst and von Schleinitz embraced some of western Meissen, the Vogtland, the Ortland of Franconia, and the greater part of Thuringia (though that part was riddled by extensive tracts of non-Wettin land, such as the city-state of Erfurt).

Indeed, the division seemed contrived to lure Albrecht, who had already shown a preference for Thuringia and Torgau to take the poorer half.[30] To further bait that trap, Ernst and von Schleinitz added an enormous requirement of 100,000 gulden to take the better half. They had misjudged Albrecht. No fool, he selected the better half anyway. Once settled, who could make the lion pay?[31] His half had most of Mark

Meissen, the esteemed southeast portion that also embedded those royal cities so special to the heart of every Wettiner: Dresden and Meissen.

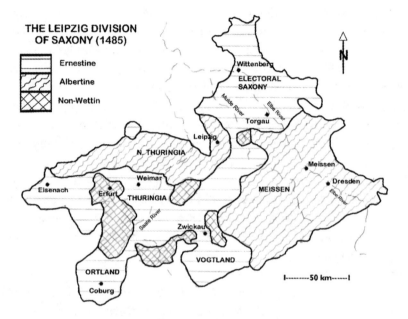

Figure 2: Simplified from Blaschke (1985) and Schwiebert (1950)

Nevertheless, Ernst's ugly half, splintered and inferior though it was, did have the original electorate added to the north. In its entirety it was definitely a territory most sovereigns would envy. After all, a man needed three days to ride a good horse from the southern boundary in Franconia through sprawling river-fed forests and fields to the northern boundary by Brandenburg. In the same way, a man needed three days to ride from the western boundary near Hesse to the eastern boundary abutting Albrecht's half.[32] Great stone fortresses, belonging to the sovereign, loomed from heights. Trees, never out of sight, yielded hardwoods for every use: the dominant beech for tool handles, but also the hornbeam for iron-tough gears and the oak for enduring furniture. Forests offered inexhaustible nuts and woods for fuel. The fretworked canopy sheltered game, especially wild hogs and the prized red deer. Lowlands cleared for farming rippled with wheat, barley, rye, flax, and oats. Cattle, horses, sheep, and goats milled over the rougher pasturelands. Vegetable gardens, pigs, and sundry fowl surrounded robust farmhouses. Orchards hung heavy with pears, apples, plums, and cherries. Rivers teemed with waterfowl and silvery fish. Tending this horn of plenty were hundreds of thousands of the freest, least discontent countryfolk in the empire.[33]

These bountiful feudal lands graced the territorial sovereign with hard cash. In the 1480s, the rent from nobles and countryfolk still rivaled the income from silver.[34] In addition, the ruling prince controlled the roads, including the "Low Road," the major southwest-northeast trade route that crossed what later came to be called "Ernestine Saxony." Tolls, tariffs, and safe conduct charges from the sovereign's roads poured into the coffers. In addition, no small amount of money came from protection contracts with imperial cities Mühlhausen and Nordhausen and with the city-state of Erfurt. Another source of income, less significant, was the disjointed judicial system that extracted fines and penalties. Taxes, erratically collected, brought in money to an even lesser degree. Nevertheless, in an era when annually a laborer might receive twenty gulden or a lawyer two hundred gulden,[35] total income every year to the elector ran into many tens of thousands of gulden.

This was the Ernestine Saxony that young Frederick assumed upon Ernst's death, not yet one year after Ernst and Albrecht sealed the Leipzig Division. The document of that legal separation named seventy towns and cities in Ernestine Saxony. The most populated of these were Zwickau, Torgau, Weimar, and Wittenberg. Still, these four had less than five thousand inhabitants each and probably little more than two thousand—mere villages compared to the great cities of the empire such as Augsburg, Nuremberg, Magdeburg, and Cologne.[36] Demeaning for any territorial prince of the first rank was the lack of a university. As events would prove, troubling in particular to young Frederick was also the lack of any religious focus such as the Chapel of Three Kings in the city of Meissen where the Wettiners buried their electoral princes. Overall, Ernestine Saxony virtually shrieked to worldly outsiders that it was little more than a rough frontier with scarcely one thread of finery.

Coupled with the need of refinement was the urgency to reform the government, if for no other reason than governance had been in a shambles since the Leipzig Division. Subjects and officials were bewildered as to whom and how they served. Complicating the outlook for Frederick even more were his duties as an electoral prince, for he was now no ordinary prince, not even an ordinary imperial prince. The responsibilities of an electoral prince were much greater than the responsibilities of other princes of the empire. These seven electoral princes or "electors" had been enfeoffed since 1356 by the Golden Bull with the right to elect the "king of the Romans." This king expected soon thereafter to be crowned emperor of the Holy Roman Empire by the pope. At the right moment, then, an electoral prince such as Frederick was indeed a kingmaker. According to the Golden Bull, which codified electors who had in truth been serving since 1257, one elector had to be the king of Bohemia; three electors had to be the archbishops of Mainz, Trier, and Cologne; and the remaining three had to be the secular princes from the Palatine, Brandenburg, and Saxony.[37] The Golden Bull also designated the Saxon elector to be the high marshal of the empire. Moreover, during an interregnum of the highest imperial office, the Saxon elector was the administrator of the eastern portion of the empire.

FREDERICK'S SEASONING

"The uninformed can be the master of no one"[38] was a proverb of the time, perhaps even muttered against Frederick. He knew that in 1486 he was the same age that his father, Ernst, had been when he began his rule in 1464. Just how well had this young prince Frederick been prepared for the responsibilities of a secular elector?[39] His father had been ashamed in 1480 in Rome when he was unable to talk to Pope Sixtus IV in Latin.[40] For Ernst, this lack of knowledge that an ambitious imperial prince needed, this dearth of Latin, the language of all educated people of the Christian world, seems to have arisen from the parochial attitude of his own father, Frederick the Meek. Frederick the Meek was so Saxon that in 1458, when Pope Calixtus III tried to offer indulgences in Saxony, the elector demanded half the proceeds; he had "inspectors" at every sale making sure he received every pfennig.[41] Despite his father's insular attitude, Ernst and his mother, Margaretha, knew very well that Latin was a cornerstone. She was the sister of the Habsburg emperor, the aunt of the Habsburg king Maximilian. Just as certainly, Ernst's wife, Elisabeth, knew Latin was a cornerstone. Elisabeth was a princess of the ruling Wittelsbachs of Bavaria and her brother Duke Albrecht IV was known as the shining linguist of the time, rivaled perhaps only by Maximilian.

But none of the maternal influences meant anything if Ernst resisted the world outside Saxony as his own father had. From Frederick's birth in Torgau on January 10, 1463, Ernst must have vowed his son would never blush before anyone. Ernst would prove again and again how perceptive he was. Who could better instill his children with the niceties as well as the necessities of a court life than his mother and his wife? In about 1470, he instituted the Women's Quarter (*Frauen Hof* or *Frauenzimmer*), a virtually independent court from his own.[42] All the younger royal boys and girls immersed themselves in this separate Women's Quarter. Soon after, in 1471, Ernst by letter approved his mother to supervise Frederick; the boy was to learn Latin and French as well as the other necessities of a sovereign.[43] Thus Frederick was being sculpted into one of the better educated princes such as those of Bavaria, Burgundy, and Austria.

Although Frederick had an older sister, Christine, and a younger sister, Margarete, he probably had faint contact with them as a boy other than seeing them during their two daily meals (mid-morning and late afternoon) in the women's dining room.[44] Excepting mothers and grandmothers,[45] in day to day activity the female side of any noble court existed prudishly separate from the male side. Frederick was much closer to his brothers and male cousins; until the breakup of the common household in 1482, he lived alongside his brothers and Uncle Albrecht's sons. For example, in 1476, before Frederick's brother Ernst left for his ecclesiastical career in Magdeburg, seven royal boys lived in the common household: Frederick (13); his brothers Ernst (12), Albrecht (9), and Johann (8); and the cousins George (5), Heinrich (3), and Frederick (1). Older Frederick had to seem the "older brother" even to his cousins. Although Ernst and Albrecht soon left this group, the others remained together another six years.[46]

Margaretha surely wrote her brother, the Habsburg emperor Friedrich III, about this sober child. Did she convey to the emperor that the child was conscientious and trustworthy? Did she conceal that the boy, much like the emperor himself, was deliberate almost to a fault? Soon enough, however, the royal ladies yielded Frederick to a formal education. At age 10, Frederick had come within the sphere of the scholarly priest Ulrich Kemmerlin, probably at whatever Wettin residence the priest was needed. By 1474, Frederick at age 11 had his own "young lords" court at Torgau for thirty-two weeks with at least one of his brothers and fourteen servants.[47] Kemmerlin taught reading, writing, mathematics, and yet more Latin. Kemmerlin no doubt rigorously taught Latin as much more than a language but also as "art" in that the selections in Latin imparted mental discipline and cultural knowledge.[48]

It is implausible Frederick also studied under the humanist Fridianus Pighinucius, obscure except for his acquaintance with renowned humanist Conrad Celtis. Although documents prove Pighinucius tutored Frederick's brother Ernst, who was only one year younger, this occurred years after Ernst left for Magdeburg.[49] In any case, Frederick did learn Latin, and he even had favorites in Latin such as Terence and Cato, both of whom spun elegant aphorisms so similar to proverbs. It seems likely, because of their pervasive popularity for children, that he learned as well the animal stories of Aesop, each with an attached moral.

Throughout his life, Frederick was fond of German proverbs. He considered proverbs virtually equal in wisdom to the Bible.[50] It was common, moreover, among all people in this time of illiteracy to quote proverbs. Even the literate nobility quoted proverbs, including some that targeted themselves. Some jibes were merely sour: "Where noblemen are, there are fancy sheets." Many were acid: "When Adam hoed and Eve spun, where then was the nobleman?" Some ran bitter: "Where there is a carcass, then don't worry where the noblemen and ravens are."[51]

The time of Frederick's youth did not stand out as a creative time in the empire for literary fare; Gutenberg's invention of the 1450s was ready and waiting for the printing explosion that was yet to happen. Frederick must have listened often to the old songs of chivalry and love from the minstrels who came and went. No doubt he read or listened to the wit of Wolfram von Eschenbach's thirteenth century Arthurian epic *Parzival*.[52] Frederick possibly read the *Sachsenspiegel,* an essential compilation of Saxon laws from that same century.[53] He probably heard accounts of the *Heliand,* the Old Saxon saga from the ninth century. Its mixture of New Testament and ancient pagan elements was provocative.[54] Could the Christian God conquer the inexorable forces of time and fate? Although the wealthy Wettiners might have possessed a copy, it is unlikely Frederick would have labored through the Low German alliterative poetry so tortuous to read.[55] Besides that, its pagan doubts were firmly answered by a much advanced Roman liturgy.

Frederick's later life confirmed that in his youth, probably reinforced by Father Kemmerlin, he deeply believed the tenets of the Roman Church. There is nonetheless solid evidence that astrology intrigued him lifelong as it did many other contemporaries,[56] even the humanists (although his early confidant Dr. Mellerstadt in Leipzig carried on a highly audible harangue against astrology).[57] Most people of the time believed not only that the stars and planets forecasted events but also that two-headed calves and other sports of nature revealed the future. The safest course for a Christian prince was strict observance of traditional church discipline. As a tot, Frederick probably already knew "The pious regret nothing."[58] Reading the Bible was not a normal part of church discipline, though Frederick could have read the Latin of the sanctioned Vulgate Bible. Fundamental to piety was learning the vast accumulation of church rituals and requirements on the church calendar.

The 1480 catechism in German by Dietrich Kolde detailed the duties of a Christian.[59] The essence of duties to the Church was threefold obedience: to the seven Holy Sacraments, to the Church's interpretation of the Ten Commandments, and to the five "commandments of the church." These latter five were weekly attendance at Mass, annual confession, annual communion, designated fasting, and obedience to clerical jurisdiction. By church law, clerics could punish the disobedient by excommunication, refusal of burial in church grounds, and other means. Sins were legion, the worst being idolatry, the next murder. The church formulated at least sixteen categories of sexual sins.[60] Least offensive was an "unchaste kiss"; not much worse was fornication. The worst were five categories of sins "against nature." Self-gratification was a graver sin in the eyes of the church than raping a woman. Frederick no doubt realized early on that most nobles and many clerics themselves winked at most of these sexual sins. Noblemen had few reservations in gratifying themselves with women below their class and not much more for those within the nobility.

The sin that was truly perilous was one that was also a civil crime, a transgression that would fall under the elector's own jurisdiction. Frederick had to witness the administration of justice[61] in various entities under his father. Imprisonment other than short internment was seldom an option in those days. Throughout the empire, torture was a standard step in the legal processing of a defendant once accused by witnesses (more than one witness as in the Bible) and indicted. Few accused, guilty or innocent, held out under torture pursued in well-established stages of increasing degradation and pain. Punishment was public and watched excitedly "amid the noise of the crowd and the smell of frying pork sausages from butchers' stalls put up for the occasion."[62] The penalty of death was usually only for murder, treason, or theft. The executioner "mercifully" beheaded the highborn but pitilessly hanged most others.

Burning and the horrific breaking on the wheel for heinous crimes were less frequent. Murder of an infant could require burial alive or drowning. Local officials were leery of executions on holy days and festivals, though the anticipation and gore were highly popular, simply because a visiting sovereign so often pardoned criminals as a grand gesture. Theft and fraud were the most common crimes, punished occasionally by death but routinely by loss of fingers or ears. Some received public humiliation or banishment. Rape and adultery were definitely serious civil crimes, even capital crimes, though hard to prove.[63] Convictions for heresy and witchcraft, the foodstuff of gossips for centuries, were actually rare.

On a more pleasant subject, music was an everyday presence in the Wettin court, usually very brassy. Saxons were known throughout the empire for their trumpeters. These musicians were the most admired and the best paid. Ernst would loan them to other courts for special occasions, but if the best were not returned, he sent them a hard reminder. Documents from 1484 suggest that for his own playing, Frederick preferred the lute, a popular stringed instrument of the time.[64] Animals were also favorite diversions of the court, besides the usual many dozens of falcons, dogs, and horses.[65] Menageries were maintained at many locations. Several kinds of deer were ubiquitous. Bears had been common at Torgau and Meissen for decades. Other creatures included wolves, lynxes, eagles, waterfowl, songbirds, monkeys, and peacocks. Exotic beasts amused the royals, though sometimes the imports did not survive long. Among these in Ernst's time were a camel and a lion.

Frederick had many male influences. Within the Wettin court, Frederick's uncle Albrecht without doubt influenced him.[66] Did Albrecht's ominous restlessness make Frederick wary later of the possible discontent of his own brother Johann? Uncle Albrecht moved out of the electoral shadow of his brother Ernst to make a name for himself as a military leader. In 1471, in part because of his marriage to the daughter of the recently deceased King George Podjebrad of Bohemia and in part because it was in the interest of Saxony, Albrecht, with thousands of knights and foot soldiers, fought futilely for the contested throne in Bohemia. In 1475, at Neuss on the lower River Rhine, Albrecht was the "emperor's great marshal and flagmaster"[67] at the side of the imperial field general Albrecht "Achilles."[68] Both fought Charles the Bold of Burgundy[69] (ironically, a territory gained by Maximilian only a few years later through marriage to Charles's daughter Maria). Although a fierce and cruel warrior, Albrecht was widely admired by Saxons. In 1476, he even put aside his bloody sword to travel with a great entourage to the Holy Land. On his return, he resumed his imperial military career and rose ever higher in command.

That Frederick himself was versed in the ways of the knight is undeniable. As a youth, in Dresden while riding up to the barrier for his turn to joust, he overheard a woman in the crowd blurt, "Oh, what can that young child show!?" This disturbed him so much at the time that he could still recall it years later for Spalatin, his secretary and biographer.[70] How rarely he must have heard harsh words in his exalted station. Even as a child he undoubtedly wore the finest armor available and fought hard. A contemporary told Spalatin that the elector fought as hard as anyone in jousts.[71] Early on, Frederick developed a love for the great hunting lodge at Lochau, where red deer and wild boar[72] abounded as well as wolves and bears.[73] Hunting and jousting were not only for pleasure. Standing firm in the face of danger was no small element of the joust and the hunt. To shirk these knightly aspects was unthinkable for a prince of the time[74] unless he had already been slated for a religious life as had Frederick's brothers Ernst and Albrecht.

Frederick prepared himself well for the risk arising from combat, the joust, or the hunt. Nevertheless he lived in a time of abrupt death in many forms. One danger above all seemed to later observers to have caused in Frederick a fear of death that ballooned into a phobia: the threat of plague.[75] Plagues were real enough; in half of the twenty-five years prior to 1487, somewhere in the empire, plague raged.[76] Nuremberg alone during those twenty-five years had five severe outbreaks; similarly, Erfurt had four.[77] Two forms of plague seemed ever ready to strike, and both were deadly. Deaths in towns mounted into the hundreds and in cities into thousands. Ernst had to move his court temporarily to Coburg in 1484 from fear of the plague.[78] That was too late to save Frederick's mother, Elisabeth, who died of plague that March at age 41.[79] It is plausible the death in May that same year of Frederick's seventeen-year-old brother Albrecht, who had begun a life in the church, was also from the plague. In 1487, the first altarpiece Frederick commissioned featured St. Mary, "most often invoked as a protector in times of war or against the plague."[80]

Outside the Wettin court, Frederick spent time in the court of Mainz when his brother Albrecht had taken an ecclesiastical position there. In addition, Frederick undoubtedly visited the courts of powerful relatives, including Uncle Albrecht IV of Bavaria and even the Austrian court of his grandmother Margaretha's brother, the emperor.[81] He had probably also visited the court in Burgundy of his Great-uncle Maximilian, for somewhere Frederick polished the skill to speak, read, and write French. All highborn princes also began attending "diets" at an early age. Not only would Frederick have gone with his father the elector to *Landstags* (territorial diets) within Saxony but he also would have gone to *Reichstags* (imperial diets) "out in the empire." Some claim that in 1481, Frederick, at age 18, went with Uncle Albrecht to the *Reichstag* in Nuremberg.[82] More certain is that, in 1486, Frederick at twenty-three and Johann at eighteen attended the *Reichstag* in Frankfurt with their father.

Many other possibilities arise for Frederick's preparation. His father and Uncle Albrecht had traveled in rarified air. The atmosphere was colorful and festive. Perhaps in 1474, Frederick at eleven had been with father Ernst and Uncle Albrecht when they traveled to Amberg east of Nuremberg for their niece's marriage to Prince Philipp of the Palatine.[83] Was Frederick in the procession from Saxony that entered Amberg with three hundred subject knights, all dressed in flaming red? Did he note at the dance the amazement of nobles from the Palatine and Bavaria when Saxon musicians with their convoluted trumpets covered a range of notes never heard before? Did he see his father and Albrecht dance with each other? Did he watch the jousting tournament won by Uncle Albrecht, a tournament so hotly contested that a knight from Bavaria died of injuries?

Without doubt there were many festive occasions. In 1476, Frederick certainly numbered among twelve hundred resplendent Saxons and Thuringians at his brother Ernst's installation in the city of Magdeburg.[84] It seems likely that in 1478, Frederick at fifteen attended the extravagant wedding of his sister Christine to Hans, Crown Prince of Denmark. Frederick, however, did not accompany his father and his "two hundred mounted retainers dressed in black livery, their horses in jeweled halters" to Rome in 1480.[85] That grand opportunity lost for Frederick to meet the pope seems reasonable only in light of Ernst's growing distrust of Albrecht. Did Ernst leave seventeen-year-old Frederick behind to observe and report the activities of Albrecht and even Ernst's own advisers?[86]

Frederick's greatest mentor was surely his father, Ernst. Father Ernst was pious enough for a prince, taking Frederick and Johann in 1482 to a

Franciscan monastery in Jüterbog for an overnight s4tay and confession.[87] There is nevertheless evidence Ernst enjoyed himself outside the marriage bed.[88] But what more can be gleaned of Ernst himself? What can outsiders believe of this influential prince whom history ignores except for venting contempt on him over his decision to divide the most powerful territory in the core of Germany? Ernst never even earned a sobriquet. Yet he was able to gain from Rome two splendid ecclesiastical positions—Mainz and Magdeburg—for his sons, as well as gain the coveted Golden Rose for himself. He managed powerful marriages of his daughters to the future king of Denmark and to the House of Braunschweig-Lüneburg. He also encouraged and achieved major institutional reforms in Saxony.[89] Nonetheless, Frederick's confidant Spalatin was said to have described Ernst as competent and prone to moderation—except a tendency to abrupt rages.[90] Was this Frederick's own assessment? If true, did this volcanic temper erupt, and then simmer for weeks and months? Did it result in the Leipzig Division? Did Frederick resolve never to fall prey himself to this destructive loss of control?

Records prove that before his father's death, Frederick made demands on subjects in the name of the elector.[91] Ernst's concern for his sons' survival may have prompted him to bring Frederick as well as Johann into governance early. If so, Frederick learned from high-powered officials such as Chancellor Johann von Mergenthal and the notorious schemer Hugold von Schleinitz. Did Frederick question from this experience the custom of the time to use as councillors powerful nobles with their own personal ambitions? On the other hand, did he surmise those who were not powerful tended to become sycophants? Young Frederick had to have met the main councillors residing at the electoral court and everyone down to the grooms. If nowhere else, he encountered them while dining. Judging from later evidence,[92] at meals the constant retinue of the elector numbered more than one hundred, with places assigned at tables of ten. In reality, Frederick undoubtedly saw everyone of influence except some of Ernst's officials (usually called *Amt* men) scattered in towns about the territory.

In summary, in 1486, Frederick was a trilingual, well-traveled young prince who was acquainted not only with all the powers in the electorate but also with the mightiest figures of the empire. He was in truth related to almost all the most powerful families of the empire. It was a time when those who ruled called each other "cousins," assuming with good reason a real blood connection or at least a marital bond of some kind. Although these "cousins" quarreled among themselves, it was a rash and unwise act for one to turn violently against another. The violence occasionally came from within the immediate family. Witness the Brother War. Nor did the nobility of countries outside the empire feel the same restrictions as those within. Beyond the eastern border in 1486 two dangerous factions were seething with impatience to test Frederick's mettle . . .

PERILOUS FIRST MONTHS OF RULE

All of young Frederick's weighty preparations meant nothing if he was too much the rabbit to retain his position as the electoral prince of Saxony. External dangers did exist. And they were immediate. In 1486, at the *Reichstag* in Frankfurt, the six "German" electors, bullied by Emperor Friedrich III, had elected his son Maximilian king of the Romans in the absence of the seventh elector, the king of Bohemia. The Bohemian king Vladislaus objected to this election of Maximilian.[93] In truth, the election in Frankfurt had violated the terms of the Golden Bull. Vladislaus and his Hungarian allies were particularly upset with the electors of Brandenburg and Saxony, whose territories abutted their own. Shouldn't their sympathies be with their neighbors and not with the Austrians?[94] Moreover, because the two electorates of Brandenburg and Saxony shared a defense pact, it meant little in the long run which electorate the Bohemians and Hungarians attacked first; the other electorate had to fight too. It was also of no importance that Ernst, weeks before he died, had been the one to cast the vote for Maximilian at the *Reichstag*. Frederick and his Saxons would bear the consequences.

Vladislaus had in his complaint an ally, the Hungarian king Matthius Corvinus. Corvinus was not simply a rapacious lout. Like war-loving Maximilian, Corvinus embodied many of the admired traits of the time. He was multilingual, accumulated a notable library, and as a patron of the arts flaunted artists, poets, and humanists in his court. Moreover, he buffered the empire from the Ottoman Turks. Corvinus also claimed part of the rule of Bohemia himself. Therefore, in his eyes, he was also the Bohemian king; hence he, too, was the elector who had been wronged. Most likely he was the driving force behind the complaint. In contrast to Vladislaus, he was truly menacing. He had already proven he was as formidable as the imperial power. He had captured the Habsburg stronghold Vienna in 1485 and no doubt had designs on the empire itself.[95] Was Saxony his next stepping-stone? Matthius Corvinus and Vladislaus were to meet in the Bohemian city of Iglau within days after Ernst's death. Could anyone doubt that untested Frederick was one topic of their discussion?

Even as Frederick mourned father Ernst at his burial ceremony in Three Kings' Chapel in Meissen, he must have worried. Threats lurked on all sides of the new elector's territory, perhaps even inside. Younger brother Johann had been accompanying Frederick and his father often to functions inside and outside Saxony. Johann was only eighteen years old, but as the younger brother decreed to rule in some capacity yet knowing in reality his role would be nominal, he, just like his uncle Albrecht many years earlier, had thrown himself fully into the ways of a knight. A princely family expected a younger brother to follow a military career if he could not or would not contend for a powerful ecclesiastical position. Johann had firmly embraced this martial course; none was keener on the joust. Horses, leather, steel, and sweat were sweeter to Johann's nose than any flower. Frederick must have known he had to mollify this younger brother.

Johann was not the only Wettiner who might have been interested in the electorate. Who knew if Uncle Albrecht, a pet of both the emperor and his son King Maximilian, might not decide to reunite Saxony by overthrowing untested Frederick? Many throughout the empire would cheer such a move because it would set up again a powerful entity to keep the ruling Habsburgs from running roughshod over the imperial estates. Just weeks before Ernst's death, the emperor had been only too happy to sanction officially the division of Saxony; divided Saxony was less a rival to the House of Habsburg. Even so, if a crisis arose, who would fault a warrior like Albrecht for seizing power to save the honor of all Saxony?

In the meantime, Frederick had to take the reins of Ernestine Saxony. Swayed by his father throughout the years, Frederick had learned to prefer Dresden as his residence and, to a lesser degree, another residence on the moody River Elbe: his birthplace, Torgau. Because Uncle Albrecht now reigned in Dresden, Frederick gravitated in general to the Hartenfels castle in Torgau during the first half of the year and to the residence castle in Weimar the rest of the year.[96] Furthermore, because the Wettiners intentionally spurned permanent residences, the sovereign's court had to be mobile.[97] Frederick also made the effort to "live" in a number of towns; occasionally he even visited the old rundown Ascanian castle at Wittenberg. Of course, he relished stays in the opulent hunting lodges at Lochau and Colditz.

Emperor Friedrich III was to confirm Frederick at a future *Reichstag*. In the meantime, the fledgling had to evade some of the greatest predators in and out of the empire. He awaited the outcome of the meeting in Iglau between the Hungarian Corvinus and the Bohemian Vladislaus. No Saxon had reason to trust the Bohemians. It had been little more than fifty years since thousands of "Hussite" soldiers invaded Saxony with hundreds of their dreaded war wagons.[98] Only the Swiss rivaled the Bohemians in ferocity and ingenuity. Although Vladislaus was a weak leader, his partner Corvinus was not. The Saxons, fueled by their knightly skills, were fierce enough, but similar to citizens of other imperial territories, they won by superior numbers and courage, almost never by military genius.

Frederick and Johann Cicero,[99] his counterpart in Brandenburg, soon heard the outcome from Iglau. Corvinus and Vladislaus demanded extravagant remuneration from the two electoral princes.[100] Demands from Corvinus had teeth. He had taken much of Austria, including prized Vienna, from the emperor because the emperor had not paid 400,000 gulden that Corvinus demanded. In January 1487, Frederick and Johann Cicero, in the face of an attack by the Bohemians and Hungarians, appealed to the empire for military aid. Was this also the moment for Albrecht to seize the reins of power from Frederick? Albrecht as yet showed Frederick nothing but cooperation, but what if threat of war and the safety of Saxons demanded his total command of the situation?

What were the dispositions of Frederick's other neighbors?[101] In addition to previously discussed Bohemia to the east, Brandenburg to the north, and intermeshed Albertine Saxony, Frederick's most powerful adjacent neighbor was Hesse to the west. This territory under Landgrave Wilhelm was well-disposed toward Saxony. Many of Frederick's other adjacent neighbors were territories of counts and lords, chief among them Schönburgs, Hartensteins, Wildenfelsses, Tautenburgs, Schwarzburgs, Stolbergs, and Mansfelds. In general, they cooperated but were defiantly independent. Only slightly less independent were the bishoprics of Meissen, Merseburg, and Naumburg,[102] imperial fiefs ruled by bishops who were essentially territorial lords. Once nearly embedded in one Saxony, the Leipzig Division had made all of them more difficult to dominate. Toward Frederick, Naumburg was most cooperative, Merseburg least. Other neighbors were the powerful archdiocesan territories of Magdeburg and Mainz and the equally powerful dioceses of Würzburg and Bamberg—all of them, for the moment, friendly. Additional neighbors were abbeys, imperial cities, and city-states, as well as entities that defied definition. Frederick's neighbors typified the murkiness of the empire: numerous and diverse to the very limit of comprehension.

And who advised Frederick in this time of difficulty?[103] It was not the schemer von Schleinitz. The Saxon high marshal had outwitted himself. All his hereditary properties were in Albrecht's half. He quietly slipped away from the Ernestine court.[104] Frederick significantly abolished the office of high marshal. His chief advisers in the first months were other incumbents who had served his father: *Hofmeister* Hans von Doringberg, Chancellor Johann Seyfried, and *Rentmeister* Hans Guntherode.[105] None of these appeared in the chamber registry book of 1487 and 1488 that listed Frederick's fifteen closest advisers.[106] Of these fifteen, four were of the titled nobility: counts from the families von Gleichen and von Stolberg. The other eleven were with less certainty all untitled nobility (collectively called knights): Heinrich and Götz von Ende, Otto and Dietrich Spiegel, Doctors Mellerstadt and Schrenk, Heinrich Löser, Ernst von Schonberg, Hans von Obernitz, Dietrich von Stenz, and Cristoffel von Lipsk. Notable in these earliest days because they were university graduates were Mellerstadt and Schrenk.[107] Assuming from their worth to Frederick over the next years, other advisers probably included Michael von Denstedt, Hans Hundt von Wenkheim, Conrad von König, Hans von Leimbach, Siegmund von Maltitz, Hans von Minkwitz, Heinrich von Starschedel, and Anselm von Tettau.

The engagement of Frederick's sister Margarete with Duke Heinrich II of Braunschweig-Lüneburg had occurred in Leipzig in better days. For once, the two power-marriage partners had at least probably seen each other because, years before, Heinrich had been a guest of the Saxon court at Rochlitz. In February 1487, Margarete, at sixteen, married eighteen-year-old Heinrich at the duke's royal residence in Celle. The young prince had just assumed his reign of this considerable territory northwest of Ernestine Saxony. Yet the Braunschweig territory had once been much larger, one more example of a large dynasty shredded by poorly defined or poorly enforced inheritance rights. However splintered it was, the Braunschweig extended family was threaded throughout the empire. The marriage of Margarete and the previous marriage of Christine to the future king Hans of Denmark reflect a strategy of Ernst that to compete with the growing strength of the Hohenzollerns (that is, the Brandenburgs) to the north, the Wettiners needed stronger alliances with other northern neighbors.[108] Religious appointments of Ernst's sons Albrecht and Ernst also fit the northern strategy.

Frederick's eastern neighbors remained a worry, though the Saxons heard King Vladislaus was having trouble enlisting support for any attack on Saxony and Brandenburg. Would his much more dangerous ally Corvinus feel, in view of that poor alliance, it would be more prudent for him to tend to the defense of his recent conquest of Austria? The Austrian situation was also the reason Uncle Albrecht had no time for his Ernestine nephews. He had become the emperor's commander in chief, preparing a campaign to retake Austria. Albrecht's participation angered Corvinus even more against the Saxons.[109] Albrecht had been granted feudal rights to some properties east of Saxony under the control of Corvinus. Where would Corvinus try to take his revenge? In Austria or in Saxony? Was it significant that Iglau, the meeting place for Corvinus and Vladislaus, had been only a four- or five-day march directly southeast of Dresden, the heart of Albertine Saxony?

Frederick, during the early months of his rule, signaled his interest in influencing church matters and spiritual behavior. He initiated ecclesiastical changes, especially among the Franciscans so favored by the Wettins.[110] Brother Johann was active in this effort too. They prodded for reform in the Franciscan monasteries in Torgau and Wittenberg. Pope Martin had suggested reform in this begging order of monks in 1430. Now Frederick wanted this "Martinian" form of stricter, more pious behavior implemented in the monasteries. This was not only to make them more self-sufficient; Frederick generously endowed and supported these cloisters. His territory enveloped about one hundred monasteries and foundations. They were located in any town of size, but they were especially concentrated in the dioceses of Mainz and Halberstadt in western Thuringia and the Ortland (Coburg area).[111] Less than thirty in his territory at the beginning of his reign were reformed or in the process of reforming.[112]

It is probable that Frederick's father, Ernst, had planned to push reform himself. He had achieved a remarkable concession in 1485 from Pope Innocent VIII.[113] The pope expressly permitted the Saxon sovereign to reform both exempt and non-exempt monasteries of his territory if necessary. In all these matters, Frederick included Johann; his father had wished this. Moreover, Johann was more likely to remain a loyal partner. One unspoken reason undoubtedly was that Frederick was preparing to launch an aggressive effort on more than one front that would become obvious only during and after his confirmation as elector at the upcoming *Reichstag*. To do this Frederick needed a loyal Johann.

FIRST *REICHSTAG* AS SAXON ELECTOR

"What a bird is, one knows by his song and feathers."[114]

Every prince knew the value of "representation"[115] or "presentation," that is, the public display befitting his office. It was not merely a display of power to intimidate. It was a deliberate, well-planned effort to show all the qualities of a prince most admired at the time: physical courage, power, generosity, thoughtfulness, intellect, curiosity, piety, nurturing, loyalty, and other virtues. Representation included among other methods jousting, symbols, rituals, stagings, music, coins, books, and funding. It was costly to carry out. To be totally effective, every representation had to be as public as possible. In the empire, no one surpassed King Maximilian at pomp; and he lagged behind the Italians. Frederick's first venture into this demanding, highly visible trial was in the first spring days of 1487 at the *Reichstag* in the imperial city of Nuremberg.[116] The impression he gave "out in the empire" was of great importance.

On March 28, Frederick and his well-armed entourage emerged from dense forest north of Nuremberg. Across a half mile of cleared flats loomed one of the gems of the empire.[117] Inside the great three-fold walls with more than one hundred towers lived twenty thousand citizens, among them the empire's finest artists and craftsmen. Frederick and Johann rode in through one of the west or north gates near the Kaiserburg fortress with several hundred horsemen in armor;[118] no doubt all the knights in the same vivid color, a showy arrival only a powerful prince could do. Triumphant harmony by his paid musicians amplified his importance; his court employed nine permanent musicians, all trumpeters but for one drummer.[119] Frederick's procession exhibited all the splendor of the well-orchestrated processions that began jousting tournaments. He was unlikely to forget one iota of flags, banners, staffs, or indeed any symbol of Saxon rule. Peers had to be noticing he was already a master of protocol.

The money-starved emperor had called for the *Reichstag*.[120] At that time, *Reichstags* still occurred only as mandated by the emperor, an indication of how subordinate the estates were in the imperial view of governing. A *Reichstag*, always held in an imperial city, was nevertheless no trifling event; hundreds of masters and thousands of servants were involved for several weeks, often for several months. They burned time and money. For Frederick, this *Reichstag* was a succession of grand occasions.[121] On April 18, the emperor crowned humanist Conrad Celtis poet laureate of the empire.[122] Frederick had championed this honor for Celtis, as indirectly acknowledged in 1486 when Celtis dedicated to Frederick his most significant work, *Ars versificandi et carminum* (The Art of Writing Verses and Poems).[123] Here is clear evidence that Frederick was far from a newcomer on the imperial scene. Moreover, he recognized that the work of Celtis was important, one of the first impulses of the humanistic groundswell from the south spreading over the empire. That Celtis was the son of a peasant suggests Frederick was open to talent regardless of social position. By crowning Celtis, the emperor indirectly honored Frederick himself.

That was only the first triumph for Frederick at the *Reichstag*. On May 23, Frederick finished negotiations for a renewed "inheritance protectorate" of Ernestine Saxony with Albertine Saxony, Brandenburg, and Hesse. This kind of agreement among upper nobility dynasties was more and more popular. It served to define boundaries, protect inheritance, and determine succession if a family died out. Implied also was some degree of mutual assistance in military difficulties. Such protectorates were only as dependable as the integrity and willingness of the parties involved. Frederick's father, Ernst, had signed a similar agreement with Bohemian king Vladislaus in 1482. That agreement seemed of little value in 1487. Still, the protectorate renewed among both Saxonies, Brandenburg, and Hesse afforded some comfort to Frederick.

An even greater event occurred on May 23. The emperor enfeoffed Frederick as elector. From then forward, without doubt, he was Elector Frederick III of Saxony. He was the sixth Saxon sovereign named Frederick in the line of Wettiners that went back to Frederick I of the

Bitten Cheek, who began his reign of Mark Meissen in 1292. Frederick I the Warlike had been the first Saxon elector, enfeoffed in 1423. It was convention at the time to begin numbering from one again after the third use. The only interruption in this almost two hundred-year-long chain of Saxon sovereigns named Frederick was Frederick's father, Ernst. That was only because Ernst's older brother, of course named Frederick, died before he could assume the reign.

On June 3, Frederick and Johann hosted a great feast. All the princes and noble women at the Nuremberg *Reichstag* attended, as did the most important patricians of the city.[124] Records show the chefs served twenty courses. Frederick and Johann must have offered a wide spectrum of the animal kingdom, from pork to peacocks and from turtles to eels. Highlighting courses were "subtleties," dishes designed to amaze and amuse, such as a "baked" pie spewing forth live birds. No doubt the best wines from Rhine vineyards flowed freely too. Throughout the day, the Saxon brass entertained, even at the dance that evening. The brothers surely followed custom (records prove Frederick did in later years) in hiring for the dance unattached ladies—the younger and more willing, the better.[125] Later yet, patricians and highborn nobles gambled at cards. Cautious Frederick on such occasions seems to have won or lost only hundreds of gulden, not thousands, as some patricians and nobles did.[126]

As to the business of the *Reichstag* itself, young Frederick and the other territorial princes were cynics. Nothing was to happen this time but the usual sad sequence of imperial politics. The emperor needed resources. The technique of Friedrich III was well worn. The emperor was mute in the meetings, and then cornered each individual prince or prelate privately to muscle money or soldiers from that person, while attempting to give nothing significant in return.[127] If pressed, in true Habsburg fashion he promised marriages, fiefs, and other rewards that he might or might not deliver later. Although ancient for the time—he was seventy-one—and considered sluggish by his detractors, the emperor was in truth doggedly effective. At Frankfurt the previous year, the emperor had given the estates nothing but empty promises. In return he received a colossal triumph: the electoral princes elected his twenty-six-year-old son Maximilian king, assuring his succession to the imperial throne. The electors had foolishly surrendered all their future leverage.

Voting for the king was the privilege of the curia of seven electors. On any issue other than the election of the king, all three curiae of the imperial estates voted. The electors remained the most influential curia, deliberating first and then meeting with the "curia of princes." This "curia of princes" consisted of some two hundred fifty non-electoral princes, counts, other titled nobility, and prelates. Within this curia, about ten princes, especially those of Hesse, Württemberg, and now Albertine Saxony, dominated. Only after the curia of electors and the "curia of princes" had resolved their differences and agreed on an issue did they meet with the third curia.[128] It was inevitable that the vote of this third curia of sixty or so free imperial cities meant nothing; its influence was an illusion.[129] Within the empire, with no voice whatever, were about two thousand families of lower or untitled nobility (knights), hundreds of thousands of burghers from roughly three thousand non-imperial cities and towns, and more than fifteen million countryfolk (*Bauern*).

In 1484, a new force had arrived among the electors: forty-two-year-old archbishop of Mainz, Berthold von Henneberg-Römhild. This carried sad irony for Frederick, for Berthold had replaced Frederick's younger brother Albrecht who had succeeded Diether von Isenburg in 1482.[130] At first, Berthold seemed a toady to the emperor and his son. How false that notion proved to be! Berthold had a vision of organizing the empire internally in a way that would benefit the estates, not simply help solve the problems of the House of Habsburg. The Habsburgs' concerns were real enough. Because their holdings were on the most peripheral parts of the empire, they scuffled constantly with France, Switzerland, Italy, Bohemia, Hungary, and even the Turks. In any case, by 1487, Berthold was truly emboldening all the estates. Although the three curiae of electors, princes, and imperial cities that voted at the *Reichstag* were well established, the emperor had learned to circumvent matters easily by inviting only those he trusted. Now the estates, encouraged by Berthold, resisted. Those present would not approve funds for the empire until the missing estates voted, present or absent. Berthold and others won change on another matter of great importance: the curiae could now negotiate among themselves in secret. No longer were the eyes and ears of the imperial circle in attendance to intimidate. In 1487, as in no previous *Reichstags*, both the curia of electors and the curia of princes had become boldly independent. Under Berthold's influence, the curiae were now talking of a constitution.

Procedurally, the curiae were so much stronger at the 1487 *Reichstag* that the emperor had to employ more subtle tactics. Friedrich III became more the fox, less the wolf. A long-standing grievance of the electors and princes was lack of an imperial judicial court. The emperor's "concession" to the final compromise of the 1487 *Reichstag* was that he allowed the concept of an imperial judicial court to be drafted for study.[131] In return, the estates approved money for the emperor, but in their new defiance they set rigid conditions on the funds. They would furnish money only for relief of the Austrian properties captured or threatened by Corvinus. To assure this outcome, they would give the money only to the Brandenburg elector Johann Cicero. He would in turn disburse it only to the imperial commander in chief of the military, Frederick's uncle Albrecht. The old emperor had won just in time the previous year the guarantee of his son Maximilian as his successor.

At Nuremberg in 1487, new elector Frederick probably listened far more than he talked in the now secret discussions of the curiae. Besides Frederick and the dynamic Berthold, four other electors completed this most powerful of the curiae. Johann Cicero of Brandenburg, at thirty-one, was also a newcomer. More senior members were Archbishop Hermann of Cologne, at thirty-six an elector for six years, and Philipp of the Palatine, at thirty-eight an elector for ten years. Grand old prince of the electors was Archbishop Johann II of Trier. Although only fifty-two, the archbishop nevertheless had been an elector for thirty years. First becoming an elector at only twenty-two himself, the archbishop may have warmed to twenty-four-year-old Frederick. Doubtless they all welcomed him, for whatever political skirmishes ensued, these five electors remained uppermost in Frederick's esteem the rest of his life.[132]

Regardless of Frederick's real or perceived role in the political maneuvers during the 1487 *Reichstag*, after it was over he was in good standing both with the curia of electors and, perhaps more importantly at the time, with the imperial circle. Frederick was not so naïve to think that the Habsburgs were indifferent to his assets of silver. Still, he knew advantages flowed from imperial approval. This tentative harmony with the Habsburgs was some assurance for the safety of Ernestine Saxony against all potential enemies, with the exception of formidable Corvinus.

Autumn 1487 would indeed bring a chill from the east as icy as the usual piercing winds.

CHAPTER 2

VISIONS OF A MANY-EYED PRINCE

(1488–93)

> "One who has to watch over territory and
> people can not sleep the entire night."
> —Motto displayed by Frederick the Wise[1]

FLEDGLING YEARS OF DANGER

The *Reichstag* was a great success for Frederick, but one king of the east was not impressed. He was not Vladislaus, but the potent Corvinus—that same Hungarian king who had beaten the Habsburgs in Austria and seized their jewel, Vienna. How much easier would be an invasion of Ernestine Saxony? Corvinus could skirt his army east of the Erzgebirge through friendly lands, adding ferocious but leaderless Bohemians along the way, and then at Breslau (today's Wrocław) sweep west. The horde could rush like the bitter eastern winds right along the convenient "Low Road" into the heart of Ernestine Saxony. The spearhead did not even have to cross one large river until it reached Frederick's favorite residence at Torgau, on the River Elbe. His Hartenfels castle was commodious but militarily weak.

Frederick had no realistic defense against Corvinus.

Yet the threat from Corvinus on the eastern border of Saxony waxed and waned. Was Corvinus master of feints? Or was he, like King Maximilian, frequently overwhelmed, even redirected, by his own machinations and schemes? For Frederick, every anxiety subsided only to yield to another.[2] The old fox had stirred. The latest maneuver of Emperor Friedrich III came to light, much to the discomfort of all the imperial princes. Disappointed in the resistance from the estates at the

1487 *Reichstag*, the emperor decided the Swabian League could deliver his might within the empire.[3] This league, named for the old duchy of Swabia running from the River Rhine across to Bavaria, enveloped some twenty-six cities and many nobles, knights, and prelates. It had existed before 1487, but this was its latest form. And it was daunting.

The emperor actually concluded an agreement with the Swabian League in February 1488, ironically about the same time the Flemish city of Brugge revolted over taxation and loss of privileges under the Habsburgs. When Maria of Burgundy died in 1482, Maximilian became regent of Flanders for their son Philipp (the Fair), who had assumed the rule. Brugge citizens captured Maximilian. The electors convened for their own electoral diet, or *Kurfürstentag*, in April 1488 in Würzburg, ostensibly to develop a plan to free Maximilian.[4] Frederick himself did not attend, but his advisers were there to again appeal for help, especially from their ally Brandenburg, against the threat from Vladislaus and Corvinus. This refrain revealed how deeply disturbed Frederick was about danger from the east.

The emperor was concerned only about his son. To free the ceaselessly ambitious Maximilian, he appealed to the most senior electoral princes—those from Cologne, Trier, and the Palatine—and one on the rise: Frederick.[5] Some in the imperial inner circle sniped that the four electors negotiated halfheartedly. Yet by May, the citizens of Brugge, salved by promises of relief and peace, released Maximilian. If Frederick had not already learned from his father how well the Habsburgs kept promises, he learned immediately after Maximilian's release. Against his captors, the king "declared feud"; that ancient feudal violence had not yet been prohibited. He began to muster an imperial army to punish the Flemish. Maximilian did have cause. During his internment of fourteen weeks he had witnessed almost daily from his cell window over the city square the torture and execution of his soldiers and collaborators.[6]

Frederick learned in August that two half-brothers of the electoral prince of Brandenburg who governed a province in Franconia had committed it to the Swabian League.[7] They assured the adjacent powers, Saxony and Hesse, that their entry into the league in no way impaired the inheritance protectorate with Brandenburg. They touted the peaceful character of the Swabian League, an assurance no rational prince could believe. Later in the year, the emperor asked Frederick to protect the Swabian League within his territory. Later yet, the old tinker began to worry the league would become too powerful; in the wrong hands, it could threaten the Habsburgs. Then the old manipulator urged no more nobles or cities to join the league. Frederick had no interest in joining a league allegedly set up to provide the emperor military muscle. Many suspected the emperor also intended to use the league to stave off any efforts by the House of Wittelsbach to form a continuous territory from the Rhine to Bavaria. The elector of the Palatine to the west and the ruling family of Bavaria to the east were Wittelsbachs. Nothing sizeable lay in between their territories but the duchy of Württemberg, a major remnant of the old Swabia. The emperor, as well as every other noble, knew the Swabian League was at its strongest in Württemberg.

While anticipating all the externals that potentially threatened Saxony in his first years, Frederick was slow to reform his territorial government.[8] Whether it resulted from Uncle Albrecht's greater experience or more from Albrecht's pressing need for money because of his imperial military duties in Hungary and Flanders, Albrecht reformed the financial administration in his part of Saxony. Before this reform, the *Oberzehnter* administered only revenue from mining; Albrecht's own "chamber" administered the rest of the territorial revenue. That changed. The *Oberzehnter* now managed nearly all revenue in a central treasury permanently seated in Leipzig. The "chamber" shrank to a mere disburser of money for the ducal household in Dresden. Also notable is the fact that Albrecht's highest financial officer, the *Oberzehnter* Jakob Blasbalg, was a wealthy Leipzig merchant—not a nobleman.[9]

Before the 1485 Leipzig Division, Ernst and Albrecht had established the highest territorial judicial court (*Oberhofgericht*) in Leipzig to take precedence over numerous provincial courts (*Hofgerichte*). Albrecht re-established the *Oberhofgericht*, inactive since the division, for his duchy. Frederick, already exhibiting the trait of extreme caution, seemed content to observe the reforms of his much more experienced uncle. Frederick did, however, change key officials of his immediate staff. Heinrich von Ende replaced Hans von Doringberg in the highest ranking advisory position of *Hofmeister*. Von Ende was from Kayna, all his holdings well within Ernestine Saxony. From the first, Ende had all electoral administration "firmly in hand."[10] Frederick also appointed Franconian Hans Hundt von Wenkheim "keeper of the door" (*Türknecht*). This position was not trivial. Because the "keeper of the door" controlled the privy purse, he enjoyed rare immediacy with Frederick.

In 1488, Matthias Corvinus yet again complicated life in the Saxon court. Corvinus was only forty-five, but like so many privileged who ate "well" of mostly meats, he suffered painful, debilitating gout. His health in general was failing. He had as his only progeny a sixteen-year-old bastard son, Janos. Prompted by his decline, Corvinus developed two plans to leave Janos an inheritance. The king's backup plan was to surrender his Habsburg conquests in Austria in return for the emperor's promise to honor Janos as successor to the throne in Hungary. This he did not want to do. His primary plan, therefore, was to bequeath his son the rich territory of Silesia that he already controlled as a concession from the Bohemian king. Silesia abutted both Albertine Saxony and Brandenburg. The Silesians rebelled after learning the plan of Corvinus.[11] They would accept no boy ruler, even less a Hungarian boy ruler. Although Corvinus subdued the rebellion, the situation simmered. Silesia was already a contentious issue with Brandenburg and therefore also with both Saxonies because of their alliance pact.

In February 1489, Frederick met the concerned allies in Jüterbog, a town in the territory of Magdeburg. This large ecclesiastical territory abutted Brandenburg and Ernestine Saxony as well as Silesia. Attending were Frederick, his ubiquitous brother Johann, the Elector of Brandenburg Johann Cicero, and Frederick's brother Ernst, who was the archbishop of Magdeburg. Ernst had always followed his father's lead but since his death had become much more independent.[12] Representing Albertine Saxony was Duke George, only eighteen but already self-assured and belligerent; he virtually ruled Albertine Saxony because his father, Albrecht, was absent so often as the empire's highest field marshal. Those gathered in Jüterbog agreed to raise an army against Corvinus of fourteen hundred knights ("horses" in the vernacular, because knights always were mounted) and fifteen thousand foot soldiers. Brandenburg declared war; records are unclear if either of the two Saxonies declared war.[13] In any case, skirmishes broke out. Saxons reported Hungarians were within two days of Torgau. Yet it was a war that no party savored. Corvinus, in deteriorating health, seemed to lose heart as the pointless skirmishing dragged on; he jeopardized his much more valuable Austrian conquests by stretching his resources so far north. What if the Poles suddenly jumped into this northern war? What if the Habsburgs attacked him in the south?[14] The parties negotiated peace in May. Once again, the threat from Corvinus subsided.

Because of the threat of war, Frederick and Johann had not attended the *Reichstag* convening in the spring of 1489 in Frankfurt. They sent only envoys led by the *Hofmeister*'s brother Götz von Ende and the lawyer Otto Spiegel. Flamboyant King Maximilian dominated the *Reichstag*.[15] He appeared anxious to accommodate the estates on reform. He threw out a sop by agreeing to defend the estates against foreigners— but first he must have funds. Elector Berthold was leery. He wanted imperial commitment first, in particular to a central judicial court and to the maintenance of the "public peace" (necessitating a prohibition of feuds). Only then would he endorse the funds Maximilian wanted, though the reformer suspected they were only for Maximilian's personal adventures. Many thought the king never tired of conducting war.[16] The result of the *Reichstag* was half-hearted, yielding only unfulfilled promises from both sides.

Frederick had to be disappointed to miss the 1489 *Reichstag*. *Reichstags* were not always held annually. Because of Maximilian's captivity in Brugge, there had been no *Reichstag* in 1488. The next one would most likely not be until 1491. The reason? Maximilian's revenge. It wasn't enough that the Habsburgs had manipulated trade so that Brugge, once the greatest market town of Flanders, was diminishing in commerce so fast it was being replaced by Antwerp. The imperial army would visit Brugge in 1490, led by the emperor's chief field marshal, none other than Frederick's uncle. Albrecht, also by order of the emperor, carried the title now of supreme governor (*Generalstatthalter*). In Brugge, Albrecht would successfully suppress resistance in a "protracted and gruesome" way.[17]

A *Reichstag* in 1491 would result for Frederick in a gap of four years between highly visible imperial events—opportunities for Frederick to publicly display himself as the perfect Christian prince. Even that gap could grow if he was unable to attend the next one. Leaving his electoral territory when it was under threat from Corvinus or anyone else was not possible. He could only contain his anxiety and pray that events would allow him more freedom of movement in the future. This freedom was a necessity, for as his vision unfolded for himself and his Electoral Saxony, it would reveal that one part required him to accomplish a significant presence "out in the empire."

This Frederick could not do while rooted in Saxony.

"YOU INHERITED SPARTA, NOW ADORN IT"

The young elector launched a strategy on at least two fronts. Notably lacking from a multi-faceted plan, though, was a power marriage for Frederick. Father Ernst at only nineteen married Elisabeth of Bavaria. Uncle Albrecht had married at twenty. But this missing strategy for Frederick in his early twenties may be due only to lack of documentation. Negotiations were secret. No attempts prior to Frederick's trip to the Holy Land in 1493 are recorded, though rumors exist. Elector Ernst may have tried in 1485 to match Frederick with Danish royalty.[18] This is plausible. In 1478, the elector had arranged the marriage of his daughter with Hans, who by 1481 became king of Denmark. A second plausible rumor involved a match with a Brandenburg princess arranged by Frederick's aunt Anna, widow of Brandenburg elector Albrecht Achilles.[19] Other rumors involved a match in Jülich-Berg, a match among the royals of Poland, and even marriage to a daughter of the Russian czar. Another possibility is that Frederick more than admired Maximilian's bright daughter Margarethe, born in 1480.

Success with Margarethe would be enhanced with the success of his imperial efforts. Of Frederick's known strategies, one was for him to become a prince of first rank in the imperial circle. The many immediate rewards in gold, property, and influence that would flow from imperial favor completely justified such a strategy. In addition, imperial favor afforded some degree of protection for his territory. Because such an ambition would require Frederick to be "out in the empire" much of the time, he had to be able to leave Saxony in control of someone he trusted beyond question. That was none other than brother Johann. At only twenty-one, Johann was already more involved than Frederick in military and tax issues of the territory.[20] He was capable enough to administer the territory with the advice of Frederick's top councillors. These men also had to be trustworthy.

The second known front for Frederick was the original electoral land (*Kurlande*) in northern Saxony. Frederick's activity in 1489 makes it clear he had already devised a "*Kurlande*" strategy to advance the fortunes of his portion of Saxony.[21] The Leipzig Division had severely diminished his territory. He intended to address Ernestine Saxony's three greatest flaws: no grand residence,[22] no university, and no religious center. All three he envisioned in the heart of the original electorate to the north, specifically located in what was then a rundown town—little more than a village built on a mound of sand dumped by the River Elbe.[23] Settlers from the flatlands of Flanders, dumped there themselves in the twelfth century by Albrecht the Bear, had glorified this white mound of sand as "white mountain."[24]

Frederick had his mind's eye on Wittenberg.

In 1489, Wittenberg inspired admiration in no one who had traveled anywhere. Even if a traveler had never been out of Saxony, that person still could have tasted the grandeur of Dresden or Leipzig—even grudgingly appreciated Torgau since Uncle Albrecht had enhanced it. If a person had traveled out in the empire itself, Wittenberg was a sorry sight indeed, a mere east-west strip of wooden buildings and neglected stone edifices from forgotten times. A man on foot could stride along its inglorious main strip and rid himself of it in less than fifteen minutes; on a fast horse, he could free himself of it in two minutes. The Ascanian nobles of the electoral land that was defined in the famous Golden Bull of 1356 had already built Wittenberg into a walled town with a castle, Castle Church, town church, and Franciscan monastery. The River Elbe fed a moat outside the walls and one canal within. No sovereign since the Wettiners gained the electorate in 1423 had shown any special interest in the town. Like they had done in other villages, the Wettiners installed some *Amt* officials in Wittenberg to collect money from the townspeople and countryfolk. The locals struggled but managed a living off the sandy soil. Many were said to relieve their drudgery with home-brewed beer.

For most Saxons, the desolate place was even on the wrong side of the River Elbe. A timber bridge one cart wide had once allowed Saxons to cross the Elbe from the south side, but savage winter ice had ripped it out nearly thirty years before the beginning of Frederick's rule. Only ferry and boat traffic reached Wittenberg from the south. Almost immediately in his reign, Elector Frederick had ordered construction of a new Elbe Bridge, timber again but much sturdier with icebreakers.[25] The twelve-columned oak bridge arched high enough in the middle for boats to pass underneath; it was wide enough on top for wagon traffic. Was accessibility and increasing trade Frederick's principal motive? It is more likely Frederick as early as 1486 had a grand vision for this homely town mired in sand.

It could scarcely be coincidence that Konrad Pflüger as early as 1487 was "in steady pay with the elector" and in 1488 he was "living in

Wittenberg."[26] Pflüger was the greatest master builder in Saxony, the acknowledged favorite of the Wettins since his mentor Arnold von Westfalen, architect of the castle Albrechtsburg and cathedral in Meissen, had died in 1480 or 1481.[27] Konrad Pflüger had actually been responsible for finishing Arnold's masterpiece, the Albrechtsburg. Pflüger was a jack-of-all-trades in construction and excelled in vaulting ceilings as no one else since Arnold. Frederick was rarely in Wittenberg, so Pflüger's physical presence in the homely town could mean only one thing. He was there to carry out some essential building project. It is even possible that he had already helped with the challenging construction of the Elbe Bridge.[28]

By 1489, workers began to raze the old Ascanian castle.[29] No small undertaking, the colossal jumble of stones and billowing dust revealed to the most uninformed bumpkin that important further development was in Wittenberg's future. By this time, all or most of Frederick's plan for Wittenberg had jelled. It was within his power to create for Ernestine Saxony one great center with a grand residence, a religious center, and a university, though he would need the pope's authorization for a university or at least permission from the emperor. Yet why had he chosen Wittenberg? He adored Torgau, also on the Elbe and close to his beloved hunting lodge at Lochau. He doubtless chose Wittenberg because it was in the original electoral land (*Kurlande*) defined in the Golden Bull; in case of a dire political event, it was the least likely of any town to be shuffled into another jurisdiction.[30]

The Castle Church dated from about 1338. To honor the dying request of his wife, Kunigunde, the future elector of Saxony Rudolf I had erected the church adjacent to the castle as a memorial chapel to serve the Ascanian dynasty.[31] Kunigunde had been from a royal family in Poland; her brother became the great Polish king Casimir III. The All Saints' Foundation had maintained Kunigunde's memorial church since 1353, possibly a result of Kunigunde's wish or possibly because Rudolf was present at the Bohemian royal court in Prague in 1339 for the consecration of the All Saints' Chapel there. The All Saints' Foundation was appealing to nobles in that it answered only to the pope. In effect, the local nobility controlled the foundation. Further suggestion of a connection with Bohemia is the fact that of the five altars known to have existed in Rudolf's original All Saints' Church in Wittenberg, two altars were dedicated to saints that were patron saints of Bohemia: Sigismund and Wenceslas.

Kunigunde's memorial church in Wittenberg was not the mold for the Wettiners' Three Kings' Chapel (later known as the Princes' Chapel) at the west end of the cathedral in Meissen.[32] The Wettiners built Three Kings' Chapel in the 1420s to serve not only as their dynastic memorial chapel but also as the burial site of the Wettin electors of Saxony. The memorial church in Wittenberg was not the burial place for the Ascanians.[33] The chapel in Wittenberg also differed in that it served as a reliquary shrine. When Frederick began his rule in 1486, the chapel still contained a collection of relics amassed by the Ascanians.[34] Eight reliquaries held more than two hundred relics of Christ and various saints. Included was a thorn from the crown of Christ given to Rudolf I by Philipp VI, king of France.[35] Among other relics were remnants of Sigismund and Wenceslas, probably received as gifts from the Bohemian royals. Nevertheless, until Frederick's arrival, the Wettiners showed scant interest in the Wittenberg church or its relics. The church served mainly as space to store the castle library.

Did this small but superb collection first fire Frederick's zeal for collecting relics?[36]

Many motives can explain Frederick's well-known enthusiasm for relics.[37] One motive was that he was truly pious. He and Johann in 1488 and 1489 had taken numerous pilgrimages to churches and shrines all over Saxony, including Meissen. Motives other than piety, however, can explain an enthusiasm for relics. As sovereigns had realized throughout Europe for centuries, a collection of remarkable relics in a shrine could create renown for its possessor. Bamberg, Nuremberg, and Würzburg even touted by 1487 some form of catalog or *Heiltumsbuch* of their sacred relics.[38] Frederick surely knew of these. Another motive was money gained by selling indulgences from purgatory for venerating holy relics. This method of raising money had been widely practiced since the first Crusades centuries earlier. So a popular reliquary shrine would not only gain fame for its possessor but also bring in significant revenue.

Frederick's plan to attract attention and money to Wittenberg, thus to himself and Ernestine Saxony as well, must have evolved into an even more sparkling vision. One of the mottos he later displayed in Greek meant "You inherited Sparta, now adorn it."[39] He was going to adorn Wittenberg, the drab village of wooden shacks and weathered stone, until it became a glittering showcase boasting a renowned reliquary shrine, a great university, and in the midst of it all, a grand residence of the Elector of Saxony.[40] The beauty of his plan was that during all the years of dusty, noisy construction, Frederick planned to be "out in the empire," enhancing the fame of Ernestine Saxony and his own reputation as one of the leading princes of the empire.

He had already shown the emperor and son that he was willing.

IN THE BOSOM OF THE HABSBURG EMPIRE

In spring 1490, Frederick and Johann were both at the court of King Maximilian in the Tyrolean capital, Innsbruck. Evidence suggests that now the brothers were often together "out in the empire," leaving the reigns of Saxony in the sinewy hands of Heinrich von Ende. Frederick, moreover, was now the king's most prominent companion.[41] Maximilian was the first cousin of Frederick's father, Ernst, but the king was less than four years older than Frederick. Maximilian and Frederick had known each other since childhood, even tested each other in the joust as devotees of knightly ways. They were virtually cousins.

One can speculate they thought alike, probably even sparked new ideas off each other on how a prince should present himself. Regardless of differing political objectives, which a prince was obligated to champion if the welfare of his subjects was at stake, they admired each other. Frederick later said of Maximilian that he was the most gracious man he had ever known.[42] It is no stretch that Frederick considered Maximilian an older brother as well as a mentor.

Through all the years, Maximilian remained openly fond of Frederick. Spalatin, a confidant of Frederick, wrote of this:

> I have seen my miracle, how his imperial Majesty—resplendent in walking and standing before all electors, princes, and estates—recognized him (Frederick) more then all other electors and princes. Such waving, such hand gestures, such behavior from his Majesty if he stood too far from his Majesty causing delay, that certainly if the waving did not help, his imperial Majesty stepped from his throne and pulled this elector closer to him.[43]

Maximilian was cavalier and irrepressible. One of his most endearing qualities was his way of poking fun at himself. He supposedly quipped to

Henry VIII, "I am called His Most Invincible Majesty, but this also does me an injustice because I have often been overcome."[44] On another occasion, Maximilian was alleged to have laughed aloud and later explained, "I laugh to think that God has committed his spiritual rule to such a drunk and nasty cleric as Pope Julius and his civil rule to such a goatlike climber as I am."[45]

Maximilian was in Tyrol to assume the government from bungling, unpopular Archduke Sigismund, a cousin of Maximilian's father. What should have been a prosperous country was in continual financial stress from Sigismund's extravagant spending. Apparently his fifteen-year-old child bride in 1484—none other than Uncle Albrecht's daughter Katharina—remained too tame for the fifty-nine-year-old Sigismund, rumored to be a well-practiced whoremonger. Sigismund began raising money by selling land to the Wittelsbachs, a ploy that riled Tyrolean nobles much more than his lifestyle. Tyrol abutted the holdings of the Wittelsbachs—Munich was only one hard day's ride distant—and the danger to the Habsburg dynasty was obvious. The emperor, who fumed constantly over the Wittelsbachs as his main rivals for power, was more than alarmed. Sigismund had to go. Somehow the old fox persuaded his cousin to abdicate and settle for an annual salary.[46] No doubt the rake Sigismund preferred a pension to extinction. Maximilian, with Frederick at his side, arrived in March 1490 to take the helm.

At the bidding of the emperor, in the meantime, Frederick became a reluctant representative of the empire to negotiate with Rome a crusade that Pope Innocent VIII supposedly wanted.[47] In reality, Cardinal Peraudi, a zealot for crusades, was behind it. The plan was grandiose. Three armies under guidance of the Holy Roman Emperor would conquer the Balkans, Constantinople, Egypt, and Jerusalem. All in three years.[48] It was hopelessly ambitious. Moreover, at the time, the emperor's restless military head Maximilian was keeping one eye on Hungary and the other eye on the duchy of Brittany.[49] The imperial princes did not want a crusade either. Even the pope, in poor health, had little enthusiasm. All but Cardinal Peraudi were satisfied to leave the pretentious plan dormant.

The singular event of 1490 was the death of Corvinus. What a thorn was removed! His demise in early April was sudden, as liberating for Frederick and Saxony as warm breezes of an early spring. The Hungarian king had no stolid successor. Janos, seventeen and naïve, was easily shunted aside by Hungarian nobles. Of course Maximilian claimed the crown of Hungary, but they repulsed him too. Vladislaus prevailed only through the strength of the Hungarian nobles. Elsewhere the gains of Corvinus dwindled away. By the middle of August, the empire recovered Vienna and the rest of Austria. Maximilian exploited the weakness of Vladislaus and tried with limited success to conquer Hungary. By November, the imperial army conquered Stuhlweißenburg,[50] historically a royal stronghold and close enough to Budapest to yield concessions. Swiss allies and their ingenious new concept of using "lansquenets" on foot (early form of infantry) in addition to knights on horse led to Maximilian's uncharacteristic lightning victory.[51] The following year, Hungary paid Maximilian 100,000 gulden and even conceded him the right to succeed Vladislaus if this one left no heir. The unceasing activities of Maximilian also had gained him by proxy the hand of thirteen-year-old Anne of Brittany. The Bretons believed France or Britain would swallow them unless Anne, heiress to the duchy, allied Brittany by marriage to the Holy Roman Empire.

MYRIAD ENTITIES TO GOVERN IN HIS SAXONY

By early summer 1490, Frederick and Johann were back in Saxony. In the administrations of both Saxon lines, they were careful not to issue sweeping ordinances for their individual territories.[52] The intermeshing—even blurring—of rights and properties from the Leipzig Division made the princes leery of changes that might damage the rights of some of their subjects. Much of territorial business, therefore, involved joint action with Albertine Saxony. Albrecht's Ducal Saxony was also a partner in the defense pacts renewed for ten years or more with the imperial cities of Nordhausen and Mühlhausen.[53] A prickly problem was how to divide extensive property controlled by the Wettins in Silesia. The area in two large blocks was as large as one-fifth of Frederick's territory. The northernmost block contained the cities of Storkow and Beeskow, the southern block the cities of Sorau and Sagan. Albrecht wanted to end joint control but Frederick, always cautious and deliberate, would agree only to rotate management of the properties every three years.

Frederick promoted Hans von Leimbach to *Rentmeister*, the highest financial office in the electorate. Leimbach, about forty-five, had first endeared himself in Colditz to Frederick's paternal grandmother,

Margaretha (the sister of the emperor). Small wonder patrician Leimbach, then living in Leipzig, was knighted in 1478. By the 1480s, he was listed as one of the four richest men in Leipzig, owning not only considerable property and mining interests throughout Saxony but also a financial firm in Nuremberg.[54] He had proven in every way that he merited Frederick's highest financial office. Yet cynics must have noted that, except for his official title, Leimbach was virtually a functional twin to Albrecht's *Oberzehntner* Blasbalg, also a wealthy merchant of Leipzig but appointed three years earlier. Five years after Uncle Albrecht had revived the highest territorial court (*Oberhofgericht*), Frederick in 1493 followed suit.[55] Now, however, the two Saxon territories were combined in one *Oberhofgericht* that would alternate meeting at Ernestine Altenburg and at Albertine Leipzig.

Finance would remain a major concern. Frederick had inherited not only the debts of his father but also the debts of his uncle Wilhelm's rule of Thuringia. Frederick would demonstrate he was frugal, at least compared to other princes who ran debts into hundreds of thousands of gulden. Uncle Albrecht dealt with monetary problems as well. In 1490, the divided Saxonies, who minted in common, developed a united monetary exchange.[56] With few exceptions, the Saxons minted silver coins. In 1491, for the first time Frederick's image appeared on a coin.[57] This was, of course, one form of "representation." The Zwickau *Zinsgroschen* became known as the "bearded groschen," because from Frederick's right-facing profile jutted a very prominent beard. Although capped, his hair fell to the shoulders and over the forehead almost to his eyebrows. Over his right shoulder he held the electoral sword. The other side of the "bearded groschen" showed the coat of arms helm of the Albertine duchy of Saxony. The "standard" coin of the empire was the Rhine Gulden, worth about twenty times as much as an equivalent sized silver coin. For large expenditures, silver was inconvenient. Frederick once wrote in exasperation to Johann, who was to join him at a *Reichstag*, to bring some "good money," that is, gulden of gold.[58] Even that gold coin had become inconsistent, slowly decreasing its gold content. Other coinage was even less reliable. The Wettins nevertheless mandated one gold Rhine Gulden equal to twenty-one of their own silver groschen (*Spitzgroschen*) or forty-two of their half-groschen (*Schwertgroschen*). To ease the problem of currency exchange, the Wettins established monetary agreements with neighbors. For example, in 1492, they agreed with Hesse to mint equivalent coins of the same weight containing the same amount of silver.

From the first, by necessity Frederick had involved himself in the details of administrative and judicial functions. He "knew the law by heart" and could govern "with a flick of the wrist."[59] Frederick suffered no insubordination. When the Torgau city council attempted to exclude the elector from local *Amt* business, they found themselves in 1488 relieved of all administrative and judicial duties. Frederick well understood the importance of the *Amt* office and its chief officer, the "*Amt* man" (*Amtmann*).[60] The *Amt* office, the smallest administrative unit in his government, referred not only to the office and its officials but also to the spatial district.[61] The territory of Electoral Saxony unfortunately was even more complicated than some three hundred coalescing *Amt* offices; interspersed with the hundreds of *Amt* office areas were many dozens of properties held by religious entities and noble lords.

Some referred to the *Amt* man by an older term with a military connotation, the *Hauptmann*. The *Amt* man had both administrative and judicial powers. Working for the *Amt* man was his deputy, the *Schösser*, the proverbial "tax collector." Assisting was a *Geleitsmann*, an escort who, among other things, provided passage. Helping also were bailiffs, foresters, lake masters, scribes, armed knights on horse (*Knechte zu Ross*), and foot soldiers (*Knechte zu Fuss*).[62] The *Amt* officials were not all powerful. In some cases they were subordinate to other authorities, such as the mayor (*Bürgermeister*) in a city or even the *Schultheiss* in a village. The position of *Amt* man in some *Amts* was particularly distinguished. Among these many plums were Torgau, Colditz, Weimar, and Altenburg. It is no surprise that many had stepped on that rung as they climbed the ladder into the highest circle of electoral officials. Of all sovereign territories, Saxony had, from ancient times, one unique position in its scheme of administration. There were about one hundred *Schriftsassen*. Each one spoke directly to the electoral circle, essentially acting equivalent to *Amt* men. These *Schriftsassen* were usually powerful knights or, in some cases, leaders of cities.

Frederick administered the *Amt* system rigorously. One later noted that Frederick "completely clamped down the lid on his *Amt* people and Schössers" and added with pinched fingers, "no further than that did he trust them."[63] *Rentmeister* Hans von Leimbach administered all the finances and accounting of the numerous *Amt* offices as well.[64] There were "accounting commissions" of Frederick's highest advisers to review written records of the *Amts* and even hearings in which *Amt* officials had to account for their activity. One of Frederick's favorite proverbs, which reflected his attitude in almost all his relationships, seemed even more appropriate for these accountings: "One should not believe everything like it has been said."[65] The focus of all this was to establish and protect the sovereign's rights. Yet controversies between the *Amt* officials and the electoral advisers did not always end in the advisers' favor. Occasionally, Frederick or Johann would side with the *Amt* people. It was politically unwise to abuse this essential network of local administrators.

Crises of every kind arose, and the elector had to deal with them. They might involve a fire in a village or an epidemic or a food shortage. The elector had to try to provide assistance. On the other hand, he had to be aware of economic conditions. Influenced by his competent financial advice, he imposed an export tax on grain, which was leaving Saxony all too readily. Not all directives were wise or successful. He once issued a territorial ordinance on maintenance of roads and control of crime that was so vague it proved unworkable.

AGE-OLD PIETIES

Frederick surely heard the cynical proverb of his time: "Today pious, tomorrow devilish."[66] That could be no truer for anyone than for a prince. He and Johann nevertheless did not neglect their piety.[67] In July 1489, they had taken a ten-day pilgrimage in Saxony from Jena to Naunhof.[68] Several days they were in Albertine Saxony. Due to a number of years of bad weather during harvest, especially for fruit, in April 1490, Frederick issued an order for his Saxons to appeal to God for good weather through "special processions und pilgrimages."[69] Beginning in June, he personally journeyed to shrines from Vogelgesang (near Torgau), Wittenberg, Magdeburg, and Angermünde to the Holy Blood shrine at Wilsnack in Brandenburg.[70] The latter was three bleeding eucharistic wafers from the church that burned in 1383. Bleeding hosts were such common "miracles" from that time that many, among them cardinals of the church, refused to recognize them. On the other hand, many venerated the Wilsnack shrine, including Frederick.[71] He journeyed there with his father and brother Ernst in 1484 after the death of his mother, Elisabeth. The renowned English mystic Margery Kempe had been there in 1433, even before a great new church was built from the money that poured in.

In 1490, Frederick sponsored the printing of "The Heavenly Treasure Trove," a booklet by Johann von Paltz.[72] The black-robed Augustinian had preached before Frederick and Johann in Torgau. Frederick was so impressed, he requested some of the sermons be printed. To the silver-conscious princes, Paltz had presented four sermons metaphorically as lodes of silver ore. (1) How contemplating suffering and wounds of Christ leads to healing our own sins. (2) How restraining bad thoughts planted by evil spirits helps to obey Holy Sacraments. (3) How the Good Death can save the soul of someone who has done no good at all. (4) How anointing with oil works to prepare the soul for eternity. Some of the "lodes" (sermons) Paltz developed into "shafts" of further piety. The booklet of Paltz became relatively widespread and popular for an age of general illiteracy.

Significantly, Paltz said salvation was not necessarily through good works but through the death and suffering of Christ. Observance of the Sacraments was enough. This faintly foreshadows the revolutionary message to come more than twenty years later: salvation was not through good works but through grace.[73] Not much may be assumed about Frederick's acceptance of the piety of Paltz in its particulars. For example, Paltz regarded pilgrimages as a snare of the devil and even specifically condemned Wilsnack.[74] Frederick's willing promotion of the sermons of Paltz suggests that from his first days of rule he was open-minded to a well-argued discussion of theological differences, even if they contradicted his own beliefs.

Theology of the time was not monolithic, not even within one religious order. Piety itself varied from that of Augustinian Paltz, in essence "massive Marian piety in conjunction with the propagation of monasticism and indulgences," to "its precise opposite," the long-standing piety of Cistercian St. Bernard of Clairvaux with concentration on Christ and emphasis on discipleship.[75] Frederick, who never failed to hear Mass daily,[76] probably practiced the gamut. That was a characteristic mindset of the time. It was optimism grown large: within a plethora of elements, some even contradictory, there was order.[77] Among Frederick and the lay population, this plethora of piety did not result in tension. In the universities, conversely, the myriad philosophies, pieties, and theologies with a strong undercurrent of humanism—an intellectual stew that had never existed in such abundance before—was stimulating many to vigorously debate theology and philosophy.[78]

The Wettins of Frederick's time favored the Franciscans.[79] This was not unusual. Franciscan theology, championed by Bonaventure and honed by William of Occam in the fourteenth century, was prominent if not dominant throughout the empire. Frederick, in addition to urging reform in the Franciscan monasteries in Torgau and Wittenberg earlier, also did that in Altenburg in 1489. Every prince had his own personal father confessor (*Beichtvater*). Frederick's personal father confessor from 1486 to 1491 is not documented. Possibly his father confessor died in early 1492, because Frederick clearly made it known then to the Franciscan provincial minister that he wanted Jakob Vogt transferred to Torgau. Franciscan Vogt, who had served at Meissen, was then serving at Nordhausen. Vogt was transferred to Torgau.

Jakob Vogt was no theologian, probably not even a preacher. Yet it was Father Vogt who Frederick sent to deliver gifts to Princess Margarete of Anhalt.[80] Vogt was also especially useful in procuring relics. "Vogt obtained the acquisition of many relics for the foundation church, which he arranged and kept in Wittenberg. Here he received room and board not with his religious brothers, but in the castle."[81] Father Vogt was trustworthy and discrete with a good sense for business, perhaps even a shrewd sense. Moreover, he was not just a clerical lackey; he was respected by scholars, including the later reformers in Wittenberg.

His appeal to Frederick may be understood in part by also looking at the Franciscans in general. Their vow to observe a rule of poverty and renunciation of the world was much stricter than other orders. Franciscans served laymen in particular, emphasizing pastoral duties. Similar to the Augustinians, they venerated the Holy Mother, and in Saxony they venerated her mother, St. Anne, as well. They also focused on the incarnation of Christ and His suffering. They expressed piety in the admiration at the stations of the cross and the worship of the altar Sacraments. They stressed the Mass and Confession. The barefoot Franciscan girded his gray robe with a white cord, from which hung the "Seraphic Rosary" with seventy beads. Using the rosary, he recited the Apostles' Creed, one Our Father, and then three Hail Marys. After each ten repetitions (one decade), the pious meditated on the mystery of Christ.[82]

Frederick probably carried such a rosary and was in full sympathy with the Franciscan form of piety, yet he was also open to other forms. After all, the proverb said, "If one is devout, that is everything."[83]

REICHSTAGS: NUREMBERG 1491 AND KOBLENZ 1492

Christmas of 1490 flaunted a great snowfall. Then the winter became deadly—one of the worst in decades.[84] It seemed eternal cold settled on the empire. The great Rhine froze over from Basel to Cologne. Snow persisted into May, killing vines and buds of fruit trees. When the frigid attack ended in June, Frederick was only too ready for a trip to the *Reichstag* in Nuremberg. He had no doubt, though, about his representation all those bone-chilling months. He had not attended a *Reichstag* in four years. He did not disappoint. In the June 1491 Corpus Christi procession at Nuremberg, Frederick caused a stir when, instead of riding with the king and other princes in the procession, he trudged on foot, looking humble but showing his "bright sword" for Christ.[85] Maximilian must have been shocked but proud of the showmanship of his protégé.[86]

The Nuremberg *Reichstag* itself was the usual tired product of the ancient emperor. The princes, still dominated by Berthold, had to remind the emperor bluntly that it was useless to keep holding diets to supposedly deal with imperial matters if he refused to summon all the imperial estates.[87] Once again, the old fox had failed to notify all the estates. Once again, he had called the *Reichstag* only to ask for more money. Now Maximilian not only squabbled with Hungary, for he had not given up on capturing its crown, but he also parried with France.

The estates at the 1491 Nuremberg *Reichstag* proceeded in a puzzling way. Instead of demanding reform in return for their support, they asked for reconciliation between the Swabian League and the House of Wittelsbach. That wasn't too surprising, because four of the electors were in the line of fire. Apparently they felt that with their innumerable alliances, this conjunction would plunge the empire into an internal war. Ironically, the Wittelsbachs were as resistant to change as the emperor, stating their aversion to yielding to any imposition pushed on them by the empire.[88] Only after futilely voicing this concern did the old issues reappear. The emperor seemed ready to grant one slight concession— regular *Reichstags*—if that was a concession at all. Many of the estates considered *Reichstags* a nuisance that just wasted their time and money. The estates wanted real judicial reform; the emperor wanted commitments to help militarily. Several times, imperial allies tried to divorce military support from judicial reform. Frederick joined the electors of Brandenburg and Cologne as well as others to protest this maneuver. Finally, Maximilian recast the entire list of grievances in such a way that no agreement was possible. Lack of any subsequent action by the emperor, or for that matter by the estates, exposed the *Reichstag* as all posturing and talk once again. No one could deny, though, that the princes (and many prelates) enjoyed the banquets, willing women, and gambling.

After the *Reichstag*, in December 1491, Anne of Brittany—supposedly betrothed to Maximilian—through convoluted political moves by Pope Innocent VIII and France married the French king Charles VIII. She was only fourteen years old. A well-traveled story said that Anne was so unhappy with her coerced marriage, she arrived for her wedding with her servants carrying two beds. This marriage was a colossal double blow to Maximilian. His daughter Margarethe had been betrothed since the age of three to Charles VIII. The French king had her dowry. Even if Maximilian had not possessed the archetypical feudal mind, this affront was more than ample reason for war. As a contemporary expressed it, "Such a disgrace can be washed off only by blood."[89] The imperial circle generated pamphlets to inflame the empire. The pamphlets lamented the "Bride Robbery" and reviled the "hunchbacked king" Charles VIII.[90] The imperial estates yawned. To them, it was just another case of Maximilian's risky ambitions for the House of Habsburg. Maximilian had to wage war against France with almost entirely Tyrolean troops.

Nevertheless, Maximilian, displaying his usual optimism and high energy, was right back at the table with the estates in the autumn of 1492. At the *Reichstag* of Koblenz, he presented an elaborate proposal for administrative reform of the empire. The estates saw it only as a framework for collecting an imperial tax. Berthold embraced it but only to revise it with an ax. First, he gutted the imperial army, the administrative arm that was to collect the taxes. Next, he insisted the emperor and the king pay their portions of the tax before the others paid. Berthold suggested a final agreement would be concluded a few months later. Such a meeting never happened. In truth, the *Reichstags* had become charades. It was all too plain that too few voices were for a true confederacy of territories. The driving forces within the empire were dynastic. And Frederick was no different.

Yet sometime after the *Reichstag*, Frederick performed a delicate mission for Maximilian. The king still sought a power marriage, apparently much harder than Frederick sought his own. Frederick corresponded with the House of the Duke of Milan (Ludovico Sforza) in order to obtain for Maximilian particulars about the duke's daughter Bianca.[91] The following year, Frederick would be in Venice at the same time Beatrice d'Este, the Duchess of Milan, was there.[92] He had to conduct his queries in greatest secrecy, because Maximilian did not want his father to know about it. Old Friedrich III contemptuously called the Sforzas "a dynasty of shoemakers." Bianca Maria Sforza's ancestry was indeed singular. Her grandfather Francesco Sforza was a commoner, but he rose to a military enterpriser (*condottiero*) so successful and so well connected that he became the Duke of Milan. It was an extremely rare feat. Frederick learned that the Duke of Milan desperately wanted his daughter Bianca to marry an emperor. His offered dowry of 400,000 ducats would squelch any qualms of Maximilian about her humble past.[93] All assumed the twenty-year-old, widowed at age 10, was still a virgin. Whether or not she was actually present, Frederick concluded doe-eyed Bianca was trim and passably attractive.

Did he describe her as well as the connoisseur Maximilian could describe a woman? In 1477, Maximilian had written a friend about his bride, Maria of Burgundy, "I have a lovely, good, virtuous wife . . . small of body, much smaller than 'Rosina,' and snow-white; brown hair, a small nose, a small head and features, brown and grey eyes mixed, beautiful and expressive. Her mouth is somewhat high, but pristine and red."[94]

Frederick's report pleased Maximilian. Bianca was neither ugly nor fat, but she had a mountainous dowry. The wedding would be negotiated.[95]

BEFORE HOLY LAND: ACTIONS LAUDABLE AND VILE

His cities on the River Elbe—Wittenberg and Torgau—continued to occupy Frederick. In Wittenberg, the master builder Konrad Pflüger planned the construction of an enormous three-winged structure that would be both castle and church.[96] Pflüger's plan did not simply overlay the old Ascanian castle and the old All Saints' Memorial Chapel. Although Pflüger had to raze the old castle to prepare the new foundation, that activity did not affect the old All Saints' Chapel. The chapel would still stand several years later.[97]

In Torgau, Frederick intended to build a Chapel of the Holy Cross, one so delightful it would later be called the "Beautiful Church" (*Schöne Kirche*).[98] Before he left Saxony for the Holy Land in the spring of 1493, he would see the cornerstone in place. At Torgau, he also was set on replacing the old ice-battered wooden bridge across the River Elbe with a proper stone-pillared bridge. A section had been torn out since 1471.[99] Frederick learned conditions for a bridge over the Elbe by the Hartenfels castle were poor because of the bottom conditions and the strength of the current. So he deferred action until he could consult various builders all over the empire.

Frederick was not myopic. He saw beyond the River Elbe. In the years 1491 through 1493, he approved construction on existing castles in three locations: Eilenburg near Leipzig, Vogtsberg (near Plauen in the Vogtland), and also Weimar.[100] He wanted to distribute major work throughout his territory. Like any enlightened sovereign, he knew what a boon such construction projects were to the local subjects.[101] One scholar noted, "From the moment he assumed power in August 1486 at the age of twenty-three until his death ... Frederick kept an army of master builders, painters, sculptors, carpenters, wood workers, and stone masons busy throughout the Ernestine Wettin territories renovating or replacing old family residences, their adjoining chapels, and local churches and monasteries which had fallen into disrepair."[102]

In 1492, Frederick successfully petitioned Pope Innocent VIII to appoint Johann III von Schönberg the new bishop of Naumburg, a diocese entirely embedded in Ernestine territory. The appointment was contrary to chapter wishes and showed the influence of a powerful territorial prince like Frederick. Johann was nephew of his predecessor Dietrich IV von Schönberg, whom Frederick had dominated. In February 1493, Frederick stunned his new bishop of Naumburg by ordering him to expel the Jews from his diocese, just as Frederick himself was doing throughout Ernestine Saxony. Frederick wrote Bishop Johann III that the Jews were enemies and despisers of the Christian faith. The Jews caused "pernicious trouble to your subjects and ours, from which daily complaints are carried to us."[103] It could be no coincidence that his brother Ernst, archbishop of Magdeburg, was carrying out an expulsion of fourteen hundred Jews from the forecity of Magdeburg. Ernst turned their synagogue into a chapel of St. Mary (*Marienkapelle*) and changed the name of the vacated Jewish Quarter (*Judendorf*) to Quarter of St. Mary (*Mariendorf*). This definitely seems revenge over a great bone of contention between Jews and certain Christian elements at this time. The Jews were impolitic enough to point out the Hebrew of a passage in the Book of Isaiah that Christians translated, "Behold, a virgin shall conceive and bear a son, and shall call his name Immanuel," is more correctly translated, "Behold, a young woman shall conceive and bear a son, and shall call his name Immanuel."[104]

Veneration of Mary was not the only cause.[105] The status of Jews among Christians had changed in the thirteenth century. Before the change, the Church was influenced by St. Augustine, who viewed the Jews as belonging in the Christian world—clearly a presence proved by the Holy Scriptures. Moreover, according to some, such as Thomas Aquinas, the Jews in the New Testament had actually recognized Jesus as their Savior, perhaps even the Son of God. In 1103, Holy Roman Emperor Heinrich IV had the leading lords of the empire swear to peace for the Jews.[106]

In the thirteenth century, however, the two dominant religious orders, Dominicans and Franciscans, began to attack the Talmud of the Jews. The Talmud was post-biblical writing by rabbis, or so-called rabbinical literature. The Talmud in the eyes of Dominicans and Franciscans had become dominant among the Jews. The Jews, the two orders claimed, had drifted from Mosaic Law. As a result, for Dominicans and Franciscans, the Jews were now as unwelcome in the Christian world as Muslims and heretics.

Contempt for Jews did not abate. In Frederick's youth and early rule, literate people widely read fierce polemics against Jews. In 1474, Dominican Peter Schwarz preached such rants, which were published the following year in Esslingen and Nuremberg. More hostile yet was "Description of the Atrocities of the Jews" by the Franciscan Alfonsus de Spina, printed and reprinted since 1471. The messages were incendiary: The Jews murdered God. The Jews hated the Christian Church. The Jews wanted the wealth of Christians, even their blood.[107] The *Pharetra catholicei fidei* would appear in 1495.[108] Bearing the hands of the Franciscans, the *Pharetra* is a manual not for converting Jews, but for convicting "the worthless Jews who have been repulsed by God." Although it appeared after 1493, this manual reflects the angry undercurrent of anti-Semitism in the Franciscans. Frederick relied most of all on Franciscans for spiritual guidance. Perhaps his reason was not religious. He may have had covert political reasons or he may have been prodded into it by brother Ernst, but such a harsh action of expelling the Jews did not surprise his contemporaries.

THE HOLY LAND PILGRIMAGE AND ALL IT BESTOWED

Uncle Albrecht had journeyed to the Holy Land in 1476. He turned thirty-three on the trip.[109] Fifteen years before that, Albrecht's uncle Wilhelm (the Brave) at age 36 had made the pilgrimage. Now in 1493, Frederick at thirty had decided to travel to the Holy Land. The four grand ways to display one's reverence for God (according to Spalatin) were "church-building, adornments, relics, and pilgrimages."[110] Frederick was ready to add the greatest pilgrimage of all. If one could afford it, there were many other good reasons for such a journey. It offered prestige among men. How many could say they had walked where Christ walked? How many in the empire could make such an expensive, perilous journey? For a nobleman, it bestowed the precious knighthood of the Holy Sepulchre. And the trip offered immense spiritual rewards: hundreds of years of indulgences and forgiveness of all sins.

On the other hand, mortal danger traveled with the pilgrim.[111] Uncle Albrecht, despite his mother's anxious warnings, left Saxony for the Holy Land with an entourage of 119 fellow pilgrims.[112] Eleven died during the sea voyage from Venice to the Holy Land. Few things were more horrifying than the thought of being trussed in burlap, weighted down, and thrown into the depths of the sea. That is why those with money paid the captain in advance to prevent such a ghastly end. The captain would preserve them until they could be buried on land. Others with Albrecht died while ashore. Some may have died fighting. At Jaffa, his party fought Mamelukes and killed two of them. For many reasons, one real possibility for a pilgrim was death.

Frederick was acutely conscious of the possibility. He, who had lost his mother and brother to the plague, who had lost his father during a hunt, who had long endured bone-breaking jousts, had never prepared a will. Yet on February 19, 1493, exactly one month before his departure,

Frederick made out his first will.[113] He willed money for poor students to attend a university, suggesting Leipzig or Erfurt, but hinting that in the future such a student attend a university in his territory. For his own funeral, he explicitly named reformed monks and pious priests. His burial site was not to be in the Princes' Chapel in Meissen, but it was to be at the Benedictine monastery Reinhardsbrunn, which lay in forested hills near Eisenach in Thuringia. For his burial, the monks would receive one thousand gulden. Frederick and Johann had taken a personal interest in the monastery, visiting in 1492 and using their papal authority to convince a recalcitrant abbot to resign.[114] If reform failed at Reinhardsbrunn, Frederick was to be buried in Meissen after all. Loyal Johann, who would remain in Saxony, would see to it.

On March 19, 1493, Frederick began his pilgrimage to the Holy Land for his expressed reasons of "special intimacy and devotion."[115] That day, he departed Torgau in a ceremony at the Church of St. Mary, followed by a procession through a throng of citizens.[116] His brothers, Johann and Ernst, were at his side the entire day, including the half-day ride to Eilenburg. From Leipzig the next day, Frederick traveled to Naumburg. From there to Nuremberg, he took a way similar to Albrecht's: through Saalfeld, Coburg, Vierzehnheiligen (Jena), and Bamberg. From Nuremberg, he took his own route through Augsburg and Landsberg into Austria. His contingent snowballed as he journeyed south. Spalatin later indicated ten were from Franconia, Swabia, and Bavaria; fifteen were from Vogtland.[117] Frederick's entourage was larger than that of his uncle Albrecht in 1476; various records combine to account for about 190 by the time they sailed at Venice, compared to Albrecht's 119.

The invaluable accounts book for the entire journey was kept by "keeper of the door" Hans Hundt von Wenkheim, who managed the elector's privy purse.[118] Details of the pilgrimage were preserved from Hundt's record and recollections of Frederick years later to Spalatin.[119] Of course Frederick's most essential advisers remained in Saxony with Johann (although several on the trip became key advisers later). The only other prince on Frederick's trip was Duke Christoph of Bavaria, the forty-four-year-old younger brother of Frederick's mother.[120] Other titled nobles were Philipp von Anhalt, Heinrich von Stolberg, Adam von Beichlingen, Balthasar and Hans von Schwarzburg, Heinrich von Gera, and Anarg von Wildenfels.[121] Untitled nobles (knights) and advisers consisted of Sebastian von Mistelbach, Heinrich von Schaumberg,

Degenhart Pfeffinger, Konrad Metzsch, Rudolf von der Planitz, Hans von Feilitzsch, Caspar and Haubold Pflug, Sigmund and Konrad von Maltitz, and finally Heinrich von Bünau of Teuchern.[122] Vital among Frederick's companions were his confessor, Jakob Vogt, and physician, Martin Pollich von Mellerstadt. Other religious and scholarly pilgrims numbered ten. And what prince would be without his fool? The jester Hänsel entertained Frederick at least to Venice.[123] Also mentioned was Johannes Moler (or Maler, suggesting an artist).[124] The presence of an artist is plausible for a thorough sovereign like Frederick, though no works are known to have survived. For every one of the ninety or so notables mentioned for Frederick's pilgrimage, there was more or less one servant.

After the initial journey of eighteen days, the entourage stayed more than one week in Linz.[125] Maximilian was in Freiburg-im-Breisgau.[126] The Habsburgs were trying to resolve their conflict with France.[127] Both sides would win and lose. Maximilian was to recover the greater part of Margarethe's dowry, no doubt not enough in his eyes. In addition, his duchy of Burgundy seemed at last stable, which he knew was a bitter pill for the French. On the other hand, Maximilian conceded much. All documents of the "Bride Robbery," especially the marriage contract between Anne of Brittany and Maximilian, were to be destroyed. The French had asked Maximilian for a free hand in Naples. He appeared uninterested, but perhaps agreeable.[128]

But the outcome with France was not the reason Frederick lingered in Linz. Emperor Friedrich III, at seventy-seven a Methuselah for the time, was gravely ill. His circulation had become so poor that one leg ached inconsolably. Physicians had already amputated the gangrenous lower part. But more than that pain in his leg cast the great castle in gloom. Sometimes the emperor even refused to see Maximilian.[129] It was rumored the old fox had hidden treasure, though some thought that was just his ploy to obtain loans from financiers. Maximilian wondered, nevertheless, just what his cranky father had hidden from him. Frederick lingered in Linz because the emperor wanted him to stay longer. Had they a special bond? Was it Frederick's honesty that appealed to the old emperor? As Frederick would recall, "Perhaps he suspected he would not see him again."[130] Yet the old fox had made the same pilgrimage himself in 1436, so he knew there was a window for favorable weather through the Alps that was unforgiving. Frederick finally said farewell and continued to Innsbruck.

As so many travelers did, from Innsbruck they went on to cross the Alps through the Brenner Pass. In mid-April, the warming pass was friendly again, with snow only in shaded areas. The pilgrims descended into the Venetian Republic. Uncle Albrecht had ventured through a patchwork of Italian-speaking territories to visit Mantua, Florence, and Rome on his nine-month pilgrimage. Frederick, always cautious and frugal, proceeded straight through Sterzing and Treviso to Venice. He arrived at the enormous city on April 29. It was routine at the time to stay in Venice nearly one month to make preparations; indeed Frederick would not embark until May 23. First, they contracted their ship. Then they arranged for stabling their mounts and for lodging those in the contingent not making the voyage. In the markets of Venice they purchased whatever else they needed for the trip: "groceries, linen clothes, straw mats, cotton covers, soap, drugs and dishes, oil against lice, herbs against fleas, a chest for belongings, a pack for provisions and a collecting bucket."[131]

The voyage was in one ship (galley or "*Gallehe Paschardi*").[132] These were not small but great vessels powered by both sail and oars, requiring crews of 120 to 180 "rowers, and officers, steersmen, and sail-trimmers."[133] Life was easy for the rowers with a fair wind or hellish with no wind, forcing them to row to exhaustion. The boatswain rained curses and blows. The captain or *padrone* was lord over all. The vessels varied little from one another. Passengers could number up to two hundred.[134] Wealthy passengers had cabins at the stern (rear) of the ship. Next in comfort were bunks below these cabins. Most voyagers slept midship, head next to the side of the ship on shoulder-to-shoulder mattresses. Unfortunately, these were not on the deck but in the hold, reached by climbing down a ladder. There was little light, less ventilation. Worse yet, they slept below horses and livestock endlessly trampling on the deck boards.[135]

The Dominican friar Felix Faber, who made the pilgrimage voyage in 1480 and 1483, wrote of the most inconvenient aspect of the voyage other than death.[136] Every pilgrim had beside his cramped sleeping place a clay pot for urine and vomit. Passengers stumbling through the dark and tossing seas frequently dumped the pots. To defecate during the day, passengers lined up to the two privies on the bow of the ship. An old salt advised Faber to do this several times a day, whether he felt the urge or not. Too often it would be inconvenient; if neglected, constipation could become severe. Night was the worst time. Trying to reach the privies in the dark was difficult. Climbing directly over the side and hanging on to the gunwale was perilous but common. Some never made it to either option, enraging fellow passengers. Naturally in his cabin Frederick did not endure such disgusting conditions, but most of his fellow travelers did.

Sea itineraries to the Holy Land were rigid unless altered by severe weather. In routes seasoned by the centuries, the galleys skirted the east edge of the Adriatic Sea, much of the route along the hostile Turkish Ottoman Empire. Half of the four-week voyage to the Holy Land was sailing; the other half was visiting port cities on Venetian-controlled islands on the way. Frederick stopped in Kandia (today's Crete), Rhodes, and Cyprus. To travel openly as a prince would attract unwelcome attention. Just as Uncle Albrecht traveled as "Junker Albrecht from Grimma," Frederick also traveled under another name.

Since the middle of the thirteenth century, the Mameluke sultan in Egypt controlled access to Jerusalem and the holy sites. Christian pilgrims had to register after arriving in the port of Jaffa and wait for permission to disembark.[137] Frederick's galley sailed into the Jaffa harbor on June 21 and lay in anchor three days before they set foot on shore. The Mamelukes then detained the pilgrims overnight while they were further "certified." The pilgrims must have been consoled in that their religion declared they were now in a special state of grace, virtually absolved of sin. In the meantime, the *padrone* procured guides and supplies for the excursion to Jerusalem and Bethlehem.

Frederick traveled as a Moorish warrior. On June 26, they stopped to rest at Ramla, a very significant city at the time. Officials hassled their *padrone* over lack of proper papers, a very common occurrence for pilgrims. Usually such difficulties could be smoothed over by money. At midnight, they departed in the cool of the night for Jerusalem. The next day, on June 27, after two days of hoofing up the long incline, Frederick and his entourage reached Jerusalem.[138] The purchase of three horses in Venice, recorded in Hans Hundt's accounting book, suggests Frederick did not ride the traditional donkey as so many pilgrims did.[139] Ancient Jerusalem in daytime was as hot as any city he had ever known. Burning winds scorched his face and lungs as he had never experienced before. Frederick lodged at the Hospital of the Knights of St. John, not far from the tightly guarded Church of the Holy Sepulchre.[140] One highlight of any trip to Jerusalem for a nobleman was being dubbed a knight of the Holy Sepulchre. This carried future obligations, among others, to hear Mass daily and to protect the Christian Church and its servants. On the evening of June 29, Frederick was knighted by Heinrich von Schaumburg, already a Knight of the Holy Sepulchre from his previous visit. Then Frederick knighted other nobles in his party. Only a Knight of the Holy Sepulchre could wear the "Jerusalem Cross," a crutched cross with smaller crosses in each of the four quarters. The five crosses were symbols of the traditional five wounds of Jesus.

Deadening heat or not, Frederick visited all the main sites in Jerusalem and Bethlehem. The pilgrims had to be careful with the Mamelukes. Many visitors were self-important, and the Mamelukes themselves were touchy—both parties only too ready to take offense. In previous pilgrimages by Wettins, several incidents were recorded.[141] One of the party of Wilhelm the Brave came too close to the Muslim Dome of the Rock, which many pilgrims thought was Solomon's Temple, and suffered a heavy fine. He was lucky. One in Albrecht's party who actually looked inside the Dome of the Rock was caught by the Mamelukes and beaten.

The visitors were no angels. Although some were deeply devout, others intended to take as much of the Holy Land back home with them as possible. They chipped and gouged pieces from walls, floors, and columns. Angry reprimands from Franciscans, the ubiquitous religious order in Jerusalem, had little effect. Even protests of fellow travelers could not stop the onslaught. In Albrecht's party, Hans von Mergenthal, the first Saxon *Landrentmeister*, virtually salivated over the prospect of taking home pieces of the Holy Sepulchre. He recorded in his chronicle that it was "covered completely with marble that one can strike loose from it at night." Albrecht himself took back to Saxony a large piece of porphyry gouged from the "Temple of Solomon."[142]

Some pilgrims were skeptical, not of the truth behind the holy sites but of the validity of the sites themselves. Even the friar Felix Faber believed the Mamelukes created many false sites and even more false relics. He wrote that the "infidels . . . set out for sale wood said to be part of the Holy Cross, and nails, and thorns, and bones, and many other things of the same kind, to delude the unwary and cheat them out of their money."[143] One of the most despicable relic frauds stemmed from the slaughter of the innocents described in Matthew 2:16 in the New Testament.[144]

Felix Faber wrote of this fraud:

> It is a fact that Saracens and Mamelukes receive the bodies of still-born children, or of children who have died soon after their birth, slash them with knives, making wounds, then embalm the bodies by pressing balsam, myrrh, and other preservative drugs into the wounds, and sell them to Christian kings, princes, and wealthy people as bodies of the Holy Innocents . . . for these infidels know our ardent desire for the possession of relics.[145]

What irony to find later in Frederick's relic collection in Wittenberg a relic "held especially worthy," "an entire corpse of one of the innocent little children and Martyrs," which, according to the description of 1509, "was safely inside a silver coffin with crystal and gilt flowers."[146]

At Jaffa or on the return voyage pilgrims might find their *padrone*, who by the nature of the sea-faring business could be as fierce as any knight, demanding more money.[147] In 1476, Albrecht's *padrone* at the end of the voyage demanded more money.[148] The *padrone* waved a list of financial losses suffered because of the actions of Albrecht's group. On Rhodes Albrecht's party had stayed too long, he claimed. On Crete Albrecht's party had stayed too briefly and ruined the opportunity to buy sugar there. There is no record of how the dispute was resolved. Albrecht could be a violent, brutal enemy. He and his party had already killed two Mamelukes in Jaffa over such a demand.

When Frederick's party returned to Jaffa on July 4, the truth had leaked out that he was a rich prince. His presence perhaps became known after he met the sultan of Egypt who flattered Frederick by concluding "from the strong hands and arms of this young prince that he sprang forth from an exalted family."[149] How could the sultan have made such a judgment? Did the Saxons demonstrate the joust for the sultan? Frederick's escorts were furious, demanding more money. The fracas must have simmered down; no fighting is recorded. Peace-loving Frederick probably silenced them with money.

On the return voyage at the stop in Rhodes, the Order of the Knights of St. John welcomed Frederick on July 16, for this time he and his uncle, Duke Christoph of Bavaria, announced they were great German princes.

Their hosts installed the two princes in a special guest house. Frederick ordered "a laudable Mass" in the cloister church, attended a feast the Hospitallers held to commemorate successfully defending their fortress against the Turks, and, as honored guests, Frederick and Christoph marched in a procession with the resident archbishop who was also a cardinal. The pilgrims stayed one week.

Figure 3: Frederick III of Saxony c. 1496 by Albrecht Dürer (Gemäldegalerie in Berlin), courtesy of The Yorck Project.

Frederick's greatest collecting triumph of the pilgrimage was on Rhodes. He was able to purchase a small monstrance of gold, which enclosed the thumb of St. Anne, mother of the Holy Virgin.[150] Although Frederick had "ardently" collected on the pilgrimage, one scholar lamented "very little effort has been made to ascertain what relics these might have been."[151] Known for certain are items not relics at all: coins, stones, rings, and enameled boxes.[152] Known as well are two great Turkish tapestries and six smaller ones he also bought at Rhodes. These smaller ones may have been the ones reported in an inventory as "six beautiful great carpets with murals" in Frederick's study at the hunting mansion in Lochau.[153] Many acquisitions will never be known because Frederick gave them away as gifts. Although it is plausible, it is uncertain that a Greek liturgical book with the text of the four Gospels of the New Testament, probably originating in the eleventh century in Constantinople, was one of Frederick's acquisitions in 1493.[154]

The cross of gold inlaid with precious stones that Frederick presented to the All Saints' Foundation in Wittenberg may have housed relics from his 1493 Holy Land pilgrimage. Andreas Meinhardi recorded the contents in the cross in 1508:

> It contains some of the linen with which Christ was girt when He washed the feet of the apostles; also part of the pillar of flagellation; part of the sepulchre of the Lord; of the place where Christ prayed; of the place where Christ was born; of the place where the Holy Cross was found; of the wood of the Holy Cross; of the sepulchre of the Virgin Mary; and of Saint John the Baptist; part of Mount Olivet, of the stone where Christ was seized, of the manger of the Lord, and of Mount Cavalry.[155]

Tragedy struck at Rhodes during the pilgrims' week-long stay. Frederick's uncle, Duke Christoph of Bavaria, became too sick to travel. Left behind with attendants, Christoph died on August 15. He was only forty-four years old. He was buried on Rhodes at the St. Anthony Church.[156] At the next port in Kandia (Crete), Frederick himself became severely ill. He would have nightmares about his near death at age 30 for years to come.[157] Too much heated wine followed by a warm bath was the diagnosis of Dr. Mellerstadt, who some credited with saving Frederick.[158] Frederick nevertheless recovered by the time they docked in Venice.

There the Duke of Venice informed the pilgrims that the ancient Habsburg emperor, Friedrich III, had died.[159] No doubt the duke also passed on the news that Maximilian had concluded his peace pact with France and he had indeed made the concession regarding Naples. Frederick must have flinched when he heard that detail. The French had a free hand in Naples, and that hand probably was honing a sword.

Frederick returned to Austria in September to learn surgeons in June had amputated the rest of the old emperor's gangrenous leg. The tough old ruler had no effective anesthetic during the sawing. He joked that the empire would now limp on one leg.[160] He never recovered, but stubbornly fought death until August 19, just short of reaching age 78. He (and his severed leg) had yet to be buried.[161] Maximilian was not in Innsbruck to greet the pilgrims. He was busy on the southeast border of Habsburg territory implementing a "military border." The Turks had, with some success, attacked Croatia and Untersteiermark. Maximilian's future bride Bianca Sforza, however, had been in Innsbruck recently. Hans Hundt on September 16 recorded, "Two oxen has the 'queen' made as a gift to my gracious Lord."[162]

On October 30, 1493, Frederick arrived to a well-orchestrated welcome at Torgau. Hans Hundt had expenses entered in his accounting book for the pilgrimage totaling about 14,000 gulden.[163]

CHAPTER 3

IMPERIAL BEAU TO DISENCHANTED FOE

(1494–98)

"There are many things easy to say but difficult to do."
—Proverb favored by Frederick the Wise[1]

ELECTORAL SAXONY GROWS AND BUDS

No doubt the glow of oil lamps warmed Frederick's cold winter days as he huddled with his builders over plans. The direct object of one of his favored proverbs, "Every work praises its master," surely in his mind referred more to himself than the master builder.[2] The work would reflect on the merits of the sovereign. His plans were many. The effort continued in Wittenberg on his new castle. When he returned from the Holy Land, he set the cornerstone for the castle[3] (just as he would soon set the cornerstone for the new Elbe Bridge at Torgau). Although the master builder in Wittenberg was Konrad Pflüger, even in the early stages the hands-on construction was supervised by Claus Roder.[4] Pflüger must have kept one eye on the Wittenberg complex, but he was, after all, the preferred master builder of all the Wettins. In the middle 1490s, he was also fully involved in two major projects underway in Albertine Saxony: the Sts. Peter and Paul Church in Bautzen east of Dresden and the St. Thomas Church in Leipzig.[5]

Pflüger's three-winged complex in Wittenberg seemed an incomplete "*Wehrbau*," a simple rectangular fortress with an inner courtyard (in this case, the east wing was absent).[6] The south wing contained the principal living quarters of the Wettins and the north wing was to be the church. The west wing, which also contained some living quarters, mainly served for the business of the other two wings. Unlike the other two wings, it joined the city wall.[7] The three stories of the south wing were spacious with high ceilings. The exterior of the south wing facing the River Elbe had relatively large "curtain-arched" windows, an innovation of Arnold von Westfalen that featured faux drapery on the stone arch.[8] The window glass was both colorless and green-brown.[9] The roof was not flat, but steeped like the church roof. The south wing had two large gables facing south and one large gable facing east. The outlines of the stone gables were stair-stepped. One generous rose window probably adorned the wall under the east gable, illuminating the third floor.[10] Later sources hint that the cellars of the wing were in themselves impressive.[11] The tower at the juncture of the south and west wing twinned the church tower with its ornate, crowned Gothic spire of four sides. On the courtside of the two junctures were spiral stairways, hidden behind a loggia exterior with gable above. The two massive towers faced all comers to the west outside the city wall. They obviously had potential for cannon towers.

Pflüger's style used arches sparingly in the castle, so the living areas themselves would have flat ceilings. This happily increased areas available for later artwork. Frederick's rooms would cover the third floor of the south wing, receiving light from three sides. Hidden in the thickness of the outside wall was a standard fixture for a prince of the time: a "secret pleasure room."[12] Small chambers (*Gemächer*) offered space throughout the castle and towers, some for the innocent purpose of storing archives and some for not so innocent purposes. Hidden (secret) chambers were "*heimlichen Gemächer.*" Frederick's secret pleasure room was so cleverly designed, it was not apparent from the inside or the outside. The interior of Frederick's great living quarters of several rooms in the Elbe wing measured thirty-six strides west to east and twelve strides south to north (one stride equal to one meter).[13] That was by no means the limit of Frederick's personal domain. His bedroom in the adjacent west wing was eight by ten strides (also with a secret room).[14] He had yet another adjacent room inside the massive walls of the southwest tower, a circular room possibly eight strides in diameter. In the tower was yet another room above this one; it came to be used as the quarters for Frederick's frequent guest brother Ernst, archbishop of Magdeburg. Frederick's brother Johann occupied a suite of rooms on the third floor, adjacent to the northwest tower.[15] In truth, Frederick and Johann were not there that often, and much less often at the same time.

Occupants found the castle not as cleverly hospitable as it may sound. Although the builders moved beyond their predecessors' crudity of a linear sequence of rooms, they still did not arrange the rooms thoughtfully or use hallways to make access effective. This was "typical for the German late Gothic and early Renaissance," that is, "without a suitable solution of the access possibilities."[16] In other words, if the prince occupied a room at a time demanding complete privacy, access to another room may have been for that time impossible.

The inside décor was to be lavish. This was no problem for Frederick with his superb tapestries as well as a staff of master artists to paint, sculpt, and carve. Although the Wittenberg castle would be more or less complete in its basic structure by 1496, its interior was not fully decorated until several years after that.[17]

In Torgau, the Chapel of the Holy Cross proceeded to completion as reassuringly as the Elbe Bridge project proceeded with constant headaches. Frederick seems to have had no obstacle getting incentives from Rome to help build the bridge. He had by 1490 received a papal decree from Innocent VIII that allowed so-called "butter money."[18] For twenty years, any electoral Saxon subject who donated yearly the twentieth part of a Rhenish gulden to the building of the bridge had permission during Holy Lent to eat "milk products and butter." Frederick received the decree because he was going to build a small chapel of St. Anne on the bridge. The bridge itself was a much greater challenge. The River Elbe was remarkably constant through Frederick's territory, much wider than the strongest man could throw a stone yet rarely deeper than one man standing on another.[19] The current, though, was capricious. Next to the Hartenfels castle, it was maddening. Frederick had no one in his electorate capable of planning a bridge in such difficult current. As he so often did, he appealed to the council members of Nuremberg, that most resourceful city. In 1494, Hans Behaim arrived in Torgau to design the project and recommend suitable builders.[20] The master builder would be Paul Dolenstein. The difficulties of construction nevertheless would plague Frederick for many years to come.

Adoration of St. Anne, shown in this Torgau case by the small chapel, was just one of the vast number of ways to venerate her daughter, the holy Virgin. The Wettins seemed particularly drawn to St. Anne. Frederick received in 1494 from the new pope, Alexander VI, a bull that allowed his territory to celebrate July 26 as St. Anne's Day.[21] This promotion of St. Anne was not unique to Frederick. His brother Ernst, the archbishop of Magdeburg, was also doing that. Cousin George promoted St. Anne in Albertine Saxony as well. Anne was the saint of miners, so essential to Saxony. Apocrypha collected around the cult of St. Anne. Many believed Mary was her only child and that Mary, too, was the result of a virgin birth.

From 1496 to 1498, the years of Frederick's absence from Saxony, construction went on not just in Wittenberg and Torgau but in other parts of his territory as well. Funds continued for construction at the castle in Eilenburg, a three- or four-hour ride northeast of Leipzig.[22] In 1497, the project was completed. No doubt one factor was the town's presence on virtually the last leg of the "Low Road" trade route into Leipzig. Greater factors may have been the favor the Wettins had shown the castle as a residence in the past and now, in Frederick's time, its convenient proximity to Leipzig. Ernestine officials frequently had business in Leipzig. Grimma received funds for construction too, a costly long-term project to renovate their castle complex.[23] Grimma was also an old favorite of the Wettiners. Grimma was as near Leipzig as was Eilenburg, but Grimma lay to the southeast. Grimma had an influential champion. The *Amtmann* was Sebastian von Mistelbach. Mistelbach went on the pilgrimage to the Holy Land with Frederick, who dubbed him a knight there. Mistelbach also had jousted in tournaments against Frederick at least once and against Johann three times.[24] All this was before 1495.

It is possible Frederick considered these old fortresses at Eilenburg and Grimma, both on the River Mulde, important strategically because they were the nearest protection for a dangerously narrow neck of Frederick's territory between Albertine areas. A man could walk across the neck in half an hour, ride a good horse across it in four minutes. Cousin George had definitely shown a tendency to irritate and hinder the Ernestines whenever possible.

Although as a Wettin conscious of not favoring one residence too much, Frederick nevertheless favored living at Torgau and its nearby hunting mansion at Lochau. No doubt his great tapestries and trophies from the Holy Land first appeared to his court in Torgau. It was in the Hartenfels castle and possibly in Lochau that he enjoyed most often the improvements of his court music. The Wettins had long enjoyed trumpeters, but Frederick's taste had evolved in the imperial court.[25]

Records from 1491 and 1492 document for the first time "singers." One was Adam of Fulda, later recognized as Frederick's choirmaster.[26] It is clear he had established a court choir (*Vokalkapelle*).

The Torgau court (and church) also enjoyed an organ. Again, records from 1492 show for the first time an organist, a musician named Linhart. Organ construction was in its infancy in Saxony but that would not have stopped Frederick from acquiring a top instrument elsewhere. And just as he had borrowed Hans Behaim from Nuremberg he borrowed Paul Hofhaimer from the imperial court. The Austrian was widely recognized as the greatest organist of the empire and perhaps of all Europe. He composed and astonished royalty as he could improvise effortlessly for hours. At Frederick's expense Hofhaimer visited Torgau in 1495 with his wife and daughter on the occasion of a tournament. Hofhaimer trained four organists for the electoral court at this time or shortly after.[27] No doubt the master performed as well.

Frederick also commissioned art of a visual nature.[28] Since 1491, he had accumulated work from Paul Moeller, a goldsmith in Nuremberg. His first purchase of silver tableware and several platters amounted to the significant sum of 353 gulden. In 1495, he and Uncle Albrecht commissioned Peter Vischer the Elder, head of Nuremberg's leading bronze casting foundry. For 240 gulden, Vischer prepared a memorial plaque for Ernst's tomb in Meissen. Frederick had an affinity for Nuremberg. Not only did he appreciate its concentration of masters in every field but he also had good friends among the nobility and the patricians of the city. Surely by 1495 he was hearing from these elites about the city's twenty-four-year-old artist freshly returned from Italy and on the brink of greatness.

MAXIMILIAN AND HIS GREAT *REICHSTAG* OF 1495

Maximilian publicly married Bianca Sforza in a grand ceremony March 16, 1494, at Hall in Tyrol. The Duke of Milan was so happy, he gave Maximilian a further dowry of 200,000 ducats. By mid-year 1494, Frederick was once again focused on imperial matters. Two of his favorite electoral princes were about to go to war—against each other. Philipp of the Palatine was quarreling with Berthold of Mainz over the rights Berthold as archbishop had granted Bingen, a city within the territorial jurisdiction of Philipp. Maximilian, who had no shortage of his own wars to fight, did not want the princes wasting resources against each other. He managed to calm the difficulty by June. Because Philipp was a Wittelsbach, he of course came out somewhat an embittered loser.[29] To worsen his attitude, Maximilian made Berthold his archchancellor (*Erzkanzler*), the head of the imperial chancellery (*Reichskanzlei*).[30] Maximilian was king in the strictest sense of law but also recognized by all as the *de facto* emperor.[31] Maximilian had appealed to Frederick for military help if it had come to that. Perhaps this led to what happened next. A cynic might have said Maximilian wanted his two most influential electors close at hand.

In July, Maximilian also enlisted Frederick into his imperial machinery.[32] Frederick's service as a royal adviser began July 14 for one year. Either he or the emperor could terminate the contract earlier. On the other hand, both could agree to extend the contract. Frederick would in addition provide two hundred knights and their horses.[33] His compensation was to be 22,000 gulden annually but paid quarterly. Collection would be messy. Maximilian assigned to Frederick taxes due the empire from fourteen cities, including Nuremberg, Augsburg, and Lübeck. Frederick was not naïve about how well Maximilian paid his debts. The empire owed his uncle Albrecht 300,000 gulden and that amount was just from his military efforts in the Netherlands.[34]

Uncle Albrecht was going to try to bring the matter to a head before the 1495 *Reichstag*. Maximilian was determined not to meet with Albrecht at the *Reichstag* because the angry Saxon field marshal had previously openly tongue-lashed him over the debts. For once, Maximilian could not finesse his way out of an embarrassing situation. Councillors feared what the two hotheads who fancied themselves knights of old might do to each other if they met again. If a brave man such as the emperor half-feared Albrecht, what does that reveal about his brother Ernst's fears many years before? At one low point with Maximilian, the volcanic Albrecht "sent his lieutenant Wilwolt von Schaumburg to his lord's worst enemy, the King of France, and offered to enter the King's service if the latter would help him collect that debt."[35]

Any official of the empire could only hope other benefits made service to the empire worthwhile. Frederick no doubt judged it useful, for as recorded, "the Saxon elector was sometimes alone, sometimes with his grace Prince Johann, in the court of the Holy Roman Emperor Maximilian, and many years of service followed in upper and lower

German lands."[36] Frederick passed seamlessly from the Holy Land into territorial administration into imperial ambitions. By late July 1494, he was in Aachen, west of Cologne, to join Maximilian's grand procession to the Netherlands.[37] Frederick was often in the Burgundian city of Mechelen, which was between Brussels and Antwerp and no more than half a day's ride from either city. Charles the Bold embraced Mechelen in the 1470s and moved institutions such as the highest judicial court there. Of course it had a grand residence.[38] Mechelen remained much favored.

In September, Frederick rode in a tournament in Mechelen. He rode against Saxon knight Sebastian von Mistelbach in the *"rennen und stechen."*[39] In this joust, both Frederick and his opponent struck their lances solidly against each other. As a result, both were unhorsed. Imagine traveling at a gallop, stopping instantly from a blow to the chest, then falling back from a height of a horse and striking the earth in sixty pounds of armor. Frederick may have broken his arm. For a number of days after that fall, his arm was in a sling.[40] This injury was particularly ironic because the goal of Burgundian jousting was to splinter the lance on the opponent's shield and lessen injuries. In contrast, German jousting was extremely violent, with the object of unhorsing the opponent. The German saddle with a low backrest allowed unhorsing an opponent on impact; the Netherland "Kiri" saddle had too high a backrest to allow that easily. The lances were different too. The German lance was stouter than the Netherland lance, which was designed to splinter.[41] Maximilian, however, was influencing the Germans to embrace the gentler ways of Burgundy. Perhaps the two Saxons had jousted the German way in spite of that.

At banquet in Mechelen a month earlier, Frederick had sat beside Maximilian's daughter Margarethe on the left-hand side of the emperor. Rumors arose that he might win her hand. Margarethe had been jilted by the French king, but at fourteen she was hardly damaged goods. Her appearance, despite long golden hair so common in the Habsburgs, was not alluring, and her demeanor was grave. Even more so than her father, she had a "protruding lower jaw which was to be the hall-mark of Habsburg family inbreeding in subsequent generations."[42] Her eyes were squinty and pink-rimmed as if she had been weeping, her mouth bubbly in an unattractive way. She was aloof and touchy.[43] Because of her childhood in the French court, she was far more French than German. But she did have desirable qualities. Certainly she was intelligent and well versed in all courtly ways, and she was, after all, the new emperor's daughter. It is probable Frederick already knew of Maximilian's marriage plan for his daughter and silently laughed at the rumors.[44]

Maximilian was riding high. Not only had he acquired a queen with a massive dowry, but he also was manipulating a spectacular double marriage between the Habsburgs and the powers of Spain.[45] His son Philipp would marry Juana, daughter of King Ferdinand of Aragon, and Margarethe would marry Don Juan, only son of Ferdinand and Isabella. Don Juan was to be successor to the unified crowns of Castile and Aragon. In addition, Maximilian had established governance in Tyrol, reconquered Austrian lands, and even encroached into Hungary to gain significant concessions. He had stalemated the Dutch and placated the French. He curried favor with the pope and thus his imperial coronation by pretending he would lead a crusade against the Turks. In the north, Emperor Maximilian planned to dissolve the guardianship of his sixteen-year-old son Philipp and make him sovereign of the Netherlands and Burgundy.[46] The Peace of Senlis with France in 1493 had already stipulated that.

The treaty with France had other consequences as well.

A careless concession to France about the city of Naples had given the despised Charles VIII an opening and he rushed toward it.[47] By late summer of 1494, the French king crossed the Alps with his military might of 25,000 men, including 8,000 dreaded Swiss.[48] The French force stormed into the lowlands to conquer Florence, Lucca, Pisa, and Siena. No Italian wanted to fight. One day before the new year, the French arrived in Rome and Pope Alexander VI scurried to take refuge in St. Angelo castle. Everyone around Charles VIII begged him to depose the pope for his blatant corruption and total lack of spirituality. The king faltered. He could not bring himself to violate the pope, and he demanded nothing but a cardinal's hat for one of his favorites, the bishop of St. Malo. The weakness of Charles VIII appalled the ruthless menagerie that supported him. He pushed on to Naples, his only legitimate reason for being in Italy. In February 1495, the French easily conquered Naples.

Meanwhile in the north, Maximilian had joined Venice, Milan, and the corrupt pope himself in a motley league of opponents to the French. The "Holy League" convened in March. Maximilian rallied the members. The envoy from Venice was giddy as he wrote of thousands of imperial knights under Duke Albrecht of Saxony and the Margrave of Brandenburg flooding across the Alps into Italy.[49] The League, however, bought the services of a veteran *condottiero*, Francesco II of Gonzaga, the Duke of Mantua.[50] The troops were dominantly Venetian. Alarmed, Charles VIII tried to flee up the west coast of Italy with wagonloads of booty. Two days south of Milan the Venetians were waiting. There in July 1495, the armies collided in the mud and rain at the "Battle of Fornovo." Although the French fought hard and killed many Venetians, they lost the battle because they lost their booty. They left Italy with little more than what is thought to have been the first outbreaks of syphilis from the New World. Their subsequent spreading of the disease would give it its most notorious name: "the French disease."

Maximilian had dedicated the Worms *Reichstag* in 1495 to "the rescue of Italy."[51] In its outcome, though, the *Reichstag* was far more relevant to issues of the imperial estates. It was to be the most significant *Reichstag* since the Golden Bull in 1356.[52] Maximilian was anxious for it. In January, he summoned Frederick and the estates to Worms for the *Reichstag* to begin in late March. Simultaneous with the opening was the appearance of a polemic tract "Dream of Hans von Hermansgrün" (*Traum des Hans von Hermansgrün*), dedicated to the Saxon elector Frederick. The writer, dubbing himself half literary man and half swordsman, hinted he served Frederick or his brother Ernst, the archbishop of Magdeburg. Also implied was that the writer's concept of imperial reform was Frederick's. The writer advocated an all-powerful emperor served by princes only too willing to fund his every wish. Frederick had to know the writing actually originated from the court of Maximilian and was designed to influence the princes at the *Reichstag*. The ploy was crude and transparent. The princes were far too sly to be influenced by such a tract. Yet the tract shows how highly the imperial court of Maximilian perceived the good name and considerable influence of Frederick.

The situation was what seemed the eternal one for *Reichstags*. The estates wanted reform. Maximilian wanted not reform but money. The reformer Berthold of Mainz—also ironically Maximilian's archchancellor—was now extraordinarily aggressive in his demands. He conceived a new imperial ordinance (*Reichsordnung*), actually a first step toward a real constitution first proposed in 1487. Its aims were a declaration of public peace (*Landfrieden*), a chamber court (*Kammergericht*),[53] and a defense against foreign invasion; he threw Maximilian a crumb with a subsidy for a campaign against the Turks. Berthold supported his ordinance by precise notions about how to implement it. He proposed an imperial governing council (*Reichsrat* or *Reichsregiment*) of seventeen members to sit permanently in Frankfurt.[54] The emperor could appoint its president. The estates controlled all the other seats: the electoral curia provided six; the curiae of the princes, prelates, and cities provided the remaining ten. The electors would monitor the activity of the council. Berthold clearly intended this imperial governing council to be the *supreme central authority in the empire*. It was to impose the needed reform throughout the empire. It would supervise the activities of the chamber court and execute the judgments. It would maintain the peace within the empire (including quashing the so-called robber barons). It would negotiate with foreign powers and, when necessary, supervise all preparations for war against outsiders. Its activities would be financed by universal imperial taxes. The whole proposal was stunning. Berthold had sensed the one potent moment with a new emperor and had gone for the entire prize!

The emperor (or king) was peripheral, virtually irrelevant, in Berthold's proposed plan. None of the estates was sorry about that. Maximilian's odd and seemingly erratic political activity disturbed everyone.[55] If anyone believed his political activity had a direction, they also believed it was aimed at advancing the Habsburg dynasty. Yet disillusionment with Maximilian did not necessarily mean they supported Berthold's reform. The cities objected from the first to strengthening central authority in the empire. They already had no more than nominal power and suspected empowering the electors in particular would not better their future. In the curia of princes, the especially powerful princes of Hesse and Bavaria did not want Berthold's kind of reform. In the curia of electors, the most powerful secular electors in the empire—Johann Cicero of Brandenburg and none other than Frederick himself—opposed central authorities for judicial actions (chamber court) and for governance (imperial governing council). The resisting princes were called the party of freedom (*Libertät*).

Frederick's strong opposition led some to suspect that as Maximilian's imperial official, he was merely acting for Maximilian. Negotiations went on for weeks. No one wanted to come away from another *Reichstag* with nothing to show for it. Berthold and the reformers began to concede to the unyielding Freedom Party on almost every point. This was illustrated well with the negotiations over an imperial tax dubbed the "Common Penny." It also showed that Frederick was acting in his own interest, because he and the Freedom Party steered the dialogue in a way that definitely did not benefit Maximilian. They managed to lower the tax rate. They shifted the primary burden from the princes to the other estates and those millions not even represented in the *Reichstag*. They limited the tax to four years. Their final triumph was making the collection of the "Common Penny" virtually voluntary.

The Worms *Reichstag* of 1495 claimed progress of sorts, considering how little the participants had achieved in previous *Reichstags*. The four-month (late March–early August) meeting—no doubt interspersed liberally with religious displays, feasts, jousts, gambling, and enjoying women—touted three achievements. Permanent Public Peace (*Landfrieden*) was accepted by all. A manifestation of that was prohibition against declaring feuds. Enforcing the prohibition would be another matter. The Worms *Reichstag* also claimed the creation of a chamber court. This was a hollow triumph for the estates, stopped just short of real success by Maximilian. The reformers wanted an imperial chamber court (*Reichskammergericht*), not under the thumb of the emperor. Maximilian wanted an emperor's chamber court (*kaiserliches Kammergericht*), clearly within his sphere, and he received it. The third achievement was the imperial tax, though the Freedom party led by Frederick and Elector Johann Cicero of Brandenburg had whittled it down until it oppressed only those who could afford it the least.

The *Reichstag* clearly showed that by 1495, Frederick had emerged as one of the most powerful political influences in the empire. Could Frederick have swung the pendulum to Berthold's real concept of reform? Possibly. Could he have swung the pendulum to completely blocking reform except for the passage of a viable imperial tax to benefit Maximilian? Possibly. Conversely, evidence indicates Frederick already firmly and openly advanced the interest of territorial sovereigns. He helped neither reform nor the emperor.

Proof came that the French recognized his rising status in the empire and his influence with Maximilian. Perhaps they also recognized in Frederick a willingness to negotiate and a reluctance to fight. Early in 1496, the French king Charles VIII wrote Frederick no doubt to discourage Maximilian's further Italian plans.[56] Frederick's response is unknown.

HOPES AND DEMANDS OF EMPIRE

"One *Reichstag* only gives birth to another" was an old bitter joke attributed to the council at Basel.[57] Indeed, Maximilian called another *Reichstag*, this one for Lindau in the fall of 1496. Until then he planned his campaign in Italy with the Holy League. The league feared the return of Charles VIII. Maximilian's first goal was to drive the remaining French troops from Italy. By the time he was prepared to campaign, the *Reichstag* had already started. Frederick did not attend, probably because he knew the estates were almost unanimous in opposition to Maximilian's Italian adventure. He was nearly alone in supporting the Italian adventure, even at one point pledging four thousand knights on horse.[58] The other estates refused to give any money or soldiers. Even Maximilian's own advisers tried to talk him out of it. His financial situation was dire. Where had the 600,000 ducats gone? His officials in Worms with Queen Bianca pleaded with him to send money. The queen and her ladies were so short of money, she claimed she had only three or four days of food left.[59] She also had to pawn her linen and underwear.[60] Maximilian must have sighed wearily, knowing from his *Hofmeister* that the court of his spoiled wife was spending as much as 20,000 gulden in a month. The emperor obtained loans from the Augsburg financial wizards, the Fuggers, and pushed ahead.

Maximilian envisioned conquest and triumph.[61] He actually had a plan in which son Philipp would join him with his Burgundians. Imperial troops, mustered for the Italian campaign by Frederick and various high nobles including George (the Rich) of Bavaria, would storm into Lombardy to capture Asti, north of Genoa. Then the emperor and his son would crush the French. Maximilian did indeed make it to Genoa. Because of limited money and weak allies in Italy, he sailed with only about four thousand troops from Genoa to Pisa. The French grudgingly admired Maximilian: "If he had only four twigs he would rush into a fight."[62] Some French were garrisoned at Florence, which became his first goal. As a prelude to Florence, he decided to take Livorno. He failed that minimal task. He had nothing left to do but return to the empire. Italians now scorned him. When the Italians began to realize Charles VIII was not returning due to political and financial difficulties, they regarded Maximilian as a pest not that much different from the French. One of the ambassadors of Venice (Maximilian's most reliable partner) later wrote of the emperor's traits:

> He is of excellent parts, and more fertile in expedients than any of his advisers, yet he does not know how to avail himself of any single remedy at the right moment; while he is as full of ideas and plans as he is powerless to execute them. And though two or three methods lie open to his intellect, and though he chooses one of them as the best, yet he does not pursue this, because before its fulfillment another design which he considers better has suddenly presented itself. And thus he flits from better to better, till both time and opportunity for execution are past.[63]

In April 1496, Frederick and Johann had been in Nuremberg for five days. A reasonable explanation for the visit is that they were there at that time for the feast of the Holy Lance. Although they probably arranged a private audience, in any event they saw for themselves the annual display of imperial crown jewels, the Holy Lance of St. Longinus, a fragment of the True Cross, a piece of the tablecloth from the Last Supper, and other highly regarded relics.[64] Thousands of pilgrims venerated these precious items on the upper gallery of a tower on the Nuremberg's main market. As usual, this endowed each witness with indulgences.

Also at this time, Frederick sat for Albrecht Dürer to have his portrait painted. Why did Frederick's own court painters not paint him? He had at one time "Jhan of the Netherlands," but this Dutch master departed in 1495. He had two other court painters.[65] It is plausible he was painted by one or more of them. Perhaps he was dissatisfied. One can assume that as a rising imperial official, Frederick wanted the best. Or perhaps it was simply because he was already in Nuremberg and friends told him about a young genius. No doubt one of Frederick's many acquaintances among the artists and goldsmiths recommended the twenty-four-year-old Dürer. The youth's father was Dutch-trained and the deceased emperor's "favored goldsmith," as well as friend and neighbor of Michael Wolgemut, Nuremberg's reigning jack of all trades in art.[66] Wolgemut operated the largest workshop in the city and was a gifted businessman. He subcontracted much work and once parleyed the commission for an altar in Zwickau into a colossal fee of fourteen hundred gulden. Albrecht Dürer had been Wolgemut's student since the age of fifteen, when he already showed superior skill at drawing and engraving. Wolgemut's task was to transform Dürer into a painter.[67] Dürer learned the basics, then at eighteen traveled off and on for four years, including trips to Basel and even to Venice. Now he was to perform his first real commission for one of the most powerful men in the empire.

The portrait (fig. 3, page 56) was stunning, "quite incomparable" in German art up to that time.[68] The Italian-influenced Dürer portrayed Frederick not in front of a window, as was so often done in the southern empire, but in front of a pale green wall. Shadow on the wall made Frederick three-dimensional. The Saxon elector in somber black is imposing. He is stern, defiantly confrontational, "the imperious glance . . . commanding rather than courting the attention of the beholder."[69] He is as virile and potent in full beard as he was immature and weak just ten years before in the portrait by a Nuremberg master. Once again he is wide-eyed, but the effect is completely different. The eye is absolute authority. That eye was on the open, approachable side of the face. The eye on the dark side is unapproachable, secretive. Dürer made this dark eye remote and menacing. This was a brilliant "representation" of Frederick's character: half of him open but intimidating, half secretive and dangerous.

Did Frederick approve? We only know he gave young Albrecht Dürer two more commissions, both to be magnificent altarpieces in the Wittenberg church.[70] Dürer would elevate Frederick's patronage to a level of greatness; Frederick would elevate Dürer's reputation. "Once the Saxon Elector had broken the ice, religious commissions, too, began to come to Dürer from such leading families as the Hollers and Paumgartners."[71]

Frederick's marital status in late 1496 was still in flux. He was now thirty-three, his cousin George twenty-five. Both had been negotiating for princess brides with the royal house of Poland. In 1494, Frederick had sent his court painter Jhan to Cracow.[72] One can assume the Dutch master painted both Barbara, sought by George, and Elisabeth (born in 1482), sought by Frederick. Both were among the seven daughters of the deceased Polish king Casimir IV. They were also sisters of the current Polish king Johann, as well as sisters of the often mentioned Vladislaus of

Bohemia. No doubt painter Jhan conveyed to these two sisters sketches of their suitors. This exchange of likenesses was common for the time.

Competing with Frederick's attempt was the simultaneous courtship of Elisabeth from Joachim Nestor, twelve-year-old son of the Elector of Brandenburg.[73] Frederick's effort failed, perhaps because the Brandenburg envoy influenced the Polish royalty.[74] On the other hand, George triumphed. He married Barbara on November 21, 1496, in Leipzig.

Evidence in the form of a booklet suggests that Frederick had a romantic notion about someone during this time.[75] A note added sometime later to the item stated, "This booklet was found among Elector Frederick's own and dearest old papers." It was an illustrated knightly romance titled "History of the stag with golden antlers and the princess of the fountain" written by Frederick's own chancellery official in Torgau, Augustin von Hamersteten. It was dated "the evening before Palm Sunday 1496." In the story, the elector is embodied by the central figure, a knight who tracks the stag with the golden antlers and, thereby, in the woods discovers a beautiful woman by a fountain. She confesses to him that she must live with an old man in an unfortunate marriage. The knight offers his services, which she will accept if he first travels to the Holy Land. After his return, she will summon him. Here the history ends. It seems unlikely this is referring to a fourteen-year-old Polish princess, because the fictional woman is married. What it apparently shows is Frederick's frustrated desire for a relationship with a particular woman bound in an unhappy marriage.

Maximilian had reached the Lindau *Reichstag* in February 1497, just before its conclusion after five months. He read a bitter indictment against the estates for abandoning him during his campaign in Italy. Almost nothing had been accomplished either in Italy or Lindau. All parties agreed for the first time on a *Reichsabschied*, an agreement between emperor and estates drawn up in proper legal style that summarized all the settled issues during the *Reichstag*. Frederick enjoyed a small triumph. Although Frederick was absent, his representative aggressively pursued the office of imperial vicar (*Reichsvikariat*).[76] This was the official in charge of the empire when the emperor was out of the empire. Frederick claimed it as his hereditary office. It was potentially an exceptional position because Maximilian was often now "over the Alps." If the officeholder was strong enough to cow the estates, he had real power. He could hold judicial court, present church benefices, draw an imperial income, and bestow imperial fiefs. The new emperor or returning emperor later had to approve these matters; nevertheless these privileges for the imperial vicar were substantial.

Frederick's move was stunning in its audacity, because the position had been conceded in 1356 in the Golden Bull to the Palatine elector. Even though the Habsburgs disliked the Wittelsbachs, it signals Frederick's sense of his own influence. The Palatine elector Philipp petitioned for the position lawfully his, but Maximilian would grant the position of imperial vicar to Frederick before the Lindau *Reichstag* ended. Like all events in the empire, there were many machinations driving this one. The force behind the Palatine elector was thought to be Berthold of Mainz. Perhaps correctly, Maximilian himself considered the office only applied during an interregnum; he wanted to appoint his son Philipp his deputy when he was out of the empire. Had Maximilian anticipated that his move to appoint Philipp, whom the Germans scarcely knew, would be blocked? And did the petition of the Palatine elector indicate it would indeed be blocked? Perhaps the imperial circle was behind Frederick's move, which was really then a countermove. At least Maximilian would have in Frederick one of his strongest supporters in charge, not a Wittelsbach.[77]

But that was not the only plum for Frederick. In winning the office of imperial vicar, he also won the title of imperial governor (*Reichs-statthalter*). This put him near the top of the power pyramid just short of the summit, immediately below Maximilian. Whether Frederick felt he really had that power is not known. Certainly he loved the title, and no doubt would use it fully in his representation. Better known is the attitude of Maximilian. Just as he granted power to his son Philipp in the Netherlands, this empowerment of Frederick by Maximilian might be a preemptive move anticipating and voiding a future move by another. In this case, the other was Berthold, not the Palatine elector. Berthold had aggressively attempted to use his position as imperial archchancellor in the 1495 *Reichstag*, and his own fellow electors thwarted him.

Frederick's new imperial office of *Statthalter* required him after 1496 to attend the imperial council (*Hofrat*[78]), whether Maximilian was there or not. He tidied up his territorial matters. His construction projects in Wittenberg and Torgau were proceeding. In Wittenberg, construction of the two residential wings of the new castle was nearly complete. Workers were well under way constructing the new All Saints' Church.[79] Only the Elbe Bridge in Torgau was faltering. In his territorial administration, Frederick's *Türknecht*, Hans Hundt von Wenkheim, seems to have moved beyond that office. It is possible as an older man, he no longer wanted to follow Frederick around in the imperial entourage. Records mentioned him as Landvogt of the Saxon Palatine and also as a judge on the *Oberhofgericht* in Leipzig.[80] He was in no sense put on the shelf. Along with Heinrich von Ende, Heinrich and Hans Mönch, Hans von Obernitz, and Hans Leimbach, he was one of the six key personnel governing Electoral Saxony while both Frederick and Johann were "out in the empire" for two years.[81] Degenhart Pfeffinger, a Bavarian only twenty-five years old, replaced Hans Hundt von Wenkheim.[82] Son of a hereditary marshal in Lower Bavaria, Pfeffinger had no more joined the Saxon electoral court than he had gone to the Holy Land with Frederick. He also seriously collected relics and coins, interests sure to please the prince. In 1496, Frederick also appointed Johann Flehinger his chancellor, replacing Johann Seyfried. The office of chancellor had been evolving from administrative duties into financial oversight; its lack of definition handicapped its influence and success.[83]

UNDONE BY THE "SWABIANS" AND WILLING WOMEN

Although Maximilian had granted some of the estates their wish for a chamber court by 1497, due to its disagreeable form (*kaiserliches Kammergericht*, instead of *Reichskammergericht*), it became apparent he and his imperial circle would use it to punish uncooperative estates and favor their friends. Frederick was the recipient of such favor. In August 1497, Maximilian's chamber court confirmed in elegant legalese that the privilege given by King Sigismund in 1423 to the Saxon electoral prince was still valid. In Saxony, electoral subjects would have their day in a judicial court only before the dukes of Saxony and their *Amt* officials. Only plaintiffs who could prove their rights had thus been violated would have access to the imperial judicial court.[84] On the other hand, the chamber court (*Kammergericht*) punished the uncooperative Swiss. Even Berthold had been behind it, wanting to show the power of the *Kammergericht* by punishing the Swiss districts of St. Gall and Appenzell. The Swiss, freedom-loving and fierce, were mercenaries through and through. An enlightened imperial circle, and Berthold as well, could have induced the loyalty of the Swiss—despite their hatred of the Swabian League menace, the common penny, and just about anything imperial—with promises of Italian properties. Instead, the Swiss, smarting from imperial interference and promises of real money from France, were ready at any provocation to turn on Maximilian. "You can't conquer us with spear and halberd," they snorted, "even less so can you with pen and ink!"[85]

In early January 1497, Frederick had met Maximilian at Innsbruck.[86] This began, on Frederick's part, eight months of unbroken service to the emperor. Maximilian traveled constantly, while Frederick appears to have remained in western Austria. Most of his time he corresponded with France. When Maximilian resided in Imst in July and Innsbruck in August, Frederick joined him. Otherwise, Frederick was involved with negotiations with France. Through alliances, the French were outstripping Maximilian on every front.[87] Apparently Europe had watched and decided cash-poor Maximilian with enemies everywhere would be the loser. In February 1497, Ferdinand II of Aragon concluded an armistice with the French. France outwardly talked of peace and expressed no further interest in Italy. That drew the attention of the Italians to the raw ambition of Maximilian in northern Italy. So the Holy League, no more than a hollow shell as an alliance, bolted to France and Spain. The pope, Milan, and Venice formally joined the armistice in April 1497. Yet no one had to be reminded just how dubious the convictions in such an alliance as the Holy League were.

In April 1498, Charles VIII, the despised one, struck his head on the stone lintel of a door. Bleeding inside his head threw him into a coma, and he soon died. Maximilian learned of the death while hunting chamois with a crossbow west of Innsbruck.[88] He lost no time planning how he could frustrate the French in their decision on the king's successor. Charles VIII was the last of the Valois line that went back to 1328. No successor had a completely clear claim on the throne.[89] The obvious successor was the king's cousin Louis, the Duke of Orleans, who also happened to be married to the dead king's sister Jeanne. But others could challenge. Contenders were three-year-old Francois of Angouleme and nine-year-old Charles de Bourbon de Vendome.[90] Yet no one had the stomach to fight for children against a well-connected, wealthy claimant.

The opportunity for Maximilian that lay in the offing was the status of the widowed Queen Anne. The queen was obligated to marry the successor of Charles VIII. But because Louis was already married, the queen would presumably return to Brittany. This plum of a territory would no longer belong to France. Maximilian began scheming at once. Should he divorce the disappointing Bianca and claim Anne himself? Then, as if he willed it, the powerful Cardinal Peraudi proposed that very idea. Maximilian should divorce Bianca and marry his former promised bride, Anne of Brittany. Peraudi indicated this was also the wish of Maximilian's son Philipp and the one man who could make sure it would happen, the pope.[91] Alexander VI would agree to the annulment and of course expected a crusade in return. But this plan was too callous for Maximilian, the romantic.

But they all underestimated how callous Louis himself could be. In a lurid development, Louis claimed Jeanne, his wife of twelve years, was so deformed physically that they had never consummated their marriage. This despicable behavior by Louis was possibly made easier by the fact that he genuinely did not like this wife Charles VIII had forced on him at his tender age of eleven. To bolster his case, Louis emphasized their complete lack of children.[92] To prevent the annulment, she swallowed her pride and produced evidence of consummation overwhelmingly in her favor. She was spitting against a maelstrom. One of the most corrupt popes of history was final arbiter.[93] Alexander VI leaped into the victory parade of Louis and granted the annulment.

Frederick was thrust into this new pulse of French dominance to represent the empire. The new king of France Louis XII or his advisers rushed to one diplomatic triumph after another. Soon France had allied with the kings of England and Spain and most crushing of all to the imperial circle, Maximilian's own son Philipp! Archduke Philipp was conceding to France nothing less than Burgundy itself. Maximilian had indulged Philipp, believing he could still control him and Burgundy. How wrong he was. Only seventeen years old in early 1498, Philipp's goals far exceeded his ability to bring them about. He intended to implement his father's coronation as emperor, win over the electors, and have himself elected the new Roman king.[94] This would guarantee his own succession to the imperial throne. But his vision did not stop there. He envisioned an alliance of Burgundy, France, and the empire. Nothing could stop such a power. So he had secretly negotiated with the French, who proved far more skilled than his own advisers. In the process of bringing all this about, he was surrendering Burgundy to the French.

At the urging of Maximilian, Frederick rushed to Metz to negotiate and try to salvage the situation. He and Duke Rene II of Lorraine dickered with the French for three months. Maximilian, meanwhile, assured the French he was raising a massive army to stop the implementation of their negotiations with Philipp. If Frederick failed, Maximilian would wage war to win back "what was his."[95] And still the estates only grudgingly threw him crumbs of support. Even the Holy League balked. Privately Maximilian vowed to defeat France and swore vengeance against the pope and Venice as well. Openly he intentionally appeared indecisive to confuse his enemies. He turned to his last resort in Ulm. The Swabian League would help him. By the end of June, Maximilian bragged of two thousand knights on horse and ten thousand infantry. In July, Frederick returned to attend the *Reichstag* in Freiburg-im-Breisgau. The French had prolonged the negotiations because every day they grew stronger, and support for the money-poor Maximilian dribbled away.

Maximilian's inner circle now included Frederick as governor (*Statthalter*), the highest office below the emperor. In the absence of the emperor, he was but one of two who could sign decrees. That esteemed level of authority also belonged to the chancellor, Dr. Konrad Stürzel. Frederick's first cousin George (the Rich) of Bavaria, a cantankerous old duke who seemed to have little power,[96] was *Hofmeister*. Graf Heinrich von Fürstenberg was high marshal (*Hofmarshall*), a noble with military expertise. Maximilian's high secretary was Zyprian von Serntein. Among the members of intimates to the emperor was chamber secretary Matthäus Lang, bishop of Gurk. These men were essentially the royal councillors. Berthold of Mainz was archchancellor, but in practice he was left out of the circle. Frederick was genuinely powerful, seen that way by all. But that was no assurance he could influence Maximilian.

Frederick had dedicated himself to an intense two-year effort in imperial affairs. One could cynically believe this was the lesser of two evils, for the time period was riddled with exhausting *Reichstags*, always of the same nature. Berthold wanted reform; Maximilian wanted money, especially the common penny the estates agreed to collect. Because of Frederick's imperial duties, he sent representatives to the unproductive *Reichstags*. He could not avoid the Freiburg *Reichstag* of 1498.[97] Maximilian was exasperated. He demanded from each estate a straight answer as to who would give the common penny and who would refuse to give it. Employing a method used by the old fox, he insisted on talking to each prince personally. Frederick did not escape the interrogation. In the summer of 1498, he had in large part collected the common penny and would hand these funds over soon to Maximilian's treasurers. He would collect the remainder with all diligence.

Sometime in 1498, a noted Florentine sculptor, Adriano Fiorentino, was in Maximilian's court.[98] Possibly he rendered Maximilian in bronze or another medium, but most definitely he did a life-size bust of Frederick in bronze. The portrait is more idealized than the earlier one in oil by Dürer. Nevertheless, the wide yet stern eyes are there. The relatively short upper lip, this time with no moustache, appears truly depicted. The age around the eyes is shown by crows' feet. What seems "enhanced" is the firm chin, so protruding, it has misrepresented the lower lip and gives the face a sloping large-jawed look. Also unnatural is the nose, more or less correctly proportioned but the aquiline shape straightened with the tip not turned raptorishly down but neutral. The hair is massively thick around the head, presenting a bulky, lionesque countenance.

By mid-1498, Maximilian owed Frederick and Johann about 65,000 gulden.[99] To maintain their interest, he or some in his inner circle prodded the Milan officials to hint that Frederick could rule a territory in northern Italy, enlarged considerably after they double-crossed Venice and conquered them. To appease them immediately, cash-poor Maximilian bestowed some of his stake in northern Italy, the so-called "Görz inheritance," in the midst of the territory of Friaul. This old countship of Gorizia lay near the edge of the Adriatic Sea, a day's ride east and north of Venice. It included among its castles those of Cormons, Belgrado, Latisana, and Castelnuovo. The countship was impressively large and lushly pleasant in the southern sun. Who could resist such compensation? This bestowal served two purposes for the emperor. He got rid of that debt of 65,000 gulden and obligated Frederick intimately to Italy. Now when Milan and imperial forces attacked Venice, how could Frederick refuse to support the emperor with money and troops? Just to sour the sweet deal a bit, Maximilian retained the right to redeem the properties. Frederick was enthralled with the balmy properties, though he realized the difficulties of their possession. They were far too distant from Saxony. The political situation in Italy was as changing as the wind.[100]

Is it possible Frederick worked on Maximilian's conciliar order of 1497? The order in 1497, followed by that of 1498, in effect edged Berthold of Mainz out of the imperial circle, in violation of the 1495 agreements at Worms. Even Frederick had to be concerned with the new conciliar order of February 23, 1498, which named him the emperor's permanent deputy over the imperial court council *Hofrat* but not over the imperial court chamber *Hofkammer*. The diminution of Berthold and possibly Frederick, too, was the work of the so-called "Swabians" who began to dominate the imperial inner circle behind Maximilian's back. The "Swabians" included Lang, Stürtzel, Serntein, and Count Heinrich VII von Fürstenberg. Many believe the "Swabians," especially Serntein, began to control Maximilian by feeding him "beautiful women and virgins" to satiate his insatiable sexual appetite.[101] The emperor, not yet forty years old, craved comely women. He had twelve illegitimate children of contemporary record.[102] He bore the marks. "In 1497 the king had had a noticeable attack of syphilis (*morbus gallicus*) in the form of mouth-sores whilst sipping wine with the monks at Fussen, as recorded in their monastic chronicle."[103]

Frederick no doubt discerned with dismay and disgust the machinations behind this debauchery of Maximilian. It must be noted that the emperor himself recruited this assembly of Swabians. He did not inherit them from his father. He, as his father before him, had embraced Swabians, perhaps a reflex against the possibility of the two great territories of the Wittelsbachs joining into one enormous territory that could topple the Habsburgs. The Swabians, with Maximilian's complete approval, had squeezed out Berthold of Mainz. The Swabians, probably not without the emperor's assent, diminished Duke George the Rich in importance every day. The duke's role as *Hofmeister* was soon an illusion. Most shocking of all, the Swabians undermined, deceived, and irritated Maximilian's highest official, Frederick. Apparently Maximilian was oblivious.

The final insult came on September 12, 1498, when Maximilian issued an order from the imperial chancellery.[104] Of course the Swabians were behind it. It was a devastating setback for Frederick. The Swabians apparently had convinced Maximilian that Frederick had too much authority. Besides that, Frederick was not strong enough against reform, even opposing the emperor on some issues such as Maximilian's most recent request for money to fight the Turks. Moreover, Frederick had not been able to stop Philipp's mad plan to surrender Burgundy in his negotiations with France. Therefore, the drastic order from Maximilian of September 1498 transferred all execution of imperial business that had been reserved for Frederick to the chancellery and Stürzel. The Swabians were ultimately destructive to Maximilian's efforts to enlist help from his empire by driving out Berthold and Frederick.[105]

BITTER DEPARTURE FROM MAXIMILIAN

"Johann had accompanied the emperor on his expedition through the Franche-Comte and Lorraine; in October 1498 he rode from Metz to Louvain. He departed hastily from there at the end of October and met his brother in Freiburg in the middle of November."[106] Abruptly on November 10, 1498, Frederick left the imperial council.[107] The brothers and their entourage returned to Saxony after an absence of two years. Maximilian reeled as if awakening with a hangover. What had happened? When Frederick personally stayed away from the *Reichstag* in Worms in late November 1498, Maximilian sent his own messenger to Frederick, pleading with him to come, together with his brother Johann, to the next *Reichstag* (in Cologne) and also for him to assume his imperial position again.[108] To the *Reichstag* in Worms Frederick sent as his Saxon representative Heinrich von Bünau.[109] Frederick's thought process is preserved in a murky way in a report by official Bünau on his discussion with Berthold of Mainz. Bünau spent eight hours with the archbishop. Berthold himself was in poor health. Usually composed, the discussion about Maximilian's inner circle agitated him.

To protect Frederick's privacy, the letter from Bünau is couched in allusions and hints no doubt obvious to Frederick but to few others. Several reasons for Frederick's departure can be deciphered. Frederick openly worries for his territory and subjects. He has delegated his duties for two years. Also implied is that, at the imperial court, some accusation had been made against Frederick. He was convinced nothing in the imperial circle would improve as long as "two officials" remain. Although unnamed, no doubt one is the malicious chamber secretary Matthäus Lang. The other is less certain but most probably Zyprian von Serntein, though possibly Heinrich von Fürstenberg. Berthold told Bünau he greatly regretted Frederick leaving the imperial court. He believed Frederick had prevented the imperial circle from being even more corrupt than it was. He also believed Frederick was the one prince who could do the most for the empire.

One scholar believes the imperial chancellery order of September 1498 was only the final straw.[110] Frederick had been extremely unhappy before that. He thought he had negotiated a peaceful solution between France and the empire. Then it became obvious to him that neither France nor the imperial circle had negotiated in good faith. His own imperial circle had betrayed Frederick. In a sense, Maximilian, through his debauched distractions, had betrayed him.

Many in the emperor's court besides Maximilian and Berthold were sorry to see him go. His friend the Duke Rene II of Lorraine wrote Frederick that it "pained him that this imperial prince ... himself up to now so loyal and lofty ... and he ... would have ... endeavored futilely to reach a[n] ... agreement for peace between the Roman imperial Majesty and the king of France" and Rene II "had even sensed his absence in the imperial court. For when he [Frederick] had been in the imperial court, then things went very well."[111]

Frederick's position as imperial governor (*Reichsstatthalter*) in the imperial council (*Hofrat*) would remain vacant.

CHAPTER 4

HASTY RETURN TO SAXONY

(1499–1505)

"I have seen many principalities and territories,
but never one that I wanted (more than Saxony)."
—Frederick the Wise[1]

ELECTORAL INITIATIVES

By March 1499, Frederick and Johann issued an administrative order worded much like recent orders by the imperial inner circle.[2] The similarity in wording did not mean Frederick modeled his electorate after the imperial circle. This 1499 order only set in legal terms (borrowed from the imperial circle) procedures already in place for years, probably before the *Leipziger Teilung* in 1485. Four advisers (apparently Heinrich and Hans Mönch, Hans von Obernitz, and Hans von Leimbach) presided over by the *Hofmeister* Heinrich von Ende[3] had to be at court (*Hof*, not the judicial *Gericht*) at all times. This court council (*Hofrat*) of five was to meet daily. A majority vote decided issues. The *Hofmeister* was bound by this vote. The court was usually in Torgau or Weimar, but occasionally in Coburg, Jena, and Altenburg. Only "grave and difficult matters" were to be presented to the princes, along with the advice of the council. There was no formal provision for the estates in the electorate (as there was, for example, in Brandenburg). Scholars Maria Grossmann and C. A. H. Burkhardt believed that Frederick was so powerful by 1500 that he no longer needed to consider the views of his territorial estates on foreign matters.[4] It should be noted that matters that could be decided by local *Amt* officials were not to be presented to the council unless it was to appeal such a decision.

All "grants, confirmations, recesses, decisions, missives, and other matters" going out from the electoral court had to comply with wishes of the council (*Hofrat*) of five or the princes. A comparison of the imperial council with the Saxon electoral council shows a great difference in focus. The imperial council was strongly political and occupied with foreign problems as well as conflicts between "imperial" objectives and "Habsburg territorial" objectives. The Saxon council focused internally on the administration of electoral governance and justice.

All evidence indicates pervasive congeniality for this period of electoral activity; Frederick inspired this atmosphere. Many anecdotes, especially out in the empire, indicate he had a remarkable ability to calm and persuade. In any event, the Saxon circle of power—Frederick and Johann, and the council of five—seemed wholly cooperative. Both Frederick and Johann operated as a unit, though Frederick had a much greater interest in administration. Both Heinrich von Ende and Hans von Leimbach had to subdue their domineering personalities in the council to the welfare of the electorate. There is no hint of a corrosive personality such as Hugold von Schleinitz or Matthäus Lang.

Although the harmony remained, the homogeneity caused also by long familiarity and aristocratic standing would begin to dissolve in 1501 with the inclusion of juristically trained Chancellor Dr. Johann Mogenhofer.[5] He had been Archbishop Ernst's key adviser and chancellor for ten years. Perhaps brother Ernst bragged too much about his abilities. In the trend of the times throughout the empire, advisers from the nobility were being replaced by university-trained advisers. Mogenhofer not only met that criterion but began the active recruitment of advisers with similar training. This for Electoral Saxony began the influx of university-trained men as key advisers.[6] Moreover, Mogenhofer, unlike his predecessor, became a regular member of the council (*Hofrat*). He more than held his own within the council. He was apparently a much stronger personality than his predecessor Johann Flehinger, though his ascendance might also have been due to a sharp redefining of his office. The chancellor abandoned financial concerns (to the *Rentmeister*) to offer political and legal advice.[7] In any event, documents indicate Mogenhofer joined and possibly surpassed the influence of *Hofmeister* Heinrich von Ende and *Rentmeister* Hans von Leimbach.

Of major consequence was the influence of the Saxon court language on the German language.[8] Moreover, the Saxon development of administration, as well as its language, was also intertwined with the imperial development of the same elements by the Habsburgs. To span the empire, the imperial circle—more or less influenced by Frederick—developed a "supraregional" language. Naturally this claim is not without controversy, but educated people at the time, including Martin Luther, thought this was the case.

> I employ the common German language in order that both High and Low Germans may understand me. I speak according to the Saxon Chancery which is followed by all the princes and kings in Germany. Emperor Maximilian and Elector Frederick, Duke of Saxony, have thus united the German languages of the Roman Empire into one definite language.[9]

Frederick's influence was everywhere in the empire, even though his interest had shifted to his territory and its multitude of endeavors. As always, he was concerned with ecclesiastical responsibilities. There were about one hundred monasteries and foundations in Electoral Saxony, of which Frederick clearly favored the minority that had reformed. Perhaps he thought reform was satisfactorily underway, because as a territorial prince, he seemed in these years after his return to Saxony more involved in construction than reform. His interest at this time was clearly aimed at Wittenberg. In 1503, he had given the Augustinians the old Holy Spirit hospital property to the east near the Elster Gate. Although the slaughter grounds were not much farther east outside the walls, and their stench wafted well within the walls, Vicar Staupitz was grateful for the concession.[10] In 1504, the Augustinians began building their new monastery. Over time, Frederick would give the Augustinians several thousand gulden for the monastery. It was well worth it, considering that in the first years Staupitz would bring more than one hundred monks either to study at the university or to teach there. Frederick expected as well that the monastery would furnish some space for classes. Later the Franciscans would receive funds from Frederick to refurbish their monastery north of the town square near the wall.

Another aspect of a secular ruler's interest in church matters was to make sure the ecclesiastical powers did not exceed their authority and encroach upon his own sovereign rule. On July 14, 1500, in Naumburg, advisers of the princes met with representatives of the bishops of

Meissen, Merseburg, and Naumburg to discuss possible new territorial regulations. The princes intended to dilute the authority of the powers of the religious *Amts* and the judicial courts (*Gericht*) of the bishops. The effort by Frederick may have been a feint. Opposition from the bishops must have been spirited. This sweeping intervention by ordinance never happened.[11] Many instances of dispute, however, did arise through the years.

The truth was that the Wettins had long ago subdued the bishops almost to a vassal status. The prince could demand military help and taxes from the bishopric if he wished. In addition, the Wettins had gained power over the appointment of the chapter deacons in the bishopric of Meissen. Although the princes did not have such power in the bishoprics of Naumburg and Merseburg, they were allowed two chapter seats in each. In practice, they controlled the composition of the chapter seats, which were occupied almost exclusively by Saxon nobles.

The three bishopric dioceses became predictable. Their allegiances were flagged clearly by the Leipzig Division in 1485. The Meissen bishopric had remained tied to both parts. The Naumburg diocese was allied to the Ernestine part. The diocese of Merseburg had been attached to the Albertine part. Not surprisingly, the Ernestine success with these bishoprics was pre-determined by this. Issues with Naumburg were resolved easily; issues with Merseburg with difficulty, if at all. Success with Meissen was somewhere in between, though the Meissen bishop's authority was increasingly attacked by Frederick's aggressive cousin George.[12] Second, the reaction of the three bishops to most circumstances was predictable simply because, in a world of ever-changing authorities, these bishops were long ruling. Bishops of all three of the dioceses remained unchanged from 1492 to 1514. Handpicked by Frederick, Naumburg's Johann III von Schönberg, who would last until 1517, was friendly to Ernestine Saxony. At the Cologne *Reichstag* in 1505, Frederick and Johann even insisted the Naumburg bishop served them and not the empire.[13] Moderately reasonable with Frederick was Meissen's Johann VI von Salhausen, who would live until 1518. The third bishop, predictably the most difficult for the Ernestines, was Merseburg's Thilo von Trotha, who was to die in 1514 (concluding a staggering forty-eight years of rule).

SURLY SWISS SPURN MAXIMILIAN

If Europeans thought the Swiss were ferocious mercenaries on foreign soils, they could only wonder how the Swiss would fight if they were fighting for their homeland. Maximilian was soon to find out. Due to Swabian influence in the imperial circle, the Swiss felt threatened. The Swabians probably hated only the Wittelsbachs more than the Swiss. Although other principalities had resisted the resolutions of the 1495 Worms *Reichstag*, Maximilian had not singled them out for punishment as he did the Swiss. Conflict erupted over control of Umbrail Pass from Tyrol to Italy. Once again it was primarily a Habsburg problem. In late January 1499, imperial troops pillaged the Benedictine Convent of St. John at Müstair, located in that region. Their Swiss allies arrived too late but killed several imperial soldiers. Imperial forces called for help from the Swabian League and in the meantime plundered the burg of Maienfeld.

By March 1499, the Swiss were fighting imperial troops reinforced by the Swabian League.

Beginning with the battle of Bruderholz, the Swiss, usually outmanned, compiled an astonishing sequence of victories. Moreover, the war had shifted almost entirely to Swabian territory and Habsburg lands bordering the Swiss Confederation. From the Netherlands, Maximilian rushed to the war zone. By the end of April, he was there personally to conduct the war.[14] The war front was extensive, running from northernmost Italy north through the Alps, then swinging west along the southern shore of Lake Constance, to run all the way to Basel where the Rhine turned north. The Swiss attacked all along that front, and even when outnumbered they thrashed Maximilian's forces. The pomposity of history's self-proclaimed "last knight" was amplified by Maximilian reciting his accomplishments to Willibald Pirckheimer so the famed Nuremberg writer could chronicle his great feats. Pirckheimer was there to captain the Nuremberg contingent in battle.[15]

No greater testament to Swiss ferocity and attitude could be found than the battle of Dornach in July. While Maximilian led troops around Lake Constance, in the west, near Basel, Frederick's old "thorn" from the imperial council, Count Heinrich von Fürstenberg, marshaled imperial troops. Fürstenberg led a force of two thousand mounted knights and fourteen thousand foot soldiers. Incredibly, this massive force was mauled by the Swiss. Fürstenberg died in the first assault. The Swiss left three thousand of the imperial forces dead at the end of the battle. Many in Fürstenberg's force were high-born. The city of Basel appealed to the Swiss to allow the removal of the dead nobles from the battlefield. The Swiss answered, "The nobles must lie with the peasants."[16] The Swiss themselves would make any sacrifice. Their people not in the military had been eating grass to stay alive.

Not only had the imperial troops suffered far more deaths than the Swiss, but in battle after battle they lost their artillery. Finally the Swabians refused to fight any longer for Maximilian. The terms of the peace treaty signed in Basel on September 22, 1499, humiliated Maximilian. The Swiss knew how to rub salt into his wounds. They cast the war not in terms of Maximilian enforcing an imperial ban on the Swiss, but in terms of two estates of the empire fighting: the Swiss Confederacy against the House of Habsburg. The treaty referred to Maximilian as the Duke of Habsburg.

The Swiss War was yet another failure of policy by Maximilian. Even more, the Swiss were in effect lost to the empire. The Confederation remained a member in name only. The Swiss should have been natural allies in Maximilian's mission to expand the empire into Italy, because they coveted the foothills and plains of northern Italy. The Habsburg and Swabian aristocrats disdained the Swiss as coarse farmers, nothing more than backward mountainfolk to be used as foot soldiers for pay. Countless quotes from Maximilian and others in his favor refer to the Swiss in terms of contempt. One suffices. Maximilian in his declaration of war berated the Swiss as "ill-conditioned, rough, and base peasant-folk, in whom there is to be found no virtue, no noble blood, and no moderation."[17]

Small wonder the countryfolk in the southern empire began wondering if they could throw off their oppressors too.

In July, the imperial forces were crushed at Dornach, and the French forces crossed the Alps to attack Milan. Since April, the French had pacts with Venice and the Swiss. The month the Swiss made peace with Maximilian, the French had taken Milan. Maximilian was at a low point in prestige, influence, and money. He had proved once again how little he accomplished with money and soldiers. Nearly everyone, including his son and Frederick, had turned from him. He had only his corrupt "Swabian" advisers and the Habsburg territories. Berthold of Mainz saw this as an opportunity to "recover the empire."[18] The *Reichstag* in Augsburg in 1500 would be the moment.

THE SHAM IMPERIAL GOVERNING COUNCIL

Frederick would not forgo this great event, the most important *Reichstag* since Worms in 1495.[19] Berthold of Mainz aggressively raised all reform issues anew. Even the annual *Reichstag* was under fire, for it had been thrown to the estates in 1495 as a sop in place of any permanent authority such as a council. The annual *Reichstag* was supposed to monitor the maintenance of the eternal peace, supervise use of the common penny, and guide foreign policy. Of course, the mechanism had failed. Neither emperor nor estates cooperated. Absent estates did not consider themselves bound at all by *Reichstags*. Witness the Swiss.

Nevertheless, Maximilian always needed money. Hence in December 1499, he sent a summons for a *Reichstag* in Augsburg. He sent another in March 1500. The affair was to start April 10. Augsburg was no mean city. The imperial city lay in Bavaria between Munich and Ulm. With at least thirty thousand citizens, it was one of the largest cities in the empire, much larger than any city in the two Saxonies. It was shockingly ancient, founded in the lifetime of Christ by Romans who named it after Augustus. Citizens of renown lived there, including the most notable financial family of the empire, the Fuggers. It also boasted artisans and armorers known throughout Europe. In many ways it rivaled Nuremberg.

Berthold had matured his thoughts on a cohesive empire. It was clear the great dynasties would not submit to an imperial concept for protection. These dynasties included the Habsburgs, Hohenzollerns (Brandenburgs), Wittelsbachs, and Wettins. Therefore, they could only be drawn in by a system that emphasized the emperor and the electoral princes. Maximilian was compliant. Negotiations were secretive, allowing only speculation as to who may have been the driving forces. Nevertheless, the final summation (*Abschied*) announced ordinances that approved the administration of eternal peace, the imperial *Kammergericht*, and imperial wars, and most telling of all, an ordinance dated July 2, 1500, for the establishment of an imperial governing council (*Reichsregiment*).

First, to the delight of nearly all, the imperial governing council was to replace the annual *Reichstag*. The members of the council would meet permanently in Nuremberg. In addition to a multitude of duties, the imperial governing council would also handle money matters and keep accounts. Head of the council was the emperor, though he had neither the right to vote nor veto. Presumably he directed the proceedings. The twenty voting members included permanently the six electors (excluding Bohemia) or their deputies. The *Reichstag* and the emperor had to select the remaining fourteen voting members of the council. Burgundy and Austria each had a member (surely a concession to the emperor). From the "curia of princes" there were four: one secular prince, one religious prince, one prelate, and one count. Two more came from the imperial cities. The remaining six—untitled nobility (knights) or university-trained professionals—came from the newly created geographically defined "imperial circles," which were not to include any electorates or Habsburg lands. All members except the emperor and the electors served only one quarter annually.

Although it had glaring problems of execution, such as so many required quarterly selections, it seemed a commendable start. For the first time, the cities actually had more than nominal representation. In addition, untitled nobility and university professionals were included. Not included in representation, and undoubtedly not even included in the thoughts of any attendee of the *Reichstag* for one second, were the vast majority of people in the empire: the countryfolk. On the other hand, it could not have escaped anyone's attention that the emperor had become a figurehead. The imperial governing council had replaced him as sovereign! The council decided virtually everything, including the conduct of war. The members swore an oath to the empire, not to the emperor.

Maximilian accepted it all with his uncommon grace—and perhaps a sly glance or two. He took the opportunity on August 8 to praise Frederick lavishly "because of services of his ancestors to emperors and empire and because of his special loyalty and his services."[20] Then he advanced Frederick successfully as his own deputy, that is, the head or governor (*Statthalter*) of the imperial governing council. Of course, Frederick had no vote, but his own representative would vote for his electorate. His annual compensation was a pittance for a Saxon elector: six thousand gulden. His duty also excused him from negotiating with the French, which he was still doing on occasion, as remarkable as that seems in view of its futility.[21]

The official starting date for the imperial governing council in Nuremberg had been September 16, 1500. Enthusiastic Berthold arrived September 21. Maximilian arrived October 24, one week before Frederick. Frederick must have noted sourly that Maximilian had once again refused to pay him all the money he owed him. Perhaps that is why Frederick excused himself from the council for physical reasons less than one month after he first arrived in Nuremberg to take his seat.[22] Nevertheless, at Maximilian's urging Frederick returned to the council before year end. Frederick wanted the council to succeed, but he was discovering that though the princes enjoyed stripping Maximilian of his powers, they really did not want to take over Maximilian's troublesome duties. An example was Duke Albrecht of Bavaria, who could not even be persuaded to participate. On the other hand, the imperial governing council found to its dismay that Maximilian's envoys were also negotiating some kind of truce in Italy with France. The French must have delighted in the bumbling, stumbling empire. The emperor and the council temporarily agreed on one thing: they refused Cardinal Peraudi's attempts to sell indulgences in the empire. The reasons differed. Maximilian was angry with Pope Alexander VI. The estates did not want to be exploited. Maximilian, however, must have realized he could funnel off money for his enterprises. He changed his mind. The council resisted but finally caved to his machinations. Therefore, indulgences would be peddled in the empire.

Despite Berthold's bold plan, the council sputtered. Administratively it faltered. Documents stemming from the council had to be reviewed by the emperor, and Maximilian was rarely available. To make matters worse, the twenty members themselves were often absent. Underlying their lack of enthusiasm was the fact that many estates did not want the council to succeed. It was just one more interfering power. Frederick himself seemed not unsympathetic. The truth was that Maximilian wanted it to succeed but only to his liking: weakly, just enough to take care of some of the more tedious duties. Frederick had resisted his role, but after Maximilian assured him that he had good intentions toward him and the estates, the *Statthalter* reluctantly took on an imperial duty with small chance of success.[23] He had many projects in Saxony coming to fruition. Frederick himself left the council twice in 1501 to return to

Saxony. Was it frustration at the council's baby steps? Frederick was not one to explain. The final flaw was the council's inability to enforce its decisions. Neither the will nor the physical reality was there. The council simply expired in March 1502, without "song or sound."[24] Berthold was not the only one to realize any meaningful reform of the empire was dead, but he may have been the only one who cared.

LOVE AND DEATH AMONG THE WETTINS

Great events happened in 1500 within the House of Wettin.

On March 1, Johann, now thirty-one, married Sophie, eighteen-year-old daughter of Duke Magnus II of Mecklenburg.[25] Sophie was a petite, milky-skinned redhead with blue eyes.[26] The duchy of Mecklenburg was substantial. The recently reunited duchy sprawled along the North Sea, abutting Pomerania to the east. The wedding in Torgau on the Sunday before Lent launched a vigorous celebration that ran through the onset of the fasting time on Ash Wednesday. Guests actually started arriving two days before Sunday.

Frederick and Johann received Uncle Albrecht and his son George outside the city. Then the procession entered Torgau. In the Albertine entourage were ladies, the bishop of Merseburg, and numerous counts and knights. All in all they employed 545 horses. To honor Johann, they wore bright red garments with "To Happiness with Joy" embroidered on the right sleeve. The sight of all the powerful Wettins together again must have thrilled the Saxons. Fierce Albrecht was almost legendary. The same day, Heinrich, the Prince of Braunschweig, arrived with his Wettin wife, Margarete, sister of Frederick and Johann, in a procession of 478 horses. This reception of royal entourages was repeated numerous times. All were escorted to their lodging. By the time all had arrived before the wedding, Torgau was flooded with 11,500 guests and their 6,500 horses.[27]

The Saxon court could not rival Burgundy in finery, but the scale was colossal. Frederick had to arrange loans for the spectacle. Beds were borrowed as far away as Bavaria. Dishware was borrowed from cities all over Saxony. Armed guards trickled in from the electorate until two hundred were there. In view of the armor and weaponry carried by battle-hardened knights in the various entourages, the electoral guards seemed more suited to enforce Frederick's order during the celebrations. The hosts stocked food and drink in enormous amounts. Cousin George alone sent six vats of wine and eighteen barrels of beer along with wagons of carp and pike. Frederick and Johann had three-tier grandstands constructed in the marketplace for the ubiquitous jousting and other tournament games. Of course, tapestries, shields, and crests adorned the lodgings, the dance hall, and the locations for "knights' games."

Everywhere sounded trumpets, flutes, and drums. Every day the nobility jousted and played. The wedding actually took place in the church on Monday, administered by the bishops. Johann's brother Ernst, the archbishop of Magdeburg, sanctioned the actual marriage.[28] Each day after a midday meal, the guests, including the bride, watched plays and the tournament games. Citizens and guests sat on rooftops, walls, or any height to observe the festivities.[29] Games mimicked Carnival. One day in the square, bizarrely-costumed performers went through their antics. They were led in by two wild men with a wild little girl, the three blowing a motet on two flutes and a trombone. A faux hunter hunted a deer and a fox. A wild man riding a lion "jousted" a bear riding a wild man. All four costumed characters went crashing down.

Then began the actual jousting. This sport, of course, was favored by many nobles but was especially a pet of the bridegroom. At the evening dance, the hosts highlighted winners of the day and rewarded them. One noble who distinguished himself was none other than Hugolt von Schleinitz, obviously a relative of the infamous old high marshal who had manipulated the 1485 Leipzig Division. Every evening they danced, often hours after midnight. After more than five days of intense activity, the thousands of guests departed. Only the bride's father (Duke Magnus), her mother, and her brother stayed a few days longer.

Wedding negotiations often took ten years for great princes. One peculiar aspect of Johann's marriage is that the arrangement seems to have taken only six months. It's not implausible that Frederick, the great planner, had decided at thirty-six in 1499 that he was not likely to be the fountain for future Ernestine electors. Absorption by the Albertines was unthinkable. That left only Johann. Why had Frederick decided he was no longer a probable progenitor? There is evidence to support a thesis that Frederick was losing interest. And what could dull a quest for a woman more than already having a "special" woman? In a letter in 1498, Frederick wrote his cousin George, who had competed successfully against him for a Polish princess, that he was still seeking a match. "We are riding off to Frankfurt to seek a marriage through our uncle

Landgrave Wilhelm the Younger (of Hesse), though I can also be seen with pleasure in the world as a paramour, although if (in the future) I liked another one, then with that special one I also have it would be hard to free myself."[30]

From the deliberate, cautious Frederick, the admission was a stunner. Frederick had taken a mistress. He lamented it would be hard to give up this special woman if a match were made. Frederick was in Freiburg-im-Breisgau that August 4. Who was this woman from whom it would be hard to free himself? Was she traveling openly with him? Did he see her only where she resided? And where was that? The most likely answer to fit the timeframe of 1498 is that Frederick met her earlier in his own territory (he had been virtually absent from his own territory since 1496) or since 1496 perhaps in a city such as Nuremberg, Augsburg, or even Freiberg.

A mistress of short duration would be of little interest even to the gossips of the time. Princes had their way. The relationship of Frederick to the woman assumed more dimension when she gave birth to a boy.[31] The affair took on major dimensions when this boy, Sebastian (also called Bastien or Bastel), no doubt by 1500 or so, toddled around at the court of Frederick. Perhaps the boy lived inconspicuously in the women's quarters at Torgau. If so, his mother was most likely there also to attend him. The strongest clue to her identity was to be provided years later by what was supposedly said at table by Luther.[32] Luther knew much about the true nature of the court as well as the gossip. He referred to the probable makeup of the children, so Luther's reference to the woman as the "Wantzlerinne" has weight. Bernhard Watzler is mentioned in Frederick's last will.[33] An official, perhaps even a messenger, to the electoral court named Watzler occurs in a number of documents.[34]

Concrete evidence exists from 1525 that identifies her as Anna, the stepdaughter of Kasper Dornle.[35] She and Frederick face each other in an elegant circular compact of about 22 cm diameter. Their portraits, with specific identities engraved, are carved on pear wood mounted in walnut wood. Such intimate couplings in compacts were popular at the time. Frederick is in his sixties. Anna is an attractive woman of about forty, round-faced with fine but full lips and a straight, thin nose. Her face and the tilt of her neck convey the image of a statuesque woman. She wears a stylish cap over hair that just covers her ears. The cap and hair indicate she is not a married woman nor is she young and unmarried. Kasper

Dornle was a prominent merchant of Nuremberg. Frederick had intimate friends there, especially the patrician Anton Tucher. One can speculate Frederick met Anna possibly about 1496 and was smitten with her. And what young patrician woman could resist one of the most powerful princes of the empire?

Speculation about the woman goes yet further. Because Frederick commissioned so much art and it was common at the time to insert portraits of real people into religious works, it is not unreasonable to suppose Frederick's companion may be among them.[36] Moreover, when a work depicts Frederick and an accompanying woman, that woman is even more significant. Three works of that nature exist and are noteworthy, because the woman in each appears to have the same likeness. They were done by Lucas Cranach, Frederick's court painter since 1505. Cranach is somewhat suspect because he tended to stylize women, though round-faced women with sharp features seem not to have been his choice. The most graphic and compelling of Cranach's three is his so-called Torgau altarpiece of the Holy Kinship, a triptych dating from 1509 and now in Frankfurt. In the same side panel, in front of Frederick (reading a book) is the woman with two children. She is, not surprisingly, attractive with auburn hair and fine features. In Cranach's so-called Princes' Altarpiece (c. 1510–12) in Dessau, Frederick peers from the left and Johann from the right in adulation of the Christ Child. Assuming Cranach would never have depicted Anna as the Holy Mother, it is possible that the woman beside Frederick is Anna (and the woman beside Johann is Sophie). More compelling is Cranach's woodcut "Ladder of Bonaventure." Framed by the beams of the ladder and two rungs are Frederick and a woman.[37] Frederick is definitely older and plumper; so is the woman, more round-faced than before although she retains her sharp nose.

Identity aside, the evidence that Frederick had formed a strong attachment by 1498 and had nudged Johann into a marriage by 1500 sets up a new dynamic in the Ernestine Saxons. Many had speculated Uncle Albrecht had been biding his time, as both Frederick and Johann showed little desire to marry as they grew older and seemed less and less likely to provide heirs to the electorate.[38] Now what did Albrecht think? Probably he had long ceased thinking of that avenue. Maximilian had bestowed the hereditary governorship of Friesland on him in 1498, partly to compensate for his years of iron-fisted service all over the empire and partly to compensate him for unpaid debts of several hundred thousand gulden. Ruling Friesland as deputy at the moment was his son Heinrich (the Pious). Albrecht counted himself lucky indeed. How many princes have two principalities to leave their sons? George would assume Albertine Saxony. Heinrich would take over Friesland. Albrecht had already issued a "Father's Order," insisting Saxony be ruled by the firstborn son (the first firm documents of primogeniture for Saxony) and never be divided.

Uncle Albrecht did not yet return to Friesland, coincidentally also on the North Sea and flanking Mecklenburg to the west.[39] Albrecht attended the *Reichstag* in Augsburg beginning in April. Heinrich, in the meantime, had lost control of Friesland. He had no skill for governance, and the Frisians were about as fierce and independent as the Swiss. Albrecht rushed back and by June 1500 had subdued the uprising. He was a cruel master. Always hard, he took even more traditional rights from the Frisians. During the last stage of his suppression, the siege of Groningen, Albrecht sickened. An illness swept his army, and Albrecht was taken to Emden. He died there at age 57. His heart remained in Friesland,[40] but the rest of his corpse would be buried at Meissen near his brother Ernst in a ceremony in January 1501.[41] This funeral marked the beginning of a new reign in the duchy of Saxony. Duke George was close to Frederick, but he was no longer the five-year-old looking up to his thirteen-year-old cousin. He was now twenty-nine years old and quite a hard man himself.

ELECTORAL SAXONY BURSTS INTO BLOOM

By 1501, Frederick's plan for Wittenberg was ripening. He, however, did not neglect the rest of his territory. In 1499, he initiated construction in two key castles in western Thuringia. Treffurt castle was as little known as the other was famous. The Wartburg was a castle of legend already in Frederick's time. The ancient Romanesque castle complex, started by Ludwig the Springer in the eleventh century, was in the next century frequented by the famous minstrels Walther von der Vogelweide and Wolfram von Eschenbach, as well as St. Elisabeth. Its days of renown would only grow.[42] Frederick was still renovating the castle at Grimma. Two other construction projects—the castles at Weimar and Coburg— were no doubt to please Johann and his new bride. Johann had already been partial to Weimar, though he found Torgau pleasant enough. After his marriage, he favored Coburg. He made it clear that he planned to hold his court there.[43] He and his court may have been there in 1500 when there was a fire at the castle.[44] Frederick was concerned enough about repairing Coburg, especially the roof, that he sent Hans Behaim there. Construction began in 1501.

Yet Wittenberg was clearly Frederick's own priority.

How dear this Wittenberg showcase had been to Frederick is evident from years of frequent reports of construction progress (with some local gossip as well) sent to him wherever he was.[45] The two residential wings of the castle had been virtually complete since 1496, as far as basic structure. Although not completed by 1501, the church was in an advanced stage of construction. Frederick now had another reputable court painter, Jacopo de Barbari from Venice.[46] He was probably the first noted Italian artist to work permanently in the empire. He was accomplished but by no means young. Already sixty, he nevertheless painted in Frederick's castles. Judging from reports, much work was focused on the Wittenberg castle.[47]

From the description of Frederick's grandest room at the eastern end of the Elbe wing, much can be assumed for other rooms. The room was paneled with the finest wood. This allowed hanging paintings on canvas or on wood. It also allowed the portrayals to be moved from one room to another. Some visitors reached Frederick's quarters on the third floor through the "Hall of Colors," the great hall in the west wing. This space was intended also to serve university law students. The hall itself blazed with four scenes from ancient Rome: "On one wall was the scene of a Roman youth waiting for a senator, on another Scipio cleaning out his camp, while on a third were scenes from the lives of Roman Emperors, and on the last wall was the slave Marcus Antonius dying in the defense of his master."[48] Trial scenes embellished the walls of a smaller room off the great hall. Another small room boasted scenes from Greek mythology: "Liberation of Andromeda by Perseus," "Hercules Taking the Golden Apples from the Hesperides," and "Scenes from the Argonauts."

Just off the great hall was Frederick's bedchamber (with yet another "secret room"). The walls of the bedchamber displayed the release of Andromeda, scenes from the sagas of Hercules and the Argonauts, allegories of fortune and righteousness, and even coats of arms of Thuringia and Saxony. Beyond that was the "Stammstube," or "ancestral room," in the southwest tower. On the ceiling were canvasses with all the coats of arms of the Wettin dynasty. Apparently the crests were on a background of gold somehow combined with Jehovah to show their divine right. On the wood-paneled walls hung portraits of twenty-four princes, not just Wettins but also their Ascanian electoral predecessors. The most recent prince was Frederick himself.

Unclear today are the precise locations of the bedchambers of Johann and his wife. Contemporaries, however, noted in Johann's chamber paintings depicting scenes from Ovid's *Metamorphoses* and the tragic fable of "Pyramus and Thisbe" as well as biblical portrayals of "Absalom's Death" and "David and Bathsheba." Appropriately, representations of conjugal love and loyalty graced the sleeping chamber of his wife, Sophie. Artists adorned these many rooms year after year. Although splendid, the décor could never be considered finished. The quality of these works should not be underestimated. Frederick employed masters of the first rank. For example, Albrecht Dürer, though not physically present, undoubtedly contributed commissioned paintings that were mobile. That the master from Nuremberg was actually there is possible but unlikely.[49]

One artist of the first rank was physically there: the prolific Lucas Cranach.

Cranach may have been employed by Frederick in the area of Coburg between 1495 and 1500.[50] This is plausible; Lucas Cranach was already twenty-three in 1495 and the son of an artist in Kronach. Although the town was not in Frederick's territory, it was an easy one-day ride east of Coburg. Johann may have seen his work at Coburg or nearby, then probably alerted Frederick about this rising talent. The young artist intensified his skills in Vienna from 1500 to 1504. His Viennese works were not at all "works of youth" but mature masterpieces.[51] He was in Frederick's court by 1505.[52] Cranach would be a fixture in the Ernestine Saxon court for nearly fifty years. He was an artist of enormous energy and painted with speed that amazed even fellow artists. He was also a gifted businessman, perhaps learned from his father. He worked his "no nonsense" way into Frederick's favor at once and benefited greatly in prestige and wealth. In just three years (1508), Frederick would knight him and then send him to the Netherlands to paint portraits of Emperor Maximilian and his grandson Karl. In 1505, Cranach would put his roots down in Wittenberg, the most important project on hand being the production of altarpieces.[53] It is unlikely he was a factor in the appearance of the castle or the Castle Church before 1505 or even during 1505.[54]

As for the church itself, construction, though rapid for the time, spanned the years.[55] Not only the artworks were unfinished, but the actual vaulting of the ceiling was still underway in 1503, no doubt supervised by the master of that technique, Konrad Pflüger.[56] The church was fifty-three strides (meters) long and fifteen strides wide. The nave or spine of the ceiling was twice as high as the width of the church. The north main wall outside of the church was strengthened by six narrow buttresses. Between the buttresses were tall windows of almost colorless glass, in contrast to the castle's alternating colorless and green-brown glass.[57] Each window was three strides wide and six times that in height. The south side of the church was connected to the west wing of the castle; therefore only four buttresses on the east end were needed. Similarly, the south side had only three of the towering windows. The east end of the church had a polygonal apse. The west end abutted a tower (topped by a pointed and crowned Gothic spire) that formed the intersection of the church with the castle. The steeped roof was shingled and had an ornate steeple[58] toward the east end.

A long planked walkway led to the main door (below the third great window from the east) in the north wall. On each side of the door stood statues of saints (probably Sigismund and Wenceslas) by sculptor Klaus Heffner. Apparently Heffner was Saxon and had been heavily employed as a carver of stone and wood on both the castle and the church since 1492.[59] A second planked walkway led to a door (below the fifth window from the east) in the north wall near the tower. There was yet a third, little-used entrance in the tower itself.

Inside the church, mirroring the exterior buttresses, were piers that did not rise all the way to the ceiling. Both the north and the south side had six bays, but the sides were not mirror images due to rapid construction that led to discrepancies.[60] "Unlike most Gothic churches with their naves, aisles, and short transept, which included a choir for the clergy and an apse for the altar, this church had but one main nave or, rather, an extended choir."[61] This design at the time was unique to Arnold von Westfalen, who had preceded Wittenberg with a similar design for the church at Meissen. In essence, Frederick's builders "constructed a three-aisled *Hallenkirche* with a two-story nave elevation, capped by elaborate ribbed vaulting (Pflüger's sole contribution to the overall design), that was distinctly divided between lower and upper halves."[62] At the west end, facing the distant main altar, there was no organ and choir loft but three galleries of seats. Perhaps the only décor honoring Frederick as the sponsor was below the main gallery on the north wall. There on the façade of the "royal choir," a stone frieze displayed sixteen coats of arms representing permutations of dynastic houses of nobility in his Wettin ancestry: Meissen, Braunschweig, Austria, Masovia, Bavaria, Milan, Braunschweig-Lüneberg, Henneberg, Pomerania, Görz, Scala, Saxony-Lauenberg (the Ascanians), and Berg.[63]

Some doubt exists as to what décor was inside the church at its consecration.[64] Accounts of a few years later say that enclosing the high altar on three sides were four exceedingly high quality gold and silk tapestries of the Passion. Most churches display a font for Baptism and christening. Often the font is by a master as well. Yet the sources on this are silent for the Castle Church. Baptism, no doubt, was performed by the town church, which indeed boasted a font from 1457 by Hermann Vischer the Elder. Frederick's holy relics were housed in the interior of the Castle Church within a shrine or vault. They were displayed on tables in a second location, leading to confusion over whether they were in or near the main choir, or perhaps near a door on the southeast side that opened into the castle courtyard. A great stone screen separated the choir from the church attendees. Permanently displayed in some location was a panel portraying Frederick's trip to the Holy Land. At the southwest corner of the church directly above the Marian Chapel and lower gallery were Frederick's private chapel and viewing gallery. One could access it only from two doors. One was from the first floor of the castle; another was from an apartment in the church tower reserved for Frederick or whomever he desired there.

The church itself, though its structure was incomplete and many of its commissioned altarpieces would take several more years, was consecrated by Cardinal Peraudi in 1503 on January 17, Frederick's fortieth birthday.[65] Only two weeks later, Peraudi sent Frederick a bull granting various indulgences to the visiting faithful.[66] Thanks to the Ascanians, the All Saints' chapter already possessed the extremely valuable "portiuncula indulgence" of St. Francis, "which remitted the punishment and guilt of *all* repented sin, which otherwise could be obtained only in Asissi" on All Saints' Day (November 1).[67] It was so popular in Wittenberg that special confessors had to be available.

Moreover, when the relics were displayed each year on the Monday after *Misericordias Domini* (Second Sunday after Easter), the viewer of *each* holy relic earned an additional indulgence of one hundred days and one quarantine. One quarantine excused the viewer from the penitential exercises of one Lenten season. These were staggering rewards for viewing the relics, which numbered by this time about five thousand. The scholar Brecht stated, "We cannot speak here of anything but a pious intoxication with numbers, which carried one's preparation for the life to come to dimensions no longer conceivable."[68] Nevertheless, it was undeniable that this indulgence-laden piety would make Frederick's church a magnet for pilgrims.

Frederick's planned sensation, at least twelve stunning multipanel altarpieces in the bays tied to the liturgy and calendar of the Church, was in the beginning limited. Nevertheless, three superb altarpieces are known to have been there by the consecration.[69] Those lucky people attending the consecration had to be stunned. One (now known as the "Arrest of Christ" triptych) was by Frederick's first great court painter, "Jhan of the Netherlands." The center panel depicted Christ in the Garden of Gethsemane, with His long night of agony in the background and His betrayal and arrest in the foreground. The interior side panels show illuminated symbols of His suffering after arrest, among them the crown of thorns, the cross, the lance, and the nails. Naturally, such a vision would be particularly appropriate for meditation on Good Friday.

Also present were two altarpieces by Albrecht Dürer.[70]

One, now known as the "Dresden Altarpiece," is thought to have been another triptych.[71] Dürer, who had already traveled extensively, shows the influence of Venice and the Flemish. Other than not being foldable, the side panels are not controversial. They portray Anthony Abbot and Sebastian, the two saints most frequently called upon at the time for protection against the plague. Two of Frederick's closest family members had presumably died from this scourge in 1484. In addition, the plague had raged through Saxony again in 1494 and into 1495. Frederick commissioned the altarpiece in 1496. As he had done before in 1487 for an altarpiece, he also invoked Mary against the plague. The center panel is controversial, because Mary's baby Jesus is depicted in such a bloated corpse-like way. Some believe the artist was not Dürer, yet the three panels seem even today tied together as a whole. Skeptics explain that a later artist tied them together, perhaps even Dürer himself. In any event, the altarpiece could be useful in a number of ways for the church calendar.

Dürer's second altarpiece, the "Seven Sorrows of the Virgin," also was not foldable.[72] The polyptych had a central panel of Mary surrounded by seven smaller panels. Unlike the other altarpiece, this one seems conventional. Her sorrows were specific in the church. They occurred at the prophecy of Simeon, during the flight into Egypt, after losing the Holy Child at Jerusalem, seeing Jesus on His way to be crucified, standing at the foot of the cross, after Jesus is taken down from the cross, and at His burial. Dürer's panels vary from this sequence only slightly. He depicts nothing that could be seen as a burial. Perhaps there was a slightly different version of the "Seven Sorrows" in the empire at the time. The church calendar would have embraced this conventional work by Dürer during the year; since the 1400s, the "Seven Sorrows of the Virgin" were observed the Friday before Palm Sunday.

The altarpieces must have been a visual sensation to the average pilgrim. And what did incoming visitors see of Frederick's showcase city itself?[73]

Most visitors came from the south either by ship on the River Elbe or by a trade route from the south. A few hundred paces north of the Elbe, a deep moat surrounded a walled city. The crenulated walls and towering gatehouses promised unwelcome visitors all the murderous refinements of the time. The walls allowed three gates named for their destinations: the Coswig Gate on the west, the Elbe Gate on the south, and the Elster Gate on the east. The walls defined a triangle, one long side facing the Elbe and the shorter two sides forming a point to the north. Significantly, the north side offered no gate, only the Franciscan Monastery nestled there inside the point. The main street of Wittenberg, called simply the "Long Lane" (*Lange Gasse*),[74] was no more than a fifteen-minute walk directly between the west gate and the east gate. Just south of the western Coswig Gate, perhaps anchored to the wall, were Frederick's new castle and church. The towers from these buildings were sharply crowned. One-third of the way along the "Long Lane" from the castle was the town square with market, *Rathaus*, and the old, lofty red-bricked St. Mary's town church. Between the castle and the square and to the north were well-trafficked facilities of the time: stables, three bathhouses, and at least one *Frauenhaus* with its prostitutes.[75] Scattered mainly east of the main part of town were a few hundred homely wooden buildings. Near the eastern gate was a hospital, but Frederick had decided it was to come down, to be replaced in a short time by an Augustinian monastery.[76] And beginning around 1501, near the eastern gate, Konrad Pflüger was razing whatever was necessary to build Frederick's university. By 1503, he would erect the three-story Frederici Collegium (Frederick's College).[77]

Frederick would at last have his university.[78] The need was obvious for his electoral territory. Whether he first solicited the pope or not, he obtained permission from Maximilian, who sent him a charter letter dated July 6, 1502.[79] Maximilian liked to promote education and his charter letter urged the usual goals of a university modeled after the exemplary schools in France and the empire. Perhaps Frederick asked Maximilian first in order to flatter him. Frederick was in no way alienated from Rome; Cardinal Peraudi consecrated his Castle Church in Wittenberg as well as his chapel at Lochau that very year.[80] What it meant in practical terms was an absence of ecclesiastical funding locally or from Rome. In any case, the university would formally open October 18, 1502.

Two men masterminded the actual curriculum and faculty of the university: Martin Polich von Mellerstadt, its first rector, and Johann von Staupitz, first dean of the faculty of theology. Both were old friends of Frederick. Their temperaments were poles apart. Mellerstadt was as volcanic and profane as Staupitz was soothing and devout. Mellerstadt embraced humanism; Staupitz had no fondness for humanism, yet theologically he was far ahead of his time, already aware of the critical importance of God's grace. Frederick's new university had statutes that repeated almost word for word those of the University of Tübingen—no wonder, because Staupitz had received his doctorate there only a few years earlier. The influence of Staupitz was enormous. He lured from Tübingen Sigismund Epp, the first dean of the faculty of liberal arts (for undergraduates), Wolfgang Staehelin, the first dean of the law faculty, and the jurists Ambrosius Volland and Hieronymus Schurff. The faculty, including deans of the four disciplines (liberal arts, theology, law, and medicine), were virtually all due to Staupitz.[81] The faculty covered a wide range of theological and philosophical beliefs, from humanism to the older scholasticism. The first year, 416 students matriculated. The number would drop sharply from that the next year.[82] The drop was not because students discovered, despite Frederick's glittering new buildings, the desolation that was Wittenberg. It was the presence of the plague.[83] Nevertheless, the first year was a notable success. Most students were

Saxons, and many were in religious orders, especially the Augustinian order.

RANCOR AMONG THE WETTINS

No amount of planning can prepare a sovereign for every twist of fate. Any Saxon like Frederick knew he could not control nature and fate. Although Frederick was bringing to fruition his great plan for Wittenberg, that was no protection against the River Elbe flooding in August 1501. Much of the harvest was ruined. The following year, the harvest was spoiled again, this time by heat and lack of rain. The year 1503 was bittersweet. On June 30, Johann's wife, Sophie, gave birth to Johann Friedrich. The Ernestine Saxons had one more possible successor to the electoral position. Sadly, Sophie did not recover from the birth. Johann, after three years of marriage, was a widower with an infant son.

Frederick was having problems with his brother Ernst, the archbishop.[84] The two had helped each other through the years, both enthusiastically pursuing grand construction projects. In 1501, Frederick tried to gain control for Ernst not of the religious offices of Magdeburg and Halberstadt, which Ernst already occupied, but the government *Amt* offices.[85] Ernst would have truly been a territorial prince with that success. The *Amt* of Mainz was also included in Frederick's effort. Frederick, knowing Berthold was mortally sick, possibly could have eased Ernst into a position where he could soon gain the archbishopric of Mainz. Because it included the electoral dignity, this archbishopric was far more powerful than Ernst's current archbishopric. Frederick was shocked and annoyed when Ernst declined.[86] Two dioceses were enough, shrugged Ernst, seemingly oblivious to the impact on the Ernestine Wettins.[87]

Cousin George was also troublesome.[88] "There had been still tolerable agreement between the Ernestiners and Albrecht, but friction and quarrels were the norm after George followed Albrecht (September 12, 1500)."[89] Frederick bore George's deliberate provocations. Two major problems were constant.[90] George had his officials harass wagoneers, trying to bully them from the Ernestine Low Road to the Albertine High Road at the Albertine village Senftenberg.[91] Also, the two Saxon lines never could agree on the enormous proceeds from the silver mines at Schneeberg and Annaburg. The irritations between the two Saxonies, moreover, were myriad: controversies about the repayment of loans, interpretations of contracts, and encroachments of individual civil officials. Always George played on the trust of his cousins.[92] Frederick would mutter again and again, "Ach, my cousin George."[93] Albrecht had left George enormous debts.[94] Although Frederick may have been sympathetic, he was also pragmatic. He eventually refused all direct personal negotiation with George.[95] They still corresponded as cousins, but in Frederick's eyes, George was two-faced and unbendingly malicious in his protection of Albertine interests. One of Frederick's favorite proverbs explained his deep disappointment in George: "One should not speak lightly, but whatever one does say, that one should keep."[96]

MAXIMILIAN HITS HIS STRIDE

Frederick was not "sullen" about the empire and Maximilian.[97] He cooperated when asked to perform duties, though, like the other princes, he held back money. He still opposed indulgence preaching, because the so-called Turkish Crusade money somehow would land in Maximilian's hands for yet another war against anyone but the Turks. The imperial governing council had died by 1502. On March 21, Maximilian officially reclaimed from Archbishop Berthold of Mainz the imperial seal. That by no means marked the end of opposition to the emperor by Berthold. Maximilian's "thorn" took a new direction. In perhaps the most blatant opposition yet to Maximilian, the electoral princes met in Gelnhausen in June 1502.[98] Frederick had passed through Gelnhausen many times before, because it was a mere day's travel east of Frankfurt on the route to Saxony.

The attendance of the electors of Mainz, Cologne, Brandenburg, and Saxony themselves at the Electoral Prince Meeting proved its importance. Attending for the electors of the Palatine and Trier were representatives. Maximilian made a futile attempt to intrude on the proceedings. He knew only too well their thrust. Thwarted, he sent envoys who met privately with individual electors and did everything possible to undermine the meeting. Maximilian proposed all the electors meet with him in August. They spurned him. In July they officially withheld all help against Turkey. Moreover, they indicated how threatened they felt by the imperial circle when they formed an assistance pact to protect their electorates. The Council of Electors (Kurfürstenrat) agreed to meet annually in Mainz, Frankfurt, Gelnhausen, or Fulda. Before the next meeting, they were to confer with their estates so that they, too, could send representatives. The meeting bore the bold stamp of Berthold. Frederick, however, was in accord.

The electoral princes revealed the intensity of their resistance when they did not even wait until the next year. In November they met again, this time in Würzburg. Maximilian forbade the meeting. Frederick attended. Berthold's most outspoken ally now was the Palatine elector. Although the two had their own differences, they had a common enemy in Maximilian. Defiantly, Cardinal Peraudi also attended. He, too, had fought with Maximilian. The old cardinal (age 67 in 1502) was Commissioner of Indulgences in the empire and Scandinavia. Maximilian refused the cardinal entry into the empire up to 1501. Peraudi considered excommunication. Suddenly all was harmony. No doubt Maximilian and Rome had attained a mutually agreeable distribution of indulgence funds. The electors knew from sad experience, no matter how many safeguards they attached to the funds, Maximilian somehow obtained his war money. Was Peraudi a spy?

In any case, Maximilian railed that the electors were traitors and friends of France. Then he tried to resurrect the imperial governing council. This ploy to give the princes a token voice in his government would no longer work. Maximilian need not have worried. The princes' interest in their own meetings waned. They fell back to sending only representatives, then agreed to meet every two years. As Berthold's health plummeted in 1504, the "revolution" of the *Kurfürstenrat* was sure to die with him. As always, the demands of their own territories trumped all else.

The fate of one man turned the empire upside down in 1504. In December 1503, the Duke of Bavaria-Landshut George (the Rich) died. This first cousin of Frederick had fathered five children with his wife, Hedwig, a princess of Poland.[99] All three sons died before Duke George. Two daughters lived, one of which was becoming a Benedictine nun. The other daughter, Elisabeth, age 23, was since 1499 the wife of prince Ruprecht of the Palatine. Although Ruprecht was the twenty-two-year-old son of the Palatine elector Philipp, he was not the successor. His older brother Ludwig was heir. Salic law prevailed in the empire; daughters could not inherit rule. George (the Rich) intended to circumvent the ancient law by bequeathing "officially" his duchy to Ruprecht. The greater duchy of Bavaria was split in two lines: George (the Rich) had ruled Bavaria-Landshut, and Albrecht, with brother Wolfgang, had ruled the Bavaria-Munich line. Frederick sympathized with Albrecht, whom the law clearly favored. He sent two hundred knights to support Albrecht.[100] For pacific Frederick, this military support was unusually generous.

Maximilian seized the opportunity to increase his wealth and punish his old nemesis, the Palatine elector Philipp, who backed his son Ruprecht. In no time at all, Maximilian shelved his plans for Italy and Turkey. The Bavarian-Munich Dukes Albrecht and Wolfgang promised Maximilian disputed territories in the Inn Valley and other border areas. Maximilian, in turn, enfeoffed George's Landshuter inheritance to Dukes Albrecht and Wolfgang. Ruprecht waited for no one. His forces situated in the castles of Landshut and Burghaufen took by force the cities Dingolfing and Landshut.[101] The law of the sword would prevail. All vassals of the Palatine elector were obliged to help his son.[102] There was no lack of volunteers for Maximilian and the other side. The Landgrave of Hesse and the Duke of Württemberg were only too eager to settle scores with the Palatine. And one could not forget Maximilian's Swabian League either. All these participants, though supposedly helping one line of Wittelsbachs, leaped at the chance to crush another line. Seeing yet more opportunity, Maximilian threatened to take the electoral dignity from the Palatine and transfer it to Tyrol, no doubt with his son Philipp the Fair in mind as the new elector.

The Palatine forces could not sustain a war against so many enemies. They had to fight on two fronts, and their enemies quickly overran the home front. Although Ruprecht and his father mustered an army of perhaps thirty thousand, they wanted to win in Bavaria with minimal damage to lives and property. This strategy, as their military leaders such as George von Rosenberg knew only too well, was not feasible. The other side, with about as many soldiers, never had such inhibitions. For once, Maximilian had the upper hand. He had, after all, been fighting off and on most of his adult life. He and the Swabian League had the stomachs for it. In August 1504, among his own troops in Landshut, Ruprecht sickened from severe dysentery and died. A few weeks later his wife, Elisabeth, died. The war was lost. In September, the Palatine elector agreed to an armistice. But his fighting forces were unaware. In what could have been a colossal irony, two days after the armistice Maximilian was almost killed by Bohemian mercenaries at the battle of Mengersbach. The emperor rode in front of his attacking troops and confronted the Bohemian foot soldiers who used long lances with hooks. The hooks were intended for mounted knights in armor. They hooked the emperor and yanked him from his horse. Only the quick intervention of Erich I, the Duke of Braunschweig-Lüneburg,[103] who stormed the position with his own knights, saved Maximilian's life.

Maximilian took advantage of the mishap.[104] Within weeks, the imperial poet laureate Celtis had penned the great event in glowing lyrics, Hans Burgkmair had designed a woodcut, and yet another happening in the graced life of the emperor was in print and distributed. Yet the war was not over for everyone. South of Munich and northeast of Innsbruck, the fortress Kufstein held out in October. Maximilian led the siege himself, no doubt incensed because this was in the very territory he was going to obtain from Duke Albrecht.[105] Maximilian promised the commander Johann von Pienzenauer safe conduct if the holdouts surrendered. Pienzenauer refused. He firmly believed, despite Maximilian's twenty-four cannons, that no more than fifty men were needed to hold the great fortress. This was old wisdom. It was false against the giant cannons that Maximilian had sent from Innsbruck. No walls could withstand a constant barrage with the one hundred kilo iron balls delivered by the artillery. Pienzenauer surrendered. Maximilian demanded "blood justice" (*Blutgericht*). Pienzenauer had refused safe conduct. The emperor personally watched his henchman execute Johann von Pienzenauer and seventeen of his comrades. When it was over, eighteen heads littered the grounds before the fortress.[106] Maximilian defended his harsh judgment by emphasizing these were imperial subjects fighting their own emperor. This, he claimed, had not happened for centuries.

Maximilian felt he was on the mountaintop. He and his advisers continued their high-handed ways. In June 1505, with no input from the estates, Maximilian resurrected the chamber court (*Kammergericht*) in Augsburg and forbade it to accept any appeals from Burgundy. The *Reichstag* he called for in Cologne that same month was well attended.[107] Certainly Frederick and Johann were there. Maximilian wanted money of course. This time the estates were compliant. There was nothing like the emperor thrashing one of the electors to attract their attention. They assured Maximilian they would assist him in his military effort to gain the crown of Hungary for the empire. In 1490, Hungary had conceded him the right to succeed Vladislaus if the Hungarian king left no heir, but apparently Vladislaus was living too long. Maximilian also asked for and received commitments to another Rome campaign.[108] Then the Palatine elector Philipp, whom Maximilian had disliked anyway, was brought to his knees in the *Reichstag*. He was the loser in the Bavarian war of succession in every way but one: he did manage to retain his electorate. Only Frederick and Johann publicly stood by the side of Philipp.[109] That reflected the depth of their loyalty to other electors. Near the end of the *Reichstag*, Maximilian wanted to meet with Frederick and discuss a new imperial governing council that Frederick would head. Maximilian, however, first had to go to Aachen before meeting with Frederick. That was the opening Frederick needed. He waited two days and left full speed for Saxony.

In the summer of 1505, Maximilian was at his highest peak of power. He dominated the imperial estates. In 1504, he had arranged a marriage of his four-year-old grandson Karl with five-year-old Claudia, the only direct heir to the French throne at that time. Her dowry was to be Naples, Milan, and Burgundy.[110] The next month, Queen Isabella of Castile died, moving Maximilian's son Philipp closer to that throne. A stunning sequence of deaths—Juana's only brother, Don Juan, as well as her only sister, Isabella of Asturias (Queen of Portugal), and her sister's infant son Miguel—vaulted Juana to heiress of all of Spain. Only Philipp's mentally unstable wife, Juana, stood between Philipp and rule of Castile, and only Juana's aging but formidable father, Ferdinand of Aragon, stood between Philipp and rule of the entire Spanish kingdom.[111] The thought was inescapable to Maximilian that this was the ideal time to see to it that Philipp would be guaranteed as his successor. The plan would be to launch his campaign toward Rome and, after military success there, to coerce Julius II to crown him emperor at long last. With that crown officially his, Maximilian could motivate the imperial estates to vote Philipp the king, just as his own father had done for him in 1486. Maximilian did not even gloat when his great adversary Berthold of Mainz died in December 1504. How could matters turn any more favorable for him?

CHAPTER 5

CONSUMMATE TERRITORIAL PRINCE

(1506–12)

> "Constancy lasts the longest."
> —Proverb favored by Frederick the Wise [1]

BLACK DAYS FOR MAXIMILIAN

"One misfortune seldom comes alone." [2] The year 1506—the summer and fall of wormy fruit—brought Maximilian a nightmare end to all his plans. [3] Perhaps they were too grandiose and too obvious. In May, French king Ludwig XII dissolved the marriage contract of his daughter Claudia with Maximilian's grandchild Karl. [4] France also began stirring up trouble in Geldern again. In July, the Hungarian queen Anna gave birth to a son—at last an heir to the Hungarian throne. Within days, Maximilian would scramble to make peace with Hungary. Still intact, though, was Maximilian's plan to acquire Spain, obtain the imperial crown from the pope, and have son Philipp the Fair declared king of the empire.

Philipp the Fair had married Juana of Castile in October 1496 as one half of a double marriage bond between the empire and Spain. The other half that wedded Maximilian's daughter Margarethe to Don Juan had already dissolved with the death of Don Juan and the brief marriage that resulted in no living children. Philipp and Juana, however, had borne fruit—two sons and three daughters by 1506. Juana had been declared heiress to the thrones of both Aragon and Castile even though she was deranged; Ferdinand would be her regent. Whether Philipp's constant infidelity caused her mental woes or only worsened them was not known.

Surviving a near fatal sea voyage, the married couple returned to Spain from the Netherlands at the end of April 1506. Events would prove

Juana was in the first days of yet another pregnancy. Castilian nobles who hated and feared Ferdinand of Aragon helped Philipp muscle his way toward the throne of Castile. Another triumph loomed for the Habsburgs. Although Juana was sovereign, Philipp was the king of Castile, and much more glory awaited him if he outlived King Ferdinand.

Philipp did not. In September 1506, fighting a fever, Philipp the Fair suddenly died. Some speculate a multitude of problems wore him down: "serious informal charges by his demented wife Juana; pressures from financial worries; afflicted by the disputes of his Burgundian courtiers with Castilian grandees; disturbed by the amassing French troops on the Spanish and Burgundian borders; worried because of the hostility of his father-in-law."[5] After Philipp's death, Juana displayed her mental state in all its madness. She would not permit anyone to bury Philipp but for months kept a vigil on his casket, frequently having it opened so she could see his body.

"My God, why have you forsaken me?" Maximilian scrawled in the margin of a document.[6] He was distraught but sane. He believed the French poisoned Philipp and was still saying that publicly at the *Reichstag* in Constance the following year.[7] Maximilian was not one to wring his hands long in anguish. He was always planning. His plan of course involved war, this one against Ferdinand. Maximilian pondered the likelihood of the French taking orphaned Burgundy while he was attacking Spain. His foe, Ferdinand, acted more rapidly. He had an iron grip on the Spanish situation by mid-1507, including the regency of Castile and the confinement of Juana.

In March 1507, Maximilian had transferred to Archduchess Margarethe the guardianship and regency of Philipp's children as well as the governorship in the Netherlands. Maximilian had little choice but to negotiate with Ferdinand about the inheritance rights of Juana's children. Ferdinand was surprisingly pliable. He was hot-blooded enough even at age 55 to believe he would father a direct heir himself with his recent bride, Germaine (niece of French king Ludwig XII). She was a nubile, dark-eyed nineteen-year-old, and Ferdinand had already fathered eleven children—six of them bastards. So young Karl, at seven the present heir to the Spanish thrones, remained in the Netherlands with his sisters Eleonore, Isabella, and Mary. He would be thoroughly the product of his twice-widowed aunt, Margarethe. Karl would become fluent in French, Dutch, and Latin.[8]

WOES FOR FREDERICK, THEN TRIUMPH

One small example of Maximilian's apocalyptic downward spiral is provided by Frederick himself. Maximilian had demanded of Frederick money and one hundred "horses." On September 22, 1506, he repeated the demand. Frederick not only did not supply money or "horses," he did not even bother to answer Maximilian. Other imperial estates watched Frederick closely for guidance in dealing with the Habsburg circle. Grim days were ahead for Maximilian.

The year 1506 was not a good year for Frederick either. Heinrich von Bünau, two years younger than Frederick and perhaps his closest adviser, died.[9] At the Worms *Reichstag* in 1495, a riding accident crippled Bünau so severely, he walked stiff-legged the rest of his life. The rough, hard men of his time called him the "stilt-walker" ("*der Stelzner*"). It had been Bünau who had stayed with Frederick in his long days out in the empire, Bünau who had conferred at Frederick's request in 1498 with Berthold of Mainz in great intimacy about Frederick's feelings, Bünau who had gone with Frederick to numerous *Reichstags*, Bünau who represented Frederick with the French king Louis XII in 1500 and 1501, Bünau who, in addition, even served Frederick on the Saxon *Oberhofgericht*. Bünau was the Saxon nobleman in transition. His friends included arch-humanist Conrad Celtis and the scholar-alchemist abbot Trithemius. Bünau himself studied Greek. Vincentius of Ravenna called the well-educated and very erudite Bünau the most important member of Elector Frederick's court.[10]

In 1506, Frederick also reached a new low in his relationship with his brother Ernst, the archbishop of Magdeburg. To preface the political activity, however, one must consider a tragic turn in Ernst's life. In 1499, symptoms of the "French disease" (syphilis) first appeared in Ernst.[11] In 1503, he revealed to his confidant, Prince Magnus of Anhalt, that he followed procedures set by his doctors. First symptoms were similar to those of the plague—pox and aching pain—but if fatal, "French disease" took a long, painful course. Maybe Ernst thought otherwise. That same year he prepared his will. At the time, little was known about the disease. It is clear, though, that Ernst thought it was a sexual disease. By August 1505, he visited a cloister hoping for intercession from St. Wolfgang. The abbot there recorded their esteemed visitor had "contracted a severe disease and everywhere on his body heinous pox broke out as small pustules and persisted." This was the Ernst that Frederick confronted in 1506.[12]

The relationship was so rancorous that the two met in February with brother Johann in a strange debate.[13] Frederick and Ernst were so unhappy with each other, they sat in different rooms. Johann not only delivered the points to each brother, but he was to act as mediator and ultimately as judge. Ernst started by revealing his complaints against Frederick. In 1487, Frederick had done nothing militarily to help Ernst in a dispute between Ernst and their sister Margarete's husband, Heinrich von Braunschweig-Lüneburg. Second, Frederick had done nothing in 1500 to help Ernst gain the archbishopric of Mainz. Third, just the previous fall Frederick had refused Ernst asylum against an outbreak of plague. Fourth, he was certain Frederick conspired against him with Elector Joachim of Brandenburg to damage his archbishopric and even the city of Magdeburg. Last and not least was Frederick's intractable behavior with Cousin George. Why couldn't Frederick cooperate?

Frederick must have winced when he heard Cousin George embedded in Ernst's complaint. Frederick admitted to Ernst no wrong doing on any count. He patiently countered every charge. In 1487, he wanted to avoid war, not start war. In 1500, he well knew Ernst wanted no part of the Mainz succession; there was written confirmation of that. Regarding refuge from the plague, Ernst had insisted on occupying Altenburg. Frederick had informed him that electoral officials already occupied the Altenburg residence. Frederick knew, moreover, that Ernst had found asylum in his own diocese of Halberstadt. The fourth point he answered by pointing out that no alliance of Electoral Saxony existed either with Brandenburg or with Ernst's archbishopric. Lastly, Frederick would be most happy to settle things with Cousin George if he were reasonable.

Next came Frederick's charges against Ernst. Frederick had spies everywhere, but he did not say how he knew of Ernst's abuses. Frederick was firmly convinced that Ernst intrigued behind his back with Cousin George. Ernst snubbed his own Ernestines by awarding Coadjutor of the archbishopric to a brother of Cousin George. Frederick also knew Ernst had said in public that Frederick is not a man of his word. Frederick knew as well that Ernst referred to Frederick's companion Anna with the slur "*pübin*." The term *pübin* (or *bübin*) signified at best a concubine or at worst a whore. Ernst even lied that Frederick wanted to marry her.

Lastly, Ernst told Johann secretly that Frederick was going to sell the jewels that the elector and Johann collected together. This last lie angered Frederick more than anything. No one on earth was dearer to Frederick than Johann.

Ernst replied defiantly. His most disrespectful reply was that he wanted to award Coadjutor of the archbishopric to an Ernestine. He was unable to do that, however, because there was no Ernestine offspring with any social standing. It was clear to Johann that neither of his brothers would relent anything. He urged Ernst to forget what had happened so the three could stand again "as one man." Ernst then committed further outrage. He said he wanted it all in writing. If he broke the contract, he would not demand his share of his father's inheritance. If Frederick broke the contract, he would pay Ernst his inheritance. Johann was shocked. He knew Ernst had renounced his inheritance before their father died. He refused to even mention the "contract" to Frederick.

Johann tried to make a wise judgment. All previous happenings should be forgiven and forgotten. The brothers should "spare no effort" in being brotherly and friendly. They all agreed. What else was there to do? Just days later, the futility of honestly dealing with Ernst was confirmed. Ernst apparently had asked Maximilian to rule on Ernst's claim on Electoral Saxony if Frederick, Johann, and Johann Friedrich were all dead. Maximilian's assent to Ernst became known. It was a monstrous deceit behind the backs of his two brothers and Johann's three-year-old son. Further dealings leaked out. Ernst would then cede the electorate to Cousin George in return for an annual payment of ten thousand gulden. In fact, Ernst had made that secret written agreement with Uncle Albrecht before 1500! In August 1506, Ernst renewed the agreement with Cousin George. The final insult came that month when George brazenly volunteered to mediate the three brothers' differences.

Ernst, fancying himself a scholar with humanistic training, had even tried to involve himself in Frederick's new university in Wittenberg. At least that threat was gone. Even so, the new university in Wittenberg had anxious moments. Enrollment had plummeted from the opening year. The year 1506 was bad for the fledgling university (for the second straight year).[14] Not only did the neighboring territory of Brandenburg open a new university at Frankfurt on the Oder, but worse yet was that plague had broken out in Wittenberg. The university convened in Herzberg on the Elster, a rough village in easternmost Ernestine Saxony. Many students left. Even some top faculty left, including Greek authority Hermann Trebelius and the noted Italian jurist Petrus of Ravenna.[15]

Yet Frederick's faculty and his university would return to Wittenberg the next year and recover. His Augustinian friend Johann von Staupitz was a miracle worker.[16] He went to Rome for the business of the Augustinians and came back with a bull in hand from Pope Julius II that validated the university.[17] It also established the connection between the university and the Castle Church All Saints' Foundation. Therefore, the income that would sustain the university was finally established. Five main sources of funds were now in place: (1) foundation wealth of All Saints, (2) direct electoral payments, (3) fees from tuitions and graduations, (4) fines and rents from the student quarters, and (5) funds from lectures and practices. The emissary Staupitz's greatest accomplishment would reveal itself at the 1507 *Reichstag* in Constance.

Frederick continued aloof. He did not show up when the 1507 *Reichstag* began at the end of April.[18] Nothing indicated his importance more than the estates hesitating to conduct business without him. Maximilian could not wait for Frederick, but on May 6, he presented his plan for an Italian campaign. He emphasized how he had protected the imperial borders, especially against the French. He could not keep himself from scolding the estates who had helped so little. Still, they could help now, because the borders were under attack. Moreover, he had a plan to campaign in Italy and restore the Holy Roman Empire.

Decades of *Reichstags* permitted a predictable response from the estates. They had little interest outside the empire. What about the chamber court (*Kammergericht*), they asked. Who would rule the empire while Maximilian was in Italy? The Palatine elector Philipp was under the imperial ban because of the 1504 Bavarian Succession War. Maximilian proposed a committee of estates for the time of his absence. The estates rejected that. Frederick finally appeared in mid-June, just a few days before France and Spain announced a mutual defense treaty. It was no surprise that Maximilian had to appoint him the governor (or vicar) of the empire (*Generalstatthalter des Reichs*). Frederick was to administrate all business in the name of the emperor. He would oversee the use of the laws and keeping of the peace, act on all matters reaching him, and punish those not obeying him or the chamber court. In addition, he had the right to meet imperial estates altogether or individually. All activity was to be logged and every outgoing document personally signed by Frederick. Only Elector Philipp of the Palatine objected. In exchange for Maximilian's concessions, the estates granted him 120,000 gulden for his Italian campaign.

Then came in Frederick's eyes his own great triumph of the *Reichstag*. At the 1507 *Reichstag*, a bull from Pope Julius II was read. The pope directed "all archbishops, bishops, abbots, and prelates of the entire Holy Roman Empire" to send parts of their relic collections to Frederick.[19] It is likely Frederick had campaigned for this honor for a long time, perhaps with popes prior to the installation of Julius II in November 1503. Just how Frederick merited this colossal gift from Julius II is not clear, but the highly persuasive Staupitz had visited the pope the previous year. This special privilege fit perfectly Frederick's grand plan for the Wittenberg showcase.[20] Staupitz may have explained Frederick's grand purpose, emphasizing an attraction for pilgrims from all over the empire. The question remains as to what the pope received in return. Because Julius himself had grand plans that were stunningly expensive, perhaps the prospect of a flood of indulgence money from one of the few incorruptible imperial princes may have been the deciding factor.

HABSBURG IMPERIAL ADVENTURES *AD NAUSEAM*

The *Reichstag* took on no new complexion in 1508. Frederick angered the imperial court by openly opposing Maximilian's requests for help against Venice. The emperor's men reproached Frederick for being "treacherous" to the emperor.[21] In that year, two of the original electors died. Both had been present at Frederick's first *Reichstag* as an elector at Nuremberg in 1487. Philipp of the Palatine, so recently cut down in size by Maximilian although an elector for thirty-two years, died at age 59. Archbishop Hermann of Cologne, a man of peace much like Frederick, died at fifty-eight. Only Frederick now survived of those 1487 electors. Those five electors, even contentious Philipp of the Palatine, were dear to Frederick's heart.

Therefore, in 1508, Frederick's fellow electors were Joachim of Brandenburg, Ludwig V of the Palatine, Archbishop Uriel of Mainz, Archbishop Jakob II of Trier, and Archbishop Philipp II of Cologne. As electors, the five had a combined seventeen years of experience in the curia of electors, compared to Frederick's twenty-one years. Frederick, who had always rigorously insisted on proper protocol, was more than ever the "source" for all matters of that procedural nature. Over the next five years, Frederick, with little enthusiasm for *Reichstags* and their dreary futility, nevertheless dragged himself to Worms in 1509 and Augsburg in 1510. To the double *Reichstag* of 1512 in Trier and then Cologne he sent representatives.

Frederick was the "old man" of the curia of electors in more than a figurative sense. It was clear by 1510 that he was in crippling health. Virtually on his forty-seventh birthday, he wrote Maximilian—possibly in response to one of the emperor's numerous hunting invitations—that in the previous half-year he had not ridden a horse more than three miles (three "German miles" were about twenty-two kilometers).[22] Did the elector suffer from hemorrhoids? Did he now have chronic back pain? He already suffered from the aristocratic diseases of the day such as gout and not only kidney stones but gallstones as well. Broken and fractured bones from jousting, though healed, may have ached.[23]

One who had once traveled incessantly on horse, Frederick now had to move about in difficult and time-consuming coaches (or, even worse, sedan chairs). Coaches and wagons of the time had no mobile axles and not even primitive suspension systems such as slings and braces.[24] Traveling on the smoothest, straightest road was at best twice as slow as travel on horseback. Workers preceded by hours Frederick's personal coach, trying to smooth the roadbed as much as possible.[25] A royal traveler could tolerate no more than about four hours of such travel, in which he advanced possibly three or four "German miles." A more comfortable form of transportation was the "sedan chair," virtually a chair enclosed in a box suspended on two poles and carried by men. With teams of relief carriers, such a devise could also travel three or four German miles but over a longer day. Traveling to a *Reichstag* from Saxony in such a fashion would be possible but exasperating.

Yet Frederick traveled. In 1511, he traveled to Stuttgart to attend the wedding of Duke Ulrich of Württemberg with Sabine, the Duchess of Bavaria.[26] In 1512, he met Maximilian in Nuremberg before the *Reichstag* began in Trier.[27] That same year, he sent representatives to the *Reichstags* in Trier and Cologne. It was not surprising some suspected Frederick, poor health or not, selectively used his health as a diplomatic weapon.[28] In Nuremberg that year, the emperor wanted to discuss the Teutonic order and the pressure it was getting from the Polish king. Maximilian probably also tried to lure Frederick back into imperial politics with a figurehead position. Frederick had his own pressing problems with Erfurt and Hesse. In addition, he was now distressed over Jülich-Berg.[29] In 1483, old Emperor Friedrich III had enfeoffed Frederick's uncle Albrecht with future access to the territory of Jülich and Berg. In 1486, the newly elected king, Maximilian, had expanded the claim also to Elector Ernst and his heirs. Finally, in 1511, Herzog Wilhelm of Jülich and Berg passed away. Frederick, as well as George, expected the territory now to come to the Wettiners. But the political situation had changed in thirty years. Herzog Wilhelm's daughter Maria had married the powerful prince Johann III of Kleve, who not only claimed the territory but, worst of all, occupied it. Moreover, Maximilian needed prince Johann of Kleve as a staunch ally against always rebellious Geldern. Predictably, Maximilian did not satisfy Frederick, and Frederick did not satisfy Maximilian.

Frederick was not alone. The new electors were as cool as their old predecessors were to Maximilian's endless foreign battles. The emperor, though a real military force within the empire, proved less and less competent in his border ventures. He had to crown himself emperor in Trent in 1508, because Pope Julius II (so much like Maximilian himself in his reckless adventures) was not about to officially give Maximilian such a plum. Yet in 1509, in league with the pope, Maximilian began a campaign against the territory of Venice. Twice the Venetians soundly thrashed the imperial forces. The pope then allied himself with the army of France, which conquered the Venetians. One scholar stated, "When he took on Venice after 1509, it proved to be the graveyard of his international reputation, leading furthermore to the virtual bankruptcy of South Tyrol and Inner Austria."[30] It was clear Maximilian, though ever brave and willing, was now regarded a military feather-weight. This phase of his northern Italy wars would limp on for a total of eight years. Participants and alliances were ever changing. During that span, the warring parties included, of course, the Holy Roman Empire, the Papal States, and the Republic of Venice, but also France, Spain, England, Scotland, the Duchy of Milan, Florence, the Duchy of Ferrara, and the Swiss.

TOIL AND TURMOIL IN SAXONY

The dispute with Cousin George grew in intensity. Issues remained the same. The Albertines used high-handed tactics to try to divert traffic from the Ernestine Low Road to their own High Road. George had demanded tribute from the proceeds of the silver properties, though his father, Albrecht, never had. George issued mandates. Negotiations seemed endless. The bishops of Naumburg and Merseburg tried to mediate with no success. The estates of the two Saxonies negotiated, their lack of enthusiasm for the monetary squabbles of the princes only too apparent but their fear of war real. The advisers of the two Saxonies negotiated, but they were bound by the iron wills of their sovereigns. Among many grievances, the Ernestiners felt George owed them twenty thousand gulden. George refused to acknowledge the debt. It may well have been the Ernestiners who first hinted at war as the last remaining solution, though they later denied it. Frederick was to have said once, "I shall not start anything, but if I must fight, you shall see that it will be I who end it."[31] With so many voices gabbling back and forth, the situation only worsened. At last, their great uncle intervened. Although Maximilian might fail in foreign warfare, within his empire he had just recently smashed the Palatine in the Succession War. He still had the Swabian League to crush territorial disputes. His communication of February 1508 to the Ernestines and the Albertines ominously forbade them from resolving their dispute by war: "To act against this mandate is in no case advisable."[32] Thus, the cousins cooled off. The disputes remained unresolved.

Another contentious issue boiled in 1508.[33] It involved the city-state of Erfurt and the always uncooperative George. Erfurt was an irregular area, somewhat circular and about five German miles across.[34] Erfurt's status was confusing. It was in part imperial, in greater part subject to the archbishopric of Mainz. Although the archbishop was legally its rightful lord, Erfurt disdained that liege and gave him neither obedience nor service. The Wettins under Ernst had gained in 1483 a protection contract with Erfurt, in which the city-state paid annually 1,500 gulden to their "patron and protector." The Wettins came to regard Erfurt as a possession, so much so it was included in the Leipzig Division of 1485 as common property to both lines. The Saxon princes came to regard it their right to intervene in Erfurt affairs.

Confusion and resistance erupted in May 1508 when the city-state of Erfurt had to pledge *Amt* Kapellendorf to Frederick. The city-state had done it to salve some of its enormous debt. The citizens of Erfurt erupted, although the *Amt* Kapellendorf was just one of eighty-nine villages governed by Erfurt, and it was so small and so distant from the city of Erfurt, few probably knew anything about it. It was the spark that ignited dissidents already fuming about increased taxes, especially as they became aware of the city's long-concealed mismanagement and mountainous debt of 550,000 gulden. Just who was responsible? A mob hanged Erfurt's most powerful politician Heinrich Kellner—not in effigy. Students rioted, seriously damaging the well-regarded university. Who should straighten the mess out? The lower class burghers supported Mainz. The upper class and most university professors, except the humanists, preferred Saxon protection.

The turmoil became known as the "Mad Year" and it was no trifle.[35] Murder was common. Mainz and the Saxons needed to reach agreement and resolve the chaos. George cooperated with the Ernestiners at first, feigning only mild interest.[36] Then he began his duplicity. He approached Archbishop Uriel of Mainz independently. How better could he play the two sides against each other—with him ultimately getting some concession as the deciding influence? Meanwhile, murders continued. Frederick worried that Maximilian, who was not fond of Erfurt, would tire of the waste and ban Erfurt, just the first step to virtual imperial possession. Frederick's advisers told him the Ernestiners themselves could take control of the city and keep the lid on until the situation could be worked out. An attack and conquest would cost only five men. Frederick is said to have replied, "One is too many."[37] They tried a trade blockade, including food. Nothing calmed the situation. The misery dragged on.

Erfurt became one more problem that could not be resolved because of Cousin George. And yet another developed. Landgrave Wilhelm II (the Middle) of Hesse died July 11, 1509.[38] His heir, Philipp, was only four years old. Oddly, the predecessor of Wilhelm II (the Middle) as ruling landgrave was still alive. Wilhelm I (the Elder) had been confined since abdicating in 1493 due to mental illness.[39] He still remained a wild card in any machinations for power. In any case, Philipp obviously had to be protected in a regency, but it was unclear who that regent would be. The will of Wilhelm II (the Middle) in 1506 had designated five Hessian knights led by Ludwig von Boyneburg. A second will of 1508, thought by the knights to be the result of coercion of a deranged man dying from syphilis, appointed as regent his young twenty-four-year-old wife Anna of Mecklenburg (none other than a younger sister of Johann's deceased wife, Sophie). A third possibility—probably a universally acceptable compromise could have been the boy's uncle, powerful Archbishop Hermann of Cologne. But Hermann himself died the previous October. The Wettiners of Saxony also loomed as a possible regent or at least an arbiter by reason of contractual agreements such as the renewed hereditary contracts of Saxony with Hesse and Brandenburg.

If the Wettins and the Hessian Knights had presented a united front, the young wife Anna would have lost her claim. But the Wettins were not united. Cousin George decided he would support Anna. His son Johann was promised to Elisabeth, daughter of Wilhelm and Anna. Also the disputed last will of 1508 specifically favored George. In the case of Anna remarrying, it was George who was to become her successor as regent. For the present, both the Hessian knights and Anna accepted the fact that the Wettins would mediate. But because the Wettins were not in agreement among themselves, the affair dragged on, though Frederick managed to help the Hessian knights become virtual regents. In January 1510, the Hessian knights took Philipp into their custody. The knights were intractably opposed to Anna ruling as regent.

Anna would prove to be a firebrand. She appealed to none other than Maximilian. He ignored her. She appealed again two months later, agreeing to relinquish the regency for herself if she could at least raise Philipp herself. By July, Maximilian softened enough to ask the Hessian knights to let Anna have custody of Philipp for the next three years. The knights, led still by Ludwig von Boyneburg, refused. They essentially had won the dispute, but then Boyneburg overplayed his hand. To eliminate Anna totally from any possibility of gaining the regency he tried to restore mentally-ill Wilhelm I (the Elder) to power. The wife of Wilhelm I, Anna of Braunschweig, jumped on the opportunity, but she did not intend to share power with Boyneburg. She had her own allies. Soon two factions of Hessian nobles were competing. By 1511, scuffles broke out. The Wettins actually had to send twelve hundred armed mounted knights and three thousand foot soldiers to help Boyneburg.[40]

Thus gyrations continued, permutations confusing enough already with two Wilhelms, each married to an Anna. The Wettins, who could have firmly resolved the issues if they could have agreed among themselves, were frequently called on to "mediate." Like the instability in Erfurt, the Hessian regency controversy would drag on for many years. Both Anna of Braunschweig and the Hessian knights of Boyneburg appealed to Maximilian at the Trier and Cologne *Reichstags* of 1512.[41] This resulted in the imperial decision known as the "Cologne Contract," mandating medical care for Wilhelm I, though the Hessian estates continued to regard Philipp as heir. If Philipp were to die, then the Hessian estates were to swear allegiance to Wilhelm I. It was a half-baked solution. The end of the squabble was an illusion. Philipp's mother, Anna of Mecklenburg, not a part of anyone's solution, was not deterred.

ARRIVALS IN THE ELECTORAL SAXON COURT

The arrival of Lucas Cranach to the Saxon court (*Hof*) marked the beginning of significant additions and changes. Two key advisers faded from the scene. Heinrich von Ende was no longer *Hofmeister* after 1507. His age is uncertain, but the fact that he had accompanied Duke Albrecht to the Holy Land in 1476 indicates he was probably near the age of sixty. Hans von Leimbach, on the other hand, is known to have been in his early sixties in 1509 when he resigned as *Rentmeister*. Both men were well into "old age" for those days. It is also possible the rise of Chancellor Johann Mogenhofer in Frederick's inner council cooled their enthusiasm for administration. As his sons demonstrated later, Leimbach had suffered financially under Frederick, repeatedly loaning him his own money. Loaning money to a sovereign brought influence to the lender but often little return of money. Degenhart Pfeffinger, close to Frederick as "keeper of the door" and in charge of the privy purse, was now called "chamberlain" or "treasurer" or "finance minister." Although his title was tentative, his power and influence were not.

The year 1508 brought a new face to the court, one that would in a quiet, dignified way also have power and influence. George Burkhardt was a twenty-four-year-old priest from Spalt near Nuremberg and he went by the name "Spalatin."[42] His contemporary Christoph Scheurl described him as "a small man with very fair hair and a friendly, fine, slightly blushing face."[43] Frederick was familiar with, and even preferred, the learned humanist approach to religion and education.[44] He had solicited the advice of Mutian (Konrad Muth), an influential humanist and mystic in the Erfurt area, for a tutor for Johann Friedrich. Mutian had suggested George Spalatin. Pfeffinger then interviewed him and recommended him to Frederick. Pfeffinger would become a warm friend to Spalatin. Court life was alien to Spalatin, but he learned quickly. Although Frederick respected Antiquity and his contemporary humanists, he was in the external forms of court life "absolutely late medieval."[45]

Spalatin began teaching five-year-old Johann Friedrich in January 1509. Although Johann Friedrich was his main pupil, Spalatin apparently had six other small boys.[46] It is reasonable to assume Spalatin also instructed Frederick's own two sons Sebastien, about ten, and Friedrich (usually called Fritz), possibly eight. All evidence indicates the two boys were at court, illegitimate or not. Spalatin stumbled at the start. He talked over their heads, and as a tanner's son he had no appreciation whatever for the knightly virtues the boys craved. Duke Johann himself loved the ways of knights. Interfering in the process was Johann's *Hofmeister*, Thuringian knight Ernst von Isserstedt, who knew exactly how to appeal to the raucous hearts of boys. Scheurl lamented to Spalatin as late as 1511 that "everybody knows, our prince is not receptive yet at his age to your learning."[47] Eventually, consoled by the patient advice of Mutian and Frederick, too, Spalatin won the boys over and was able to instruct them in humanistic ways and the sciences. Later, the older Johann Friedrich would regret Spalatin no longer taught him.[48]

Spalatin excelled in manner and discretion. From the beginning, Frederick relied also on Spalatin to translate Latin documents.[49] Before the year 1509 was out, court painter Lucas Cranach had done Spalatin's portrait, tangible proof of the young scholar's worth to Frederick.[50] Spalatin no doubt showed his natural diplomatic skills to a sovereign known to be a stickler for words. By 1510, Frederick trusted Spalatin so much he asked him to write a chronicle of Saxony. In doing so, Spalatin had to communicate with many nobles and religious superiors to access documents. In 1511, Frederick rewarded the twenty-seven-year-old Spalatin by making him a canon in the St. George Foundation at Altenburg, virtually a lifetime benefice that paid well. Like most benefices of that kind, it did not even require residence at the foundation. In 1512, Frederick asked Spalatin to acquire books for the electoral library to be housed in the Wittenberg castle, as well as to curate those books already owned by the elector.[51] This required Spalatin to communicate closely with the faculty at the university in Wittenberg to determine as well their needs for the library.[52]

Christoph Scheurl had arrived at the university in 1507.[53] The twenty-five-year-old Nuremberger was trained in Italy in law and the humanities. He was a well-connected patrician, his uncle Anton Tucher particularly friendly with Frederick. The elector probably appreciated young Scheurl's assessment of him published in 1506 from a speech in Bologna by Scheurl. According to Scheurl, Frederick founded the University of Wittenberg with the aim of genuine scholarship. Frederick transformed Wittenberg from a village of wood and bricks into a city of marble. Scheurl lauded the church Frederick not only built but also filled with sacred relics and privileges for his subjects. But Frederick was more, insisted Scheurl. He was just. He appreciated music and could not only read several languages but also wrote with beauty and ease.[54]

Scheurl became the new rector of the university, a one-semester appointment, and then in 1508 he assumed a real position of power as dean of the faculty of law.[55] He drew up new statutes for the university, still mostly based on the statutes of Tübingen but also partly on the statutes of Bologna. Each of the four faculties of liberal arts, theology, law, and medicine also had its own statutes.[56] The new statutes of the faculty of theology for the first time officially recognized the *via moderna*, or "nominalism," as a part of the curriculum. The *via antiqua* or "scholastics" had able representatives in the Thomist branch (among them Mellerstadt and Andreas Karlstadt) and the Scotist branch (among them Nikolaus Amsdorf). For a while, the *via moderna* was taught by Jodocus Trutvetter, a highly regarded scholar from Erfurt. He, however, felt abused, especially by outspoken and abrasive Mellerstadt—enough to leave by 1510. In 1507, the faculties had totaled thirty-seven (twenty-one in liberal arts, eight in law, five in theology, and three in medicine).[57] It is notable that in Wittenberg in the time from 1507 to 1512 many more arrived who would figure greatly in later events[58]—no one more than Staupitz's replacement as professor of the Bible.

Staupitz had served Frederick and his university for years.[59] As general vicar of the Augustinians as far away as the Netherlands, Staupitz felt much burdened by his lectureship on the Bible in the theological faculty at Wittenberg. He found a solution. He pressed a young priest into the position. Possibly Staupitz told Frederick an amusing story about the youth, who realized he was not only to take the place of Staupitz as professor of the Bible but was to preach as well. The youth complained his strength "was already used up." He would not survive more work. Staupitz shrugged; if that happened, the Lord needs "assistance of clever people" like the youth up there too.[60] If Frederick never heard that story, he at least heard the appeal for fifty gulden for the young man's needs for the doctoral ceremony in October 1512. Frederick surely knew Staupitz intended this young doctor to replace him indefinitely at the university. Perhaps someone pointed out to Frederick that the young doctor achieved at twenty-nine what many scholars did not achieve until the age of fifty. Besides that, the priest sprang from Thuringian countryfolk. One scholar asserts, "Thereafter Frederick the Wise had a continuing interest in the future professor."[61] The future professor was Martin Luther.

In 1507, Frederick had initiated fortification of Wittenberg.[62] This was an expression of his growing concern for the security of the city. "In great houses are great worries" was a proverb he reportedly said.[63] He had, after all, poured his money and soul into the somewhat isolated showcase of his electorate. The value of his relics, including their lavish containers, might be tempting to some. Strengthening the fortification of Wittenberg would continue for years. Towers and cannons on the city walls were critical. A city was defended not only by stone and steel but by blood—a standing force of soldiers trained for anything possible. Frederick particularly wanted good cannoneers, and he gave them gifts as well as money. Practice, he urged them. Here the expertise of brother Johann must have been useful; he had always leaned more toward military matters than Frederick.

THE WITTENBERG SHOWCASE GLITTERS

Since the consecration of the Castle Church in Wittenberg in 1503, Frederick added by 1512 nine more altarpieces of grand artistry. The altars were in the nave, main choir, and upper galleries.[64] Typically, the side altars provided devotion to male and female saints as well as their relics. Altars of Christ and the Virgin Mary were central, located along the nave and choir spaces.[65] Two of the new altarpieces were by Albrecht Dürer. One, possibly finished as early as 1504, is the magnificent "Adoration of the Magi."[66] It was placed near the pulpit in the church. Every Saturday, the altarpiece probably was key to recitation of the Little Office of the Virgin. Its annual liturgical significance was on January 6, the feast of Epiphany, when the birth of the Messiah was proclaimed to the world.[67] The "three kings" (Magi) was a popular depiction. Frederick, with Johann and his cousins, funded another version by a Dutch painter for the Meissen church to honor Uncle Albrecht. Archbishop Ernst of Magdeburg commissioned Hans Baldung to do yet one more version. Between two of the Magi is Ernst himself standing tall and imperious, looking very much the brother of Frederick and Johann.

In 1508, Dürer added "Martyrdom of the Ten Thousand." This represented a post-biblical legend of Christian prince Achatius (also one of the "Fourteen Holy Helpers") and his ten thousand soldiers, who were martyred by armies of the east. The painting shows the Christians martyred by crucifixion, beating, and falling off a cliff. Standing in the middle of the chaos is Dürer himself and a plump man thought by most to be Conrad Celtis.[68] Frederick may have commissioned the work because he saw an earlier woodcut of the martyrs done by Dürer. The painting not only honored Frederick's favorite humanist Celtis but, most of all, drew attention to the elector's own relics of the Ten Thousand Martyrs. Because of that, some speculate this painting was not an altarpiece but hung in the relic chamber. If an altarpiece, it provided a devotional image to help viewers venerate the relics.

Hans Burgkmair was another young artist (only twenty-seven in 1500) who caught Frederick's attention. In 1505, the Augsburg native Burgkmair finished a triptych for an altarpiece for Wittenberg.[69] He painted eight early Christian martyrs on the panels, of whom Frederick is known to have had relics of at least seven. The saints are Sigismund and Sebastian (center panel), Eustace and Valentine (left interior wing), Christopher and Vitus (right interior wing), and Roche and Cyprian (exterior wings). Five of the saints are among the "Fourteen Holy Helpers." Liturgically, the altarpiece covered the eight feast days of the saints. On any of these feast days, a visitor at the altar would receive one hundred days of indulgence.

Frederick also commissioned devotional sculptures for the All Saints' Church. Few artists were more highly regarded than Thuringian sculptor Tilman Riemenschneider, who had worked in Würzburg many years. In 1506 he was at least fifty years old, not only at the peak of his craft but also an influential city councillor. Evidence exists that Riemenschneider produced for Frederick that year a large, "very artful and subtly crafted" wooden crucifix, painted in lifelike colors.[70] Although it later burned in the church fire of 1760, its appearance is not too problematical, because Riemenschneider created numerous crucifixes that still exist. Liturgically, Friday vigils and masses dedicated to the Holy Cross undoubtedly centered on this crucifix.

Only Christoph Scheurl's 1511 written description of a stone "Double-Madonna" (or "Double-faced Madonna") is proof that such a sculpture by Conrad Meit of Worms once existed in the church.[71] Meit's work "was most likely a free-standing work in-the-round, set on a marble pedestal. One face showed the blessed Virgin Mary as Queen of Heaven, encircled by 40 musical angels . . . (the) opposite face of Meit's sculpture displayed a more down-to-earth Mary holding a bunch of grapes (symbolic of the Eucharistic wine) just beyond the grasping hand of the Christ Child."[72] Any Marian sculpture offered almost unlimited opportunities for worshipers during the year to practice devotion.

Other major works of art that Frederick had commissioned for the liturgical calendar and the observance of relics in the Castle Church were by his accomplished court artist Lucas Cranach. In 1506, Cranach finished a triptych "Martyrdom of St. Catherine."[73] She is yet another of the "Fourteen Holy Helpers." Roman Emperor Maxentius martyred Catherine for converting his wife and protesting his own paganism. Poorly rendered in the work are Frederick and Johann, prominent among the witnesses to the saint's beheading. Also on the triptych are no less than ten other women saints: Christina, Ottife, Genevieve, Apollonia, Dorothy, Agnes, Kunigunde, Barbara, Ursula, and Margaret, the latter among the "Fourteen Holy Helpers." Frederick possessed relics from all of these saints except Genevieve. The altarpiece is clearly the female counterpart of Burgkmair's eight Christian martyrs. Similarly, Cranach's altarpiece offered many opportunities for devotion.

In 1509, Cranach completed another triptych, now dubbed "Altarpiece of the Holy Kinship."[74] In the central panel among playing children, Cranach depicts the Virgin Mary and her own mother, St. Anne, who holds baby Jesus. Cranach portrays in one interior wing a well-rendered Frederick (reading a book as St. Anne's legendary second husband, Cleophas) behind two male children and a woman who is apparently St. Anne.[75] The other interior wing shows his brother Johann (or arguably Frederick again) in a similar setting as St. Anne's legendary third husband, Salomas. As noted above, a Marian depiction offered almost unlimited opportunities for worshipers during the year. The intrigue of these works from a historical standpoint can hardly be overestimated. Besides showing Frederick as Cleophas in the interior wing, it may also depict his real-life companion, Anna. In the background of the central panel, a man is portrayed who is without doubt Emperor Maximilian. In the foreground of the center panel, to the left of the Virgin Mary sleeps an old, diminutive jester. He could well be Claus Narr, the legendary jester of Frederick's court.

The last major work of art that could have been in the Castle Church in 1512 is Cranach's so-called "Dessau Princes' Altarpiece."[76] It may have been in the Marian Chapel in the church. The Holy Virgin and Child dominate the central panel, with the saints Catherine and Barbara in adoration. The side panels feature Frederick and Johann with their favorite saints: the elector with Bartholomew, Johann with James the Greater. For the first time, Frederick appears with a much fuller face, suggesting that before the altarpiece was done (1510–12) he had gained considerable weight.[77] He appears with a form-fitting wire mesh cap (*Drahthaube*) to hide receding hair, in contrast to Johann who is shown with a full head of hair, even locks on his forehead.[78] Liturgical use of the altarpiece is obviously tied into Christ and Mary as well as the four saints. Possibly it was used also for "daily, weekly, and monthly observances for the benefit of living and dead members of the electoral house of Saxony."[79]

Frederick's preference for Bartholomew may have begun by about 1500.[80] His partiality has several possible explanations.[81] Most likely is the fact that Frederick had particularly fine relics of the saint.[82] He believed he had forty-five relics of Bartholomew: "5 particles from his hand, 1 particle of his jaw, 1 particle of a tooth, 2 entire teeth, and 6 skull fragments; and a bejeweled monstrance contained 29 other particles of the disciple's holy remains and his entire facial skin."[83] His *entire facial skin* was housed in a splendid jewel-covered monstrance of gold, emphasizing its extraordinary importance.[84] A weaker possibility for Frederick's preference is that Bartholomew was a saint favored by miners, though Bartholomew was just one of several saints. Similarly, several, including Bartholomew, were thought to intercede against plague. Yet another possibility, even less likely, was that in a popular tradition Bartholomew was the only disciple of Jesus who was of noble birth.

This dazzling array of religious art greeted the worshipers every day of the year. Worshipers flooded in. The resulting numbers were colossal.

Masses were celebrated at the twenty altars so often that for the year they numbered several thousands. During the year, the church burned more than forty thousand candles and thousands of pounds of wax.[85] In 1507, the church was incorporated into the university.[86] Endowments to the All Saints' Foundation came from thirty towns as well as parishes, priories, and one chapel. In 1508, the clergy and musicians responsible for daily worship ("large choir") totaled thirty-one: twelve canons, four vicars, seven chaplains, and eight choirboys. The scholar Robin Leaver noted, "The same year (1508) a new set of partbooks was begun, manuscripts of polyphonic settings of liturgical texts by such prominent composers as Josquin, Isaac, Obrecht, among others," commenting further that "the repertory sung at the daily masses and offices was extensive and included many polyphonic settings of Propers, more than was usual than in similar contemporary foundations."[87]

The foundation supported provosts, deacons, archdeacons, cantors, custodians, scholastics, syndics, vicars, chaplains, canons, and choir boys—fifty-five in all, and growing. More than half also served on the faculty of the university, easing Frederick's own funds needed to operate the university. The Castle Church even began to serve the university as its main assembly hall; it hosted scholarly disputations, even graduation ceremonies. Considering the castle housed much of the law portion of the university, it was becoming clear how Frederick had integrated three entities into one. To question whether or not this integration was planned or just an afterthought is to ignore how patiently over twenty years Frederick and his key advisers had created a bustling, viable complex from nothing but rubble.

Some relics were always on display in the church. Occasionally even indulgences were available.[88] Yet if worshipers came on the Monday after *Misericordias Domini* (two weeks and one day after Easter Sunday) they would see all the relics in dazzling silver and gold containers. Veneration of the relics earned the worshiper staggering indulgences. In the spring of 1509, Frederick printed and released the lavishly illustrated Wittenberg Catalog of Relics (*Wittenberger Heiltumsbuch*), designed and crafted by Lucas Cranach.[89] It was to coincide with structural completion of the All Saints' Church in 1509 and the annual exhibition of the relic collection on the Monday after *Misericordias Domini*. A second edition of the *Heiltumsbuch* appeared in 1510. To make the Monday after *Misericordias Domini* even more rewarding, Julius II sweetened the indulgences. On

April 8, 1510, he issued two papal bulls for All Saints' Church that would, among other things, increase the indulgence for every relic viewed to seven years and seven quarantines.[90] Frederick now had 117 elaborate gold and silver containers (reliquaries) holding 5,005 relics.

Other such relic catalogs preceded the Wittenberg Catalog of Relics, but it far surpassed them.[91] It was eighty-eight pages in quarto-format. Frederick's *Heiltumsbuch* was a special publication for special people. Evidence suggests about one hundred copies in paper and an additional dozen copies in parchment.[92] On the front of the second edition was a woodcut portrait of Frederick and Johann, yet another example of representation. Frederick was depicted as the devout Christian prince, large conspicuous rosary in hand. Johann stands slightly behind him, one empty hand showing. Although intended to look serious and devout, the two appear morose, especially Johann. It was a composite by Cranach from other sittings. Frederick, marked by his large eyes and broken nose, wore his net cap. Johann differed distinctly in his almond eyes, straight nose, and full head of hair. According to Olivia Cardenas, Frederick's representation image remained this way from 1507 to 1522.[93]

The book itself combined text and image to make it a virtual tour. Every reliquary of the 117 was depicted, its own makeup described. The relics in each reliquary were also explained. Even the indulgence for each of the 117 was provided. The reliquaries were displayed in eight galleries, arranged according to the Litany of All Saints. They more or less ascended in holiness, ending in divinity.[94] In the numerous relics of gallery 1 and gallery 2 ("Holy Virgins" and "Female Martyrs") was the glass of St. Elizabeth, well-known because it is the only known survivor of Frederick's entire collection of relics.[95] The actual glass of St. Elizabeth (at Veste Coburg) seems to match well the drawing in the "Weimar sketchbook" that predates 1509 and was done by various artists.[96] Cranach's *Heiltumsbuch* woodcut shows the glass itself much embellished as well as being set in an elaborate silver base and the upper rim ringed with silver. Did Cranach enhance the relic to make it and its holder look more Italianate (Renaissance) in décor? Did Frederick approve of this to aggrandize his collection even more? Both are possibilities, not only for the *Elisabethglas* but also the other relics. One need only to look at the mountains towering behind the Castle Church in the Wittenberg Catalog of Relics to know Cranach did indeed embellish. Mountains exist, but not near Wittenberg.

Examples of the "Holy Confessors" in gallery 3 are a statue of St. Jerome feeding a lion (in the desert) and an elaborate container for St. Sebald's rib. Galleries 4 and 5, "Holy Martyrs," had no lack of relics. A large silver and glass shrine contained the entire body of one (child) of the innocents. Another was an elephant tusk modified into a four-legged "steed" on which rode King Nebuchadnezzar; this was to honor the three youths (Shadrach, Meshach, and Abednego) tossed into fire. Gallery 6, "Holy Apostles and Evangelists," included the above described facial skin of Bartholomew and his other remains. Gallery 7 covered "Patriarchs and Prophets, the Holy Family, Nativity, and Ministry of Christ." Among these was a rock crystal cross. Another was a statue of John the Baptist, containing relics of this saint. No doubt also in the gallery was the thumb of St. Anne in a small solid-gold monstrance with a small window.[97]

Gallery 8 contained the most precious relics of all. They were from Christ, of course not from His body but from His passion: parts of cord, rod, scourge, and sponge. From the crucifixion were portions of nails, wood from the cross, even a thorn from the crown of thorns. Wood from the cross took the highest rank under the Christ's relics. A thorn from the crown was also especially precious, because it was regarded the first relic ever brought to the All Saints' in Wittenberg. It was the French king Philip VI's gift to Rudolf of the Ascanians: "a holy thorn from the sacred crown of our Lord and Savior in a special, golden casement."[98] Moreover, this was not just any thorn, but one that had pierced the Lord's forehead.

Many scholars have listed Frederick's relics, often with thinly-disguised skepticism and disappointment. One such list offered these rarities:

> A part of John the Baptist's garb; a part of the rock on which Jesus stood when He wept over Jerusalem; another piece from the Mount of Calvary; another from the spot where Jesus ascended into heaven; the gown of the Virgin Mary and some of the milk of her breast; a piece from the burning bush of Moses; 35 particles from the Cross; some hay and straw from the manger; the swaddling clothes; hair, a shirt, a coat, and a girdle of Christ; and 204 particles and one entire skeleton of the poor innocent babes of Bethlehem; all artistically housed in their containers of silver, gold, marble,

and other precious materials made by Paul Moeller, the court goldsmith.[99]

Another scholar listed more:

> One tooth of St. Jerome, of St. Chrysostom four pieces, of St. Bernard six, and of St. Augustine four; of Our Lady four hairs, three pieces of her cloak, four from her girdle, and seven from the veil sprinkled with the blood of Christ. The relics of Christ included one piece from his swaddling clothes, thirteen from his crib, one wisp of straw, one piece of the gold brought by the Wise Men and three of the myrrh, one strand of Jesus' beard, one of the nails driven into his hands, one piece of bread eaten at the Last Supper, one piece of the stone on which Jesus stood to ascend into heaven.[100]

Did steely-eyed Frederick—skeptical by training—believe his relics were genuine? He had to know of the widespread skepticism in his own time about relics. He had to have heard stories similar to those Father Faber told about cynical frauds from his trips to the Holy Land. Frederick no doubt knew that the authenticity of many of his relics, particularly those in galleries 7 and 8, was improbable. Yet if a relic caused the worshiper to contemplate the passion, was it still not worthy? If the worshiper received indulgences for veneration, relief from punishment, was that not worth it?

MORE GOOD TURNS FROM POPE JULIUS

Frederick had a much better relationship with Pope Julius II than did Maximilian. Frederick felt confident enough in 1512 to send his own legation to Rome to see the pope. They discussed a number of issues.[101] First, Frederick asked the pope not to enter into agreements with the emperor without the knowledge of the imperial estates. He did not expect an answer. It was only a way of registering a grievance of the imperial estates. He asked for the pope's influence with the turmoil in Erfurt. He asked for more indulgences for the Castle Church in Wittenberg, and he received, signed by no fewer than twelve cardinals, a one hundred-day indulgence for venerating the cross in his church. He also managed to lengthen by twenty years the indulgences for construction of the troublesome Elbe Bridge in Torgau and also its chapel.

Julius II knew how to dominate the cardinals, even thwart their councils. The warring Julius II was not a particularly devout pope, but Frederick had seen far worse. . . .

CHAPTER 6

LIFE IN FREDERICK'S COURT

(1513–17)

"The cross of Christ is our salvation"
—Motto on Saxon coins in 1517[1]

FREDERICK "SHARES" POWER WITH JOHANN

Pope Julius II died in February 1513. For nine years, the pope in armor had run roughshod over Italy and his cardinals as well. The cardinals wanted anyone but another warrior pope. They found the perfect antithesis to Julius II in effete, plump, thirty-seven-year-old Giovanni. He was, however, the son of rawboned Lorenzo de' Medici of the powerful Florentine family. Dubbed Leo X as pope, Giovanni had been directed into the church in childhood in order to gain rich benefices and preferments but, as was so common then, he was no priest.[2] He was a lover of the arts and pleasure. A contemporary described him as an "extremely free-hearted man who avoids every difficult situation."[3] It was naïve to think that because of his indolence Leo X would have no impact on the religious and political world. He would be a figurehead for the power that was vested in the Medicis and in the cardinals. Within months, he put the cardinal's hat on his cousin Giulio, who would be his principal minister and confidant.

Leo X received a windfall the same year he was elected pope.[4] Frederick's brother Ernst, at forty-nine, died that August.[5] Now the two powerful bishoprics of Halberstadt and Magdeburg were open. Even Cousin George jumped in line. He wanted Ernst's positions for his son Johann. Elector Joachim Nestor of Brandenburg launched a sensational effort. His brother Albrecht was too young at twenty-three to be an archbishop and, moreover, he could not hold more than one position.[6] There was one way to untangle all of those problems—*papal dispensation*. That would cost a fortune. Only the Brandenburgs could even consider it and then only because they negotiated a deal with the Fugger banking house. The Fuggers would pay the pope. In return, within his jurisdiction Albrecht could milk the indulgence trade mercilessly. Half the proceeds would go to Rome, and the other half would go to pay back the Fuggers.

Then in early 1514, Archbishop Uriel of Mainz died. Suddenly Leo X had the Primate of the Holy Roman Empire to sell, and the archbishop was one of the six influential electors. Buyers were soon standing in line. Maximilian wanted it desperately for his confidant, Matthäus Lang. With one of his own in the archbishop's chair, Maximilian would assure the election of his grandson Karl to succeed him. Yet the Brandenburgs had all the momentum and borrowed more money. Their thrust would yield unimagined benefits. The Brandenburgs, at the cost of several small fortunes, gained for Albrecht the bishopric of Halberstadt, the archbishopric of Magdeburg, and the electorate of Mainz!

This trio of triumphs shouted loud and clear that the House of Wettin had lost their struggle against the Brandenburgs. The Wettins not only would lose large ecclesiastical territories to the Brandenburgs, but in 1510 they had already lost to the Brandenburgs the position of grand master of the Teutonic order. It was no mere order of knights but a political power that controlled an enormous territory running along the Baltic Sea virtually from Brandenburg to Estonia. Few territories rivaled it in size. The Teutonic order constantly skirmished with Poland about disputed territory. The Albertine Frederick of Saxony (George's younger brother), grand master since 1497, died in 1510. His successor as grand master was Albert of Brandenburg-Ansbach.[7] About the only plum the Brandenburgs let slip through their fingers was their privilege of providing the Conservitor of the University of Wittenberg.[8] That privilege was quietly transferred to the vicar of the Augustinian Moritz monastery at Naumburg, a gain for the Ernestines. That loss for the Brandenburgs was small indeed compared to their great triumphs of 1510, 1513, and 1514.

In the meantime, Frederick, in declining health, decided to share power ("Power Sharing" or *Mutschierung*) officially with Johann.[9] It was not a division (*Teilung*) of the territory. The entire territory would revert to one ruler if either Frederick or Johann died. Frederick took all the area northeast from about Altenburg, so that it included Torgau and his *Kurlande* with his pet Wittenberg. Johann would rule Thuringia, Vogtland, and Ortland. The brothers' interests had already gravitated to these portions of the territory. Frederick still dominated all activity outside the territory, though he consulted Johann on virtually every issue. Johann now had to deal with every interior aspect of his portion. The governing by council had already deteriorated, altered by the forceful personalities of Chancellor Johann Mogenhofer and Chamberlain/ Treasurer Degenhart Pfeffinger. Now the ruling brothers had their own chancelleries and councils, yet shared many advisers as well. Any councillor of either group was subordinate to the two brothers. Either brother could call on any councillor of the other brother. The awkward Power Sharing and Johann's lack of enthusiasm put an end to any evolution in governing.[10] Johann's growing debt, lack of interest in imperial matters, and above all his lazy, even mediocre, administration of office negated any possibility of strengthening the new form of governance.[11] Yet Frederick judged it necessary, perhaps solely for some peace of mind.

The brothers set up their princely courts in their favored cities. Frederick, of course, favored Torgau, but now Johann preferred Weimar over Coburg. Did Johann's new wife, Margarete, influence him? Or was the move initiated by Frederick? For the timing of the Power Sharing seemed connected to Johann's second marriage. He married Margarete of Anhalt-Zerbst on November 13, 1513, again at Torgau but not in the spectacular magnitude of his first wedding.[12] Margarete, daughter of deceased Waldemar VI of Anhalt-Zerbst, had turned nineteen the day before. Anhalt-Zerbst was a sizeable princely territory abutting the Ernestine electorate just west of Wittenberg. Anhalt-Zerbst was respectable, but the union could scarcely be termed a power marriage for a Wettin. Some considered the bride's family definitely below the level of the Wettins.[13] Streich asserts Johann's "second 'sub-princely' marriage with Margarete of Anhalt was decidedly disapproved of by Frederick; it led in 1513 to Power Sharing of the Ernestine territory."[14] Ironically, Margarete's paternal uncle, Adolf II, would become the bishop of Merseburg the following year.[15]

Both the Ernestine and Albertine lines realized the danger of issuing unilateral proclamations. Their territories were still so intertwined it could cause great difficulties for some of the estates. A consequence of that was a real impediment to progressive governing. Although the two lines squabbled constantly, they did once in a while manage to agree enough to issue a common proclamation.[16] In 1512, both lines had stipulated in a common ordinance that Saxons should not house or accommodate anyone suspected of crime. Counts, lords, knights, *Amt* officials, and towns should examine the streets and repair them. Criminals were to be handed over to the courts and their punishment was to be carried out.[17] In 1513, a common proclamation was issued against blasphemy and excessive drinking.

In September 1513, the empire was buzzing about the Reuchlin affair in Cologne. Johann Reuchlin was a fifty-eight-year-old scholar of Hebrew who, among other achievements, had published in 1506 "*De rudimentis hebraicis,*" which contained both Hebrew lexicon and grammar. Pfefferkorn, assistant to Prior Jacob van Hoogstraten of the Dominican order at Cologne, wrote pamphlets asserting all Jewish religious writings were hostile to Christianity. He and Reuchlin began a battle of written words. To many, it was war between the Dominicans and the humanists. Reuchlin, though, was not merely a modest, retiring scholar, but had counseled Count Eberhard of Württemberg and even served the old emperor, Friedrich III, in Austria. He once tutored the Rhenish knight Franz von Sickingen, who by 1513 had brought the city of Worms to its knees and was fast becoming the most dreaded rogue knight in the empire.

In 1511, Pfefferkorn published "*Handspiegel,*" attacking Reuchlin, who answered that same year with his "*Augenspiegel.*" By September 1513, Prior Hoogstraten succeeded in bringing Reuchlin before the Dominican court to defend himself against the accusation of heresy, based upon the "*Augenspiegel.*" This was a manifestation of the infamous European "Inquisition." Powers across the empire took sides. Advised by Spalatin (who may have been in turn advised by Wittenberg's Bible professor Martin Luther), Frederick sent a letter of support to Reuchlin.[18] A great imperial prince like Frederick knew of Reuchlin's mixed career but chose to weigh in only on the religious aspect. But the affair was far from over.

FIRST BAD TURN FROM NEW POPE LEO X

Frederick continued his concubinage with his "special" woman, Anna. Concubinage was widely accepted. It was not merely a relationship between a man and a mistress. It was a relationship with a quasi-wife. It implied a man took a wife of lower social status. The weighty *Sachsenspiegel* from the thirteenth century recognized it and even allowed the couple to marry later, subsequent children receiving all rights.[19] This official marriage, of course, Frederick would never do. His disapproval of Johann's second marriage is ample proof of Frederick's strict views on the subject. Moreover, he had to keep open the possibility of a power marriage. In the meantime, his quasi-family was at court, probably the children noisily visible and the "wife" much less so. By 1513, he had at least three children at court: Sebastien, about thirteen, Fritz, possibly eleven, and an infant daughter. A fourth, the youngest son, Hieronymus, who died in childhood, may still have been alive at this time.[20]

In Rome, the cardinals were finally having their council, so long denied by Julius II. Julius himself had finally let it convene in 1512 at the St. John Lateran Basilica in Rome.[21] It came to be called the "Fifth Lateran Council." Participants included the pope, patriarchs of Alexandria and Antioch, fifteen cardinals, ten archbishops, fifty-six bishops, various abbots and generals of religious orders, and various ambassadors. Julius II conducted the first five sessions, which reveal his political purposes for allowing the rare council. The first five dealt mainly with condemning and rejecting the "council" of Pisa of 1511 and 1512 promoted by France and Maximilian. Julius II also wanted to revoke and annul the esoteric French "Pragmatic Sanction" of 1438. Of course, Julius II lost control of the "Fifth Lateran Council" by dying.

His successor, Leo X, continued the council, also motivated by political reasons. He conducted seven sessions, the last held March 16, 1517. Leo X's sessions ostensibly had three objectives: (1) achieving a general peace among Christian rulers, (2) church reform, and (3) defending the faith and rooting out heresy. For the most part, the council jockeyed around attempting to preserve church power against the Italian states, the Holy Roman Empire, France, and Spain. Not surprisingly, the council touted a crusade against the Turks. All decrees of the council were in the form of bulls. The bull from Session 9, held May 5, 1514, contained an explosive section for Frederick.

Concubinage had been deemed a legitimate form of union by the church for more than one thousand years. The Council of Toledo in the year 400 pronounced it wrong to have both a wife and a concubine, but it was not wrong to have only a concubine. Do not refuse Holy Communion to such a man, pronounced the Council of Toledo, if he was united to a concubine and the two were faithful to one another. One thousand years went by.

Then Session 9 of the Fifth Lateran Council changed it all.[22]

Those practicing concubinage—lay people as well as clerics—violated sacred canon. From princes to popes. No exceptions. Not only was it against church canon, but it must be punished severely in accord with canon law.

There it was!

Those involved in concubinage, whether they be lay or cleric, are to be punished severely. . . .

For years the church had ranted against clerics for concubinage. This papal bull urged penalties be imposed on *lay people* for concubinage.[23] No doubt the decree would still be flaunted. It was hard to enforce on secular powers. Yet Frederick was a devout Christian prince. He worked ceaselessly to present himself a devout Christian prince. This was from the pope himself. Wasn't Frederick himself all for reforming the church and its many elements? Was he to ignore this reform? For clearly the enforcement was called reform. The decree must have sickened Frederick. This was virtually the negative consequence Frederick's irritating brother Ernst had warned him about. How did Frederick respond? Evidence indicates his two (or three) sons remained at court.[24] His Anna surely became much less visible. Was she still at court? Possibly not. And wherever she was, her two-year-old daughter was as well. It may be significant that there would be no more known children for Frederick at fifty-one and Anna, who was probably only about thirty-five. This forced separation may have contributed to Frederick's depression and "severe weariness," attributed in October 1514 by his trusted envoy, Fabian von Feilitzsch, to prolonged political turmoil.[25]

A letter written by the Duchess of Rochlitz years later in 1540 to her brother Philipp of Hesse depicted a miserable existence for Anna.[26] According to the duchess, Anna was hidden away with only two ageing servants to help her. With an entourage of knights and soldiers, Frederick would visit her at night and use her for his pleasure. Everyone involved considered her just a sex partner. The children they spawned were immediately taken away by a wet nurse. This malicious letter was written decades later. The Duchess of Rochlitz would have been ten years old when Frederick's last child was born. And the duchess just happened to be the daughter of Anna of Mecklenburg and the daughter-in-law of Duke George, two people high on the list of Frederick's worst disparagers. The letter does suggest, however, that at some point Anna may have no longer been at Frederick's court.

NEW KING FRANCOIS CONFOUNDS MAXIMILIAN

Maximilian rarely had the luxury to brood. Yes, the electorate of Mainz had eluded him, but he was also facing resentment from powerful princes because in 1512 he had renewed for ten years his contract with the Swabian League. The complaining voices included Frederick and Johann.[27] Maximilian's health was so poor that since 1512 he had traveled with an elaborate coffin. His baggage also included literary works trumpeting his greatness that were to be buried with him. Yet he still fretted, for he had not ensured his successor. Then in 1516, France crowned a new king, Francois. Not only did the flamboyant Francois gain back territory for France in Italy, but he also aggressively pursued the imperial electors. Francois immediately wooed Frederick, entreating him to send his son Sebastian to live in his court.[28] Frederick politely declined. The next year an envoy of Francois spoke to Frederick of "several sacred relics such as a piece of St. Merten, a piece of Maria Magdalena, and more."[29] Again Frederick declined. Maximilian also wooed the electors to elect his grandson Karl.[30] The emperor's credibility (in contrast to that of Francois) was tarnished by years of lies and double-crosses in his brazen Machiavellian style. To all of them Frederick was a stone wall.

Maximilian was also involved in an intrigue against Poland. It seemed to begin with the emperor's negotiations in 1514 for the marriage of his thirteen-year-old granddaughter Isabella to the Danish/Norwegian king Christian II.[31] Frederick reluctantly entered into it to accommodate both Maximilian and Christian II, who was Frederick's nephew. The king, possibly from Frederick's advice, did not seek a large dowry from money-strapped Maximilian but sought, instead, an alliance with the empire against Poland. The king insisted that Saxony and Brandenburg also participate. It seemed both Christian II and Maximilian wanted Saxony, Brandenburg, and the Teutonic order as part of the contract, supposedly then intending to ally with Russia against Poland. Both Frederick and Joachim Nestor of Brandenburg wanted no part of an alliance with two sovereigns who liked nothing better than a lively war. Somehow the marriage nevertheless came off in 1515.[32] That same year, the frenetic Maximilian accomplished yet another marriage of a granddaughter, Philipp's ten-year-old Mary, with Louis II of Hungary and Bohemia.

It is possible Frederick's support of yet another scheme of Maximilian resulted in the emperor granting fair privileges to the Ernestine town of Naumburg. Prior to that, Naumburg had to defer to the fair privilege given to Leipzig. About the only other fruit from Frederick's participation in Maximilian's scheme was his satisfaction with the performance of his envoy to the negotiations.[33] Dr. Hans von der Planitz was already forty when he began diplomatic service for Frederick. Planitz came from a knightly family in Zwickau, but in contrast to the vast majority of knights, he had excelled as a scholar and taken a doctorate in law from Italy. It was a happy combination for Frederick. One of the virtues of a knight was complete loyalty. Moreover, Planitz was perceptive, shrewd, and practical. He would earn Frederick's complete trust and become significant in the coming years as his key envoy.

PROXIMAL THORNS NO LESS PAINFUL

Erfurt still simmered. The installation of the Brandenburger Albrecht as the new archbishop of Mainz did nothing to calm the situation.[34] The new archbishop was much more powerful politically than the previous one. He very much wanted to claim the city-state as his ecclesiastical domain. The Wettins (even difficult George) stood firm and prevented the new archbishop's entry into Erfurt. As powerful as the Brandenburgs had become, Elector Joachim Nestor nevertheless regarded the Saxons as a valuable ally not to be alienated. He and Frederick had a long, amiable history as fellow electors.

One of his university professors now helped Frederick's handling of Erfurt immeasurably. Drawing on a braintrust was, after all, one of the benefits to a sovereign for building and maintaining a university. The lawyer Dr. Henning Göde had come to Wittenberg in 1510 at the age of sixty.[35] He had recently been an adviser to the Erfurt council and knew intimately the conditions and the officials in Erfurt. By November 1516, Göde had helped put together a new protection contract with Erfurt, even stimulating the Erfurters to declare null and void all previous concessions to Mainz. It seemed the intractable problems of Erfurt were at an end.

If only one of Frederick's professors could have resolved the problem in Hesse. By 1514, the regency situation had reached bizarre developments. Although Ludwig von Boyneburg and his knights had custody of the young heir, Philipp, several other factions always lurked nearby trying to obtain custody of Philipp too. These factions included that of Anna of Braunschweig representing her insane husband, Wilhelm I (the Elder), and that of his mother, Anna (of Mecklenburg). In 1512, Maximilian had initiated the poorly conceived "Cologne Contract," which if nothing else cooled tempers of those combatants because they did not want to bring an angry emperor in on their heads. Both lines of Saxons were supposed to administer the contentious regency of Philipp, who in late 1513 just turned nine.[36] The Ernestines thought the Saxons had nothing to gain from the mess, but Cousin George thought otherwise. He, as usual, waited for his opportunity.

In late 1513, the rough lifestyle of knights and boys who wanted to be knights handed an opportunity to those trying to gain custody of Philipp.[37] In January 1514, Anna held her own *Landstag* and told her supporters that a servant of the knights slammed Philipp into a bench so viciously, her son was knocked out cold.[38] Anna tried to draw the Duke of Württemberg into the fracas by requesting an examination of Philipp by his physician. Boyneburg and his knights refused. Nevertheless, the Hessian estates were alarmed by news of Philipp being injured and insisted on a representative staying with Philipp until there was a resolution at the legitimate *Landstag* in Kassel starting in March.

At the *Landstag*, which Frederick did not attend, the proceedings were like a trial—accusations and counter-charges. The "injury" appeared to be a hernia. Not surprisingly, some claimed Philipp had the hernia from birth.[39] Boyneburg even produced two witnesses who claimed they heard Philipp's father say at Philipp's birth that if the baby did not have the same fault with his testicles he himself had, then the boy could not be his son.[40] Of course, Anna protested that the stories were lies. The Electoral Saxony lawyer Friedrich von Thun suggested an examination. By the time all agreed, representatives of the two Saxon lines, the three Hesse factions, Brandenburg, Mecklenburg, and Württemberg were witnesses to the examination. As to the examination, no records of the *Landstag* in Kassel discuss the subject, suggesting no conclusion was made other than that Philipp was in satisfactory health. The examination must have been traumatic to young Philipp, yet his exposure was not over. Philipp's health had to be demonstrated immediately to the Hessians. To do that, the Saxons had the boy present in the castle courtyard. Thun made a speech, proclaiming the prince's good health. Then citizens were allowed to parade by their prince, to shake his hand, and to promise him their loyalty.

The Ernestines considered the issues with Philipp resolved and wanted to conclude the *Landstag*. Anna and her supporters refused. Cousin George saw his opportunity. Even though his brother Heinrich agreed with the Ernestines, George's representative sided with Anna and her supporters. This allowed Anna's supporters to rile the citizens of Kassel that a great injustice was being done. Mobs advanced on the castle, forcing the Saxons to depart quickly. The result of the *Landstag* was that Anna gained control of Philipp, and as regent she became virtual ruler of Hesse. Naturally, she was grateful to Frederick's cousin George. She soon formed a military alliance with George and his Albertines; together they would defend Hesse from an attack by the Ernestines. George was magnanimous enough to support the Ernestines when they tried to keep Anna from taking revenge on Boyneburg and his supporters.

On yet another front, Frederick's relic collecting was jolted in 1514. The Brandenburger Albrecht had gained the bishoprics of Frederick's brother Ernst as well as the electorate of Mainz. Frederick learned that Albrecht, who had enormous debts to pay off, was voracious for sacred relics.[41] Even Albertine George began to collect relics.[42] Frederick's efforts exploded. He had not taken full advantage of his special papal privilege from 1507. Before 1513, he had about five thousand relics, an amount he considered an enormous collection that he proudly touted in his *Heiltumsbuch*. In the next three years, his various resourceful envoys would manage to triple the size of his collection. Naturally that caused his annual display to increase dramatically.

EVERYDAY LIFE AT FREDERICK'S COURT

Frederick's university continued to accumulate firstfruits.[43] The first text in Greek was printed in 1513. The faculty added the study of mathematics the following year and the study of Hebrew the year after that. Some of the faculty had the temerity to question their tie to the Castle Church. Their ignorance led to nothing. In the Castle Church complex, construction of the forecastle began in 1514.[44] This much lower structure for offices and living quarters would close off the castle into a roughly rectangular "*Wehrbau.*"

Frederick took great interest in Wittenberg, but in 1514 he at long last saw his stone-pillared bridge finished over the River Elbe by Hartenfels castle. With the "permanent" departure of Johann and his new bride to Weimar, Frederick started extensive work on the Hartenfels.[45] The accommodation of the Hartenfels before Frederick's additions was adequate enough to host grand events. He would make it more than adequate. It was the first significant construction at the castle in almost twenty years. But that construction in the 1490s paled in comparison to what Uncle Albrecht had built in the early 1480s. Albrecht had extended the old chancellery (the southwest or west wing) so extensively, it came to be called the wing "built by Albrecht."[46]

Much of Frederick's work was de-roofing portions of the wings so more floors could be added above. It is "without doubt" that the new building stone came down the Elbe from the stone quarries in the Elbgebirge (Saxon Alps).[47] The great west wing, though not as wide, was almost twice as long as the Elbe wing of the castle in Wittenberg.[48] The other three wings of the Hartenfels, at virtually the same impressive magnitude, were present in some stage of development. The four wings would eventually form a *Wehrbau* more triangular than rectangular because the west and northwest wings virtually merged into one arced wing. Frederick seems to have made major enlargements only on the west wing and the northeast wing.[49] In his paintings, Lucas Cranach more than once captured the Hartenfels (and the Elbe Bridge) of Frederick's time; it was even then an enormous, multi-storied, many towered castle. Since it was so lightly fortified, it was much more a palace than a castle.

What was life like in Frederick's court?

He reached the age of fifty in 1513. He had consorted with cardinals to condottieri. He knew the greatest poets and artists of the empire. He corresponded with kings and scholars. He was devout, but similar to other men of this time who considered themselves enlightened, he studied astrology and alchemy. He had spent years among the most advanced courts of the empire. He had learned under the master of representation and great consumer of all the fine things life offered: Maximilian. There was little more Frederick could have learned short of living in the courts of France and Italy. And he most certainly knew of these courts. What was his own court like? How did his surroundings appear? What sounds did he hear? What smells? Who were the personnel who surrounded him every day of his life? What did they wear? What did he wear? Who ate with him? What did they eat? How did he amuse himself? What was everyday life like? We stop now to survey the court life of Frederick, a powerful sovereign who was also a man.[50]

Surrounding Frederick at court in visible ways as well as imperceptible ways were about two hundred family members, visitors, officials, and servants. Near the end of 1513, Frederick's court no longer included Johann and his family. Frederick's own family included his sons and possibly his "wife" Anna. One can doubt after the Fifth Lateran Council bull condemning concubinage that Frederick maintained a separate ladies' court for Anna and their daughter, as was custom. Nevertheless, Frederick probably kept his sons with him. His closest electoral personnel were undoubtedly his council of five advisers dominated by Mogenhofer and Pfeffinger; these advisers were diluted after Johann began to borrow them frequently. Frederick's jesters were routinely nearby. Of course, Frederick's father confessor, Franciscan Jakob Vogt, was with him daily. Many of Frederick's key officials and advisers (Von der Planitz, Scheurl, Staupitz) were only occasionally at his court. His court artists such as Cranach were also frequently working on sites away from the court. Yet always there were body servants, civil servants, domestic servants, physicians, kitchen staff, weavers, tailors, shoemakers, locksmiths, soldiers/guards, crossbowmen, fishermen, hunters, stalkers, falconers (fowlers), dog-handlers, stable hands, horse-handlers (grooms), ferriers, butchers, musicians, singers, joust masters, barbers, messengers, woodworkers, carpenters, masons, potters, glassblowers, wheelwrights—virtually one or more representatives from every skill and trade at the time.[51]

As far as the physical living quarters of the prince and the members of his court, the castles may have been spacious with large rooms, but access from room to room was poor. Most were dimly lit, and though cool in summer they were heated erratically in cold weather. Furniture may have been ornate, but it was sparse and limited. The Saxon high nobility used tables, chairs, stools, benches, chests, and bedsteads. The latter had baldachins, curtains, feather mattresses, and elegant bedding. The furniture was elaborately carved for the sovereign and his kin. The chests were simple *cassoni* with hinged-top lids. Missing were cabinets with drawers. The concept of drawers existed, but it was used mainly in sophisticated travel kits. The royal rooms were not at all bleak, but decorated with magnificent artwork, tapestries, and carpets. Frederick's artists also painted windows in cheerful translucent colors. Also adorning the rooms were elegant candelabras and other fixtures. In a lavish hunting lodge, trophies—the more abnormal the better—adorned the upper portion of many walls. This splendor of living quarters of course did not extend to officials and servants. Inventories suggest they slept on everything from cots to couches to just cushions (or nothing more than straw bags).[52] Probably several slept in one room on the floor, and that room was not likely to have a fireplace or stove. A few servants slumbered in the heated rooms of their masters and mistresses to serve their every whim, even during the night.[53]

Clothing was not amassed by any but the highest nobles. A sovereign might have many extravagant furred robes, cloaks, and pairs of footwear with everything in between. For example, Frederick's father, Ernst, in one quarter of 1484 purchased fourteen pairs of shoes, one tall pair of boots, and one lined pair of boots for his wardrobe.[54] Other titled nobility may have been more or less extravagant than Ernst. Frederick was less extravagant but nevertheless splendidly attired. Presentation was too important. He wore jeweled rings and chains of gold with or without jewels. His high officials dressed well, too, especially independently wealthy ones like Leimbach. Others such as Spalatin and everyone lower in status wore a set of official court clothing.[55] They received two new sets every year. They were to wear this clothing at court until Frederick's tailors issued the next set. They were issued by position to "noble boys," "noble girls," kitchen personnel, medical personnel, household servants, stable hands, messengers, musicians, jesters, and so forth. The fabric was not elegant for some; it had to be durable. Wettin sovereigns doted on their pages and boys in all capacities. Often the court clothing would be drab brown or gray, but not for the boys. They "were resplendent in red."[56] In March 1484, summer garments were arriving at court when Frederick's mother died.[57] Ernst had the garments re-dyed black.

The best fabric was for the sovereign and his kin. Within the electorate the best fabric was from Zwickau. The very best came from the Netherlands. Frederick authorized exceptional outfits for special occasions, such as a visit from the emperor. Other occasions merited this exception too, such as making a grand entry at a wedding or a *Reichstag*. Everyone riding in the procession might be garbed in all black or in all red. Even the horses were rigged with special halters, bridles, and other paraphernalia. The prince and his kin were excepted at all other times. A festival might require a "party coat." One such coat for Frederick was fashioned from black "zendill," and adorned with a nude woman no doubt in the vein of a classic repose. Another, possibly for a grand hunt, featured on the sleeve a boar hunter with a lance. The fashion of the time—even for servants—was colorful, often making pant legs and sleeves not match but contrast. Frederick, on an outing in Freiberg, once wore an ash-colored jacket with one sleeve of black velvet embroidered in gold and pearls.[58] The men's long smooth trousers of the time were attached to a belt or a jacket but were as tight-fitting as hose with the flap of a codpiece hiding little.

Meals were twice a day—mid-morning and late afternoon—in the dining hall. Men and women ate separately. Depending on where Frederick was residing, there may have been a separate dining hall for women. If so, the young males of the royals often ate with the women. Frederick sat at "high table." Frederick's idiosyncrasies at meal are not known, but he was closely attended. Probably at least eight servants served just his table. A servant had often fanned his father, Ernst, during meals with a whisk from peacock's feathers.[59] Frederick ate with honored guests or his highest officials. Business was not discussed at high table; his jesters made sure of that. Around Frederick and below him were fifteen or so tables, each waited upon by a number of servants justified by their standing at court. Diners sat in assigned seats, usually ten to a table. No backfilling was allowed. There was, however, allowance for those who showed up unexpectedly: messengers, priests, troubadours, and in some cases wandering tradesmen if they were valued. The lowest ranked tables had only one server.

According to Spalatin, after some relative or friend cautioned Frederick about spending too much on household provisions, he replied,

"I want to give my people enough as long as I live. When another comes after me, then he can do as he wants."[60] Saxons usually drank beer with a meal. Perhaps Frederick and the high table enjoyed wine. Meat dominated the meals: farm-raised beef, mutton, pork, and poultry; wild game including boar meat, venison, bear, hare, beaver, grouse, dove, snipe, pheasant, and waterfowl; local carp, pike, and crabs as well as imported herring and cod.[61] Meats and gravies were generously spiced with saffron, ginger, pepper, cloves, cinnamon, nutmeg, and capers; sugar was also regarded a "spice." Other farm products at the tables were honey, eggs, butter, milk, and cheese from goats and cows. Bread from rye and wheat was eaten in great quantities at table. Fruit was both fresh and dried: pears, apples, plums, cherries, and currants. Almost an afterthought were rice, millet, oat porridge, and vegetables in season such as peas and cabbage.

MUSIC, GAMES, AND UBIQUITOUS JESTERS

Life at court during the day choked the air with sound.[62] The court lacked the contemplative silence of a monastery or a convent. Supplies poured into the courtyard on rattling wagons pulled by clomping, whinnying horses. It was rare, especially at Torgau, when there was no cacophony of hammers and saws performing construction and repair around a castle complex. Nor were the workers silent or expected to be.

It was all the more important to blunt the noise within the castle and in the surrounding gardens with music. Music was pervasive around Frederick. His Electoral Saxony was a music center surpassed only by the Netherlands and the southern empire.[63] Music flowed from trumpets, fifes, drums, kettledrums, cornets, and male throats. Saxons especially loved their trumpets, no less for dancing. Even in Elector Ernst's time, knowledgeable people from other courts marveled at the range and clarity of Saxon trumpet playing.[64] Except for the lute, Frederick himself was not partial to stringed instruments, though much later events would prove Johann liked to hear the violin. Musicians were mobile, so in Frederick's time, in addition to the regular court musicians, many itinerant musicians performed, especially with lutes and even harps. The organ enjoyed great popularity too, though it is problematical whether it had a day to day presence in the court.

Frederick's father, Ernst, in 1482 employed a musical group of six trumpeters, two trumpet apprentices, and one kettledrummer. Thus it remained until 1491, five years into Frederick's reign; even the names of the nine musicians remained the same. Then his taste evolved. In 1491, he added a regular lute player. By 1503, possibly influenced by his years out in the empire, the group had grown to fourteen musicians: eight trumpeters, one bugler (*Zinkenbläser*), one lute player, two pipers, one kettledrummer, and one drummer apprentice. In 1514, Frederick scaled back to twelve musicians, possibly because Johann took several musicians to his Weimar court. The composition in Frederick's court remained constant the rest of his life: six trumpeters, one bugler, three pipers, one kettledrummer, and one drummer apprentice. The lute was gone; perhaps there were enough itinerant lute players to fill the gap. More prominent was the cheerful pipe or flute (*Zwerchpfeiff*), a one-piece cylindrical tube held crosswise with a mouthpiece and six equally spaced finger holes.[65] The salaries of the musicians reflect their worth to Frederick. Trumpeters received about thirty gulden each year. Others received less, with the lute player (before his elimination) receiving about half the salary of a trumpeter. Frederick often gave his musicians (and singers) extra money for special performances. He took his musicians (and singers) to *Reichstags*. Praise of his musicians from non-Saxons delighted him.

The human voice was considered the most sonorous instrument of all, though at the time it was male only. No "singers," however, are documented for Frederick's court before the two recorded for 1491. Then a choir seems to have evolved steadily, possibly from Frederick's experience in the court of Maximilian or the court of his son Philipp the Fair. By 1494, Frederick employed five singers and three boy singers. Frederick doted on his singers, especially the boys. He made sure they were schooled and housed properly. By 1504, there were twenty singers, half of them boys.[66] His choir of twenty or so was well compensated, eventually as well or better than his favored trumpet players.[67] Perhaps that was justified by their heavy duties, because they also had to perform church music. His singers probably sang many local folk songs in the court, but they were likely singing many of the same songs admired in the court of Maximilian. The emperor employed two superb choirmasters who were also great composers: Heinrich Isaac and his protégé, Ludwig Senfl.[68] Isaac was a master at the long popular Franco-Flemish contrapuntal polyphony. He and Senfl did both secular music as well as sacred music for church. The two differed in that Senfl was more a master of brilliant arranging than of original melody. Also Senfl, younger by thirty-nine years, moved more easily into the increasingly popular homophonic style that emphasized clarity of the words.

Outside the main castles, Frederick initiated for ambience ponds and verdant areas for strolling. Summer houses on these floral areas were favorites. Herb gardens were popular. Ponds were stocked with fish and waterfowl. Also favored were enclosures with mammals, many exotic, such as monkeys. Torgau had bear kennels. Lochau had wolves. Cages with songbirds were everywhere. A messenger might arrive at any of Frederick's castles more laden with plants or songbirds than parchment. On the grounds were archery or crossbow ranges, even shooting galleries. A luxurious touch in Torgau for the time was a covered walkway from Hartenfels castle to St. Mary's Church.

Games during the day occupied some. Lawn-bowling existed. Chess was a demanding game played by a few, card-playing less demanding but played by many. Among the men, card-playing could always lead to heavy gambling. In the evening, the privileged in the court enjoyed performing arts. Staged plays were a delight. Subjects covered the rainbow, irreverent to sacred. They were often made more exciting by casting members of the court. In addition, musical concerts of every kind entertained the Saxons. Poets read long poems, often in fawning praise of the sovereigns. A poem by Sibutus gushed *ad nauseam*:

> Duke Johann however sits in view of all on his traditional throne in the midst of the coats of arms of his ancestors. Around him a large crowd of nobles, young and old. . . . A true Godly meeting seems to be under way, and the rulers of the heavens participate in the banquet. . . . Exactly the same as a peacock when he displays his multicolored tail, the duke cocks his ears toward flattering words. . . . He wrinkles his forehead and he rotates his black eyes like an eagle. . . . From his chin a poetic black beard flows. . . . With snow-white feathers the duke decorated his head, and during the dance, towers above all other princes. . . . Electoral Prince Frederick, however, is no less skilled at arms and just as joyful about combat as Duke Johann. Both when still boys fought severe

battles in the games; they learned foreign combat customs by heart. These two for the first time introduced to us the lance fights and the tournaments in combat arenas and the new art of war with drawn swords.[69]

That poem flattered Johann more than Frederick for no other reason than Frederick had missed these particular festivities because he was attending the funeral of longtime fellow elector, Archbishop Hermann of Cologne. Yet Frederick did not starve for praise, because numerous poets showered him with praise year after year. Perhaps Frederick deserved much of the praise, because he was indeed a strong patron of the arts and he did not impose his own views on artists whether humanist or traditional. Some thirty significant literary works were dedicated to him.[70]

As Frederick became too old to joust or even ride hard, he indulged one special hobby that was popular with the highborn.[71] He made things with a state-of-the-art turning lathe. He purchased expensive tools from Nuremberg. He talked to the wood lathers he employed at his castles, discussing how to make furniture more artistically. He even competed with them, occasionally excelling them, according to Spalatin.[72] Frederick made elegant things, above all from the most precious wood, but probably also from ivory and even the fossil resin, amber. His products might have included cups, bowls, canisters, candlesticks, balls, and chessmen among other things. It is known that he made crossbow bolts as a gift for the Palatine elector. Did he also make crossbows themselves such as Elector Hermann of Cologne did? Did he perhaps make rosaries? All of these products seem likely, and if so they were of precious materials.

Enjoying special status were jesters. The varied "fools" were genuinely dear to the sovereigns of the time. Even the ladies' court had its own jesters, including otherwise unseen female jesters.[73] Their masters and mistresses mentioned them in letters with great tenderness. On the other hand, their masters could be cruel to jesters. Johann reported to Frederick a mock tournament between his own jesters Hans and Thomel. Fighting for a flask of wine, Hans struck down Thomel and won the wine.[74] Yet another time, Frederick was entertained in Zwickau by blind men thinking they were striking a pig to win it and knocking each other senseless. Humor was coarse and cruel. A story about the Wettins' legendary jester Claus Narr illustrates the cruelty.[75] Frederick's grandfather Frederick (the Meek) took the child Claus for his jester, probably in the 1430s, because he was "heartily amused by Claus's naively brutal treatment of some geese he was tending." Claus apparently lived until 1515, dying at almost ninety.[76] He played to perfection the foul-mouthed fool, but he was quick-witted and a master of repartee. Apparently once the elector asked Claus what he thought a precious stone was worth. Claus replied the stone was "so valuable he must have a wealthier jester to esteem and evaluate it."[77] The Wettins esteemed Claus so much, they placed his value at three thousand gulden for the Leipzig Division in 1485. Claus made it known at the time he thought the division was bad.[78] He ended up with the Ernestines, though all the Wettins, including Frederick, had endured the stinging jibes of Claus Narr since earliest childhood. Among Frederick's numerous other jesters were Haensel, Albrecht, and Fritz. Most jesters were dwarfs. Some were cripples or hunchbacks.[79] Not all were keen-witted like Claus Narr. Many were mentally deficient, permanently young children who said anything that popped into their heads.

COURT FAVORITES: JOUSTING AND HUNTING

Festivities were not day to day. They came often, however, to Electoral Saxony and thus to Frederick's court. As natural as seasons came the feast days and carnival (*Karneval*), year after year. They were often occasion for festivities. No celebration was wilder than carnival, the time just before the solemnity and sacrifice of Lent.[80] As far back as 1386, documents show carnival was a special time.[81] Even monks and nuns participated in nonsense, the fun usually in the form of mocking secular and religious authorities. Even the higher nobles, mocked though they were, participated. The world had to be turned upside down. Germans still have a saying that "if you are not foolish at carnival, you will be foolish all the rest of the year." At some point, the key to the city was given to a jester who would rule for a day. Frederick was present when Johann hosted the Zwickau Carnival in 1518.[82] The host and his city staged elaborate performances in the street: plays similar to the "lout" plays of Hans Sachs, an ensemble of twenty-four male sword dancers dressed in white, and another of twenty-six men doing a "wheel dance."

Craziness abounded, including a child (or dwarf) careening through the streets in a cart pulled by a dog.

There were, of course, in Saxony also weddings, town celebrations, and *Landstags*. Often enough at all these occasions Frederick's carpenters busied themselves, usually in the town square or marketplace, building grandstands around the arena for "knights' games," principally jousting.[83] Soon the stands and nearby buildings displayed the coats of arms of knights who intended to fight. They set up tents and corrals all around the perimeter of town. There they tended to their armor, weapons, and strings of warhorses. It was a rare nobleman who could resist the smell and sound of fierce knightly combat, at least to watch it and talk about it. The jousting was a spectacle with armored and colorfully decorated warhorses ridden by even more colorful knights in armor. Often the helmets sprouted antlers and great plumes of vivid feathers. The tension before the noisy clash of armor and lances was palpable.

Tournaments were a bright thread in the fabric of living for the noblemen and their ladies. Nearly half of the letters between Frederick and Johann, if one of the two had been at an occasion without the other, pertained to the nature of the jousting course, the order of weapons, and the aspects of the saddles, among other such important details.[84] Frederick had Cranach capturing the swarming complexity of the tournaments both in paintings and etchings for woodcuts. Such was the appeal of the joust as the test of manhood that, as late as the spring of 1510 at the Augsburg *Reichstag*, Frederick at forty-seven jousted Maximilian at fifty-one.[85] This was only six months after Frederick revealed to the emperor that he could scarcely ride a horse.

There were many less physical forms of competition, such as crossbow shooting, that Frederick is known to have done at other times. Nevertheless, he never lost interest in all the permutations of the tournament. Any noble, after all, had to assess armor, horses, weapons, techniques, and countless other aspects of jousting. In Torgau, Frederick had established in 1488 an armory and arsenal run for the next thirty-five years by Armory Master Ewalt Heseler. Frederick had a lifetime of purchasing and appreciating armor for its weight, mobility, and protection.[86] Frederick had contracted with the armorer Lucas Gassner in Innsbruck in 1493 on his way to the Holy Land. In 1496, he made payments to Maximilian's armorer Meister Albrecht. And even a physically ailing man could still wear such armor. As late as 1521, Planitz would be arranging the purchase of two sets of jousting armor from the Nuremberg armor-master Heyncz. Even ironsmiths Hans Eryngk and Andreas Rockenberger in Wittenberg had made armor for Frederick. Through the years, Frederick had purchased armor from Weimar, Zwickau, Erfurt, Innsbruck, Munich, Cologne, Augsburg, Landshut, and Antwerp.

Similar to all nobles of the time, Frederick also assessed horses. And luckily for him, horses could be used in his other favorite pastime. As much as Frederick loved the tournament, he probably loved hunting even more.[87] Hunting was an archetype for the medieval mindset: everything was precisely defined. Falconry at the time was virtually a science with long-trained falconers and centuries of lore. Maintenance of falcons and dogs was in itself much prescribed and often expensive.[88] Falcons ate only live pigeons and chickens, while dogs ate oat gruel and available bread scraps. Dogs, similar to falcons, needed special handlers with special equipment. In 1480, Uncle Albrecht promised himself he would keep no more than twenty-eight dogs at a time.

Hunting on horse or in a "blind" was just as steeped in detail. The great stag was the ultimate trophy. Trackers for a grand prince like Frederick returned before the hunt began with observations on tracks. They even laid out droppings on tables to examine. After deciphering the evidence of the trackers, beaters would try to direct the quarry toward blinds or onto courses for the chase. Dogs were used for the chase. Hunters often dressed in green. Although wild boar and bear were exceptionally dangerous to hunt, any armor was cowardly. A deer had to be butchered in a precise sequence with the exact tool from a field kit of dedicated tools.[89] Only a knight could perform actual butchering, the blood collected on the underlying hide. Choice pieces were impaled on a forked branch stuck in the ground nearby. The pack of dogs looked on, waiting to be rewarded with blood-soaked bread and delicacies such as the heart, lungs, and liver. Most game was eaten right way; if not, it was smoked, dried, or salted. Predators considered inedible, such as wolf, fox, and badger, were hunted for sport, supposedly thereby protecting the more desirable game.

The hunt began long before dawn. The day was so long, Frederick would stop and observe Mass in mid-morning. His favored place for hunting was the area surrounding his Lochau hunting mansion.[90] This low terrain of sand and marsh that also merged with the heath sprawled a few hours ride north of Torgau and east of the River Elbe. In the heath, groves of birch, oak, alders, and even pines were islands in a sea of whistle grass. One later observer, who obviously had no love for the area, wrote, "Everywhere one turns oneself, one sees water and sumps, from which thick stinking fogs ascend frequently, and one should believe, nobody can remain healthy one month here."[91] Frederick loved the area; it may have reeked, but it swarmed with game. The prized red deer was there, as well as packs of wild boar. But much more thrived there: bear, fox, wolf, hare, badger, beaver, game birds, waterfowl, and two other kinds of deer.

The average year at Lochau yielded hundreds of deer, even greater numbers of wild swine, uncounted smaller game, about half a dozen wolves, and perhaps one bear. Frederick tried to protect surrounding farms, yet hunts often went awry. The animals were unscripted. To him, it was unconscionable for hunters to damage a farmer's efforts and ignore their responsibility. Sometimes he compensated the farmer with money, sometimes with grain. After the hunt, the adventurers relaxed at Frederick's hunting mansion.[92] Apparently, it was a great three-winged structure (*Hinterschloss*), fronted by a "*pfeifferstul*" from which musicians in the inside loggia played into the courtyard.[93] The contemporary Hans Herzheimer wrote in 1519 that the lower floor was massive brickwork and vaulted. The upper two or three floors were wood frame. Corners were reinforced with towers. Inside the *Hinterschloss*, eighteen of the many large rooms were equipped with furnaces. One tower had interior baths with water pumped into them from the outside. On the grounds were gardens, ponds, summer houses, bird enclosures, a hothouse for tropical plants, a zoo, a shooting gallery with a running target, a bath house, and stables. Frederick knew how to relax his frequent hunting guests, who included Maximilian and the powers of the empire. His Lochau hunting mansion enjoyed lavish praise from such guests. Herzheimer gushed he had never seen the equal of Frederick's hunting mansion and its five outlying "pleasure houses." The overall design and integration of delights was unique in the entire empire.[94] Lochau was in the vein of the gourmet's "subtleties." One was nobody if one could not breezily mention a visit to the Lochau. It was one more example of why Frederick's name, even among the highest nobles, brought to mind ingenuity, taste, and excellence.

HEADACHE: WHAT TO DO ABOUT MARTIN LUTHER

In September 1516, Frederick called Spalatin away from Wittenberg to reside at his court.[95] Frederick consulted the quiet scholar in many ways. For one thing, the elector had become interested in the most touted scholar in Europe, the Dutchman Erasmus. Frederick needed Spalatin's precise Latin to correspond with Erasmus. Spalatin by that time had known for at least two years Frederick's monkish professor of the Bible at the university in Wittenberg: Martin Luther. In 1515, Johann Lang wrote Mutianus that Spalatin "venerates him [Luther] and consults him like Apollo."[96] Spalatin was awed by Luther's knowledge of the Bible and just about every other religious aspect.[97] Spalatin had surely communicated his enthusiasm to Frederick. The first proof that Frederick himself was more than slightly aware of Luther is in Luther's December 14, 1516, letter to Spalatin: "You write about the most illustrious prince speaking of me frequently and praising me."[98] In a real sense, Spalatin was becoming Frederick's spiritual mentor and Luther had already become Spalatin's spiritual mentor. By 1516, Luther was answering Frederick's questions indirectly through Spalatin about Erasmus, Reuchlin, and the gamut of religious issues.

As professor of the Bible, Luther lectured on the Psalms in 1513–15, on Romans in 1515–16, on Galatians in 1516–17, and on Hebrews in 1517–18. Bernhard Lohse interpreted the thinking behind Luther's choice of this sequence.[99] Churchmen at his time considered Psalms as prayers of Christ. Luther began to concentrate on the personal relationship of believers to God. The believers must humbly submit to God's judgment, just as Christ humbled Himself on the cross. Only this submission made it possible for them to share in divine grace. After Psalms, Luther's next choice of the letters of Paul to the Romans, Galatians, and Hebrews (the latter was at the time considered by Paul) indicated Luther's concern about the righteousness of God and the justification of believers. Although Luther did not ignore other themes revealed in these books, he clearly concentrated on sin and grace, damnation and salvation. These were the same issues that had for years made him exceedingly anxious and fearful.

During all Luther's early years in Wittenberg, Staupitz had piled more and more work and responsibility on his protégé. It was clear Staupitz intended to give him no time to brood and fear the wrath of

God. In the autumn of 1511, while Luther toiled on his doctorate, Staupitz made him the house preacher of the Augustinian monastery.[100] In May 1512, while Luther still tried to complete his doctorate, Staupitz made him the subprior of the cloister as well as director of the general studies program associated with the cloister. Of course in 1513, Luther became professor of the Bible. Then beginning in 1514, he became the pastoral administrator of the parish church in Wittenberg. In May 1515, Staupitz made him the district vicar of his order, and Luther had to supervise ten cloisters (and later, eleven) of the Saxon congregation of his order. Luther was so conscientious, he carried out every new duty to the letter, not to mention keeping the monastic rule of his order.

In the summer semester of 1516, Luther received a copy of Erasmus's breakthrough compilation of the original Greek of the New Testament from the oldest, most reliable manuscripts he could locate. This new avenue was so wide, so humanistic in its bent, it fired Luther even further in his study of the Scriptures. Heiko Oberman asserted, "He immediately set about familiarizing himself with this new tool, so shocking for Latin-oriented Christians. While he was engaged in the exegesis of chapter nine of the Epistle to the Romans, he drew—the word 'write' would be inappropriate—Greek letters in his lecture manuscript for the first time to point out a translating error in the Latin Bible."[101] It is tempting to believe Luther's "reformation discovery," i.e., "salvation is from faith alone" from Romans 1:16–17, stemmed from revelation in meaning he found in the "original" Greek. Nevertheless, Bernhard Lohse after exhaustive analysis was able to place it only in the period of 1514–18.[102]

The Scriptures were just as sacred to the Roman Church as they were to Luther. The difference developed because the Roman Church believed their traditions were in complete accord with the Scriptures. Luther began to convince himself otherwise.[103] He was powerfully persuasive, too, and rarely hid even the most abrasive sentiment.[104] Frederick found this out firsthand. In 1516, Frederick had it in his power to obtain for Staupitz the bishop's chair at Chiemsee (between Munich and Salzburg). Staupitz, worn out at fifty-six, was open to this prestige and comfort. Frederick asked Spalatin to persuade Staupitz to accept. Spalatin first checked with Luther. The blunt Luther erupted. A corrupting, administrative office for one as capable as Staupitz? Never! Luther prevailed. Spalatin informed Frederick privately. It seems both Frederick and Spalatin appreciated this blatant honesty in Luther. No doubt Spalatin toned down Luther's vitriolic message.

But how irritated Frederick must have been when he heard Luther's blatant attacks on the saints and the cult of relics! One example of the former is that Luther had asked Spalatin for St. Jerome's letters, then delivered a sermon on St. Bartholomew's Day (August 24, 1516), blasting the legends that had grown up about that very saint.[105] Bartholomew was, of course, Frederick's favorite saint. Luther's blunt character is nowhere revealed more than in his comments to Spalatin that "much pleases your prince . . . which does not please God." Luther fumed that Frederick may have been a man extraordinarily intelligent in secular matters, but in things concerning God and the welfare of the soul, Frederick was seven-fold blind. Luther blustered that his remark did not have to be kept secret. He was willing to say it to the prince himself.

That same year, one day before Frederick's special All Saints' Day (November 1), Luther savaged from the pulpit indulgences granted from the veneration of relics![106] This was his third sermon that year critical of indulgences. He preached that remission of sins from such indulgences was scripturally unsound. Among other faults, it lacked contrition and confession. Further, to think the pope could "deliver souls from purgatory is audacious." Luther emphasized that the "purchasing of indulgences in any case is highly dangerous and likely to induce complacency." Afterwards, he was told reliably that Frederick was most unhappy with his sermon. Yet by year's end, Frederick was praising Luther, certain evidence that Frederick had enormous respect for the expertise of his professor of the Bible. Frederick's attitude had been typical for him: anger but with restraint, and then reflection that perhaps it was so.

Luther surely had passed on his new thinking on the Bible to Spalatin, who no doubt passed it on to Frederick in a milder form. Frederick and Spalatin probably thought it was all no more than powerful academic probing brought on by the Erasmian work. Spalatin, like others, appreciated that Luther was never content with a literal translation but was untiringly digging for the original meaning intended by the first Christians. No one else in their sphere was doing this so thoroughly.[107] Luther believed the Scriptures were the Word of God; the medium was also the message. Spalatin came to believe this too. If

Frederick did not already believe this, he also would come to believe this.[108]

On October 4, 1517, Frederick executed a second will, suggesting his health was so poor, he saw death not far ahead.[109] He appealed in the will to brother Johann, as his survivor, to not unnecessarily burden the territory and its people with assessments and taxes. He also bequeathed more money, one thousand gulden, to be divided among fifty monasteries (excluded were religious orders of knights), as well as increased funds for masses for the dead. At last, he officially requested to be buried in the Wittenberg Castle Church. In the meantime, he was intrigued by the revelations from his professor of the Bible.

Sooner or later, the new thinking of Luther was going to attract the attention of the powers of the Roman Church at some higher level, most likely hurried upward by a theologian at Erfurt or Leipzig. Whereas the shrewd Erasmus tiptoed around volatile issues, the blunt (and possibly overworked) Luther tore into them as tactfully as a "wild boar in the vineyard."[110] His new thinking, expressed in September 1517 in his lively attack on Aristotelian-based theology or scholasticism ("Disputation Against Scholastic Theology"), could easily have done it.[111] It was radical. He attacked the foundations on which the earlier church doctors had constructed their theology. He systematically refuted every scholastic theologian by name from Scotus (d. 1308) through Ockham (d. 1349) and d'Ailly (d. 1420) to the last one, Gabriel Biel (d. 1495).[112] He did avoid mention of the great Thomas Aquinas and any of the popes. Thus his attack escaped immediate notice. Another issue altogether caused an eruption. Not surprisingly it was one that was not only theological but political and economic.

Luther publicly attacked indulgences with ferocity.[113]

Many clerics had already criticized indulgences, including Luther himself and his Wittenberg University colleague Karlstadt. They had emphasized spiritual reasons. In his early lectures, Luther did not reject the practice of indulgences in principle, but worried there was no true contrition involved. Indulgences as a tool of the church began at least as early as the eleventh century, at first affecting only temporal punishment imposed by the church. But their scope grew. Later it also included temporal punishment in purgatory. Later yet, the indulgence removed even the guilt. Eventually this grew to include the recipient's family members. On the other hand, the church officially remained silent on the scope of indulgences. Even by Luther's time, there was no common understanding of what was permitted. This made it difficult for priests doing actual pastoral work. What was the priest to do when a brazen sinner without an ounce of contrition breezily showed him his letter of indulgence? It was not an academic issue. It was a spiritual issue.

But it was also an economic issue.

The pope himself depended on indulgences to finance not just grandiose plans like the basilica of St. Peter's in Rome but the very survival of the Vatican and the Roman Church. Indulgences pervaded the life of Europe. Luther's own sovereign, Frederick, was deep into the indulgence business, rewarding each viewer of his relics thousands of years of relief from purgatory. The indulgence business, however, that sparked Luther's tirade was that of Archbishop Albrecht of Mainz (although Luther was at first ignorant of who was behind it). Because Albrecht and his Brandenburgs owed such vast amounts of money to the Fuggers, the indulgence trade after 1514 became aggressive and ugly. A cynical jingo circulated:

> As soon as the coin in the coffer rings,
> The soul from purgatory springs.[114]

A cold-eyed assessor put the sinner somewhere on a sliding scale of payment that demanded twenty-five gulden from a prince or archbishop to a promise of fasting and prayer from the indigent.[115] Woodcuts and street poets mocked this indulgence business run for the pope, Archbishop Albrecht, and the Fuggers. The coffer or chest could only be opened later in the presence of a notary by a sequence of three keys. Adjacent to Frederick's territory, one key was held by the commissioner of indulgences representing Archbishop Albrecht and the church. An agent of the Fuggers held another key. The local secular authority held the third. Luther recalled the affair in 1541 in a tract titled *Wider Hans Worst* ("Against Hans Wurst").

> It happened in the year '17 that a preaching monk named Johann Tetzel, a great loudmouth . . . traveled around with indulgences selling grace for money as expensive or as cheaply as he was able. At the time, I was preacher in the cloister and a young doctor newly come from the forge, hot and enthused for Holy Scriptures. When many people from

Wittenberg went to Jüterbog and Zerbst for indulgences . . . I began to preach with moderation that one might do something better and more certain than buy an indulgence. I had already preached such here at the castle against indulgences, and so came into disfavor with Duke Frederick, for his foundation here was very dear to him. . . . It came to me how Tetzel had preached gruesome, abominable articles of which I will mention a few. Namely: he had such clemency and power from the pope that if one had deflowered or even impregnated the Holy Virgin Mary, the mother of God, he could forgive it if that same one would put in the chest what was required. . . . Another: if St. Peter were here now, he would not have greater clemency or power than he himself had. Another: he would not trade places in heaven with St. Peter; for he had with the indulgence saved more souls than St. Peter had with his sermons. Another: when one dropped a penny into the chest for a soul in purgatory, as soon as the coin chinked in the bottom the soul flew up into heaven. . . . At the time I did not know who was to receive the money. . . . I wrote a letter with the Ninety-five Theses to the bishop at Magdeburg admonishing and pleading that he stop Tetzel and prevent such heavy-handed things from being preached, lest it might give rise to public unrest. Such was his duty as archbishop. . . . But no answer came to me.[116]

Most of Luther's Ninety-five Theses that he sent to the bishop as well as supposedly posted for discussion at the Castle Church (because it was the university church) on All Saints' Eve (October 31) were well within the bounds of academic disputations. As he had earlier expressed in sermons, he did not reject every aspect of indulgences but emphasized their use only in relieving temporal punishments imposed by the church. Again he objected to the false sense of security created by indulgences. Yet in his long list of theses, ten (forty-two though fifty-one) went dangerously beyond the bounds of disputations. Most of these ten began, "Christians are to be taught . . ." They virtually usurped the pope, because they clearly stated just the opposite of what the pope was doing. For example, thesis 43 stated, "Christians are to be taught that he who gives to the poor or lends to one in need does better than he who buys indulgences." Thesis 50 stated, "Christians are to be taught that if the pope knew the exactions of the preachers of indulgences he would rather have St. Peter's church in ashes than have it built with the flesh and bones of his sheep."[117]

Luther was a baby at politics. The first rumors of political consequence for posting the Ninety-five Theses alarmed him. It was quite natural that rumors would say Frederick was behind the Ninety-five Theses. The rumors said Frederick was jealous of Archbishop Albrecht. The rumors said Frederick encouraged Luther, because he was jealously guarding his own indulgences and resented some of his Saxons venturing over the territorial borders to spend their Saxon coins on indulgences. This misunderstanding was so wrenching to Luther that he offered to participate in any disputation on indulgences to prove it was the issue of spiritual importance and nothing else.[118] But who would give him the satisfaction? Although alarmed, Luther at this point was nevertheless still unaware of the enormity of the poison in his tirade against indulgences. His aim did not go beyond Archbishop Albrecht of Mainz.

When Spalatin finally read the Ninety-five Theses to Frederick,[119] his worldly sovereign concluded grimly, "You will see that the pope will not like this."[120]

CHAPTER 7

THE MARTIN LUTHER MAELSTROM

(1518–20)

"I believe the shoemaker about the shoes, the tailor
about the trousers, and the smithie about the iron."
—Proverb favored by Frederick the Wise[1]

SURGE OF THE PRINTED HYPERBOLE

Frederick must have been aghast—not so much at Luther's Ninety-
five Theses as at the speed they surged across the empire, then beyond.
This church-enmeshed Europe had never seen such a firestorm.
Wittenberg canon Ulrich von Dinstedt sent a copy of the Ninety-five
Theses to Christoph Scheurl in Nuremberg who had them printed.
Others also had them printed. They circulated in both Latin and German.
By December and January, copies reached Nuremberg, Leipzig,
Augsburg, Erfurt, Ingolstadt, Mulhouse, and Basel. In England, Thomas
More received a copy from Erasmus in March 1518. Albrecht Dürer was
so ecstatic, he sent Luther a gift. Johann Fleck, Franciscan prior in
Steinlaussig, told his monks simply, "He is the man who will do it."[2] Fleck
must have already known the Augustinian Luther "was the man." His
obvious source is Jakob Vogt, Frederick's father confessor, who was
assigned to Steinlaussig in 1516 and 1517.[3]

Meanwhile Luther was oblivious of the magnitude of his action. He
had sent a copy of his theses to the primate of Germany, Archbishop
Albrecht of Mainz, at the same time he had made them public for debate.
Luther wrote a humble, apologetic cover letter, which nevertheless
blistered the corrupt indulgence trade practiced by Johann Tetzel.[4]

Luther knew Tetzel was using Albrecht's name for the trafficking but apparently he thought Albrecht was ignorant of its nature.

Within one week of making his theses public, Luther wrote Frederick directly (the first known occurrence), on another subject altogether.

> I have heard that Your Grace plans, at the end of this tax period, to impose another and perhaps even heavier tax. . . . I beg that for the sake of God you will not let it come to that. I and many others who mean well with Your Grace are sincerely sorry that even the last taxation has reduced Your Grace's reputation, name, and good will.[5]

Frederick may have been amused by Luther's naive impudence.

There was a much larger issue looming. Frederick was aware of pulses all over the empire and beyond. He had informants everywhere.[6] He surely knew that Archbishop Albrecht, a twenty-eight-year-old prince who knew virtually no theology, could smell a problem for his indulgence traffic. He had sent the Ninety-five Theses of Luther to his faculty at the University of Mainz.[7] By December 17 they replied. One sentence in their response must have mildly pleased Albrecht: "We have read them and among other things we find that they limit and restrict the power of the Pope."[8] This was the perfect instrument to squash the Saxon pest. Archbishop Albrecht had already informed Leo X. Albrecht, a self-appointed patron of the arts, was above such turmoil. He would let Rome handle it.[9] Because of Albrecht's indifference, his councillors had denounced Luther to the pope not for heresy but for spreading new doctrines. The pope supposedly reacted as many elites reacted: Luther was just another monk, and a crude German at that, so perhaps he was soused on beer.

Surely Frederick also knew that by January 1518, the chapter of the Saxon province of the Dominican order met at Frankfurt on the Oder.[10] In the presence of three hundred Dominicans, Johann Tetzel, fuming over Luther, refuted Luther's Ninety-five Theses with 106 of his own.[11] The Dominicans agreed that Luther was a heretic, and they designed for the pope their own accusation of heresy against Luther. This denunciation would carry more weight than Archbishop Albrecht's communication. One of the Saxon Dominicans' own, Nicholas von Schönberg, was an intimate friend of Cardinal Medici, who in turn was the closest confidant of the pope. It is not known when this denunciation reached Rome. What was known to Frederick was that Dominicans were bellowing from their pulpits that Luther would burn within a month. They did not stop there but took swipes at the University of Wittenberg and even Frederick himself. Their threats had teeth. As recently as 1509, so-called heretics had been burned in Switzerland with the consent of Pope Julius II.

Yet Frederick also knew that the greatest threat to his Saxony was not from the pope but from Maximilian. The emperor was, as usual, entangled in numerous other enterprises. His health was so much worse than Frederick's now—whether it was advanced syphilis or a dozen other ailments sustained by a reckless life, the emperor was failing fast. He had never been more stressed by unresolved problems. He struggled to ensure his grandson Karl the title of king so that Karl would be certain to succeed him as emperor. He planned his appeal to the estates, especially the six electors, at the upcoming *Reichstag* in Augsburg. Meanwhile, Maximilian had to travel to the Netherlands to wrangle with the reluctant Karl. Maximilian wanted to arrange for his other grandson Ferdinand the assumption of the Austrian lands. He plotted with the pope for a crusade against the Turks. He probably scoffed at first over the news about Luther, as many nobles did. Just monks squabbling. Yet upon further reflection, Maximilian recognized that a Saxon monk could cause the pope enough discomfort that perhaps he would yield to the empire on some other issues. On the other hand, this rash monk might interfere with the lucrative indulgence traffic. Maximilian's inclination was to humor the pope and support a ban against Luther if it came to that. He might enforce the ban or he might not. That all depended on the pope's cooperation with his own plans.

Frederick knew all this. He knew a ban meant only as much as the emperor wanted it to mean. Franz von Sickingen, the most notorious robber knight in Germany, had been under imperial ban, but he still roamed freely. Maximilian might need Sickingen against France or even against the obnoxious Duke of Württemberg. Sickingen was, after all, one of the few superior condottieri in Germany. As a "military enterpriser," he could bring knights thundering into a fray by the thousands, almost with the snap of his fingers. At the moment the rogue Sickingen, backed by 10,000 knights and foot soldiers, was extorting 35,000 gulden from young Philipp of Hesse, who had just come of age.[12] Maximilian and Frederick both knew all this.

The first official action by the pope was in February 1518, when he asked the Augustinian superiors to discipline Luther or at least appease him.[13] The pope as yet spoke officially only of Luther's "mania for innovation."[14] The fact that not much later the pontiff suddenly granted Spalatin full confessional powers indicated that the papal politics were moving.[15] The pope, no doubt, wanted to ingratiate Spalatin and perhaps gain a confidant close to the elector. That same month, Luther heard that Tetzel was so enraged while in Berlin that he ranted about burning Luther. Tetzel was a well-spoken man with a commanding presence, who habitually threw threats at all who opposed him. Once in the Saxon mining town of Annaberg when the miners did not show proper respect, Tetzel threatened to close the mines. His threat worked, and the miners did penance for him. Because he was an official inquisitor of the Dominicans, any threat from him was alarming.[16]

In February, Luther confided to Spalatin:

> You ask me how much indulgences are worth. The matter is still in doubt, and my *Theses* overwhelmed with abuse. Yet I may say . . . indulgences now seem to me to be nothing but a snare for souls, and are worth absolutely nothing. . . . For the sake of exposing this fraud, for the love of truth I entered this dangerous labyrinth of disputation, and aroused against myself six hundred Minotaurs, not to say Radamanthotaurs and Aeacotaurs.[17]

At last Luther realized he had created a tempest, and not only he but also the university was under attack. He learned that various university faculties were being goaded into attacking him, and he sent Archbishop Albrecht a draft of an expansion on his own hastily written Ninety-five Theses. In March, Archbishop Albrecht sent the abbot of Lehnin to Luther with the request that he publish no more on indulgences. Perhaps Luther was genuinely humbled by such exalted attention (or had reflected on the damage he might be doing his sovereign and benefactor), because he was uncharacteristically meek—so much so that he agreed to back off.

Yet he did not back off. He preached a sermon ("Sermon on Indulgences and Grace") that he afterward had printed in German. It had twenty articles, and the argument was easier to understand than the Ninety-five Theses. The pamphlet squalled across the empire. Its impact was thunderous. The storm drenched not only academics but everyone.

Within the German-speaking empire, it would be the best known and most widely circulated of any Luther writing.[18]

Luther was succinct in "Sermon on Indulgences and Grace" and he supported every point with the Holy Scriptures. A major Luther scholar recently commented on the significance.

> With one sentence the traditional division of repentance into contrition, confession, and satisfaction was swept from the table as not based on or in agreement with Scripture. God requires only true contrition and conversion, combined with the intention to bear Christ's cross in the future. If God punishes sins, no man has the power to remit it. We cannot usurp God's jurisdiction. . . . Indulgences are only something for lazy and imperfect Christians.[19]

Many higher nobles, including Frederick's cousin George—Luther's most virulent enemy later—at first welcomed Luther's condemnation of Tetzel's trafficking. Their motives, however, often stemmed only from the drain of money from their own territories. As one could predict, this widespread printing of "Sermon on Indulgences and Grace" caused the indulgence traffickers to react with equal force. The chief one among them stopped ranting and went into action. Tetzel's theses appeared in Wittenberg in early May. He clearly wanted more than condemnation. Luther, he claimed, was a heretic in the same vein as Wycliffe and Huss, both of whom were burned at the stake. Tetzel went further: any power who could restrain Luther's heresy and did not do so was also a heretic.

This was a major assault on Frederick himself.

Luther recognized that these bombardments in print had to end. They must not taint his sovereign. Luther scrambled to arrange an engagement with his opponents in a public disputation so that no one could say the elector was hiding a heretic. But Luther's opponents had no desire to give him a respectable forum. Besides that, the powers in the church—all the away up to the pope, it was said—were increasingly irked by the outspoken and ever more popular Luther. Why not just let the punishment take its natural course—the Roman way?

The next triennial meeting of the reform congregation of Augustinians was to convene April 1518 in Heidelberg. Luther would attend. He would be out of the territory of his sovereign and would therefore have to face real physical danger for the first time. Frederick wrote letters for Luther to give to all the authorities on his route, advising them to do everything in their power to assist Luther. With that done, Spalatin was able to assure Luther that he would not be waylaid and carted off to Rome. Possibly Luther was told what an extremely powerful political advantage Frederick enjoyed, as Maximilian and the pope both maneuvered to select a successor to Maximilian. Unknown to Luther, Frederick also wrote Augustinian General Vicar Staupitz reminding him that when he paid Luther's fees for his doctorate, Staupitz had emphasized that Frederick was gaining a professor for his university. Frederick was not pleased to release Luther from his teaching responsibility.[20] It was a clear warning that nothing was to happen to his "professor." Over the course of four days, Luther traveled to Heidelberg on foot and supposedly incognito. About halfway to Heidelberg, powerful electoral official Degenhart Pfeffinger met Luther and his traveling companion, fellow Augustinian Leonard Beier, in the village of Judenbach while still in Frederick's Saxony.

When Luther arrived at the Palatine court in Heidelberg, *Hofmeister* Jacob Simler gushed, "By God, you have excellent credentials!"[21] Luther was backed by the force of one of the most authoritative princes of the empire.

Luther was more successful than unsuccessful at the conference. Many older Augustinians were hostile or confused. Younger Augustinians, different "by two whole octaves" according to Luther, flocked to him.[22] Among them was a sixteen-year-old Dominican, the later influential Martin Bucer. He wrote a friend in awe that "although our chief men refuted him with all their might, their wiles were not able to make him move an inch from his propositions. His sweetness in answering is remarkable, his patience in listening is incomparable."[23] Palatine Count Wolfgang, brother of Elector Ludwig, wrote Frederick that Luther "won no small praise for your Grace's university, and was greatly lauded by many learned persons."[24] Influenced by Frederick's warning, Augustinian superiors had Luther travel by wagon with the Nurembergers as far as Würzburg, then with the Erfurters on to the north, and finally with the Eislebeners who brought him all the way to Wittenberg. Luther had to gloat to Spalatin, "I, who left on foot, returned by wagon."[25] His friends in the Wittenberg cloister noted he was "stronger and fatter."[26]

The print war expanded. A serious, respected theologian at Ingolstadt, Johann Eck, prepared a refutation of Luther called *Obelisks* ("daggers" but also a word commonly used at the time to flag spurious portions of text). A copy reached Wittenberg. Eck called Luther "a Bohemian, a heretic, rebellious, presumptuous, and impudent, as well as sleepy, simple-minded, unlearned, and finally a despiser of the pope."[27] For once Luther was stunned. He had considered Eck a friend.[28] He wrote Staupitz, "I have provoked all the people, the great, the average, the mediocre, to hate me thoroughly."[29] He included an explanation of his Ninety-five Theses (*Resolutions concerning the virtue of indulgences*) that he hoped Staupitz would send on to the pope.

Wittenberg colleague Karlstadt, now converted to Luther's way of thinking, responded to Eck supposedly without Luther's knowledge. Karlstadt was already more "radical" than Luther, defiantly insisting a conclusion by a scholar backed by the authority of canon was more reliable than any assertion by the pope.[30] Eck of course had to answer Karlstadt. On May 19, Luther sent Eck his own response, immodestly called *Asterisks* ("little stars" but also a word used at the time to flag the most valuable portions of text). In his cover letter, Luther offered Eck *Asterisks* so "that you may see and recognize your ignorance and rashness; I consult your reputation by not publishing them, but by sending them to you privately so as not to render evil for evil as you did to me."[31] Yet Luther wrote his tract with just as much sarcasm and bitterness. Eck was "a godless enemy of love and a perverter of the people." Luther respected the pope; Eck was a "malicious" slanderer. After answering every point with rhetoric as acidic as Eck's, Luther concluded, "Christ and his Word are with me and I shall not fear, no matter what the entire world may do to me."[32]

Prodded by Staupitz, Luther polished *Resolutions*, his lengthy explanation of his Ninety-five Theses, which was intended to appease the pope. Spalatin had his hand in it, but Luther's original introduction was pure Luther. This new polished introduction, however, was pure electoral court, which knew how to address the pope and the curia. It also, of course, absolved Frederick and his university.

> If I were as they describe me, the illustrious Elector Frederick
> of Saxony certainly would not suffer such a pestiferous boil in
> his university, for he is probably the greatest zealot for

Catholic truth there is at the present time. Nor would the exceedingly intelligent and very diligent men of this university have tolerated me. Therefore, Most Holy Father, I cast myself at your feet with all that I am and possess. Raise me up or slay me, summon me hither or thither, approve me or reprove me as you please! I will listen to your voice as the voice of Christ reigning and speaking in you. If I have deserved death, I shall not refuse to die.[33]

Luther had *Resolutions* printed in June 1518 and the product reached the pope that same month.

BLUSTER OF THE PROFLIGATE POPE

About the same time Luther was polishing *Resolutions*, the Dominicans had their general meeting in Rome.[34] The head of the order was Cardinal Cajetan, a man of fifty-nine from Gaeta (between Rome and Naples). Cajetan was not a prince playing at church work; he was a serious theologian, so conversant with the teachings of Thomas Aquinas that he was considered a leading authority. Cajetan apparently was unwilling to pursue Luther. It was Herman Rab, Dominican provincial of Saxony, who relentlessly pushed for action against Luther. He went to the curia and convinced its attorney general, Mario Perusco, to proceed. Essentially the accusations against Luther were espousing dangerous doctrine and revolting against papal power. Sylvester Prierias, the curia expert on questions of faith (and also an antagonist against Reuchlin), cobbled together an opinion in three days. He attacked the Ninety-five Theses in general on the grounds that they did not agree with Thomism. But his real thrust was what everyone expected was Luther's vulnerability: he had attacked the authority of the pope.

By the middle of June, the pope had approved the process. These opinions of Prierias, embedded with the coarse polemical insults of the time, formed the grounds for a citation against Luther. The citation commanded Luther to appear in Rome within sixty days from the arrival of the citation and its supporting documents in Wittenberg. On July 6, 1518, Frederick received from Cardinal Rafael Riario the ultimatum agreed upon by the Curia on May 20,[35] which gave the extent to which Luther had to recant. Riario urged the elector to force the recantation. Cardinal Riario warned Frederick that if he favored Luther, it could tarnish the honor of his house. At the end of July Frederick answered Riario, stressing his lifelong obedience to the church. Frederick regretted the turmoil. He was pained to think that some thought he was behind it. May God preserve him from such godlessness.

Also in early July, Rome sent the summons to Cajetan, who was also the papal legate at the *Reichstag* in Augsburg. Cajetan sent it on to Luther. Luther received the package on August 7. By the next day he already wrote Spalatin to reveal his own plan against extradition to Rome. Extradition meant oblivion, probably death. Jurist friends in Wittenberg, probably foremost Hieronymus Schurff who had warned Luther *before* the Ninety-five Theses about taking on indulgences and the pope, advised Luther to write immediately to both Frederick and Spalatin in Augsburg. The jurists helped Luther through the legal convolutions. Luther appealed to the elector to enlist Maximilian's help in requesting from the pope a *remissio seu commissio causae suae ad partes Alemanniae*, that is, permission to vindicate himself within the empire.[36] Reuchlin had demanded the same thing against the Dominicans. Luther's first line to Spalatin revealed how shaken he was. Scholar Irmgard Höß called it a "cry": "I need your assistance now very urgently, dear Spalatin, yes, besides me the honor of our whole university needs you!"[37] He informed Spalatin what he had asked Frederick in an accompanying letter, then abruptly ended, "I am already replying to . . . [the citation of Prierias], which is exactly like a wild, entangled jungle. You will soon have the whole work, when it is completed. That 'sweetest' man is simultaneously my accuser and my judge, as you can see from the Summons. Farewell. I am occupied with so much writing that I cannot go into details."

The next development was in early August when Maximilian offered tepid support of the pope's ultimatum. Frederick knew only too well that "support" from Maximilian could disappear in a blink. Frederick himself did only what he deemed necessary to satisfy Rome and not one "*bißchen*" (tiny bit) more. While Frederick was in Augsburg for the *Reichstag* Johann Eck sought an audience with him six times,[38] but Frederick refused to see him. That did not mean Frederick remained unavailable. He saw Philip Melanchthon, his new professor of Greek. Although Spalatin had promoted Petrus Mosellanus for the position,[39] Luther had remained neutral, and Frederick had solicited the advice of the scholar Reuchlin for candidates for teaching Hebrew and/or Greek.

Reuchlin, not surprisingly, had recommended his own grandnephew Melanchthon for the chair in Greek. The twenty-year-old Melanchthon passed through Augsburg and introduced himself. He was cadaverous and frail, and he had a thin voice and a slight speech impediment,[40] but Frederick was undeterred. The youth was much like Spalatin otherwise. He was articulate and most pleasing in his manner, he knew the niceties of court, his father had been armorer to Elector Philip of the Palatine, and of course his granduncle had served in princely courts too.

Frederick had more pressing matters at the *Reichstag*. Nor did he, famously taciturn, simply react to developments; he anticipated them. He knew before his own shrewd councillors had advised him, certainly before Luther had ever suggested it, that Luther would need to be tried within the empire under the friendliest conditions possible. To accomplish that, Frederick needed help from Maximilian. Since the pope's ultimatum, Spalatin was negotiating verbally with Maximilian's minister Hans Renner for that purpose.[41] What the elector wanted was a hearing administered by a friendly cleric, the bishop of Würzburg, or even the bishop of Freising, perhaps at a friendly university (which excluded Erfurt, Leipzig, and Frankfurt on the Oder).[42]

Then came a major development. On August 23, Leo X himself wrote the electors as well as Cardinal Cajetan. The pope's letter to Frederick left no doubt as to the gravity of Luther's situation.

> Beloved Son, greeting and the apostolic blessing! . . . It has come to our ears from all quarters that a certain son of iniquity, Friar Martin Luther, of the German Congregation of Augustinian Hermits, forgetting his cloth and profession, which consists in humility and obedience, sinfully vaunts himself in the Church of God, and, as though relying on your protection, fears the authority or rebuke of no one. Although we know this is false, yet we thought good to write to your Lordship, exhorting you in the Lord . . . to escape the suspicion of doing wrong, in which Luther's rashness would involve you . . . we again exhort your Lordship, for the sake of God's honor and ours and your own, please to give help that this Martin Luther may be delivered into the power and judgment of the Holy See, as the said legate will request of you.[43]

Deliver Luther. Unmistakably final. Leo X's letter to Cardinal Cajetan left less doubt as to the gravity.

> Beloved Son, greeting and the apostolic blessing! After it had come to our ears that a certain Martin Luther, reprobate Augustinian, had asserted some heresies and some things different from those held by the Roman Church ... we, by these presents, direct you ... to force and compel the said Martin, now declared to be a heretic by the said auditor, to appear personally before you ... and when you have Martin in your power, keep him under a safe guard until you hear further from us. ... And in order that this plague may be the more quickly and easily exterminated, you may admonish and require, by our authority and under pain of excommunication and other penalties mentioned below, all and singular prelates and other ecclesiastical persons, as well secular as regular of all orders, including the mendicants, and all dukes, marquises, counts, barons, cities, corporations and magistrates.[44]

Extermination. Unmistakable a second time. Two days later Gerard Hecker, provincial of the Saxon Augustinians, received a long directive from General of the Augustinians Gabriel della Volta:[45]

> You can hardly estimate into what a mass of evils a certain Brother Martin Luther of our order and of the Congregation of the Vicar [Staupitz], has brought us and our profession. ... Luther has come to such a degree not only of noxiousness, but also of most damnable heresy, that he has not feared to lecture and dispute openly against the Holy Roman Church and the Supreme Most Blessed Pontiff, and publicly to preach his false doctrine. ... Therefore we command you under pain of losing all your promotions, dignities and offices, when you receive this letter, to proceed to capture the said Brother Martin Luther, have him bound in chains, fetters and handcuffs, and detained under strict guard in prison at the instance of our Supreme Lord Leo X.

Have him bound. There it was. A third time. Unmistakable.

Where was the equivocation? Where was the vacillation? In the day of the horse, this verdict of Rome came within months of the Ninety-five Theses. No one can doubt the papal vision of a catastrophe within the church unless Luther was exterminated. Frederick understood the enormity. As one of the faithful, why did he not deliver Luther at once? Frederick and those whose judgment he most trusted were convinced that Luther was correct in his methods. Luther based his conclusions on the deepest insight into the Holy Scriptures, the only tangible source for God's Word. It was Erasmian, except the interpreter was not a mouse muffling his voice in a cranny, but a lion who roared.

Luther had recovered some of his bluster within a few days after this blizzard of ominous news from Rome. To Spalatin he wrote, "In all this I fear nothing, as you know, my dear Spalatin." Yet he was still offering legalisms to Spalatin, no doubt prodded by Schurff. To his spiritual mentor, Staupitz, he wrote, "For neither does that citation to Rome, nor do their threats move me; you know that I suffer things infinitely worse, which would make me consider these temporal and passing thunderbolts trifles, were it not that I sincerely desire to cherish the power of the Church."[46] Here Luther referred to his *Anfechtung*, paralyzing fear of divine judgment, which he suffered so often.[47]

Concrete support of the pope by Maximilian would make it impossible for Frederick or Luther to offer any kind of long-term resistance. But Frederick had perhaps anticipated among many possibilities such a black situation. The pope and his minions had turned his world upside down. And within days, Frederick would turn Maximilian's *Reichstag* upside down.

AUGSBURG *REICHSTAG*: FREDERICK IS "LIKE A WALL"

The *Reichstag* in Augsburg had been in session since June of 1518.

The issue of the *Reichstag* that first played center stage was the crusade against the Turks. The murderous sultan Selim had gained power in 1512. In contrast to Italians or Germans who drew relatives into their power, Selim immediately executed all his brothers and nephews. He had beaten off the Persians, had conquered Syria and Egypt, and had recently armed for a large-scale attack against the West. At long last, a Turkish peril appeared true, but the threat was not against the empire so much as against Italy and the southern Habsburg lands. Naturally both Maximilian and the pope promoted a crusade.

Maximilian in some kind of final convulsion was vibrantly active. Unfortunately for the emperor, he presented to the Augsburg *Reichstag* dusty crusade plans against the Turks worked out back in the 1490s and even brought forward again in 1500.[48] The imperial estates received the plan strongly supported by the pope about as cynically and uncooperatively as imaginable. The ban on Luther imposed by the pope, unexpected by most, coupled with Maximilian's equally unexpected "support" of the ban, made the mood of the imperial estates even uglier against Rome. On August 5, 1518, Maximilian had written the pope regarding Luther, "If the authority of your Holiness and of the most reverend fathers does not put an end to such doctrines, soon their authors will not only impose on the unlearned multitude, but will win the favor of princes to their mutual destruction. ... Whatever may be righteously decided upon in this our Empire, we will make all our subjects obey."[49]

The letter seemed written not by Maximilian but by Cardinal Cajetan. The threatened "mutual destruction" would have angered Frederick. Apparently, though, Frederick and none of the other estates were aware of the letter.[50] No extra fuel was needed for the fire. The estates were so angry with Rome and their never-ending calls for crusades and crusade financing that they muttered against the "Roman Turks." Then the rancor exploded: "The pope is worse than the Turks."[51] Responding to one means advanced by Cardinal Cajetan to finance the crusade, Frederick himself angrily condemned it a "false, blasphemous indulgence."[52] The subject of a crusade was closed.

Maximilian's strategy for a *Reichstag* was a wonder of ineptitude. Next he proceeded with his plan to make grandson Karl king. He had lined up the Fuggers to finance his bribes. Again the electors thwarted him. One opponent was Richard von Greiffenklau, archbishop of Trier. He was suspected to be well bribed already by France. The other was Frederick, who had accepted no bribes. He would not make the same mistake his father had made in 1486. The Habsburgs were turning the empire into their family monarchy. The emperor was supposed to be elected. And why give up such leverage? Frederick "stood like a wall" against the pressure.[53] There could be no such vote legally. Frederick had the law set down in the Golden Bull firmly on his side. Maximilian had never been crowned emperor by the pope. He was still only king in the strict sense of the Golden Bull. How could Karl then be elected king? Would the electors of Trier and Saxony agree to elect a king if Maximilian was crowned emperor? Seemingly both agreed. This seems contrary to Frederick's thinking. Nonetheless Frederick could agree if he thought Maximilian would not be crowned emperor.

Maximilian must have been delighted. The answer to his problem was now so easy. All he had to do was instigate his ally Pope Leo X to crown him emperor, and then Karl could be elected. The pope refused. He could not crown Maximilian emperor while Maximilian was in the empire itself. It had to be done in Rome. Maximilian was furious—doubly so, because he believed there would be no coronation in Rome either. He had supported the pope's ban of Luther. "No pope, as long as I lived, has been loyal to me," he complained bitterly.[54] For a decade the popes had recognized, even if Maximilian had not, that after the Italian national estates had become stronger, the popes no longer needed the emperor as a steward of the church.[55] Maximilian could not deliver a crusade anyway.

The *Reichstag* became yet another disaster for Maximilian. But he did earn the admiration of his imperial estates. The dying emperor had performed at a high level with every ounce of energy he had. His masterful German was eloquent, his mannerisms gracious, his verve real. He was for moments at a time the bold, barrel-chested ramrod he had once been. His hair once red-gold sunshine in his prime was now gray-streaked and stringy. Spalatin recorded the wrenching scene when Maximilian took leave of Frederick.[56] His body and health were depleted. Maximilian may have doffed his red beret chivalrously, but in departing he had to drag one leg. The old warrior had fought hard—and seemingly lost every battle.

Frederick, on the other hand, had won every battle. The Turkish crusade was dead. Karl had been stopped. Maximilian knew he must have Frederick's support in order for Karl to be elected, even if it happened after his own death. Pope Leo X wanted anyone but Karl, even coming to realize that Frederick might be the next "emperor." In the meantime, moreover, with the Turkish crusade over, Maximilian had nothing to offer the pope. So the pope had let Maximilian down in crushing fashion. But had the pope forgotten Luther?

And so it happened. Maximilian, furious with Leo X, was only too glad to request a hearing for Luther in the empire. And if the pope refused, just let him try to get Luther.

CARDINAL CAJETAN REBUKES LUTHER AT AUGSBURG

On September 11, Leo X sent an order to Cardinal Cajetan instructing him to examine Luther soon in Augsburg, not in a contentious way, but carefully.[57] Cajetan could then acquit or condemn Luther, according to his own judgment. Frederick knew from personal contact that Cardinal Cajetan was a serious and well-mannered judge. He was not a partisan ranter like Tetzel. Because of Frederick's influence, he "received Cajetan's promise that he would deal benevolently and mildly with Luther, and in any case would release him, therefore not take him prisoner."[58]

Frederick had arranged everything but a guarantee Cajetan would not condemn Luther.

On September 29, in Weimar, Luther crossed paths with Frederick's party returning from Augsburg. By October 4, he was in Nuremberg. Christoph Scheurl was supposed to accompany him from there to Augsburg to be his legal adviser, but Scheurl was not in Nuremberg. It was no disaster, because two trusted electoral advisers, Johann Rühel and Philipp von Feilitzsch, remained behind in Augsburg. Instead of Scheurl, Luther's friend Wenceslas Link from the Nuremberg Augustinians went with him to Augsburg. He even loaned him a new cowl, because Luther's was so shabby. Luther had twenty gulden in his pocket, given to him by his benefactor's party in Weimar. Arriving in Augsburg October 7, Luther stayed at the Carmelite monastery of St. Anne. All this Frederick had arranged as well.

Cardinal Cajetan was a guest of financial giant Jacob Fugger. The meetings began October 12.[59] Luther knew the cardinal was a hidebound Thomist. Luther did not respect Thomas Aquinas as a teacher of the church, so he knew the road was going to be a rough one for the two of them. But it was worse. Cajetan was a cardinal. His idea of "benevolent" and "mild" to a lowly monk was not Frederick's. So to Luther, Cajetan was haughty and authoritarian. To Cajetan, Luther was a stubborn monk, eerie with deep-set piercing eyes. Cajetan made his expectations plain from the beginning: Luther was to return to the heart of the church, recant his errors, and promise not to repeat them in the future. Luther wanted to debate. Cajetan had no intention of treating him as an equal. Luther managed to wheedle out of Cajetan the main objections to his recent activity.

Cajetan clarified two disputed points. He cited Clement VI's 1343 bull *Unigenitus*, which said the treasure of the church, obtained through the merits of Christ, could be applied by the pope to remit temporal punishments. Cajetan considered this point won. The second point was theological. Cajetan claimed that Luther's demand of certain justification when one received the Sacrament was contrary to both the Scriptures and the church. Of course he considered that point won also. Luther would not agree on either point. Cajetan's arguments were not scripturally sound. Here was the divide between the two. Cajetan accepted that papal authority was superior to all councils as well as the Scriptures. The first session ended with both men exasperated at the density of the other.

Day 2, Luther appeared with Vicar Staupitz, and in the presence of four imperial councillors, a notary, and others he made a formal statement that he had always honored the church and would follow its teachings in the future just as he had done in the past. He could not recant without a structured disputation that showed him according to the Scriptures that he was wrong. The proceeding stalled. Staupitz requested Luther be allowed to answer the disputed points in writing. Cajetan granted this, perturbed that he had ever been maneuvered into the examination. Yes, the pope had requested it, but it had been the Saxon Frederick's doing. Little did Rome know just how stubborn and disrespectful this eerie-looking monk was.

The third day Luther produced his written argument. Saxon councillors Rühel and Feilitzsch gently reminded the cardinal of his agreement with Frederick. The powerful cardinal was irked. Luther dealt with point one by insisting the bull *Unigenitus* was papal law, not law based on the Scriptures. One cannot preclude error by a pope. Many papal laws had already been corrected by the church. In his discussion of the second point, Luther actually penned one of the tenets of the Reformation: righteousness (or justification) was by faith in Christ alone, according to his interpretation of Romans 1:17.

Cajetan contemptuously rejected Luther's written reply, yet he would send it on to Rome. Angered by the impudence of a mere monk, he demanded again that Luther recant; then the cardinal began to shout, and exerting his authority he threatened Luther and the others with the ban. Both sides became surly, although Cajetan dominated. Luther earlier had startled Cajetan with one winning thrust. Luther went too far, however, by sarcastically noting Germans knew their grammar. Cajetan seethed. "Go and do not return to me again unless you want to recant," growled Cajetan.[60] The cardinal is "as well fitted to deal with and judge this business as an ass to play the harp," Luther wrote a university colleague that same evening of the third day.[61]

Luther waited several days while Cajetan met with others, always with the intention of somehow breaking Luther into a recantation. Rumors floated about his arrest. Cajetan was, after all, a Dominican. And there was an old maxim about any measure being valid when dealing with a heretic. The Saxon councillors and Staupitz convinced Luther during this lull to file a peculiar formal appeal before the Augsburg notary and two witnesses requesting "the pope ill-informed to the pope better-informed."[62] In other words, the pope had not been informed well enough by his advisers to act against Luther; this legalism supposedly would keep any step Cajetan took from being final.

On October 20, after a five-day interlude of stewing and fretting, Luther convinced himself that treachery was imminent. He left Cajetan a letter stating he had fulfilled all obedience. He found the means to escape. He had considerable help, because he had to slip through a small opening in a city wall since the city gates were closed. A horse awaited him, and the inexperienced rider Luther fled, bouncing painfully in the saddle. A few days later he was in Nuremberg, warmly welcomed and entertained by Willibald Pirckheimer, whom Luther had also seen on his way to Augsburg, and his esteemed circle.[63] It is unclear how many of his circle (which had been fond of Vicar Staupitz before Luther's onset and included at times Dürer, Anton Tucher, Conrad Celtis, Sebald Schreyer, Hartmann Schedel, Lazarus Spengler, and Christoph Scheurl) were there to meet Luther.

On October 31, the saddle-sore Luther arrived safely in Wittenberg but like a fugitive, exactly one year after he supposedly posted his Ninety-five Theses. What his fate would be he did not know.

TAKING SIDES IN THE "LUTHER AFFAIR"

With the great flurry of correspondence about the "Luther affair" (*Luthersache*), it could not have escaped Frederick's notice what the great scholars and theologians were saying. Erasmus wrote Johann Lang, "I hear that Eleutherius [a name Luther used for himself for a while] is approved by all good men, but it is said that his writings are unequal. I think his Theses will please all. . . . I wonder what has come over Eck to begin a battle against Eleutherius."[64] Wolfgang Capito in Basel wrote that many considered Luther "a Daniel sent at length in mercy by Christ to correct abuses. . . . And would that he might arouse all theologians from their lethargy."[65] It did not escape Frederick's notice that the primate of the empire, young Archbishop Albrecht of Mainz, had not attacked his subject. In Maximilian's "antipathy" to Luther he had lumped him in with Reuchlin, a telling point for Frederick. Reuchlin had been acquitted.[66] At this point the "Luther affair" seemed an attack from Rome as well as the local Dominicans. Frederick had never been fond of the Dominicans. Few were.

Nevertheless, Frederick had to weigh humanist scholars' approval of Luther against the attacks on Luther from Rome.[67] Well before Luther's return to Wittenberg, Frederick knew from official channels, his councillors, and various spies more about the hearing than anyone. He had already read Cardinal Cajetan's report on the Augsburg hearings and naturally had his own report from Rühel, Feilitzsch, and Staupitz. Frederick knew how on the third day Luther had confounded the cardinal. Cajetan's report was predictably harsh, demanding Luther's immediate extradition. In the meantime, Cajetan had acted to plug a gaping hole in the argument against Luther, for in truth no pope or council had ever defined indulgences. Cajetan sent his own definition to Rome and urged the pope to issue a decree on indulgences, which he then did on November 9.

Frederick requested a summation from Luther so he could respond to the Cajetan report. In the meantime, letters from Leo X thundered down like hail on Saxony. Frederick's letter from the pope announced that the pope's special envoy Karl von Miltitz, a Saxon ("your Grace's loyal subject"), would be coming soon to visit.[68] A cynic could decipher from the unctuous letter that Miltitz held the Golden Rose for Frederick in one hand and a knife in the other to first take care of the "infected, scrofulous sheep" Luther. The pope added, "We remind your Lordship, and admonish you paternally, to act according to your reason and the virtue of a Christian prince."[69] In Spalatin's own letter from Leo X, the pope reminded him, "Wherefore we exhort you in the Lord, and paternally charge you on your duty and devotion to us" that Spalatin should advise Frederick against "that only son of Satan, Friar Martin Luther."[70] The pope sent similar letters to Degenhart Pfeffinger and other powerful advisers, as well as the Wittenberg Council.[71] Not to be neglected was Frederick's cousin George. The pope urged him to help Karl von Miltitz "execute his commission," which was to "extirpate this tare and coccle from the fertile field of the Lord."[72] He did not fail to mention Miltitz was a canon at the Church of Meissen.

Did the recipients of all these letters discuss them with another? Most assuredly. Regarding Miltitz, Frederick wrote Cousin George, "It well might happen that he would refuse to give me the golden rose unless I banished the monk and said that he was a heretic. But I fancy I can do as Clauss Narr says, go on drinking my wine and being a heretic all my days."[73] The Golden Rose fast became a joke among the powerful all over the empire because of its transparent purpose.

What could Frederick expect of this Karl von Miltitz? Miltitz was from a family of the nobility in Rabenau on the outskirts of Dresden.[74] He was related to familiar and powerful names serving the Saxon court for decades: Schleinitz, Ende, and Schönberg. His stepmother was even related to Johann von Staupitz. His father, Siegmund, had been *Amtmann* of Pirna.[75] Karl had studied at Mainz, Trier, Cologne, and Bologna. Surely it was not easy for a Saxon to advance in the Roman curia. In 1518, Karl von Miltitz had managed to obtain a benefice in the Meissen church. At twenty-eight, he was competent enough to perform as a diplomat and deliver messages, but he was not destined for the inner circle. Nevertheless, the curia thought it a brilliant scheme to incorporate this well-connected Saxon into their mission to Frederick. What they perhaps did not know was that Karl von Miltitz loved to drink wine. Or perhaps that minor vice was so common in the curia that no one thought anything about it.

In the ensuing weeks, letters and comments led some in Wittenberg to believe Rome was furious that Cardinal Cajetan allowed Luther to "escape." Suspicion grew, and everyone was talking about the "Luther affair." Luther had his ears to the ground too. He passed on some gossip to Spalatin in December 1518: "In the court of the bishop of Brandenburg they lately discussed what favor and whose support I had. Someone said: 'Erasmus, Capito and other learned men favor him.' 'No,' replied the bishop, 'these men are nothing to the pope; it is the University of Wittenberg and the Elector of Saxony that really count.'"[76]

Karl von Miltitz left Rome in November.[77] Rumors swirled like early snow. Miltitz's mission was ominous. Rome was indeed maintaining that Luther had fled Cajetan, and all considerations were void. Luther gave a farewell sermon in the town church at Wittenberg, for he thought he would have to flee. Staupitz had offered him asylum, but the emperor and the pope had long arms. Perhaps Luther could find refuge in France, as Spalatin suggested. By this time the deliberate Frederick had weighed his chances of stopping Miltitz and the consequences if he did. Frederick wrote Luther November 28; he approved of Luther's flight! While Luther ate his last meal in the Augustinian monastery three days later, a letter arrived from Spalatin. It shrieked danger: are you still there? To Luther's amazement that same evening another letter arrived, this one from Frederick in Altenburg.

Frederick commanded Luther: "Do not leave."

What had happened? Karl von Miltitz was in Augsburg in late November. He failed to see Cardinal Cajetan, who had followed Maximilian to Austria, but he did see Degenhart Pfeffinger at his Bavarian estate. From that meeting with Miltitz, who was perhaps loosened up by ample wine, Pfeffinger communicated facts to Frederick that changed the elector's mind about the inevitability of Luther's arrest and extradition. Miltitz was in Nuremberg days later. Saxon councillors Pfeffinger, Rühel, and Feilitzsch were there too, all eyes and ears. Miltitz, possibly giddy from drinking wine and enjoying his self-importance among Saxon officials, divulged that he had three papal breves that ordered him to capture Luther and deliver him to Rome.[78] Was it the wine bragging? Did Miltitz, assuming Luther would hear all, try to frighten him into submission? Luther was definitely unnerved. Two weeks later Christoph Scheurl wrote Luther. Scheurl had been with Miltitz too. He believed the legate, having experienced the sympathy of Germans to Luther and the hostility toward Rome, was himself unnerved. Miltitz would, after all, soon be deep in Saxony and subject to the powerful Frederick.

A German proverb warned a letter from a prince should be read at least three times.[79] Frederick knew this, and so he wanted his letters as clear as spring water. On December 7 or 8, after grinding through twenty revisions, Frederick sent Cardinal Cajetan the only letter he would ever send anyone in the Roman curia on Luther's behalf:[80]

> We are sure that you acted paternally toward Luther, but we understand that he was not shown sufficient cause to revoke. There are learned men in the universities who hold that his teaching has not been shown to be unjust, unchristian, or heretical. The few who think so are jealous of his attainments. If we understood his doctrine to be impious or untenable, we would not defend it. Our whole purpose is to fulfill the office of a Christian prince. . . . As for sending him to Rome or banishing him, that we will do only after he has been convicted of heresy. His offer to debate and submit to the judgment of the universities ought to be considered. He should be shown in what respect he is a heretic and not condemned in advance. [81]

Luther was elated. He gushed to Spalatin, "I have seen the admirable words of our Most Illustrious Prince to our Lord the Legate of Rome. Good God, with what joy I read them and read them over again!"[82]

Bantering back and forth about a site for future disputation had focused on either Erfurt or Leipzig, though neither university was sympathetic to Luther. Johann Eck had appealed by letter to Duke George to allow him to debate Karlstadt and Luther at the University of Leipzig. George finally granted this December 31. Also a few days after Christmas, Miltitz arrived at the electoral court then residing in Altenburg and tried to bluff Frederick; he demanded Frederick drive Luther from his territory. Did he not know Frederick had stood before Maximilian "like a wall"? Frederick coldly refused. This shook Miltitz, and he soon backed off, proposing they discuss how Luther could be reconciled with the pope. Naturally Frederick was agreeable to that. He sent a messenger to Wittenberg to summon Luther to Altenburg. Then Frederick, determined never to be a party in talks with Luther present, departed for Lochau.

Luther arrived in Altenburg a few days later to confer with Miltitz in the presence of Fabian von Feilitzsch. Luther had enormous respect for the unusually clever and sensible Feilitzsch.[83] On January 5 or 6, Luther wrote Frederick that he had agreed to do four things to reconcile himself with the pope. First, he would drop his criticism provided the other side did so as well. Next, he would write the pope admitting he had written and spoken too sharply. He would also publish a leaflet advising everyone to follow the Roman Church. Last, prodded by Spalatin and Feilitzsch, he agreed to have the archbishop of Salzburg (Leonhard von Keutschach) judge his case with the condition that there would be no recantation. Further negotiation reduced the demands to only the first and last. Frederick then became more active. Keutschach was at the time squabbling with a coadjutor forced on him. It was none other than Matthäus Lang, an old political enemy of Frederick from his days in the imperial inner circle. Lang was the worst of the "Swabians." Frederick suggested his close friend the archbishop of Trier, Richard von Greiffenklau, as arbitrator. Soon everyone, including Luther, seemed pleased, and they all agreed on Greiffenklau.

Miltitz said the pope was furious with the "dirty dog" (*Schweinehund*) Tetzel. He even asserted the pope rebuked Prierias for his attack on Luther.[84] Doubtless the Saxons did not believe this display by a diplomat who drank too much wine and became maudlin, even shedding tears. His story, though, took tangible form when after his departure he forced a meeting sometime around January 20 with Tetzel in Leipzig. He wrote Pfeffinger that in the presence of a Fugger agent he had formally charged Tetzel with embezzlement and living an immoral life. Tetzel was indeed disgraced.

DEATH STALLS THE EMPIRE

About the time Frederick was dealing with Miltitz, the emperor was traveling from Innsbruck to Linz. Maximilian had suffered a long wintery trip back from Augsburg. His debts to merchants in Innsbruck were so long-standing that they refused him service until they received payment. Maximilian answered by departing and making his way to Linz. No more than one day's ride from Linz, he had to stop in Wels. December 10, 1518, his condition was grave. Like his father, he fought to live, refusing death. He did not draft his last will until three weeks later and signed the will before witnesses on January 10. The news reached Frederick January 21, 1519, that his lifelong friend Maximilian had died on January 12.[85]

Maximilian was only fifty-nine. For all the aggravation he caused, he was an irrepressible man whom Frederick admired. Maximilian, despite Frederick's obstinacy, was openly fond of his nephew. In many ways Frederick had become a great prince of the arts and the world by emulating Maximilian.

No one in power in all of Europe would talk of anything for months except for the election of the new Holy Roman Emperor. The Luther affair seemed to evaporate. Although that relieved Luther, it offered no relief to Frederick who now had to weather the storm over the interregnum and the election of a new king. The Palatine elector, so despised by the Habsburgs, had eagerly grabbed the *Vicariat*. Maximilian's imperial chamber court, so hostile to Frederick, accepted the Palatine elector. Johann urged Frederick to claim at least half the regency role during the interregnum. The Golden Bull gave him that right. Frederick scorned more imperial burdens. War was imminent. Duke Ulrich of Württemberg tried to take advantage of Maximilian's death; within his realm, Duke Ulrich attacked the free imperial city Reutlingen. The duke had previously murdered one of his own subjects, the uncle of Ulrich von Hutten, to gain his wife as a mistress. Even the duke's estranged wife Sabine, daughter of the Bavarian Duke Albrecht, demanded action against her husband. The duke's reckless deed against Reutlingen furnished the perfect opportunity for the Bavarians. The duke had no chance against the fury of the Swabian League led by Bavarian Duke Wilhelm and assisted by the most feared condottiero in the empire, Franz von Sickingen.[86] The war against the duke, his defeat, and his expulsion would all take place in the interregnum. The Swabian League claimed the rule of the large duchy of Württemberg.

It seemed other parties seized upon the interregnum to settle scores. At the same time Württemberg erupted, the "Hildesheim Feud" discharged.[87] This feud was close to Frederick for several reasons. As interregnum vicar for that region, a role he wanted to refuse, he was responsible for keeping the peace. Also, one of the parties in the feud was Heinrich (the "middle one") of Braunschweig-Lüneburg, the husband of his sister Margarete.[88] She was forty-eight and mother of three boys and three girls, aged eleven to twenty-five. Heinrich (the "middle one") and Bishop Johann IV of Hildesheim concluded an offensive alliance in February 1519. The opposition included Heinrich (the "young one") of Wolfenbüttel and his cousin Erich I of Calenberg, both experienced military men. Much of the cause of the feud was based on petty insults not unlike those between Frederick and Cousin George. Yet this Hildesheim squabble had led to a feud and actual skirmishes.

To make the "Hildesheim Feud" even messier, Cousin George became involved. George demanded Frederick as vicar intercede to stop the fighting, but Frederick was a stickler for protocol. Neither party had contacted him, he countered. The Wolfenbüttel side seemed reluctant to fight the Hildesheim bishop. Only on May 9 did Frederick assume his role as vicar and demand a stop. By that time, both sides had been accumulating soldiers and supplies. George himself lent the Wolfenbüttel side two thousand soldiers. Philipp of Hesse (George's future son-in-law) sent one thousand soldiers to the other side. Many parties were bound by defense pacts. The feud simmered.[89]

Frederick received his notice of the imperial election from Archbishop Albrecht on February 13 in Grimma.[90] Exactly according to the terms of the Golden Bull, the Mainz archbishop notified the electors to convene in Frankfurt am Main to begin the election process June 17. The principal candidates for the election of the king of the Holy Roman empire were French king Francois and, of course, Maximilian's grandson and king of a united Spain, Karl. Also mentioned were Henry VIII, king of England, and even occasionally Frederick himself. Of all the candidates, only Frederick was also an elector. During the months leading up to the election, all six electors entertained personal pleas, offers of money, and proposals of power marriages.[91] Frederick in a double role was no exception to overtures. He thought as hard on the election as any issue. The election must be done in a just, prescribed way. He consistently answered those who sought his influence that the next king "has to be freely elected Roman king pursuant to the Golden Bull and not through noticeable obligations of 'aid.' "[92] In addition, he put his councillors and professors to work on two questions.[93] First, could a non-German be elected emperor? Second, could electors, if proven to have taken bribes, be allowed to vote? These gave rise to more questions just as relevant. Was Karl non-German? He grew up in the Netherlands fluent in Dutch and French, and although he claimed to speak German, it was dubious. And who could determine if an elector had taken a bribe? It did not have to be money. The rumor floated that the pope had offered the electors of Trier and Cologne the prestige of becoming cardinals if they supported the king of France.

Frederick, though he stated otherwise, succumbed himself to the promise of a superlative power marriage. In Augsburg the previous year, Maximilian himself had first mentioned a match between Frederick's nephew Johann Friedrich and the daughter of Herzog Johann of Kleve. Maximilian received no assent from Frederick other than the caution it should in no way be conditional on his vote. The emperor advised Karl of this, suggesting in addition that Karl should offer Frederick a bribe of 60,000 gulden and an annual pension of 8,000 gulden.[94] Karl actually bested Maximilian after the old warrior's death. He offered marriage between Johann Friedrich and his sister Katharina. Frederick did not refuse the offer but warned Johann Friedrich of the devious nature of such ploys. The French were not to be outdone. The king offered Frederick himself Anna, the twenty-seven-year-old widow of the Margrave of Monferrato. Anna was ruling Monferrato, the northwestern-most territory in Italy, in a regency for her infant son Boniface. In addition, the French king offered Johann Friedrich the daughter of his imperial ally Heinrich of Braunschweig-Lüneburg. This would have been a marriage of cousins.

It is clear that Frederick proceeded to negotiate over the greatest plum of all, the marriage of Johann Friedrich with Karl's sister. Could anyone doubt which way Frederick was leaning? It was in the best interest of his electorate and Johann Friedrich to get Karl elected. All the pledges to Maximilian at the Augsburg *Reichstag* to support Karl meant nothing now. They were made only to Maximilian, so his death voided them. On June 11, Frederick arrived by boat on the River Main. With thirty-three years as an elector, he was the grand old man. The candidate who had escaped the attention of many, though the pope considered him a better choice than Karl, was Frederick himself. The process began June 11 and took place in secret over many days. Frederick revealed virtually nothing at the time about the process but did flag some results.[95] He did not even confide to Johann in his letters, for fear they would be intercepted. No documents exist to reveal the election process. It is evident, though, that the electors had voted many times, and they had formulated quite a surprise for the victor. On June 28, the electors announced from St. Bartholomew Church that they had unanimously elected Karl, even though at the beginning the electors from Trier and Brandenburg had been unambiguous supporters of the French king. In hindsight, it is amazing that Albrecht of Mainz, the other Brandenburg, and the Palatine elector Ludwig V, who hated the Habsburgs, did not join the other two to clinch the election for the French king.

Archbishop Albrecht was in turmoil himself because of the rampant bribes. After only one day of deliberation, he came to Frederick privately wondering if the election could proceed. The archbishop of Mainz had a large part in administering the election. He had to administer an oath from each elector that said in part, "And my voice and vote, on said election, I will give without any pact, payment, price, or promise, or whatever such things may be called. So help me God and all the saints."[96] It seems Albrecht, lover of all the best things in life, nonetheless took his position seriously. And who did he seek for reliable help but the Saxon elector?

What went wrong for the French king? Obviously he could not obtain the four votes he needed. His supporters blanched at the prospect of another Habsburg. The archbishop of Trier backed off his vote for France and turned to Frederick as an alternative. He had visited Frederick virtually in the middle of the night. The electors of Palatine and Brandenburg probably also turned to Frederick, so all he had to do was cast his own vote for himself. Much speculation ensued about Frederick being elected himself but refusing the "honor." He was in poor health, and he did not intend to empty his electoral coffers for his own glory. If he had ruled the old Saxony that existed before 1485, perhaps he might have been tempted. But Maximilian for all his bluster and conquest had died virtually penniless. Credence for that short stint as the Roman king for Frederick, or at least a refusal by Frederick, is given by Spalatin.[97] Erasmus, Luther, and Johann Friedrich also believed Frederick could have had it but refused it. Spalatin believed Frederick had the votes of Trier, Palatine, and Brandenburg.[98] Moreover, the English envoy Richard Pace had said Frederick "was for three hours elected Roman king."[99]

When Karl learned what he had won with his election he, reticent as a quasi-German from the beginning, must have had sinking thoughts. The electors, probably led by Frederick and his last-minute supporters, had drafted thirty-four articles that the newly elected king had to accept: The emperor promised to protect the empire, all its separate members, and the Church and to secure to them peace and justice; to observe the regulations of the Golden Bull; to confer no office upon anyone not a German; not to make alliances with other states without the knowledge and consent of the electors; not to dispose privately of estates falling to the crown, but to use them as imperial possessions; to introduce no foreign military forces into the empire; to impose no taxes, and to call no diet, against the will of the electors; to use only the German or the Latin languages in official communications, except in places where another tongue was already usual; and to aid in improving the financial status of the electors.[100]

The electoral princes led by Frederick had tied the emperor's hands more than ever before.[101] The election became a hollow triumph at an enormous cost. The Spanish nobility was furious.[102] Did not everyone know the emperor warred constantly and pestered his nobles incessantly for men and money? Karl was not in Frankfurt. The actual coronation of Karl had to occur in Aachen, but it would not happen until the fall of 1520. In September 1517, nearly two years after Karl succeeded deceased King Ferdinand, seventeen-year-old Karl had sailed from the Netherlands to Spain. After he met his fifteen-year-old brother Ferdinand for the first time, they parted, and Ferdinand sailed to the Netherlands. Of course Frederick had met Karl. The boy was not impressive, slender with jaw long and pointed, and strikingly under-bit even for a Habsburg. He was dull and unscholarly. He stumbled in either German or Latin. His contrast to the lively, charismatic Maximilian must have struck Frederick as well as the other nobles. Karl, however, was not the fool his apish lower lip suggested.

TUMULT AT HOME

One day after Karl's election, Heinrich (the "middle one") of Braunschweig-Lüneburg attacked the other side of the "Hildesheim Feud" in full force. Heinrich of Wolfenbüttel fled, and the aggressors captured Erich I von Calenberg and more than one hundred nobles. Nobles were ordinarily ransomed for whatever they could bring in from their own fortunes, which could prove a treasure chest of money and properties for Heinrich of Lüneburg and Bishop Johann of Hildesheim. Heinrich of Lüneburg, fearing the reaction of Karl because he had actively supported the election of the French king, immediately appealed to Frederick to demand a truce and arbitrate a settlement. Envoys from the elector arranged a five-month armistice. For the moment, at least, Heinrich of Lüneburg was definitely a great winner.[103]

By the second half of July, Frederick had returned from Frankfurt to Torgau, where he was shocked to learn that Degenhart Pfeffinger was dead. Pfeffinger at only forty-eight was a victim of Frederick's great dread, the plague. His chancellor, a fellow pilgrim to the Holy Land as well as a serious relic collector, was close to Frederick. Thus Frederick had lost two of his greatest friends in a span of six months. A few weeks later, Frederick was laid low himself.[104] It was no passing sickness, but according to Spalatin he suffered for eight weeks an accumulation of dizzying fever, colic, "stone," and gout.[105] Recovery was slow, but the crippling, painful gout remained. Travel was possible only if carried.[106]

During this time, Luther, at Spalatin's request, wrote a comforting tract for the elector. In August and September he wrote in Latin "*Tessaradecas consolatoria pro laborantibus et oneratis*" ("Fourteen Consolations for Those who Labor and Are Heavy-laden"). Spalatin translated it into German, softening some of Luther's sharpness. Fourteen was the traditional number of spiritual saints or "Helpers." Luther felt Frederick may have requested this to divert him from his more biting tracts. Evidence shows, on the other hand, that Frederick sent Luther's tracts to someone in Grimma as early as Easter 1519.[107] He sent tracts to others later. It could be reasonably argued that cautious Frederick did this merely to solicit opinions about Luther's writings. Yet he did seem to relish Luther's hard-struck opinions, which Spalatin often read to him. In October 1519, the electoral adviser Markus Schart made a request that resulted in Luther's *A Sermon on Preparing to Die*. This was possibly intended for Frederick. There was long church tradition in contemplating the "good death" and preparing for it.[108]

Meanwhile, Frederick read Luther's report of the Leipzig Disputation, which took place from late June to mid-July while Frederick returned from the election in Frankfurt.[109] At first, Bishop Adolf of Merseburg on his own volition had tried to stop the debate completely, declaring the pope had issued a decree on indulgences.[110] Duke George, who had received little cooperation from his bishop or his university for the disputation he had approved, was furious. Of course the disputation started anyway.

Petrus Mosellanus, the Greek scholar at the University of Leipzig, was there. He recorded his impressions of the thirty-five-year-old Luther:

> Martinus is of medium height, haggard, and so emaciated with care and much study that one can almost count all the bones in his body. Nevertheless, he is still in the vigor of manhood. His voice rings clear and distinct. ... In his manner and social intercourse he is cultivated and affable, not at all gloomy or arrogant, always in a good humor, in company agreeable, cheerful, and jocose. No matter how hard his opponent threatens him, he is always confident and joyous.[111]

Mosellanus could have been describing mannerisms of Maximilian. It was just the way Germans wanted to see themselves.

Luther's own account of the experience describes a litany of dirty tricks by Johann Eck and his supporters to assure themselves a victory. Of interest was Luther's assessment of Duke George that he conveyed to Spalatin:

> The most illustrious prince also called me to visit him alone and talked with me at length. ... He stated that the Bohemians were greatly encouraged by me and also that with my Lord's Prayer I had caused confusion among many conscientious people. ... But I was not so dull that I could not distinguish between the pipe and the piper. I was grieved that such a wise and pious prince was open to the influence of others and followed their opinions, especially when I saw and experienced how like a prince he spoke when he spoke his own thoughts.[112]

Luther claimed victory after seventeen days of debate. So did Eck, his claim supported by noisy partisans. As to who won the actual debate, one may consider the opinion of Mosellanus:

> Luther is extraordinarily learned. Above all, he possesses such an astonishing knowledge of the Bible that he knows almost all of it by heart. He understands enough Greek and Hebrew to be able to give an independent judgment of the value of the translations. He is never at a loss in speaking, such an immense stock of ideas and words does he have at his command. But what most men blame in him is that he is more imprudent and cutting in his criticism than is safe. ...

> Carlstadt, however, is even more impetuous. . . . Eck's credit has received a great blow among us on account of the disputation. Almost everyone here is now more kindly disposed toward Martinus than before.[113]

After the debate, it became apparent that Eck was on a mission. Eck wrote Frederick, apologizing for his vehemence but explaining that he had to oppose those arrogant enough to declare that they understood Scriptures better than the Church Fathers. He accused Luther of supporting Jan Hus. Opponents had recognized that Luther's refusal to refute all of Hus, who was burned as a heretic in 1415, was an effective weapon.[114] Saxons were particularly thin-skinned about the Hussites who had later invaded Saxony. During the debate, when Luther was lured into defending a point made by Hus, Duke George blurted, "That's the plague!"[115] Impulsively on July 23, Eck rode to Altenburg and tried once again to see Frederick,[116] but again Frederick ignored him. He merely solicited the opinions of Luther and Karlstadt on Eck's letter.

Wittenbergers flooded the academic world with their own reports and retorts. They trumpeted that Karlstadt and Luther had obviously triumphed. Eck could not counter this attack, they claimed. He was a lion in person but a mouse in print. Not helping his cause were favorable reports about Luther coming from Mosellanus and even people in Duke George's own court.[117] The duke's physician, Heinrich Stromer von Auerbach, gushed in a letter to Spalatin, "The man, believe me, is worthy of being immortalized."[118]

The Luther commotion died down for months, even though Miltitz still floundered around with transparent maneuvers to entice Luther from his protection.[119] Frederick would no longer see Miltitz, and the papal envoy gave up his bluff. Miltitz did in September finally surrender the Golden Rose to Frederick's advisers in Altenburg.[120] He added the warning that if Luther was not surrendered to the pope, the entire electorate would go under the ban. The advisers feigned bewilderment. Frederick wrote to the pope that he had "stood idly by" during the Luther affair. He wanted Luther out of his territory. Nevertheless, Luther was willing to submit to a hearing by the archbishop of Trier at the next *Reichstag*.[121] Did the old elector know no *Reichstag* would be held in 1520?

Possibly lulled by the clownish behavior of Miltitz, Luther did not suspect the fury building in Rome, but Frederick did. Rome was incensed. Miltitz had squandered one entire year.[122] In January 1520, Rome geared up its entire machinery and thus began an onslaught. They badgered Frederick from every quarter. He had staked out his position clearly to Cajetan. Student problems in Wittenberg did not help Frederick's disposition.[123] University students insisted on carrying knives, because Lucas Cranach's apprentices carried knives. Rumors of Luther's assassination floated around Saxony, and he was not pleased to know that half the men in Wittenberg were armed. The groups clashed, often at night after drinking. Frederick issued an ordinance, "Articles for Peaceful Behavior," banning weapons for both groups. He set fines at three gulden, and a repeat offense could mean expulsion. He set curfew in summer at ten o'clock in the evening, in winter at nine. The president of the university fought the measures and incited the students, much to Luther's displeasure. Frederick could not be dissuaded from his ordinance, even if that hurt attendance at the university. No weapons.

Extensive reform of the university was virtually lost in the tumult in 1518.[124] It began with visitations from the electorate, spurred by complaints that some professors were not giving their lectures. It ended with significant reform, rammed through by Luther. Luther-authority Brecht summed up the reform:

> The substance of the Wittenberg university reform was the common product of the Reformation and of humanism. It consisted of rejection of scholasticism and a turn to a Bible-centered theology, which received its special accents from the theology of the Reformation. The new movement's connection with humanism secured for it a high level of scholarship and prestige, guaranteed its intellectual breadth, and prevented a complete break between it and the old educational tradition. . . . This bore fruit at once.[125]

The new curriculum plus the almost legendary figure of Luther and the growing prestige of Melanchthon drew students like a magnet in the years 1519 to 1521. "The city was swarming with students like an anthill. In the 1519 summer semester it was already being said that the number of students was rising like a flood. A year later many students had to turn back because the city was overcrowded. Luther asked the elector at that time to take steps against the prevailing inflation."[126]

Luther's intense preparation for the Leipzig debate greatly accelerated his theological conclusions. The framework of the Reformation was in his head, and he could not write fast enough.[127] In the last six months of 1519, Luther would publish twenty tracts, many of them commentaries on Scripture.[128] In one tract Luther had asserted that both wine and bread may be taken in the Eucharist, agreeing with Jan Huss. Immediately he was attacked, even Duke George now claiming that Luther was actually a Bohemian. Frederick was alarmed enough to request proof. Luther had to provide Spalatin details of his Saxon background. He did so with much wit, offering the counts of Mansfeld as witnesses to his Saxon lineage.[129] Luther knew that Frederick had asked the question, goaded by Cousin George. The duke had remained hostile since the Leipzig Disputation. He harangued everyone he could against Luther. In February 1520, Luther wrote his critics about the Eucharist in such a way that it was highly insulting to Duke George, whom he correctly suspected was behind the attack. Frederick, alarmed again, asked Luther to restrain himself.[130]

In previous years Luther had regarded the poet Ulrich von Hutten, one of the men behind *Letters to Obscure Men* in the Reuchlin affair, as repulsive and juvenile. Hutten had regarded Luther as a squabbling monk. By February 1520, both men regarded each other highly. Although Hutten was volcanic like Karlstadt (and much more violent physically), he had made a great discovery. He found a treatise from 1457 by Lorenzo Valla that proved the "Donation of Constantine" was a forgery. Rome had invoked the "Donation" for centuries as proof that the Roman Emperor Constantine had transferred his sovereignty over the Roman world to the pope. Hutten's exposure floored Luther. The monstrous deception unleashed his full fury against Rome. He slowly began to believe the pope was the biblical Antichrist of the Last Days. Luther's thinking was becoming apocalyptic.[131] The world was in its last days.

In March, Gabriel della Volta, the general of the order of Augustinian Hermits, began to hector Vicar Staupitz about Luther. By May, Staupitz would have to resign as vicar. In Rome from May 21 through June 1, four consistories discussed the imminent bull against Luther. The *Exsurge Domine* (threatening excommunication) was the worst kept secret in Christendom. Luther himself had known about it for at least three months. Numerous knights had written him to offer support, chief among them the truly dangerous Franz von Sickingen.[132] Luther wrote Spalatin that though the knights had freed him of "fear of men," the fury of the devils might replace it.

Frederick was still insisting he had been steadfastly neutral. In July 1520, he wrote to Cardinal Riario.

> I have never hitherto undertaken to defend either the writings or the sermons of Dr. Martin Luther, nor do I do so today, as I showed to his Holiness's legate Cardinal Cajetan, and to the papal nuncio Charles Miltitz, both by my letters and orally. Moreover I hear that Dr. Luther has never shown himself unready obediently to appear, armed with a safe-conduct, before just, convenient, disinterested and prudent judges to defend his doctrine in person, and, when he has learned better and more holy doctrine from Scripture, submissively to obey. . . . So no one can rightly blame me on this account.[133]

The *Exsurge Domine* bull was being delivered throughout the empire by papal nuncios Johann Eck and Girolamo Aleander. Eck had the south and Saxony. Reception was hostile but not lethal as he worked his way north. Luther had his own surprise. In August, he published in German "To the Christian Nobility of the German Nation Concerning the Reform of the Christian Estate."[134] It was wildly popular. Within two weeks the large print run of four thousand copies sold out. More were printed. Luther's friend Johann Lang characterized it as a "war trumpet" against the pope.[135] Its vehemence stunned Luther's cautious friends. Luther knew it was aggressive, but he also knew many were pleased, even stirred by it. Even fiery Duke George admitted the tract grew out of the corruption and greed of Rome that in turn corrupted the princes of the empire. Some had to notice it was unifying the voices of the nobility throughout the empire. Luther's large number of demands and their breadth surprised Frederick.

Frederick had to be finally aware that Luther and the printing press were a force beyond what anyone could imagine. Even Spalatin could not keep him informed, because Spalatin could not keep up with the directions and number of teachings spinning from the Luther maelstrom. Sometimes Frederick's optimism wilted under the Luther storm. In

August 1520, Frederick sent Johann more Luther writings, but he had to admit, "I fear they will expel from me the monk because they want to enforce on him, as one says, the ban and on everybody who is following him." He added, "God does it for the best!"[136]

KARL TAKES THE CROWN

On October 23, 1520, fifteen months after his election, Karl V appeared in Aachen to be crowned with enormous pomp.[137] Four ceremonies were required. During the coronation, the Elector of Saxony was to hold high the sword of the empire, but Frederick was not there. He tried to go, leaving Saxony in September, but traveling only as far as the Three Kings' lodging in Cologne. Aachen was still a two-day ride to the west. Gout and sickness waylaid him, and he had also heard rumors of plague there. The new king of the empire treated him with honor and came to him. Apparently in Cologne Karl assured Frederick that Luther would not be condemned without a hearing.[138] Frederick refused to see the papal nuncios Carraciolo and Aleander traveling with Karl, but they persisted. Aleander made two demands: Frederick must burn all of Luther's books, and he must imprison or deliver Luther to the pope. He requested an answer.

A few weeks later, Aleander described Frederick in a letter to powerful Cardinal Medici.

> The Saxon is certainly an able prince, but is led astray by his councillors, who are all disciples of Luther. He is angry at us, I hear, on account of a *commendam* [benefice] to which his natural son had been appointed in Rome, notwithstanding which, and although in possession of the certificate of appointment, he was obliged, on his return to Germany . . . to pay a large sum to a cardinal. The elector, who in general is a close, taciturn man, who does not easily betray his thoughts, cannot get over this, as one of his people told me.[139]

If true, there were many issues with Rome troubling Frederick.

On November 5, Frederick met Erasmus.[140] Spalatin was present as Frederick's flawless interpreter of Latin. Knowing Erasmus was as close-mouthed as he himself was, Frederick looked him straight in the eye and asked his opinion of the Luther affair. Erasmus disliked Luther's sharp attacks against the church as much as he disliked the actions of the pope.

He feared a schism in Christianity. As an adviser to Karl, was he dancing around the new king's position? "Has Luther erred?" asked Frederick. Erasmus answered, "Yes, in two things; first that he assailed the pope's crown and the other is that he attacked the monks' bellies."[141] Erasmus wanted to preserve what was good in Luther's writings. An impartial panel assembled by several rulers of Europe, including the "emperor," could judge Luther. He would thus be admonished, not by the pope but by secular powers. This did not preclude punishment if necessary.

With his conversation with Erasmuc in mind, Frederick had his advisers respond to the two demands of papal nuncio Aleander. The response was prefaced by the elector's now standard denial of being involved in promoting Luther. Frederick, however, was not willing to surrender his Saxon subject Luther, although he would allow Luther to be examined by "reasonable, educated, pious, and irreproachable judges."[142] Futhermore, until that examination, as a Christian prince Frederick would not approve of burning Luther's books and tracts in electoral Saxony.[143]

Frederick departed Cologne November 7. He sent a letter to Karl V, asking that Luther be examined at the 1521 *Reichstag* in Worms.[144] By November 17, imperial councillors had assented to his request. All seemed optimistic that the end of the Luther affair was in sight. In the meantime, Luther had another thick tract printed, his most violent one yet against the pope, even against the traditional underpinnings of the church. Nevertheless "Babylonian Captivity" was in Latin, intended for scholars. Luther was not trying to incite lay people. Its obscurity was no better protected than that of his Ninety-five Theses. "Babylonian Captivity" was an earthquake. Upon reading it, Erasmus gasped, "The breach is irreparable."[145] The long tract evaluated the seven sacraments of the church. Luther defined a sacrament as that which is directly instituted by Christ in the Scriptures. He recognized only the Lord's Supper and Baptism, grudgingly allowing penance as a third. He had disallowed confirmation, marriage, extreme unction, and ordination. His repudiation of ordination virtually destroyed the hierarchy of clericalism in the church, setting the stage for his concept of "a priesthood of all believers."[146] He had even undermined much of the Mass. The impact on ever resolving his dispute with the church was cataclysmic. The disputation had become a breach, which now had become a chasm.

If his opponents were incensed, they would soon be in flames. For that fiery notion was what Luther incarnated on December 10, 1520, with the papal bull in Wittenberg. Scholar Brecht noted, "Melanchthon, through a notice posted at the city church, invited everyone concerned about evangelical truth to assemble at nine o'clock at the chapel of the Holy Cross, which lay outside the Elster gate."[147] There in a display of defiance before a crowd of mostly professors and students, Luther and supporters burned the bull and all the papal books of law. Symbolically, this area was where the pit for burning carrion was located. Within days, Karl V voided all arrangements regarding the resolution of the Luther affair. He withdrew his invitation to Worms for Luther. All the negotiations had to begin again.

Just days before his fifty-eighth birthday, Frederick must have felt one hundred years old.

CHAPTER 8

NEW TEACHINGS
AND A WORLD UPSIDE DOWN

(1521–25)

> "There lies on earth not much for a man."
> —Proverb favored by Frederick the Wise[1]

THE GREATEST *REICHSTAG*: WORMS 1521

Luther's writing during 1520 had been prodigious. He produced four major works: "The Sermon on Good Works" in May, "The Address to the German Nobility" in August, "The Babylonian Captivity" in September, and "The Freedom of the Christian Man" in November. These four writings are virtually the foundation of the Reformation.[2] Luther may have obsessed the thoughts of Rome, but that was in no way true for the imperial circle. France and the empire, both flexing their muscles under new youthful sovereigns, were drifting toward war once again.[3] Nothing had changed. King Francois apparently felt he still had friends in the empire, even writing Frederick and other electors in December 1520 to assure them that he wanted Karl's transition to power to be peaceful. On the other hand, he wished the electors would discourage Karl from meddling in Italy. The *Reichstag* in Worms was to begin in January 1521. Emperor Karl made it clear that he, too, sought the loyalty of the estates.[4] Attending in addition to the imperial circle were 384 representatives of the imperial estates: the electors, 49 prince-bishops (including four archbishops), 31 secular princes, 65 prelates, 14 abbots, 4 religious orders, 137 counts and lords, and 84 free/imperial cities.

The fourth article in Karl's election "capitulation" in 1519 called for the renewal of the imperial governing council (*Reichsregiment*).[5] Frederick had been adamant about it, though Maximilian had seemed to be able to thwart it easily enough. Frederick saw it as a necessity, for when the emperor was absent, significant wars broke out such as the recent ones in Württemberg and in Braunschweig. Frederick wanted the imperial governing council to be a real regency in the absence of the emperor, with full power to enlist military forces similar to the Swabian League, not to make war but to prevent war. The estates, however, had let the matter die since Karl's acceptance of the articles in 1519.

Negotiations between the estates and the imperial circle on the nature of the council lasted until May. It was obvious Karl wanted a weak, ineffective council. The main distinction was that the estates wanted a permanent imperial governing council; the emperor wanted an imperial regency council that convened only in his absence. The emperor won that point. Nonetheless, six electors or their representatives plus four imperial appointees belonged to the council of twenty-two. Moreover, one of the electors had to be present or represented at all times.[6] The compromise resolution of the council was read to the *Reichstag* May 21.

That same day, Karl appealed to the estates to help him with war against France: they must send King Francois the message that the empire was united and firm in their defense. On May 23, the estates agreed to support Karl in war, believing they had agreed only to defend the empire against France or the Swiss, not to campaign in Italy. That same day, the electors, perhaps sensing the imperial governing council would be ineffectual for their interests, rejuvenated the electoral princes' association. Again, that same day Frederick departed the *Reichstag* without taking the oath. Was he disillusioned, realizing the new emperor was, after all, just another Habsburg who would reinstitute the old Maximilian gimmickry while he resisted all reform? Two days later, the emperor, who had the right, designated the governor of the imperial governing council. Did he choose Frederick, the veteran of thirty-five years in imperial affairs? No; Karl appointed his eighteen-year-old brother Ferdinand, who had been raised in Spain. The future of the council looked as grim as plague. It was yet another dismal example of why the Holy Roman Empire of the German nations never performed like a nation or an empire.[7]

Another black cloud over Frederick at the *Reichstag* had been the marriage arranged in 1519 between his nephew Johann Friedrich and Karl's sister Katharina. In 1520, Elector Joachim of Brandenburg had wryly wished Johann a better outcome than his own in marriage contracts with the Habsburgs. That June of 1520, Karl said his sister could not possibly come to Saxony while her mother was so ill, causing Frederick's brother Johann to hear many snide comments. Frederick tried to calm him. Karl, nevertheless, called Johann Friedrich, now seventeen, his "dear brother-in-law" at the *Reichstag* in Worms.[8] On May 7, Karl promised to send Katharina to Saxony six months after he returned to Spain, along with half her dowry of 200,000 gulden. Therefore, Katharina and the first half of the dowry would appear sometime in 1522. Frederick himself had been insulted by the Habsburgs in a marriage scheme. Was it to happen once again in his reign?

Frederick had seemed eager for the *Reichstag* in Worms. For once he had appeared early for a *Reichstag*—three weeks early. Did he have in mind manning the imperial governing council, then dominating it himself as governor, which the other estates would willingly allow? The answer appears to be totally unrelated. Young nephew Johann Friedrich was the honoree of the planned jousting tournament of several weeks that seems to have been the real center of attraction at the *Reichstag*.[9] Johann Friedrich competed himself, achieving modest results. In the "*rennen und stechen*" his opponents threw him four out of five times.[10] He had flair though, his horse's blanket displaying "1521" and the boastful "My luck runs on stilts." The young prince had started an elegant book on tournaments. Karl was effusive, asking him for materials on jousting. Johann Friedrich was, after all, going to be his brother-in-law.

Other business occurred at the *Reichstag*, not least among them the "*Gravamina*" (grievances).[11] Yet the presentation of these 102 grievances against the pope and the Roman Church seemed to have occurred almost concurrently with the appearance of Martin Luther.[12] Their interdependence and time for presentation had been discussed for some time prior to the *Reichstag*. Frederick's chancellor Brück had negotiated tirelessly for weeks with Karl's imperial confessor Glapion about Luther's appearance.[13] Glapion had been busy. He had also visited Luther-sympathizers Franz von Sickingen and Ulrich von Hutten at nearby Ebernburg castle and apparently removed them as an element of danger by contracting them to the emperor. But his visit accomplished more. He duped Sickingen's pastor Martin Bucer into a plot to lure Luther out of his safe-conduct caravan led by burly Imperial Herald Caspar Sturm.[14] Bucer intercepted Luther's caravan to Worms at Oppenheim and entreated him to go with him to the Ebernburg. Luther instinctively smelled a trap. Why couldn't Glapion meet him in Worms? He refused Bucer, and the plot failed.[15]

Although the lords and clerics watched jousting, gambled, and enjoyed women as they usually did, intrigues were everywhere. A smell of danger permeated the *Reichstag*. The papal nuncio Aleander had written Rome in February, "All of Germany is in an utter uproar; nine-tenths of the people are shouting, 'Luther,' and the other tenth . . . 'Death to the Roman court!' "[16] Still, there was also a sense of hostility to Luther from the imperial circle, the papal representatives and at least two of the six electors (Brandenburg and Mainz).

Frederick knew the situation was ominous and unpredictable. He wrote brother Johann before Luther's arrival, "The bishops and cardinals are against him. Would to God that I could help Martin right and proper, I would not fall short."[17] Unsaid were the dozens of machinations Frederick had already ordered.

Finally behind his escort, the imperial herald Sturm, Luther entered Worms the morning of April 16. Few events at the time were recorded by more people than Luther's visit to Worms. He stayed in the same lodging as Frederick's advisers Friedrich von Thun and Philipp von Feilitzsch (and imperial marshal Ulrich von Pappenheim) and shared a room with Frederick's advisers Hans Schott and Bernhard von Hirschfeld. The next day, Aleander and Glapion told Luther that he was to only answer their questions during the hearing and offer nothing further. That afternoon, Pappenheim summoned Luther to appear, and with Sturm he escorted Luther to the bishop's residence adjoining the cathedral. Luther entered the hall wearing the robe of the Augustinian order with its leather belt. His freshly shaved tonsure gleamed. This may have been the first time Frederick had seen his Wittenberg monk. The archbishop of Trier's adviser, Johann von der Ecken, informed Luther that he was summoned for two reasons only: to acknowledge writings published under his name as his own, and after that to affirm his books or to retract them. At the request of Luther's legal adviser, Hieronymus Schurff, someone read the titles of the writings.

Luther faltered, timidly answering in German, then in Latin. In a weak voice he asserted that replying in haste as to whether he would affirm or recant so many writings was dangerous, not to his own safety but to his soul. He needed time to review so many writings. Was he delaying or truly unprepared to answer for a pile of his writings? The imperial circle conferred with the princes. They granted Luther one day; he was to appear again the next day at the same time. Opponents gloated over his shaky start.

The next day the other *Reichstag* business delayed Luther's appearance so long that torches illumined the hall when he returned. This time his voice was loud and firm. In German he apologized for any uncomely behavior the day before; he was, after all, only a monk, not a member of the court. He then categorized his writings into three groups. This was a shrewd counter to the one-word answers demanded by the nuncios.[18] How could he not discuss each group? One group spoke of the piety of faith and morals; surely even his opposition knew they were innocent and useful for Christians. The second group criticized the papacy and corrupt practices of the church. How could he retract what even the *Gravamina* objected to about the church? The third group was directed against individuals who had attacked him. He admitted he may have been too sharp in his retorts, though he could not retract what he thought was true.

Although his own legal adviser objected, Luther went on to repeat his entire argument in Latin. Von der Ecken brusquely disputed his entire argument and asked if Luther would recant. Luther's answer would echo across Europe:

> Unless I am convinced by the testimony of the Scriptures or by clear reason (for I do not trust either in the pope or in councils alone, since it is well known that they have often erred and contradicted themselves), I am bound by the Scriptures I have quoted and my conscience is captive to the Word of God. I cannot and I will not retract anything, since it is neither safe nor right to go against conscience. May God help me. Amen.[19]

As Luther was escorted out of the hall, a Spaniard in Karl's imperial circle shouted, "To the pyre with him!" Luther was ecstatic afterward. "I've come through, I've come through." Frederick, veteran of thirty-five years of *Reichstags*, was elsewhere but uncharacteristically emotional. He was more than pleased with Luther's repetition in Latin. "Father Martinus spoke well before the lord emperor, all the princes, and the estates." Luther was, after all, his professor of the Bible and reflected on Frederick's university. The elector added, "He is much too bold for me."[20] But it was an approving censure. This may have been a turning point for Frederick.[21] Luther was no longer just a scholar like Reuchlin. He was flesh and blood, cadaverously thin but as sturdy and brave as any knight. He was a Christian of conscience—and a Saxon. Moreover, Luther's illumination of God's Word from Holy Scriptures seemed so straightforward and logical. "Things of faith should be as pure as an eye," Frederick once told Spalatin.[22]

In general, Luther supporters were well pleased. Karl V was not. On April 19, he had a statement read to the estates. He noted it was clear "that an individual monk who stood with his opinion against all of thousand-year-old Christendom had to be in error." The emperor "regretted that he had not proceeded against him and his false doctrine earlier." He would send him to Wittenberg under safe conduct. Then he would "proceed against him as against a notorious heretic, however, and he also expected that the estates, on the basis of their promise and as good Christians, would conduct themselves accordingly."[23]

The imperial estates answered April 20. They praised the fortitude of the emperor to protect the faith. Nevertheless, the estates would attempt one more time to resolve the Luther affair. After all, Luther had said he was willing to be convinced it he was wrong. Then no one could say he had not been tried fairly. The estates offered this proposal for the emperor's approval. He granted a three-day hearing. The emperor was silent on what would happen if Luther did not recant. Members of the commission numbered ten. Two were electors: the archbishop of Trier (Richard von Greiffenklau) and Joachim of Brandenburg. Duke George of Saxony and Chancellor Jerome Vehus (for the Margrave of Baden) represented the princes. Others were the bishop of Augsburg (Christoph von Stadion) and the bishop of Brandenburg (Jerome Schulze), the grandmaster of the Teutonic order (Dietrich von Cleen), Count George of Wertheim, Dr. Hans Bock from Strasbourg, and Dr. Conrad Peutinger from Augsburg. The members were about evenly split for or against Luther, though some were virtually neutral, only wanting an end to the affair.

On April 24, Luther met with the commission. Vehus, a Luther sympathizer, led the hearing. They intended to admonish Luther, not debate him. The flinty resolve of Luther obviously was still not known to most of them. After Vehus described a relatively easy way for Luther to put an end to the affair, Luther responded. He finished his response in the exact position he had taken before the emperor. The commission, except for the archbishop of Trier, left Luther. Also there with the archbishop was his adviser Von der Eck. There for Luther were Hieronymus Schurff and Nikolaus von Amsdorf, and Johann Cochlaeus was there as an observer for the papal nuncios. The discussion proceeded in a disjointed way and ended bitterly, with Cochlaeus calling Luther a madman. Cochlaeus visited Luther's lodging, still fuming, and asked Luther to renounce his safe conduct. The two of them would debate to the death! Luther treated Cochlaeus, such a transparent agent for the nuncios, as a joke.[24]

The commission fell apart. One more meaningful meeting took place with Luther debating Peutinger and Vehus for three hours. By this time Frederick had departed for Saxony, annoyed at the makeup of the commission but confident his friend the archbishop of Trier and Frederick's representatives could control the situation. The archbishop met with Luther alone. Richard von Greiffenklau, very hardnosed but just as sly, was overtly critical of Luther.[25] Frederick's trust in him made some wonder if the two friends had secretly agreed to something. Apparently Greiffenklau asked Luther himself how to resolve the situation. Possibly Luther saw the futility of further negotiations and took the approach of Gamaliel: let subsequent events reveal the will of God. On April 26, Luther was released by all parties and allowed to leave Worms.

Two days later in a letter to Lucas Cranach, Luther mocked the proceedings, "Nothing else was done there than this: Are these your books? Yes. Do you want to renounce them or not? No. Then go away! O we blind Germans how childishly we act and allow the Romanists to mock and fool us in such a pitiful way!" He then added that he would soon "be hidden away."[26]

LUTHER SWEPT UP INTO THE "LAND OF THE BIRDS"

Frederick entrusted the "kidnapping" of Luther to his advisers. He wanted no details.[27] He was so secretive that he informed brother Johann only that he would like to help Luther. This way there was no paper trail of evidence that Frederick himself had defied the emperor; at the same time, Luther was safe.[28] The so-called "Edict of Worms," issued by the emperor supposedly with the full consent of the estates, was intended to enforce the papal bull threatening the excommunication of Luther. The edict declared Luther a heretic and stated that no one was to aid Luther. Moreover, the edict demanded that any imperial subject was to take Luther prisoner and deliver him to the emperor. Amazingly, just before he left the *Reichstag* Frederick had wrangled from the emperor an exemption for himself from this mandate.[29] Frederick did not have to enforce the edict! How hard it was to refuse Frederick. He dominated the estates, as proven already by capitulation articles with Karl's election and Frederick's manipulation of the Luther affair. Karl had great plans ahead against France and Italy, and he did not want the most powerful prince in the empire thwarting his every turn.

It would be many months before facts of Luther's abduction leaked out. On April 29, Luther dismissed the imperial herald Sturm near Friedberg in Hesse. Ignoring the safe conduct restriction against preaching during his return to Wittenberg (as well as jeopardizing Frederick's plan), he preached in both Hersfeld and Eisenach. Luther insisted the Word of God must not be bound. No doubt much to the relief of those entrusted by the elector to hide Luther, on May 4 they finally sprung their plan near the fortress of Altenstein. A swarm of riders "kidnapped" Luther and rushed him off on horseback. Luther made sure he had first secreted his Greek New Testament and the Hebrew Bible.

Before midnight the exhausted monk was in lofty heights, safe inside the legendary fortress Wartburg. Surely Luther could not stir up anything from this airy refuge. Luther, who found humor in the most distressing situations, would write friends that he was in "the land of the birds."[30] Wartburg castle commandant (*Hauptmann*), Hans von Berlepsch, was as cautious as Frederick. He tried futilely to control correspondence between irrepressible Luther and the world outside.

Frederick must have heard Luther was going to translate the Greek New Testament into German. He sent a strong hint that Luther should produce some postils too.[31] Frederick had long wanted these. By June, Luther already produced "On Confession: Whether the Pope Has the Power to Require It" and dedicated it to Franz von Sickingen.[32] Was the dedication a not so subtle warning to his opponents that the knights overwhelmingly supported him? Although developed by Holy Scripture, "On Confession" was not an abstract theological tract. Its goal was to change the practice of confession from a priestly inquisition to one that was freely to God, even if no priest was there at all.

Luther learned that a colleague Bartholomäus Bernhardi of Kemberg had married in May. He knew Bernhardi would be condemned for breaking his vows. That triggered his look into the scriptural basis for taking religious vows. Luther convinced himself that vows taken to merit salvation were false to God and must be dissolved. He realized this interpretation negated vows taken by members of orders, even himself. If a vow was taken without the desire to merit salvation, it should be kept. He developed these thoughts further, finding more scriptural proof. He dedicated "On Monastic Vows" to his father, who had angrily opposed his religious life. This tract, so volatile for thousands of monks and nuns, he released to Spalatin in November 1521. Spalatin suppressed it. Frederick would not allow it.

Spalatin also informed Luther that Frederick would not allow him to attack Cardinal Albrecht of Mainz.[33] In his continuing fight against indulgences, Luther was going to publicly attack Albrecht and his "brothel" in Halle. Luther boiled a while, then exploded at Spalatin, "I will not suffer what you say, that the Elector will not allow me to write against Mayence [Mainz] nor anything that can disturb the public peace. I will see you and the Elector and the whole world to perdition first."[34] Luther could at least attack Albrecht privately. Somehow he was able to send Albrecht a letter in December 1521, in which Luther gloated, "And let not your Grace think Luther is dead," adding the threat that he would "gladly and joyfully put his trust in God and will start such a game with the Cardinal of Mayence as few people expect. . . . If you unexpectedly become a laughing-stock, remember that I have warned you."[35]

Luther became more and more contentious. His health was poor, suffering from the worst kind of fissuring constipation. He was gregarious and accustomed to being in a whirl of ideas. He had heard of Karlstadt's extreme mishandling of the situation in Wittenberg. He even lashed out at the elector for asking for spiritual writings. How much longer could the Wartburg hold him? He did not wait long. He had to return to Wittenberg. Melanchthon was the wisest head there, but he was too young, too frail to lead hot-blooded men. On December 3, Luther slipped back to Wittenberg, disguised as young knight George ("Junker

Georg"), with thick, curly hair black as soot with beard to match.[36] He stayed with Melanchthon. He was pleased with the situation. No one had been killed or even injured. Yes, a few people, especially monks and priests, had been roughed up, but was it that unusual for drinking students to rough up a monk?

But Luther was angry to hear his writings had not reached anyone there. Frederick and Spalatin were keeping him under wraps. Luther wrote Spalatin to complain about this "drop of bitterness," but he was cool-headed enough to add, "I want to keep my arrival in Wittenberg and my departure a secret [from Frederick]."[37] By December 12, he was back at the Wartburg, where he settled in to the task of translating the Greek New Testament into the German of the Saxon court. His irritation over Karlstadt's extreme behavior might have been calmed by the news that Karlstadt was soon to marry. That would take the wind from Karlstadt's sails.[38]

Yet no sooner had Luther returned to the Wartburg than a problem arose in Wittenberg with the so-called "Zwickau prophets": Nicholas Storch and Markus Stübner. Zwickau, one of Frederick's largest cities, was known for making fabric. Many rich merchants lived there and even more poor people. Since 1519, the "prophets," with Thomas Müntzer, had been developing a theology that they claimed came to them from the Holy Spirit. As the spiritually elect, the prophets and Müntzer should rule. Müntzer in particular was adept at inciting the weavers, and violence erupted. All this had happened under Johann's watch. Frederick had turned more and more "church questions" (*Kirchenfragen*) over to Johann,[39] who was hesitant to use force. What if these men were truly inspired? All three men fled before Johann took action. The two Zwickau prophets came to Wittenberg and began preaching their new theology. Frederick himself had to intervene, but he, too, hesitated. Were they truly inspired? The prophets were clever at quoting Scriptures; they outdid Melanchthon and Amsdorf in this way. Where was Luther?

Luther intended to return to Wittenberg at Easter in 1522, after occupying his time with the New Testament. He wrote Melanchthon, scolding him for being so timid with the Zwickau prophets. The fact that the prophets did not baptize infants did not bother him. Infant Baptism was not mandated in Scripture. He cautioned against jailing them as Duke George, who could not resist writing Frederick to tell him what should be done, was goading Frederick to do. Frederick icily wrote him that he wished to read nothing "that is no business for your Honor to write."[40] Because of Frederick's rebuffs, George often complained to Johann too.[41]

Luther wrote Frederick in February congratulating him on acquiring a relic and added almost as an afterthought that he was returning to Wittenberg. Unwritten was his alarm over the commotion in Wittenberg in January and February. The Zwickau prophets and Karlstadt agitated each other to more extreme views. They also riled citizens to violence. Mobs stormed both the church at the Augustinian monastery and the town church, smashing altars, removing "images," and dumping unction oil.[42] They even thought organs and other musical instruments had to be removed.

Frederick had heard enough. On February 13, he sent instructions to his university and to the All Saints' Foundation of the Castle Church:

> We have gone too fast. The common man has been incited to frivolity, and no one has been edified. We should have consideration for the weak. Images should be left until further notice. . . . No essential portion of the mass should be omitted. Moot points should be discussed. Carlstadt should not preach any more.[43]

We have gone too fast. Does that sound neutral? Frederick had for years approved reform. This statement suggests he regarded the "Luther affair" as needed reform, not a schism from Rome.

Frederick continued to feign neutrality, but his advisers did not. Even brother Johann did not. Johann had, at least to Frederick, confided his belief in Luther probably as early as 1520 and definitely by January 1521.[44] That month leading up to the *Reichstag* in Worms, he wrote Frederick, "I also am completely loathe to hear that Martin should be prosecuted, but because I trust God who will not desert us, there still are many more honest people who will do the best for Martin, for I think he is on the right way."[45] Young Johann Friedrich was even more enthused with Luther. In October 1520, the youth had written Luther to assure "him of his good will, his great inclination to his teachings and informed him that he also tries to influence the elector in his favor."[46]

Frederick must have been relieved that Johann and his son resided in Weimar.[47] They had less opportunity from there to openly "fly the flag" for Luther. Frederick knew Luther was about to bolt his hideout and wrote one of his officials John Oswald to convey to Luther that he did not "wish any improper measures to be taken, which might give rise to rebellion and other difficulties."[48] On March 5, Luther wrote back, absolving Frederick of all responsibility. He was in Borna, already on his way to Wittenberg, protected by someone far greater than the elector. Two days later, he wrote Frederick again and gave him some cover, "I humbly wish your Grace to know that by God's help I have returned again to Wittenberg, which undoubtedly is against your Grace's will, since you have never wished to be involved in this matter."[49] He explained he had to return because of the disturbances in Wittenberg and for the first time he mentioned, "I fear (alas, I feel sure!) that there will be a great uprising in Germany, with which God will punish the German nation, for we see that the Gospel pleases the common people greatly, and they receive it in a fleshly sense."[50] The countryfolk (*Bauern*) had taken the new teaching in the wrong way. There could be a great rebellion.

Both men must have sensed unrest all about them.

SACRIFICE OF FREDERICK'S GREAT SHOWCASE

Sometime in the fall of 1520 Frederick made a monumental decision. Although he gave lip service to honoring all the saints, in December 1520 he had Spalatin write his agent Burkhard Schenk in Vienna to trouble himself no longer with purchasing relics.[51] Schenk was to purchase only books. For several years humanists such as Tileman Conradi had directed blistering attacks on individuals collecting relics instead of advancing the study of Holy Scriptures. Yet in 1512, Luther himself had reverenced the relics of the Three Wise Men in Cologne.[52] The relationship of relics to the indulgence corruption had not completely soured Luther on relics. Even though so many were faked, venerating a relic to envision Christ's suffering was pious.[53] Unfortunately the faithful seldom used relics for that end. They wanted the indulgence. The more the better. And how could anyone actually venerate several thousand relics?

In the spring of 1521, the Castle Church no longer touted indulgences. How much this was due to Frederick is questionable. He was fully engaged at the *Reichstag*. That he had not sanctioned it is suggested by the fact that the All Saints' Foundation appealed to Frederick in the fall of 1521. What were they to do? Frederick approved displaying the relics but not promising papal indulgences. Perhaps Frederick and his foundation thought that would mollify Luther, who with others was actually attacking the Mass itself. Luther even wanted to abolish the choir. Was the foundation aware that in 1521 Luther was already telling Spalatin that he wished Frederick would dissolve the foundation itself? Frederick probably knew all this after the *Reichstag*. He gradually backed off his showcase of relics and indulgences; by spring 1523, the Castle Church displayed only a few relics at the high altar. The reformer's demands to abolish Mass and the choir were too much to bear. Frederick refused.

Frederick's great showcase of spectacular altars and seemingly countless relics had been virtually completed by 1520 with the addition of Lucas Cranach's massive "Altarpiece of the Holy Trinity."[54] This great triptych adorned the high altar. The center panel featured the throne of God with God the Father supporting the crucified Christ; also a dove symbolized the Holy Spirit. Shining cherub faces wreathed this Holy Trinity. One side wing featured Frederick with St. Bartholomew; the other wing Johann with St. James the Greater. The theme of the altarpiece was God's approval of Christ's sacrifice, which was to inspire worshipers to realize this was what ultimately atoned for their sins. Suspended above the altarpiece and the high altar was Riemenschneider's great crucifix. Also, symbolically facing the high altar venerating the Savior were Frederick and Johann in the form of two kneeling life-size alabaster sculptures painted to appear lifelike.[55] Hands held in prayer, Frederick wears armor, helmet by his knees. The idealized facial features appear suspiciously like the bust of Frederick by Fiorentino.

Yet the showcase was seen by fewer and fewer pilgrims. There were no indulgences. That Frederick could have backed down from his dream of many years, which was so brilliantly successful, is resounding proof that he deferred to Luther in things religious. Frederick was familiar with his writings, certainly those in German. He mulled modestly to Spalatin, "This is very important business, which I do not understand as a layman."[56] Frederick, too, had *Anfechtung*, that terrifying dread of being wrong, perhaps even unsaved. He repeatedly said he must not do anything that would act against God. In view of his own doubt, he consistently protected religious dissent unless it took a violent form. Who could know? He came to believe it was Luther who knew. Frederick followed Luther's teachings more and more at great cost to his own plans, even at the risk of losing his electorate. It wasn't Luther, moreover, that Frederick was pleasing. Pleasing God, doing God's will, was paramount.

STIRRINGS OF CHAOS IN THE ELECTORATE

Did Karl begin to punish Frederick that July in 1521? Certainly an imperial mandate came out favoring Albrecht of Mainz by obligating Erfurt to abandon all ties with Electoral Saxony.[57] After the 1521 *Reichstag*, Bishop Adolf of Merseburg chose not to know of Frederick's exemption, and he called for enforcement of the Edict of Worms, which Cousin George was undoubtedly behind. Frederick at first deflected such attempts by replying that he would consult his university about it. Frederick said little and explained less. Sometimes he did not reply at all. Even Cardinal Albrecht of Mainz made a run at him. Whether placid Albrecht was really angry is questionable. He and Frederick spent social hours with each other. Albrecht was at the Lochau with Frederick in 1519 when the news of Maximilian's death arrived. Frederick knew the Luther affair was dividing families, even the Albertine Saxons. Cousin George's disposition was not improved by the fact that his younger brother Heinrich (the Pious) sympathized with Luther from the first, denouncing the papal bull.[58] During 1521, several pastors, swayed by Luther's teachings, sought refuge in Electoral Saxony. Frederick refused no one.

Bernhardi, pastor at Kemberg, had started yet a new rebellion for pastors. In May 1521, he married.[59] Other marriages followed. Archbishop Albrecht summoned Bernhardi before the diocesan court. Bernhardi argued his plight well: he would rather suffer on earth than be damned eternally. Frederick and the Wittenberg circle not only managed to keep Bernhardi from any punishment but also saved his position. Others who were prosecuted did not fare as well. Punishment varied from depriving priests of their parishes to trying to bully them into annulling their marriages. Outcomes at first depended on how much local support a priest enjoyed, but resistance evolved. By 1524, only Bishop Adolf of Merseburg in Frederick's sphere doggedly persecuted priests for marrying. Resistance was well organized and prosecution exasperatingly slow. Frederick, the master of protocol, had no small part in the strategy.

The case of Michael Kramer seems to have eluded Frederick for no other reason than Kramer lived in Johann's jurisdiction.[60] The cleric, who resided in Kunitz in Ernestine Saxony and toiled under the jurisdiction of the bishop of Naumburg, took a wife in 1523. Through an amalgam of Duke George's meddling to break up clerical marriages and Kramer's surpassingly poor judgment, the cleric acquired a succession of three wives, the first two only too eager to dissolve the marriage. No legal means for divorce could overcome the internecine wrangling between "papists" and "Lutherans" over Kramer's wives. Duke George no doubt was delighted over this example of "immorality" stemming from the new teachings. Kramer also tarnished his reputation of a pastor who was popularizing Luther's nuanced teachings into tracts.[61]

Marriage was not the only problem with those who took vows, not even the greatest problem. While the authorities used their resources punishing a few married clerics, a trickle, then a flood of priests, monks, and nuns gushed from the churches and the monasteries. Although one cause of the massive exodus was Luther's tract "On Monastic Vows," his tract was inspired by the exodus that had already started. The exodus caused predictable chaos to institutions. It also caused unforeseen chaos to society. Unworldly people swarmed into Ernestine Saxony wanting jobs, marriage, and other facets of society for which they had never been prepared. Among a group of nine wide-eyed nuns brought by wagon into Wittenberg in 1523 was Luther's future wife, the gifted Katharina von Bora.[62]

TEDIOUS NUREMBERG *REICHSTAGS* OF 1522 TO 1524

Following the 1521 *Reichstag* in Worms, another one convened in Nuremberg only ten months later.[63] The archbishop of Trier Richard Greiffenklau sensed a crisis. Through Hans von der Planitz, the archbishop begged Frederick to attend the *Reichstag*. "Your Electoral Grace must hold firm, not become sick, worse yet not die, for your Electoral Grace was never so greatly needed as now, for your Electoral Grace knows how all matters stand in the empire."[64] This plea was weeks before the *Reichstag* started.

The archbishop was prescient. Duke George was already in Nuremberg in December 1521 as a representative of the secular princes on the imperial governing council. He bristled with an agenda. With Luther in exile, he saw a perfect opportunity to undo all the damage. He sat on the council beginning in January and informed Planitz that he was going to demand intervention in Wittenberg.[65] The third article of the council order authorized the imperial regents "to handle disputes of Christian faith in the empire with other Christian estates and authorities."[66] Had Frederick had a hand in drafting such an article? Regardless, Cousin George seized it like a sword. By January 22, he had whipped the council into issuing a mandate for Electoral Saxony.

Following Frederick's instructions, the unnerved Planitz advised the council that monastery escapees and marriage of priests were not in his sovereign's jurisdiction. Church superiors were handling that. As far as changes in the form of communion and the Mass, even biblical scholars did not agree which way was correct. Frederick always deferred to his experts on such questions. Despite Planitz's almost hysterical pleas for Frederick with his vast skill at obfuscating issues to come to the council meeting, the logic of Frederick's argument presented by Planitz seemed to freeze the council. Even Duke George was stymied. Frederick pretended to defer to church superiors, yet those church superiors did Frederick's will. The activity of the imperial governing council had deeply disappointed Frederick. It was going to accomplish nothing.

Leo X died December 1, 1522. Pope Hadrian VI wasted little time going after Frederick. In January the pope sharply reminded Frederick to proceed against Luther. In concert, perhaps, was a similar letter to Frederick from Karl V (Hadrian had once tutored Karl). Frederick answered with vague excuses about his infirmities and most of all his incompetence in theological questions. The *Reichstag* finally began at the end of March 1522.[67] It was no coincidence about this time that Spalatin was to research what had actually happened to those individuals placed under the ban or edict.[68] Jakob Vogt, Frederick's father confessor for thirty years, died April 15 in Torgau. The turmoil in Wittenberg had so shocked the aged Franciscan that he had written Frederick's sister Margarete in dismay. Just before Vogt's death, Frederick appointed Spalatin court chaplain and court preacher, not comprehensible unless Frederick was receptive to the new teachings.[69] Then in stunning swiftness, the *Reichstag* concluded after only five weeks. Luther was not officially recognized in any *Reichstag* document, but that surely was not true of the secret sessions. It was a clear indication of the enormous influence Frederick exerted even from afar.

This was further proven by the imperial governing council that convened shortly after the *Reichstag* started again. Duke George managed to make Luther and Wittenberg again the hot topic. Luther had not salved wounds by printing a tract that called those on the council "tyrants." Planitz again danced around accusations, claiming his sovereign was not always pleased by what Luther wrote. In this case it was undeniably true. Planitz turned the table on the council by pointing out that it had been Luther who had quelled improprieties in Wittenberg. Removing Luther could lead to unrest. Planitz further declared that the bishops of Merseburg and Meissen had indeed conformed to the mandate of the imperial governing council. Planitz, who had to stand up against the anger of dukes and prelates, no doubt looked forward to the beginning of Frederick's own term on the council. It began July 1, the same day Augustinian monks Hendrik Vos and Johann van den Esschen were burned at the stake in Brussels for Lutheran beliefs. Their capture and execution was pushed by Karl's aunt Margarethe, regent of the Netherlands, invoking the 1521 Edict of Worms. The threat of death in the empire was real.[70]

Frederick did appear at the council, though he suffered from gout, and he managed to lower the tone against Luther.[71] An example of how his exactitude for protocol could bring the council to a virtual standstill was his reproach for someone who had produced imperial seals in Nuremberg for the use of the council. Only the emperor could approve that. Yet the council did read a Duke George rant against Luther's disrespectful answer to a critical letter by English king Henry VIII. Frederick manipulated a bland answer from the council to George. Did anyone really want an imperial subject reprimanded by an English king?[72] Frederick did write the king a deferential apology but committed himself to nothing.[73] The governor of the next session of the imperial governing council, Palatine count Friedrich, told an Albertine Saxony adviser that the Luther affair "had been handled the previous quarter and it was not pleasant to hear of it" again.[74] In effect, no one at Duke George's level listened to him any longer. There was other business in the empire. Everyone was stunned that rogue knight Franz von Sickingen declared feud on the archbishop of Trier that fall. A mere knight attacking an elector? For once the council acted and put a ban on Sickingen. It made no difference whatsoever to Sickingen, who attacked Trier with a large force. The archbishop, Frederick's good friend, defended Trier with such ingenuity and ferocity that Sickingen backed down.[75]

Yet another Nuremberg *Reichstag* convened from November 17, 1522, to February 8, 1523. Frederick was too weak to attend, so the reliable Philipp von Feilitzsch represented him at the *Reichstag*, because as an imperial council member himself Planitz could not represent Frederick. At the *Reichstag* the papal nuncio Chieregati demanded intervention against Luther and implementation of the Worms edict. The estates stormed back. They wanted their *Gravamina* against the Roman Church satisfied. They wanted churchmen who preached only from the true, pure, genuine, and holy Scriptures. They wanted archbishops and bishops to use technically well-equipped people, who could examine sermons and teachings for their errors. One suggested a general, free Christian council in Germany. Until that happened, Elector Frederick could easily manage Luther and his followers.

It was a staggering rebuke of Rome.

Was it the continual absence of the emperor himself that made the estates so protective of their own? The *Reichstags* had become short and unpleasant for the imperial circle as well as the papal circle. Even as the threat to Frederick subsided, he insisted on his officials and university professors looking into every nook and cranny. How did one defend oneself against a mandate from the imperial council? An edict from a *Reichstag*? What were the precedents? Further attempts would be made. Frederick did not intend to be unprepared. Yet the imperial governing council was dying, more and more poorly attended.

Suddenly in September 1523, Pope Hadrian VI died. He was sixty-four, having held the papal chair less than two years.

Vitriol against Frederick spewed out. Aleander described Frederick as a "monster" to the new pope, Clement VII. Clement VII was none other than the sly Cardinal Medici, cousin of Leo X. Rome and the church hierarchy never accepted Hadrian VI, an outsider. Although he was a committed reformer, he accomplished little. In addition to the cardinals opposing all reform, Leo X had compromised the papacy for years to come. The Romans rejoiced when Hadrian died after only eighteen months. Hadrian's successor, yet one more corrupt Medici who would perform like a secular sovereign, was to their liking. Clement VII was but forty-five, promising a long reign.

The vitriol continued. Ferdinand said he would drown his sister Katharina rather than send her to Saxony, and that Frederick was destroying the well-being of the empire as well as the Christian faith.

Finally, envoys from Karl informed Frederick that the marriage of Katharina to Johann Friedrich was off. Karl was more subtle behind Frederick's back. He simply wanted to know what the pope was going to do to take care of Luther, but the pope wanted to know what Karl was going to do to take care of Luther. Both men had scant interest in solving the Luther conundrum. They were interested in their relationship, the intentions of France, and which of the three would control Italy.[76]

The third *Reichstag* in Nuremberg began January 14, 1524. Frederick attended, even coming as early as November 28. He had many good friends in Nuremberg. He also could excuse himself from the *Reichstag* early on the excuse that he had already been there for twelve weeks and was in poor health. This is exactly what he did on February 26. Hardly any negotiations had been taken up, let alone affairs of empire. Frederick had done little more than indulge in crossbow archery, about the only sport he could still perform. He did, at Karl's request, arbitrate a disagreement between Ferdinand and his adviser Salamanca. The old mediator was peerless. To Frederick's face the imperial circle was exceedingly gracious and complimentary.

The venerable elector was unmoved. He had been intimate with the master of flattery and double-cross, Maximilian. Frederick had for some time sensed the nasty purpose of this *Reichstag*. Philipp von Feilitzsch remained to represent him. The lawyer Cardinal Campeggio asked to be included in the *Reichstag*, and the estates welcomed him. The Edict of Worms was pushed hard and confirmed again. The estates, however, had softened its implementation to "as much as possible" putty. Feilitzsch protested it anyway. In Basel, the evangelical Oecolampadius, a colleague of Luther, scoffed that Frederick had "by cleverness destroyed the attacks of the opponents."[77]

Karl wrote Frederick in July 1524 that he wanted him to enforce the Edict of Worms. Frederick knew the issue was pushed by Rome, not Karl V. Frederick wrote back to remind the emperor that he had not been there during the discussion—his own representative Feilitzsch had protested against it—so Frederick could hardly be responsible for the *Reichstag* results. The discourse became illogical banter. Frederick learned that in June and July a prince diet (*Fürstentag*) had taken place in Regensburg but was attended only by Ferdinand, the dukes of Bavaria, Cardinal Campeggio, and many bishops of the southern empire.[78] Their goal was to destroy the new teachings. Count Albrecht of Mansfeld wanted to counter with an Evangelical League, but Frederick squelched the idea. It was all posturing.

LUTHER RESTORES PEACE TO WITTENBERG

After Luther's return to Wittenberg in March 1522, he had turned his attention to the changes made by Karlstadt and the Zwickau prophets.[79] Of their innovations, Luther accepted the removal of the private Masses and the mandatory oral confession as well as the words of the Mass referring to the concept of sacrifice. Although Karlstadt angrily objected to restoring anything, Luther brought back the Latin language in the Mass, the communion under one form, the Mass vestments and the elevation of the communion wafer. He had shed his swarthy knight's appearance and once again wore a cowl and displayed a gleaming tonsure. After only one week of Luther's dominant presence, cautious Schurff sent Frederick a glowing report:

> I humbly wish your Grace to know that there is great gladness and rejoicing here, both among the learned and the unlearned, over Doctor Martin's return and over the Sermons with which, by God's help, he is daily pointing us poor deluded men back again to the way of truth, showing us incontrovertibly the pitiful errors into which we have been led by the preachers who forced their way among us. ... I have no doubt that it is by the special providence of the Almighty that he has come to Wittenberg just at this time.[80]

Within seven weeks of Luther preaching moderation and obedience to authority, he had restored order.

But all was not as before with the Wittenberg circle. Karlstadt and Gabriel Zwilling had seriously damaged their reputations in Luther's circle and in the electoral circle. Luther tried to smooth over Zwilling's part, but for once Spalatin steadfastly opposed him and persuaded Frederick of Zwilling's poor judgment.[81] Luther pushed the Zwickau prophets to the periphery. Storch was uncomfortable in an academic environment and finally drifted off the following year. Stübner, however, was once a student at Wittenberg and, mellowing somewhat, he settled in, not at all unpopular at the university.[82] The turmoil had affected Melanchthon, and in Luther's absence, he even considered leaving Wittenberg. He was shaken by his inability to confront violence. He was a weak physical presence, but he excelled as a scholar, methodically formulating the new evangelical teachings.

Luther pleased Frederick immensely with his progress on the New Testament in German.[83] He had returned to Wittenberg, translation in hand. No product would better demonstrate Luther's amazing ability to work at lightning speed. He translated the New Testament from Greek to German in eleven weeks. For several weeks in Wittenberg Luther checked it with Melanchthon. Philip gushed, "Bugenhagen is a grammarian, I am a dialectician, Jonas is an orator; but Luther is all in one; no one can be compared to him."[84] His translation was not just adequate, it was breathtaking in its brilliance. In July 1522, Melchior Lotther began printing *Das Newe Testament Deutzsch*, 222 pages with 21 woodcuts apparently from Cranach's workshop. One of the first copies was rushed to Duke Johann,[85] another to Hans von Berlepsch at the Wartburg. In September the book was available for sale, selling three thousand copies in two months. By December, Luther, relying on Melanchthon and no doubt Hebraist Aurogallus, had hammered the Hebrew Pentateuch of the Old Testament into German.

Yet if Frederick thought Luther had mellowed into a docile scholar, he was mistaken.

In 1523, Luther was back on the attack. The Castle Church remained a bastion against reform. Nevertheless, Frederick had already made excruciating concessions by virtually retiring his fabulous relic collection. Luther was not satisfied. Not only did the Castle Church practice the old faith but some of the All Saints' Foundation canons were notorious for their drunkenness and whoring. Shut the foundation down, railed Luther, and use the money on the university. On March 1, he formally demanded the foundation abolish the old Mass that was incompatible with Holy Scriptures. He increased his attacks, going public. By August Frederick had Schurff and Melanchthon warn Luther to stop. The imperial governing council earlier that year had issued a mandate that no more changes were to be made. The Castle Church was a visible pet project of Frederick's. Luther was undeterred. Although Luther won over most of the foundation canons, Frederick was unmoved and would not approve more changes. Finally, Luther and his allies in the foundation wore down the few remaining defenders of the old faith. Although Frederick approved no more changes, they occurred anyway by 1525. Frederick was far too ill to resist.

Frederick's remarkable calm and sense of justice even in the midst of quarrels are revealed by his gesture to Luther at this time. In December 1524, Frederick gave Luther "the cloister itself and the garden next to it."[86] Had Frederick turned the corner at this declining point in his life, so sick and hurting that he no longer cared about maintaining his pretense of indifference?

HIGHBORN IN-LAWS

The long coveted marital connections of Ernestine Saxons with the Danes had turned sour since 1513 when King Christian I died and his thirty-two-year-old son Christian II assumed the throne.[87] Christian II was more rotten than Cousin George. George at least had principles. The new king's first vile act was denying his own mother's dowry. His mother, of course, was Frederick's older sister Christine. She appealed to Frederick. This had been Hans von der Planitz's first important diplomatic mission. Meanwhile, Frederick had been adroitly managing the marriage of Christian II with Maximilian's granddaughter Isabella. The marriage did occur in August 1515. But despite Frederick's efforts for his nephew, the hard-hearted Christian II would not give his mother a dowry.

The situation worsened.

Christian II proved as a ruler to be among those reckless adventurers so common in European royalty at the time. His tactics led to the "Stockholm Bloodbath," an infamous battle in 1520 that resulted in the death of many high-ranking nobles. His estates hated him so much that he had to abandon the throne in April 1523 and flee to the Netherlands to seek refuge with Habsburg in-laws. Not very welcome there, his court drifted to the Brandenburgs. In September 1523, much to Frederick's distaste, his nephew Christian II appeared with Elector Joachim of Brandenburg at one of Frederick's hunting mansions. Christian II already had a reputation for grand plans of re-conquering Scandinavia but no money to do it. Not surprisingly, Frederick was neutral. He was, after all, related to both Christian II and Friedrich I, the king Christian II intended to overthrow.

Christian II tried to wheedle out of Frederick grand lodging in Torgau. Frederick evaded approval. In Wittenberg, Christian II somehow convinced Luther that he was sympathetic to the new teachings and persuaded Luther to write a letter on his behalf to Frederick. It requested that Frederick arrange a pension for Christian II from Ferdinand, who was, after all, his wife's brother. Moreover, the exile would grant all future claims on Scandinavia to Ferdinand in exchange for a fief. Frederick, of course, did nothing, but he was displeased with Luther for meddling in affairs he knew nothing about. In April 1524, Electoral Saxony would enter into a pact with the new king in Scandinavia, Poland, Pomerania, and other northern territories.

Christian II's wife, Isabella, made a much better impression, yet even she was a loose cannon at times. In Nuremberg on Maundy Thursday (Thursday before Easter), 1524, she embarrassed the Habsburgs enormously when she took communion in both forms from a pro-Lutheran pastor. Frederick, Ferdinand, and doubtless many others sighed with relief when the Danish exiles slipped away in June 1524 to avoid creditors who threatened to seize their property. Christian II and Isabella settled in Brabant in the Netherlands.[88]

THE MASSIVE RISE OF COUNTRYFOLK

By the middle of 1524, Frederick and Johann became aware of the radical preacher Thomas Müntzer again. Müntzer preached in the town Allstedt in an isolated outlier of Ernestine Saxony far to the north. For once the Ernestines did not dawdle with a threat. Johann Friedrich, now twenty-one and performing administrative duties, visited the town in July to hear Müntzer.[89] A mob, thought to have been inspired by Müntzer, had burned the Marian Chapel at nearby Mallerbach on March 14.[90] Müntzer had become more radical since Zwickau. He accepted only Mosaic Law and was determined to do away with the oppressors of countryfolk. Miners were his main supporters. Johann Friedrich's ears burned from his sermon. Weeks later the young prince wrote a subordinate, "I am having a terrible time with the Satan of Alstedt. Kindliness and letters do not suffice. The sword which is ordained of God to punish the evil must be used with energy."[91]

Uprisings of countryfolk threatening mayhem had started in the southern empire in June 1524.[92] Frederick and Johann were sufficiently alarmed to summon Müntzer to Weimar at the end of July to preach. In his sermon from the Book of Daniel, the radical held nothing back. He claimed as his authority the Holy Spirit.

The man who has not received the living witness of God knows really nothing about God, though he may have swallowed 100,000 Bibles. . . . You princes of Saxony, you need a new Daniel to disclose unto you this revelation and to show you your role. . . . The sword is given to you to wipe out the ungodly. If you decline, it will be taken from you. Those who resist should be slaughtered without mercy as Elijah smote the priests of Baal.[93]

After the sermon Müntzer must have sensed or heard how the Saxon sovereigns received his sermon. He disappeared, only to reappear in September in the free imperial city of Mülhausen. Mülhausen was just outside the jurisdictions of Frederick, Duke George, Albrecht of Mainz, and Philipp of Hesse. It was a shrewd choice.[94]

The changes in the empire during Frederick's lifetime definitely embittered the countryfolk, especially those in the southern empire. Strengthening of territories and introduction of Roman law that stressed ownership of property had made their marginal existence worse. In previous centuries, the countryfolk had access to woods, small game, and fish. Now they had lost many privileges and had to pay their masters both in taxes and in service. Despite figures such as Luther who had risen from the countryfolk, they were still regarded by their masters as ugly dimwits, little more than animals that could speak. Woodcuts depicted them ape-like in face and posture. Although there can be no doubt that the mood engendered by Luther's teachings of personal freedom had made them bolder, in the south their desire to revolt festered years before Luther's fame. By 1524, the southern countryfolk were organizing, and many who had served the nobility as foot soldiers had returned to their homes with military skills and ideas.

Following the 1524 *Reichstag* in Nuremberg, Frederick preferred above all other residences his great hunting palace in Lochau.[95] For seven weeks, April 30 to June 26, he remained there. Although he sought tranquility, he could not avoid the press of the issues of the time. Magdeburg was not in his territory at all, yet in summer 1524 some Magdeburgers appealed to Frederick that they might exercise their right to pick their own minister.[96] They wanted electoral adviser Nikolaus von Amsdorf. Frederick and Spalatin carried on secretive communication with Dr. Pasca in Magdeburg.[97] They successfully installed Amsdorf, but the Brandenburgers and meddlesome Duke George erupted when Amsdorf and the Magdeburgers later wanted to change the church service.

Frederick returned to stay at Lochau from August 1 to October 11, another eight weeks.[98] Finally Frederick was again at Lochau December 8, this time never to leave it alive.[99] Lochau was furnished lavishly. In Frederick's sleeping chamber alone were three beds, two couches, and two cushions. He slept, as always, surrounded by servants. Always among them was a "barber," who practiced medicine too. Present also were vials and vials of medicines and potions, some prepared by Frederick himself. Six great tapestries graced his study. So one would not forget the main purpose of this luxurious palace, hundreds of antlers loomed above in halls. Hunting was a lost pleasure for Frederick, but at Lochau he relished the solitude and memories. Four were with him constantly: his son Sebastian, Spalatin, High Marshal Hans von Dolzig, and Secretary Johann Veihel.[100]

The Habsburg Ferdinand in the spring of 1525 was desperately negotiating with the armies of countryfolk that had gathered all over the southern empire. The moment every cleric and nobleman dreaded had come. Chancellor Leonhard von Eck of Bavaria had expressed it well as dark, dark humor: if the countryfolk organized, they could conquer "the clergy by breakfast, the nobles by dinner, and the knights before bedtime."[101] The countryfolk outnumbered all the rest of the citizenry at least ten to one, probably fifteen to one. They were hardy, sinewy people bronzed by the sun and steeled by the wind. They were tireless. Only the knights were harder.

Although the protesters were not all of one cloth, their demands to the ruling nobility seemed well represented in the "Twelve Articles." The countryfolk were entitled by Holy Scriptures to be free. They wanted to select their own preachers. Economic issues were there too: the right to obtain wood, game, and fish; the return of their confiscated meadowlands; and relief from excessive taxes and compulsive labor. There was now even an inheritance or "death" tax. Luther wrote "Admonition for Peace" in mid-April 1525 to respond to the "Twelve Articles" that he had only recently read. Although he chided countryfolk for trying to use Holy Scriptures to justify violence, Luther angrily blamed the princes and lords saying, "We have no one on earth to thank for this disastrous rebellion except you princes and lords . . . as temporal rulers you do nothing but cheat and rob the people so that you may lead a life of luxury and extravagance. The poor common people cannot bear it any longer."[102]

The grievances of the countryfolk deeply moved Frederick. On April 14, he penned his own guilt to Johann:

> Perhaps the poor people have been given a reason for such rebellion, especially by forbidding them the Word of God. In many ways the poor are being burdened by us temporal and spiritual rulers. May God turn his wrath away from us. If God wills it, then it will happen, and the common man will rule.[103]

Although Frederick knew there was a severe problem with the countryfolk in the south, he knew the problem was local as well. In early May, possibly thinking of Luther, Frederick proposed "that on their territory someone be enlisted who is known to the peasants, who has their trust and confidence, and who could negotiate with them; may God grant that these grievous and anxious matters on the territory be quieted down and the people be made satisfied."[104]

Frederick was insulated. Johann knew better. He was out in the countryside. He estimated one army of 35,000 rebels was just a few days' march from Weimar. Schmalkalden, one day's ride southwest of Erfurt, fell to rebels on May 1. Castles and cloisters were favorite targets of the rage, and many were already destroyed in southern Thuringia. Müntzer's forces in Mülhausen had started destruction as well. Perhaps Frederick knew some of this, but his attendants probably wanted to spare him anxiety. Other sovereigns were fully aware of present danger. Towns in general did not try to resist the rebels, because they did not have the military resources the princes had. Philipp of Hesse and Albertine Duke George did not have qualms like Frederick. These two sovereigns proceeded as many sovereigns did all over the empire. They tricked the gullible countryfolk into thinking that they might negotiate their grievances. As soon as the sovereigns with their well-armed, experienced soldiers had a complete military advantage, they executed the leaders and slaughtered the countryfolk.

DECLINE AND DEATH

On April 9, 1525 (Palm Sunday), Frederick heard the Gospels read in German for the first time. On Easter, one week later, he heard the Eucharist in German, but less than a week later, Frederick suddenly declined. His pain was wrenching. With bitterness he told a chamber servant, "If my dear God wills it, then I gladly depart this world; because here on earth are neither love nor truth, neither faithfulness nor anything good."[105]

On April 30, he wrote Johann apologetically:

> I do not know how to spare your grace, however, that I become ever weaker. I have in eight days had little rest, neither day nor night. I am not able to pass water, I write only tentatively, I may not eat, then I sleep painfully. . . . Dr. Auerbach who comforts me, is with me.[106]

His body was quitting him. All the well-known signs of imminent death were there. Dr. Heinrich Stromer von Auerbach, noted physician of Leipzig, would not have been present for anything less than grave illness.

Although dying, Frederick still exercised resolve. On May 4, Spalatin tried in a letter to move Frederick to approve reform of all foundations, monasteries, and the religious.[107] Was this a thinly disguised effort to approve reform of the Castle Church? Frederick did not answer. He was alert and sharp to the end.[108] On May 4, Spalatin entered Frederick's chamber, where the elector was sitting in a low chair with wheels. He offered Spalatin his hand and teased him, "You do well that you come to me; one should visit sick people." Frederick had himself wheeled to a table. There, holding Spalatin's hand, he talked of weighty matters until eight o'clock in the evening. His father confessor (Andreas Wagner from Herzberg) came after that. Just after midnight Frederick took communion in both forms, but "no unction."[109] Together Frederick and Spalatin wept.

That next morning, Frederick gathered his chamber servants and pages. "Children, I suffer so," he said. One piped up, "Gracious Lord, if it is God's will, your Electoral Grace will become better." Frederick replied, "Here nothing is better but, if it is God's will, there it will be better." He dismissed them and made confession once again to Wagner, and as if feeling regret, he again called for his chamber servants and pages. These were the faces always with him, but he had been bad-tempered with some of them.[110] He said, "Dear little children, I ask you for God's sake where I would have made you angry . . . we princes burden the poor people in all ways and that is not good." As he spoke, he began weeping. Soon everyone was crying. "Don't cry for me, children," he said. "I see that I will not be here much longer. Think of me and pray to God for me."

Later, on that day of May 5, his son Sebastian entered his chamber, carrying something. "Son, what do you have there?" asked Frederick. "Spalatin sent me something to read to you," his son answered. It was consolation from God's Word. "Bring my eyeglasses," said Frederick. "I will read it myself." Soon after, Frederick dictated a new will to his secretary Johann Veihel and Spalatin. Frederick opened his heart in this last will. "I have left 200 gulden to my God-given wife," he dictated. To his thirteen-year-old daughter who was with Dr. Pasca in Magdeburg he left 500 gulden. To his sons he was rambling but generous.

> I have told my brother several times that I intend to keep, for Fritz and Bastian, in particular each year 500 florins from a certain tin mine, to distribute the same with 20,000 florins. And besides that, I recently wrote Brother Johann, though I still have no answer, a cordial request that 500 florins be affected yearly . . . [and] on top of that, for them also the palace at Jessen together with its goods, which I brought about through a letter to Matthes Loser, near the village of Getsdorf, together with the vineyard at Jessen, fishery, and the tin mine at Lebin.

There was more.

While Frederick's second will, compared to the first, had increased the expenditures for monasteries, as well as increasing expenditures for Masses for the dead, in the third will there is no more mention at all of monasteries or Masses for the dead. In the second will he had desired burial in the Wittenberg Castle Church. The third will, however, did not mention his burial. That suggests the omissions for religious purposes were not intended. He was in great pain, thinking of the needs he must insist on for his immediate loved ones.

Finally he said, "I know no more." After a while Spalatin asked him, "My master, does the gracious elector have burdens?" "Nothing but the pain," he answered.[111]

Those were his last words. He died between four and five o'clock in the afternoon of May 5, 1525.

The next day Dr. Auerbach, in preparation for embalming, took out the entrails and noted several infirmities. Frederick's spleen and liver showed damage. There were several gallstones. The main corruption was an enormous stone in the kidney—two fingers long and jagged, the lethal stone prevented urination.[112] They lay the embalmed corpse in a coffin. Here the normal funeral process stalled. Brother Johann was directing military actions against rebelling countryfolk. Count Albrecht of Mansfeld had smashed rebels in the Harz region virtually the same hour Frederick died.[113]

Luther, divulging superstitions of the time, wrote a friend about Frederick, "He had known very little of the uprising, but had written his brother (Johann) to try all kindly measures before he allowed it to come to a battle. Thus his death was Christian-like and blessed. The sign of it was a rainbow that Philip (Melanchthon) and I saw over Lochau one night last winter, and a child born here at Wittenberg without a head; also another with club feet."[114] Melanchthon had more superstition to offer: "At the Lochau ... a spotted deer which had been tame and every year in September ran into the forest in the rutting and in October came home again.... This happened many years. But ... since Elector Frederick died the deer went away ... because it had lost its sovereign, it did not want to remain for a new and different sovereign."[115]

On May 10, with the arrival of Johann's approval, officials conducted an old-faith ceremony for Frederick at the Lochau and then conveyed him in a "tar-sealed" coffin to Wittenberg.[116] They sang evangelical songs along the way. For burial, his second will from the year 1517 prevailed. Frederick would be buried in the Wittenberg Castle Church. Moreover, that will had asked that "all temporal ostentation, as much as is fitting, [be] avoided," though he specified that his grave before the main altar should be covered with a flat brass plate and a "poured likeness" be set up at the north wall of the church. At the funeral Luther delivered two sermons and Melanchthon one Latin oration. The chorus sang "*Auf tiefer Not*" ("Our Deepest Need"), Luther's funeral hymn based on Psalm 130.[117] Johann still had not returned, but Frederick's son Sebastian was there, as well as many citizens and students of Wittenberg. Only Frederick's fourteen-year-old nephew Franz von Braunschweig-Lüneburg, a student at Wittenberg, represented legitimate relatives. The rebellion accounted for sparse turnout. It was a perilous time for anyone to travel the countryside.

Frederick was buried May 11, 1525, in the very church he had erected.

CHAPTER 9

THE HALF MILLENNIUM AFTER FREDERICK

> "Wanderer, you who look at this grave
> only with a fleeting eye: delay your
> journey here a little while."
> —Plaque on Frederick's grave [1]

AFTERMATH: BLOOD OF THE COUNTRYFOLK

On May 11, 1525, Frederick lay at rest in the floor of the Castle Church in Wittenberg, but the empire was not at rest. The next day, the Swabian League led by Count George Truchsess (von Waldburg-Zeil) crushed rebelling countryfolk in Württemberg.[2] By that time, the rebels numbered 300,000 across all the Germanic empire except Austria, Bavaria, and the far north. Their original religious aims had evolved into economic and political demands. The resistance of the ruling nobles and prelates had also evolved. Well-organized armies of trained knights and foot soldiers, aided by sly negotiators, served the nobility. They tricked the hapless, naïve countryfolk again and again. Mercy was not part of the nobles' strategy.

Four days after Frederick was buried, Philip of Hesse, Duke George of Albertine Saxony, and the Duke of Braunschweig overwhelmed Thomas Müntzer and his eight thousand rebels at Frankenhausen. Landgrave Philipp of Hesse and Duke George used Müntzer's break with the old faith as an excuse to slaughter him and his followers. The princes estimated their knights and foot soldiers killed nearly six thousand rebels at Frankenhausen. The battle itself, trained soldiers against inept countryfolk with crude weapons, was more like an execution.

That was not enough.

Landgrave Philipp and Duke George carried out formal executions, beheading fifty suspected leaders, including Thomas Müntzer.[3] God justified their lethal work, they said. The guilty leaders—both cowards and rebels that they were—had taught a false Gospel that, counter to the Lord, had led to murder, burning, and other ungodly crimes. The princes, to whom God grants the power of the sword, must punish those who profane God.[4] Johann, now Saxon elector, and son Johann Friedrich joined Duke George and Philipp of Hesse on about May 21. In a bold move they occupied Mülhausen and virtually took all rights from the free imperial city. The Ernestines were in time to see the executions.

Over the next few weeks, nobles slaughtered rebels on many battlefields. In addition, the victors executed and maimed thousands of captives. Over the empire, deaths for the rebels may have mounted to 100,000. As inexact as that number may be, no figure at all is available for the thousands of mutilated and blind "rebels" who were seen begging in villages and towns for many years to come.[5] Details are ghastly. The invoice that executioner Augustin sent to his sovereign Casimir of Ansbach-Brandenburg (west of Nuremberg) chills the soul. Augustin had performed eighty beheadings (one gulden each) and sixty-nine eyes gouged out or fingers chopped off (one half-gulden each). In the shadow of these cruel punishments, the princes banished entire families and imposed numerous other forms of hardship.[6]

The only great prince without blood on his hands had been Frederick III of Saxony.[7] Johann proceeded cautiously after Mülhausen. He knew Duke George relished the thought of capturing Martin Luther and his followers, condemning them as the cause of the rebellion and taking harsh measures, but this Johann would not allow. Johann Friedrich expressed that to Duke George forcefully.[8] On the other hand, the Ernestines wanted to punish ringleaders in their territory. With armed force, Johann and his son conducted a punitive campaign through the entire Ernestine Saxony.[9] They were almost as reluctant as Frederick to take lives. In two months they had executed several rebel leaders, yet levied fines totaling more than 100,000 gulden.

FREDERICK III UNDERSTOOD IN HIS OWN DAY

What did contemporary observers of Elector Frederick III of Saxony conclude of the prince? The honorific "Frederick the Wise" probably did not emerge in the first decades after his death.[10] Its origin seems lost. Many in the imperial circle hated him because they could not control him. Many defenders of the old faith detested him. For years the papal nuncio Aleander raged over Frederick and labeled him the "Saxon fox," the "Basilisk" (mythological reptile with lethal breath and eye), the "despicable Saxon," and finally the "fat groundhog with the eyes of a dog."[11]

But what of "friends"?

Typically, Martin Luther was brutally blunt:

> In the first place, said Luther, the fact that he is so "foolish" as to increase the services in the Wittenberg Castle Church; in the second place, he has the ambition to gather more relics in this church than Archbishop Albrecht of Mainz has in his new chapter house in Halle on the Saale; in the third place, he is building too much . . . in the fourth place, he cannot be found "when he is needed" and he neglects his duties in the affairs of government on account of his preoccupation with churchly devotional exercises. Only with Frederick's love of peace was he [Luther] entirely of agreement, for he still held that every war, even the purely defensive war, is wrong. Yet he could not suppress the suspicion that Frederick's love of peace was not based on noble motives alone, but also on the fear of injury.[12]

Yet Luther at a mellower time compared Frederick and brother Johann:

> [Johann] was distinguished by the greatest clemency, Frederick by the greatest prudence. If the qualities of the two princes had been united in one person, we would have had a prodigy. Duke Frederick seated himself, asked for counsel, closed his eyes, made note of what was said by one after another, and finally he spoke, saying, "This or that won't stand up," "This or that will be the consequence."[13]

And yet another time Luther praised Frederick:

> It's a great gift to have a good and wise prince, such as Elector Frederick, who was truly the father of his country. He governed excellently. He could fill barns and haylofts, and he

had large trenches dug in the fields to store provisions. Every year he spent twelve thousand florins on building. . . . Still the elector had enough money, for he was his own tax collector . . . and required exact accounts of his officials and servants . . . he left a very large treasure to his country.[14]

Luther's most definitive biographer, Martin Brecht, stated,

Because Luther knew how purely and chastely Frederick's heart loved the Holy Scriptures, he also loved the prince. From Staupitz he knew Frederick's dislike of those sermons that were cold, consisting only of artfulness and human traditions with no power and substance, since they could be refuted with counterarguments. The Holy Scriptures with their forceful speech, however, possessed majesty and power. Frederick the Wise demanded this from a preacher. According to Luther, this was a view worthy of a pope.[15]

Brecht further noted that in later years Luther "recalled again and again the great political wisdom of the 'Solomon of Electoral Saxony.' "[16]

And what was Emperor Maximilian's opinion of Frederick? According to Spalatin, Maximilian said to Degenhart Pfeffinger, "My nephew the electoral prince of Saxony, your sovereign, oh how wisely he has acted that he has moved neither Mainz nor Hesse to war over Erfurt. However, I have warred, and to my great damage and disadvantage . . . your sovereign acts so wisely that he does not war."[17] Certainly this flattery does not convey all Maximilian thought of Frederick. Without doubt, Frederick's very pacifism disappointed him. He preferred Frederick's uncle Albrecht who not only fought for Maximilian but used Saxon money to do it. Yet it is definite that Maximilian was fond of Frederick, singling him out and gushing over him at *Reichstags*. Was it because the emperor so seldom encountered such integrity?

Kings curried his favor. Popes favored him until Luther poisoned the water. Scholars dedicated important works to him. Great artists realized he was a perceptive and reliable patron. His fellow imperial princes revered him. He was their rock at the *Reichstags*. He had been their buffer in the imperial circle. The most active reformer of the empire, Berthold of Mainz, greatly admired Frederick. Just having Frederick in the imperial circle of Maximilian had been a "consolation" to Berthold.[18]

EVOLVED HISTORICISM OF "FREDERICK THE WISE"

After Frederick's contemporaries passed on, the evaluation of Frederick proceeded along one line dealing with his obvious protection of Martin Luther. Sometime before 1600 he became "Frederick the Wise."[19] His much longer, influential imperial involvement was forgotten. The only question asked was whether this protection stemmed from his conversion to the new teachings of Luther or whether it was due to his already well-established methods of governing his subjects. But this changed in the 1800s with the onset of Rankean source-based historiography; Leopold von Ranke insisted history be torn into shreds and reconstructed entirely from primary sources.[20] Ranke wanted history as it really happened.[21] Ranke and especially his follower Heinrich Ulmann took a dim view of Maximilian, "an unstable, fantasy-ridden dreamer, a self-serving schemer, and an Austrian exploiter, who reigned over a Germany that needed a wise and steady hand, a far-seeing statesman, and a true German patriot."[22] Virtually necessitated by the historiographers' low opinion of Maximilian were favorable evaluations of his main antagonists Berthold of Mainz and Frederick of Saxony.

Ranke gushed praise over Frederick as "the most able and prudent of all the princes of the empire."[23] "No one had contributed more to the election of Charles V. than Frederick of Saxony: by the protection which he had afforded to Luther and his university, he had rendered possible the national movement in that prince's favour. He now absolutely refused to allow Luther to be tried at Rome."[24] "His calm judgment, his well-known experience, and the universal respect paid to his acknowledged integrity and talents for business, invested him with singular authority. He might indeed at this time (1520) be said to govern the empire, in as far as it could be governed at all."[25]

Ranke, however, did see what many regarded as Frederick's weaknesses. "We are already acquainted with the character of this prince—his temporising policy, his reluctance to interfere in person, his habit of letting things take their own course."[26]

RECENT PERCEPTION OF "FREDERICK THE WISE"

In the twenty-first century there seem to be three camps regarding Frederick. One camp views Frederick at the territorial level as a sly, secretive usurper of imperial and ecclesiastical powers, as if both of these authorities were more "legal" or desirable.[27] Although this view is simplistic in that it ignores links of territorial politics to the simultaneous politics at the imperial and papal levels, the view of Frederick as frequently sly, even duplicitous, is correct.

A second camp, characterized most notably by Austrian Hermann Wiesflecker, views Frederick with a wider lens. Since 1971, Wiesflecker has published nearly four thousand pages rejuvenating Maximilian's reputation. Almost by necessity Wiesflecker at the same time has tried to diminish Frederick's reputation, noting derisively, "Except for the fact that the elector is known because he protected Luther, today he would probably be almost forgotten."[28] Are historians interested in fame or truth? Wiesflecker's contempt of the prince who stymied Maximilian again and again is overt. Frederick was a "fearful vacillator who had to improve a single letter 20 times. He loved peace and kept his head down rather than venture anything."[29]

It is amazing, then, what Frederick accomplished, for Wiesflecker elsewhere grudgingly noted Frederick "enjoyed among the electors and princes special respect."[30] He further stated that in 1498 the "defection of this high-powered man united the electoral-princely front against the king."[31] "At the Diet of Augsburg (1500), the opposition won a complete victory," admitted Wiesflecker, adding, "Maximilian had to leave the imperial power almost completely to the estates. Since the Saxon elector allied with the archchancellor (Berthold of Mainz) the king was completely isolated and forced to yield in everything."[32]

Supporters of Maximilian might indeed want to forget Elector Frederick III of Saxony.

The third camp of scholars best understands Frederick as a Christian prince, who was also a multi-leveled, pragmatic sovereign with singular honesty and conviction.[33] Heiko Oberman focused not only on the medieval core of Luther but on that same element in Frederick. A prince of the fifteenth and sixteenth century, even though secular in name, did not rule only in that sphere but was also tradition-bound to concern himself with the spiritual realm of his subjects. The duties of a Christian prince had long overlapped the duties of clerics. According to Oberman, one can understand Frederick *only* as a Christian sovereign.[34] Wider application seems merited from Heiko Oberman's specific assessment of Frederick during the 1519 election of Karl V.

Historians of every stripe have found only one statesman thoroughly praiseworthy: Frederick the Wise. A German and a man of integrity, he is considered to have been a staunch representative of the interests of the empire in a sea of corruptibility and national betrayal.[35]

Peter Schmid in 1988 concluded the common reproach of Frederick for his "clumsiness, indecision and passivity" in imperial politics is based only on his last years of life.[36] Schmid's research into the *Reichstag* activity during the years of Maximilian resulted in an opposite conclusion about Frederick's character.[37] Until 1498, Frederick not only had a special zeal for imperial politics but had considerable influence on Maximilian. After the two fell out in 1498, Frederick's continued influence on imperial politics at times crippled Maximilian.

In 1985, Martin Brecht, Luther's definitive biographer, assessed Frederick.

> As a person he was almost shy and cautious. He sought to avoid risks and conflicts as much as possible. . . . Despite all his deliberateness, Frederick knew how to pursue his goals persistently and tenaciously, and success was also not denied him. Last but not least, Frederick's political decisions were influenced by a sense of moderation and a pronounced feeling for justice. . . . He opposed an expansion of the emperor's and empire's privileges over the territories. Thus among the princes he became the leading opponent to imperial power within the empire.[38]

Last but not least is the assessment of Ingetraut Ludolphy, Frederick's most thorough biographer.[39] Ludolphy chose not to offer the biography of Frederick in a linear development but to examine Frederick in his three core roles: territorial prince, imperial prince, and Christian prince.[40] Two great inhibitions denied Frederick an aggressive territorial expansion: he did not like to use force, and from day one he spent all his money and energies trying to make a respectable electorate out of the shambles he inherited from the Leipzig Division. He kept pace with improvements in governance of other territories, but he was not himself an innovator. As an imperial prince, he had enormous influence. By 1500, he opposed strengthening the emperor. Frederick was definitely no champion of enlightened imperial reform like Berthold of Mainz. It is as a Christian prince that Frederick stands above all others of his time. From a sense of justice and Christian duty, he risked his electorate to protect the truth he thought Martin Luther revealed in the Holy Scriptures.

BIBLIOGRAPHY

Aland, Kurt. *Kirchengeschichtliche Entwürfe*. Gütersloh: Gütersloher, 1960.

Allgemeine Deutsche Biographie. Edited by Historischen Kommission bei der Bayrischen Akademie der Wissenschaften. Leipzig: Duncker & Humblot, 1875–.

Andreas, Willy. *Deutschland vor der Reformation: Eine Zeitenwende*. 6th edition. Stuttgart: Deutsche Verlags-Anstalt, 1959.

Arnold, Benjamin. *Medieval Germany, 500–1300: A Political Interpretation*. Toronto: University of Toronto Press, 1997.

Bacon, Paul. "Art Patronage and Piety in Electoral Saxony: Frederick the Wise Promotes the Veneration of His Patron, St. Bartholomew." *Sixteenth Century Journal* 39, no. 4 (2008): 973–1001.

———. "Humanism in Wittenberg: Frederick the Wise, Konrad Celtis, and Albrecht Dürer's 1508 *Martyrdom of the Ten Thousand Christians*." *Konsthistorisk Tidskrift* 82, no. 1 (2013): 1–25.

———. "Mirror of a Christian Prince: Frederick the Wise and Art Patronage in Electoral Saxony 1486–1525." PhD diss., University of Wisconsin—Madison, 2004.

Bader, Karl Siegfried. "Approaches to Imperial Reform at the End of the Fifteenth Century." Pages 225–62 in *Pre-Reformation Germany*. Edited by Gerald Strauss. New York: Harper & Row, 1972.

Bainton, Roland H. *Here I Stand*. New York: Abingdon-Cokesbury, 1950.

Bauman, Michael, and Martin Klauber, eds. *Historians of the Christian Tradition*. Nashville: Broadman & Holman, 1995.

Baumgartner, Frederic J. *Louis XII*. New York: St. Martin's Press, 1994.

Behaghel, Otto. *A Short Historical Grammar of the German Language*. Translated by Emil Trechmann. New York: Macmillan, 1891.

Bemmann, Rudolf. *Zur Geschichte des Reichstags im XV. Jahrhundert*. Leipzig, 1907.

Benecke, Gerhard. *Maximilian I (1459–1519): An Analytical Biography*. London: Routledge & Kegan Paul, 1982.

Blaschke, Karlheinz. "Herzog Albrecht der Beherzte—Ein sächsischer Fürst im Reich und in Europa." Pages 13–26 in *Herzog Albrecht der Beherzte*

(1443–1500): Ein sächsischer Fürst im Reich und in Europa. Edited by André Thieme. Cologne: Böhlau, 2002.

———. "Kurfürst Friedrich der Weise von Sachsen und die Luthersache." In *Der Reichstag zu Worms von 1521.* Edited by Fritz Reuter, et al. Worms: Norberg, 1971.

———. "Leipziger Teilung der wettinische Länder von 1485." *Sächsische Heimatblätter* (1985).

Boehme, Johann Gottlob. *Sächsisches Groschen-Cabinet.* Leipzig: Waysenhaus- und Fromman nischen Buchhandlung, 1769.

Boehmer, Heinrich. *Der junge Luther.* 3rd edition. Leipzig: Koehler & Amelang, 1939.

———. *Road to Reformation: Martin Luther to the Year 1521.* Translated by John W. Dobberstein and Theodore G. Tappert. Philadelphia: Muhlenberg Press, 1946.

Borkowsky, Ernst. *Das Leben Friedrichs des Weisen: Kurfürsten zu Sachsen.* Jena: Eugen Diederichs, 1929.

Brady, Thomas A. Jr. "Review: Imperial Destinies: A New Biography of the Emperor Maximilian I." *Journal of Modern History* 62, no. 2 (June 1990): 298–314.

Brandi, Karl. *The Emperor Charles V.* Translated by C. V. Wedgewood. New York: Knopf, 1939.

Brather, Hans-Stephan. "Administrative Reforms in Electoral Saxony at the End of the Fifteenth Century." In *Pre-Reformation Germany.* Edited by Gerald Strauss. New York: Harper & Row, 1972.

Bräuer, Siegfried. "Wallfahrtsforschung als Defizit der reformations-geschichtlichen Arbeit." Pages 15–49 in *Spätmittelalterliche Wallfahrt im mitteldeutschen Raum.* Edited by Hartmut Kühne et al. Berlin: Humboldt-Univ., 2002.

Brecht, Martin. *Martin Luther: His Road to Reformation, 1483–1521.* Translated by James L. Schaaf. Minneapolis: Fortress, 1985.

———. *Martin Luther: Shaping and Defining the Reformation, 1521–1532.* Translated by James L. Schaaf. Minneapolis: Fortress, 1990.

Brinkmann, Bodo, and Stephan Kemperdick. *Deutsche Gemälde im Städel 1300–1500.* Kataloge der Gemälde im Städelsches Kunstinstitut Frankfurt am Main 4. Mainz: Von Zabern, 2002.

Bruck, Robert. *Friedrich der Weise als Förderer der Kunst.* Strassburg: Heitz & Mündel, 1903.

Buchner, Ernst. *Das deutsche Bildnis der Spätgotik und der frühen Dürerzeit.* Berlin: Deutscher Verein für Kunstwissenschaft, 1953.

Buchner, Maximilian. "Zur Biographie des Stammvaters des sächsischen Königshauses, Herzog Albrechts des Beherzten und seines Bruders, Kurfürsten Ernst von Sachsen." *Neues Archiv für sächsische Geschichte* 29 (1908): 155–62.

Bünz, Enno. "Die Heiltumssammlung des Degenhart Pfeffinger." Pages 125–69 in *"Ich armer sundiger Mensch": Heiligen- und Reliquienkult am Übergang zum konfessionellen Zeitalter.* Edited by Andreas Tacke. Schriftenreihe der Stiftung Moritzburg 2. Göttingen: Wallstein, 2006.

———. "Die Kurfürsten von Sachsen bis zur Leipziger Teilung (1423–1485)." In *Der Herrscher Sachsens: Markgrafen, Kurfürsten, Könige 1089–1918.* Edited by Frank-Lothar Kroll. Munich: Beck, 2004.

Burkhardt, C. A. H. "Das tolle Jahr zu Erfurt und seine Folgen 1509–1523." *Archiv für sächsische Geschichte* 12 (1874): 337–426.

———. "Die Vermählung des Herzogs Johann von Sachsen 1. bis 5. März 1500." *Neues Archiv für sächsische Geschichte* 15 (1894): 283–98.

———. *Ernestinische Landtagsakten.* Volume 1: *Die Landtage von 1487–1582.* Jena: G. Fischer, 1902.

———. *Hand- und Adreßbuch der deutschen Archive.* 2nd edition. Leipzig: Grunow, 1887.

Cahill, Richard A. *Philipp of Hesse and the Reformation.* Mainz: von Zabern, 2001.

Cárdenas, Livia. "Albrecht von Brandenburg—Herrschaft und Heilige: Fürstliche Repräsentation im Medium des Heiltumsbuches." Pages 239–70 in *"Ich armer sundiger mensch": Heiligen- und Reliquienkult am Übergang zum konfessionellen Zeitalter.* Edited by Andreas Tacke. Schriftenreihe der Stiftung Moritzburg 2. Göttingen: Wallstein, 2006.

———. *Friedrich der Weise und das Wittenberger Heiltumsbuch.* Berlin: Lukas, 2002.

Chamberlin, E. R. *The Bad Popes.* New York: Dial Press, 1969.

Cohen, Jeremy. *Living Letters of the Law: Ideas of the Jew in Medieval Christianity.* Berkeley, CA: University California Press, 1999.

———. "Traditional Prejudice and Religious Reform: The Theological and Historical Foundations of Luther's Anti-Judaism." In *Anti-Semitism in Times of Crisis*. Edited by Sander L. Gilman and Steven T. Katz. New York: New York University Press, 1991.

Cordez, Philippe. "Wallfahrt und Medienwettbewerb: Serialität und Formenwandel der Heiltumsverzeichnisse mit Reliquienbildern im Heiligen Römischen Reich (1460–1520)." Pages 37–73 in *"Ich armer sundiger mensch": Heiligen- und Reliquienkult am Übergang zum konfessionellen Zeitalter*. Edited by Andreas Tacke. Schriftenreihe der Stiftung Moritzburg 2. Göttingen: Wallstein, 2006.

Cornette, James C. *Proverbs and Proverbial Expressions in the German Works of Martin Luther*. Edited by Wolfgang Mieder and Dorothee Racette. Bern: Lang, 1997.

Creutzberg, Heinrich. *Karl von Miltitz*. Freiberg im Breisgau: Herder, 1907.

Cummins, John. *The Hound and the Hawk: The Art of Medieval Hunting*. London: Weidenfeld & Nicolson, 1988.

Czok, Karl. *Geschichte Sachsens*. Weimar: Böhlau, 1989.

Dalberg-Acton, John, et al. *The Cambridge Modern History*. Volume 2: *The Reformation*. Cambridge: Cambridge University Press, 1904.

Dann, Caroline. "The Language of Ravishment in Medieval England," *Speculum* 86 (2011): 79–116.

Dark, Sidney. *The Story of the Renaissance*. New York: Doran, 1924.

Delang, Steffen. "Der Schloßbau." In *Deutsche Architektur und Plastik, 1470–1550*. Edited by Ernst Ullmann. Gütersloh: Prisma, 1984.

Delbrück, Hans. *Medieval Warfare*. Translated by Walter J. Renfroe Jr. Lincoln, NE: University of Nebraska Press, 1990.

———. *The Dawn of Modern Warfare*. Translated by Walter J. Renfroe Jr. Lincoln, NE: University of Nebraska Press, 1990.

Dobozy, Maria, ed. and trans. *The Saxon Mirror: A Sachsenspiegel of the Fourteenth Century*. Philadelphia: University of Pennsylvania Press, 1999.

Duby, Georges, and Philippe Ariès, gen. ed. *A History of Private Life*. Volume 2: *Revelations of the Medieval World*. Translated by Arthur Goldhammer. Cambridge, MA: Belknap, 1988.

Dülmen, Richard van. *Theatre of Horror: Crime and Punishment in Early Modern Germany*. Cambridge: Polity Press, 1990.

Ehmann, Wilhelm. "Johann Walter: Der erste Kantor der protestantischen Kirche." *Musik & Kirche* 6 (1934): 188–203.

Ermisch, Hubert. "Eine Hofhaltsrechnung Markgraf Wilhelms I (1386)." *Neues Archiv für sächsische Geschichte* 18 (1897): 1–30.

Eschenhagen, Edith. "Beiträge zur Social- und Wirtschaftgeschichte der Stadt Wittenberg in der Reformationszeit." *Lutherjahrbuch* 9 (1927): 29–41.

Faber, Felix. *The Wanderings of Felix Faber*. Translated by Aubrey Stewart. The Library of the Palestine Pilgrims' Text Society of London 8. London, 1897.

Fichtner, Paula Sutter. *Protestantism and Primogeniture in Early Modern Germany*. New Haven: Yale University Press, 1989.

Fischer, Robert. "Paltz und Luther." *Lutherjahrbuch* 37 (1970): 9–36.

Förstemann, Karl E. *Neues Urkundenbuch zur Geschichte der evangelischen Kirchen-Reformation*. Hamburg: Perthes, 1842.

Friedhuber, Ingeborg. "König Maximilian I., die Erbländer, das Reich und Europa im Jahre 1500." Diss., Graz, 1963.

Friedländer, Max J., and Jakob Rosenberg. *The Paintings of Lucas Cranach*. Revised edition. Ithaca, NY: Cornell University Press, 1978.

Ganss, George E. "Changing Objectives and Procedures in Teaching Latin, 1556–1956." *The Classical Journal* 52, no. 1 (October 1956): 15–22.

Gollwitzer, H., ed. *Deutsche Reichstagsakten unter Maximilian I*. Göttingen: Vandenhoeck & Ruprecht, 1979.

Gow, Andrew Colin. *The Red Jews: Antisemitism in an Apocalyptic Age, 1200–1600*. Leiden: Brill, 1995.

Gross, Reiner. *Geschichte Sachsens*. Berlin: Edition Leipzig, 2001.

Grossmann, Maria. *Humanism in Wittenberg, 1485–1517*. Nieuwkoop: de Graaf, 1975.

Haile, H. G. *Luther: An Experiment in Biography*. London: Sheldon, 1980.

Hannay, David. *The Sea Trader, His Friends and Enemies*. Boston: Little, Brown & Co., 1912.

Hänsch, Ernst. "Die wettinische Hauptteilung von 1485 und die aus ihr folgenden Streitigkeiten bis 1491." PhD diss., University of Leipzig, 1909.

Harksen, Sibylle. "Schloss und Schlosskirche in Wittenberg." In *450 Jahre Reformation*. Edited by Leo Stern and Max Steinmetz. Berlin: Deutscher Verlag der Wissenschaften, 1967.

Hartung, Fritz. "Imperial Reform, 1485–1495: Its Course and Its Character." Pages 73–135 in *Pre-Reformation Germany*. Edited by Gerald Strauss. New York: Harper & Row, 1972.

Hastings, James, gen. ed. *Encyclopedia of Religion and Ethics*. Volume 6. New York: C. Scribner's Sons, 1925.

Hausrath, Adolf. *Luthers Leben 2*. Berlin: Grote, 1905.

Hendrix, Scott. *Martin Luther: A Very Short Introduction*. Oxford: Oxford University Press, 2011.

Herz, Hans. "Zu einigen Problemen der Landsteilungen in Thüringen vom 16. bis zum Beginn des 19. Jahrhunderts." *Zeitschrift des Vereins für Thüringische Geschichte* 46 (1992).

Heyck, Eduard. *Deutsche Geschichte: Volk, Staat, Kultur und geistiges Leben*. Volume 2. Leipzig: Velhagen & Klasing, 1906.

Hildebrandt, Ernst. *Die kurfürstliche Schloß- und Universitätsbibliothek zu Wittenberg 1512–1547: Beiträge zu ihrer Geschichte*. Diss., University of Leipzig, 1925.

Hill, David Jayne. *A History of Diplomacy in the International Development of Europe*. Volume 2: *The Establishment of Territorial Sovereignty*. London: Longmans, Green & Co., 1914.

Hintzenstern, Herbert von. "Kurfürst Johann von Sachsen." Pages 98–105 in *Kaiser, König, Kardinal: Deutsche Fürsten, 1500–1800*. Edited by Rolf Straubel and Ulman Weiß. Leipzig: Urania-Verlag, 1991.

Holborn, Hajo. *A History of Modern Germany: The Reformation*. New York: Knopf, 1959.

Hoppe, Stephan. "Anatomy of an Early 'Villa' in Central Europe: The Schloss and Garden of the Saxon Elector Frederick the Wise in Lochau (Annaburg) according to the 1519 Report of Hans Herzheimer." Pages 159–70 in *Maisons des champs dans l'Europe de la Renaissance*. Edited by Monique Chatenet. Paris: Picard, 2006.

Höß, Irmgard. *Georg Spalatin, 1488–1545: Ein Leben in der Zeit des Humanismus und der Reformation*. Weimar: Böhlaus, 1956. 2nd edition, Weimar: Böhlau, 1989.

Hutchison, Jane Campbell. *Albrecht Dürer: A Biography*. Princeton, NJ: Princeton University Press, 1990.

Immenkötter, Herbert. "Albrecht von Brandenburg and Friedrich der Weise: Ein Weg zu zwei Zielen." Pages 11–21 in *Cranach: Meisterwerke auf Vorrat.* Edited by Andreas Tacke. Munich: Form-Druck, 1994.

Jäger, Albert. "Der Übergang Tirols und der österreichischen Vorlande von dem Erzherzoge Siegmund an den römischen König Maximilian von 1478 bis 1490." *Archiv für österreichische Geschichte* 51 (1873): 297–448.

Jung, Martin H. *Philipp Melanchthon und seine Zeit.* Göttingen: Vandenhoeck & Ruprecht, 2010.

Kalkoff, Paul. *Ablaß und Reliquienverehrung an der Schloßkirche zu Wittenberg unter Friedrich dem Weisen.* Gotha: Perthes, 1907.

———. "Friedrich der Weise und Luther." *Historische Zeitschrift* 132 (1925): 23–43.

Karant-Nunn, Susan. "Luther's Pastors: The Reformation in the Ernestine Countryside." *Transactions of the American Philosophical Society* 69, no. 8 (1979): 1–80.

Kirn, Paul. *Friedrich der Weise und die Kirche.* Leipzig: Teubner, 1926.

Klein, Thomas. "Politik und Verfassung von der Leipziger Teilung bis zur Teilung des ernestinischen Staates (1485–1572)." In *Geschichte Thüringens.* Volume 3: *Das Zeitalter des Humanismus und der Reformation.* Edited by Hans Patze. Cologne: Böhlau, 1967.

Kleineidam, Erich. *Universitas studii Erffordensis: Überblick über die Geschichte der Universität Erfurt im Mittelalter, 1329–1521.* Leipzig: St. Benno-Verlag, 1964.

Koepplin, Dieter, and Tilman Falk. *Lukas Cranach: Gemälde, Zeichnungen, Druckgraphik.* 2 vols. Basel: Birkhäuser, 1974–76.

Kolde, Theodor. *Friedrich der Weise und die Anfänge der Reformation.* Erlangen: Deichert, 1881.

Kötzschke, Rudolf, and Hellmut Kretzschmar. *Sächsische Geschichte.* Dresden: Heinrich, 1935. Revised edition: Edited by H. Schiekel. Frankfurt am Main: Weidlich, 1965.

Kühnel, Klaus. *Friedrich der Weise, Kurfürst von Sachsen.* Wittenberg: Drei Kastanien, 2004.

Küne, Heinrich. "Der Wittenberger Buch- und Papierhandel im 16. Jahrhundert." In *450 Jahre Reformation.* Edited by Leo Stern and Max Steinmetz. Berlin: Deutscher Verlag der Wissenschaften, 1967.

Küng, Hans. *Great Christian Thinkers.* New York: Continuum, 1995.

Langenn, Friedrich Albert von. *Herzog Albrecht der Beherzte*. Leipzig: Hinrich, 1838.

———. *Züge aus dem Familienleben der Herzogin Sidonie und ihrer fürstlichen Verwandten aus dem 15. und 16. Jahrhundert*. Dresden: Meinhold, 1852.

Laube, Stefan. "Von der Reliquie zum Relikt: Luthers Habseligkeiten und ihre Musealisierung in der frühen Neuzeit." In *Archäologie der Reformation: Studien zu den Auswirkungen des Konfessionswechsels auf die materielle Kultur*. Edited by Carola Jäggi and Jörn Staecker. Berlin: de Gruyter, 2007.

———. "Zwischen Hybris und Hybridität: Kurfürst Friedrich der Weise und seine Reliquiensammlung." Pages 170–207 in *"Ich armer sundiger mensch": Heiligen- und Reliquienkult am Übergang zum konfessionellen Zeitalter*. Edited by Andreas Tacke. Schriftenreihe der Stiftung Moritzburg 2. Göttingen: Wallstein, 2006.

Leaver, Robin A. *Luther's Liturgical Music: Principles and Implications*. Grand Rapids: Eerdmans, 2007.

Lemper, Ernst-Heinz. *Die Thomaskirche zu Leipzig*. Leipzig: Koehler & Amelang, 1954.

Levenson, Jay A., ed. *Circa 1492: Art in the Age of Exploration*. Washington, DC: Yale University Press, 1991.

Lewis, C. S. *Studies in Medieval and Renaissance Literature*. Cambridge: Cambridge University Press, 1966.

Lewy, Max. *Schloss Hartenfels bei Torgau*. Berlin: Wasmuth, 1908.

Lohse, Bernhard. *Martin Luther: An Introduction to His Life and Work*. Translated by Robert C. Schultz. Philadelphia: Fortress, 1986.

———. *Martin Luther's Theology: Its Historical and Systematic Development*. Translated and edited by Roy A. Harrisville. Minneapolis: Fortress, 1999.

Lorenz, Christian Gottlob. *Die Stadt Grimma im Königreiche Sachsen*. Leipzig: Dyk, 1856.

Ludolphy, Ingetraut. Afterword for *Das Newe Testament Deutzsch*. Wittenber: Cansteinsche Bibelanstalt, 1972.

———. *Friedrich der Weise: Kurfürst von Sachsen, 1463–1525*. Gottingen: Vandenhoeck & Ruprecht, 1984.

Luther, Martin. *D. Martin Luthers Werke: Tischreden.* 6 vols. Weimar: H. Böhlau, 1912–21.

———. *Luther's Works: American Edition.* Volumes 1–30: Edited by Jaroslav Pelikan. St. Louis: Concordia, 1955–76. Volumes 31–55: Edited by Helmut Lehmann. Philadelphia/Minneapolis: Muhlenberg/Fortress, 1957–86. Volumes 56–82: Edited by Christopher Boyd Brown. St. Louis: Concordia: 2009–.

Meinhardi, Andreas. *The Dialogus of Andreas Meinhardi: A Utopian Description of Wittenberg and Its University (1508).* Translated and edited by Edgar C. Reinke. Ann Arbor, MI: University Microfilms International, 1976.

Mentz, Georg. *Johann Friedrich der Großmütige.* 3 volumes. Jena: Fischer, 1903–8.

Midelfort, H. C. Erik. *A History of Madness in Sixteenth-Century Germany.* Stanford: Stanford University Press, 1999.

———. *Mad Princes of Renaissance Germany.* Charlottesville: University Press of Virginia, 1994.

Mock, Markus Leo. *Kunst unter Erzbischof Ernst von Magdeburg.* Berlin: Lukas, 2007.

Moeller, Bernd. "Eine Reliquie Luthers." Pages 249–62 in *Die Reformation und das Mittelalter: kirchenhistorische Aufsätze.* Edited by Johannes Schilling. Göttingen: Vandenhoeck & Ruprecht, 1991.

Mrusek, Hans-Joachim. "Das Stadtbild Wittenbergs zur Zeit der Reformation und der Universität." In *450 Jahre Reformation.* Edited by Leo Stern and Max Steinmetz. Berlin: Deutscher Verlag der Wissenschaften, 1967.

Müller, Ernst. "Die Mutschierung von 1513 im ernestinischen Sachsen." *Jahrbuch für Regionalgeschichte* 14 (1987): 173–82.

Müller, Johann Joachim. *Annales des Chur- und Fürstlichen Hauses Sachsen . . . von Anno 1400 bis 1700.* Weimar: Gleditsch, 1700.

Murphy, G. Ronald, S.J. *The Heliand: The Saxon Gospel.* New York: Oxford University Press, 1992.

Oberman, Heiko A. *Luther: Man between God and the Devil.* Translated by Eileen Walliser-Schwarzbart. New Haven: Yale University Press, 1989.

———. *The Roots of Anti-Semitism in the Age of Renaissance and Reformation.* Translated by James I. Porter. Philadelphia: Fortress, 1984.

Oechsli, Wilhelm. *History of Switzerland, 1499–1914.* Translated by Eden Paul and Cedar Paul. Cambridge: Cambridge University Press, 1922.

Ozment, Steven. *Flesh and Spirit: Private Life in Early Modern Germany.* New York: Penguin, 2001.

Panofsky, Erwin. *Life and Art of Albrecht Dürer.* Princeton: Princeton University Press, 1943.

Parish, Helen. *Clerical Celibacy in the West: C. 1100–1700.* Farnham, UK: Ashgate, 2010.

Phillips, Andrew. *War, Religion and Empire: The Transformation of International Orders.* Cambridge: Cambridge University Press, 2011.

Plummer, Marjorie. "Clerical Marriage and Territorial Reformation in Ernestine Saxony and the Diocese of Merseburg in 1522–1524." *Archiv für Reformationsgeschichte* 98, no. 1 (2007): 45–70.

———. " 'The Much Married Michael Kramer': Evangelical Clergy and Bigamy in Ernestine Saxony, 1522–1542." Pages 99–115 in *Ideas and Cultural Margins in Early Modern Germany.* Edited by Marjorie Plummer and Robin Barnes. Farnham, UK: Ashgate, 2009.

Ranke, Leopold von. *History of the Reformation in Germany.* Translated by Sarah Austin. London: Routledge, 1905.

Redlich, Fritz. *The German Military Enterpriser and His Work Force.* Vierteljahrschrift für Sozial- und Wirtschaftsgeschichte 47–48. Wiesbaden: F. Steiner, 1964–65.

Reichert, Folker. "Von Dresden nach Jerusalem: Albrecht der Beherzte im Heiligen Land." Pages 53–71 in *Herzog Albrecht der Beherzte (1443–1500): Ein sächsischer Fürst im Reich und in Europa.* Edited by André Thieme. Cologne: Böhlau, 2002.

Reitzenstein, Karl von. "Unvollständiges Tagebuch auf der Reise Kurfürst Friedrich des Weisen von Sachsen in die Niederlande zum Römischen König Maximilian I. 1494." *Zeitschrift des Vereins für Thüringische Geschichte und Altertumskunde* 4 (1861): 127–37.

Ritschel, Iris. "Friedrich der Weise und seine Gefährtin: Überlegungen und Erkenntnisse zu fünf verdächtig(t)en Kunstwerken." Pages 296–41 in *"— Wir wollen der Liebe Raum geben": Konkubinate geistlicher und weltlicher Fürsten um 1500.* Edited by Andreas Tacke. Göttingen: Wallstein, 2006.

Rockwell, William Walker. *Die Doppelehe des Landgrafen Philipp von Hessen.* Marburg, 1904.

Röhricht, Reinhold. *Deutsche Pilgerreisen nach dem Heiligen Lande.* Innsbruck: Wagner, 1900.

———, and Heinrich Meisner. "Hans Hundts Rechnungsbuch (1493–1494)." *Neues Archiv für sächsische Geschichte und Altertumskunde* 4 (1883): 37–100.

Rösener, Werner. *Peasants of the Middle Ages.* Translated by Alexander Stützer. Cambridge: Polity Press, 1992.

Rüger, Johann Gottfried. *Geschichte und Beschreibung des kurfürstlich Sächsischen Soldatenknaben-Instituts zu Annaburg evangelischer und katholischer Religion.* Leipzig: Kummer, 1787.

Salmon, Paul. *Literature in Medieval Germany.* New York: Barnes & Noble, 1967.

Schadow, Johann Gottfried, ed. *Wittenbergs Denkmäler der Bildnerei, Baukunst und Malerei mit historischen und artistischen Erläuterungen.* Wittenberg, 1825.

Schick, Ingeborg. "König Maximilian der Erste: Und seine Beziehungen zu den weltlichen Reichsfürsten in den Jahren 1496–1506." Diss. Graz, 1967.

Schirmer, Uwe. "Die Ernestinischen Kurfürsten bis zum Verlust der Kurwürde (1485–1547)." Pages 55–75 in *Die Herrscher Sachsens: Markgrafen, Kurfürsten, Könige 1089–1918.* Edited by Frank-Lothar Kroll. Munich: Beck, 2004.

———. "Untersuchungen zur Herrschaftspraxis der Kurfürsten und Herzöge von Sachsen: Institutionen und Funktionseliten (1485–1513)." Pages 305–78 in *Hochadelige Herrschaft im mitteldeutschen Raum (1200 bis 1600): Formen, Legitimation, Repräsentation.* Edited by Jörg Rogge and Uwe Schirmer. Leipzig: Verlag der Sächsischen Akademie der Wissenschaften zu Leipzig, 2003.

Schmid, Peter. "Kurfürst Friedrich der Weise von Sachsen als Reichspolitiker." Pages 47–64 in *Fortschritte in der Geschichtswissenschaft durch Reichstagsaktenforschung: Vier Beiträge aus der Arbeit an den Reichstagsakten des 15. und 16. Jahrhunderts.* Edited by Heinz Angermeier and Erich Meuthen. Göttingen: Vandenhoeck & Ruprecht, 1988.

Schulze, Manfred. *Fürsten und Reformation.* Tübingen: Mohr, 1991.

Schwiebert, Ernest. *Luther and His Times.* St. Louis: Concordia, 1950.

Scott, Tom, and Robert W. Scribner, eds. *The German Peasants' War: A History in Documents.* Atlantic Highlands, NJ: Humanities Press, 1991.

Seton-Watson, R. W. *Maximilian I: Holy Roman Emperor.* Westminster: Constable, 1902.

Silver, Larry. *Marketing Maximilian: The Visual Ideology of a Holy Roman Emperor.* Princeton: Princeton University Press, 2008.

Smend, Rudolf. *Das Reichskammergericht.* Volume 1. Weimar: H. Böhlau, 1911.

Smith, Donald J. *Discovering Horse-drawn Vehicles.* Princes Risborough: Shire, 1994.

Smith, Preserved. *The Life and Letters of Martin Luther.* New York: Houghton Mifflin, 1911.

———, trans. and ed. *Luther's Correspondence and Other Contemporary Letters.* Volume 1. Philadelphia: Lutheran Publication Society, 1913.

———, and Charles Jacobs, trans. and ed. *Luther's Correspondence and other Contemporary Letters.* Volume 2. Philadelphia: Lutheran Publication Society, 1918.

———, and Herbert Gallinger, trans. and ed. *Conversations with Luther.* Boston: Pilgrim Press, 1915.

Spalatin, Georg. *Friedrichs des Weisen: Leben und Zeitgeschichte.* Georg Spalatins historischer Nachlaß und Briefe 1. Edited by Christian Gotthold Neudecker and Ludwig Preller. Jena: Friedrich Mauke, 1851.

Spitz, Lewis. *Conrad Celtis, the German Arch-humanist.* Cambridge, MA: Harvard University Press, 1957.

Steinmetz, David Curtis. *Luther in Context.* Bloomington: Indiana University Press, 1986.

Stephan, Bernd. "Beiträge zu einer Biographie Kurfürst Friedrichs III. von Sachsen, des Weisen (1463–1525)." PhD diss., University of Leipzig, 1979.

———. "Kulturpolitische Massnahmen des Kurfürsten Friedrich III., des Weisen, von Sachsen." *Lutherjahrbuch* 49 (1982): 50–95.

Stoy, Fritz. "Friedrichs des Weisen Hoflager in Lochau in seinen letzten Lebensjahren." *Forschung und Leben: Heimatblätter des Schönburgbundes: Arbeitsgemeinschaft für Heimatpflege im Regierungsbezirk Merseburg* 2 (1928): 276–90.

Strauss, Gerald. *Law, Resistance, and the State: The Opposition to Roman Law in Reformation Germany.* Princeton: Princeton University Press, 1986.

―――, ed. and trans. *Manifestations of Discontent in Germany on the Eve of the Reformation.* Bloomington: Indiana University Press, 1971.

―――. *Nuremberg in the Sixteenth Century.* New York: John Wiley & Sons, 1966.

Streich, Brigitte. "Politik und Freundschaft: Die Wettiner, ihre Bündnisse und ihre Territorialpolitik in der zweiten Hälfte des 15. Jahrhunderts." Pages 11–33 in *Kontinuität und Zäsur: Ernst von Wettin und Albrecht von Brandenburg.* Edited by Andreas Tacke. Göttingen: Wallstein, 2005.

―――. *Zwischen Reiseherrschaft und Residenzbildung: Der wettinische Hof im späten Mittelalter.* Cologne: Böhlau, 1989.

Sumption, Jonathan. *Pilgrimage: An Image of Mediaeval Religion.* London: Faber & Faber, 1975.

Tanner, Norman P., ed. *Decrees of the Ecumenical Councils.* London: Sheed & Ward, 1990.

Tappert, T. G., trans. and ed. *Luther: Letters of Spiritual Counsel.* Vancouver: Regent College Publishing, 2003.

Tentler, Thomas N. *Sin and Confession on the Eve of the Reformation.* Princeton: Princeton University Press, 1977.

Thieme, Andre, ed. *Herzog Albrecht der Beherzte (1443–1500): Ein sächsischer Fürst im Reich und in Europa.* Cologne: Böhlau, 2002.

Thurnhofer, Franz. "Die Romreise des Kurfürsten Ernst von Sachsen im Jahre 1480." *Neues Archiv für sächsische Geschichte und Altertumskunde* 42 (1921): 1–63.

Tutzschmann, Maximilian Moritz. *Friedrich der Weise, Kurfürst von Sachsen, ein Lebensbild aus dem Zeitalter der Reformation nach den Quellen für alle Stände dargestellt.* Grimma: Gebhardt, 1848.

Ullmann, Ernst, ed. *Deutsche Architektur und Plastik, 1470–1550.* Gütersloh: Prisma, 1984.

Ulmann, Heinrich. *Franz von Sickingen.* Leipzig: Hirzel, 1872.

―――. *Kaiser Maximilian I: Auf urkundlicher Grundlage dargestellt.* 2 vols. Stuttgart: Cotta, 1884–91.

Van Dyke, Paul. "The Literary Activity of the Emperor Maximilian I." *American Historical Review* 11 (1905): 16–28.

Virck, Hans. "Die Ernestiner und Herzog Georg von 1500 bis 1508." *Neues Archiv für sächsische Geschichte und Altertumskunde* 30 (1909): 1–75.

Virdung, Sebastian. *Musica Getutscht: A Treatise on Musical Instruments.* Edited and translated by Beth Bullard. Cambridge: Cambridge University Press, 1993.

Volkmar, Christoph. *Reform statt Reformation: Die Kirchenpolitik Herzog Georgs von Sachsen, 1488–1525.* Tübingen: Mohr Siebeck, 2008.

———. "Zwischen landesherrlicher Förderung und persönlicher Distanz: Herzog Georg von Sachsen und das Annaberger Heiltum." Pages 100–124 in *"Ich armer sundiger Mensch": Heiligen- und Reliquienkult am Übergang zum konfessionellen Zeitalter.* Edited by Andreas Tacke. Schriftenreihe der Stiftung Moritzburg 2. Göttingen: Wallstein, 2006.

Wiesflecker, Hermann. "Der Italienzug König Maximilians I. im Jahre 1496." *Carinthia I* 146 (1956): 581–619.

———. *Maximilian I.: Die Fundamente des habsburgischen Weltreiches.* Munich: Oldenbourg, 1991.

———. *Osterreich im Zeitalter Maximilians I.* Vienna: Verlag für Geschichte und Politik, 1999.

Wölfflin, Heinrich. *Die Kunst Albrecht Dürers.* 2nd edition. Munich: Bruckmann, 1908.

Wrede, Adolf, ed. *Deutsche Reichstagsakten unter Kaiser Karl V: Jüngere Reihe 2.* Stuttgart: Perthes, 1896.

Zöllner, Walter. "Der Untergang der Stifter und Klöster im sächsisch-thüringischen Raum während des Reformationszeitalters." Pages 157–69 in *450 Jahre Reformation.* Edited by Leo Stern and Max Steinmetz. Berlin: Deutscher Verlag der Wissenschaften, 1967.

NOTES

CHAPTER 1: THE BEGINNING

1. Georg Spalatin, *Friedrichs des Weisen: Leben und Zeitgeschichte von Georg Spalatin* (Georg Spalatins historischer Nachlaß und Briefe 1), ed. Christian Gotthold Neudecker and Ludwig Preller (Jena, 1851), 32. Translated from German. This and all subsequent translations (unless noted) are by the author.

2. Ernst died August 26, 1486, sometime after he "fell" from his horse while hunting.

3. Markus Leo Mock, *Kunst unter Erzbischof Ernst von Magdeburg* (Lukas Verlag, 2007), 217–18, reports unpublished details exist in Thüringisches Hauptstaatarchiv, Weimar, Ernestinisches Gesamtarchiv, Urk. 673, fol. 3r. Elector Ernst lingered long enough to execute his will.

4. Hajo Holborn, *A History of Modern Germany: The Reformation* (New York: Alfred Knopf, 1959), 27–28. The Golden Bull of 1356 was a quasi-constitution of the empire. The bull detailed procedures for voting, governance, and succession. It was revolutionary not only for its specificity but for obtaining active or passive approval from all the headstrong powers involved: Pope Innocent VI, Emperor Karl IV and the most powerful princes of the empire. The emperor, however, had been elected since the ninth century by the five *Stämme* of the Germanic people, among them Saxons, then since 1257 by seven electors.

5. Ernst Buchner, *Das deutsche Bildnis der Spätgotik und der frühen Dürerzeit* (Berlin: Deutscher Verein für Kunstwissenschaft, 1953), 129–31. Regarding this portrait in the Frankfurt Städelsches Kunstinstitut (Invoice Nr. 2128), Buchner, 130, stated (translated) the "dark brown, staring eyes with the great, precipitous pupils determine the overall impression of the picture," and noted the "intensive dull pink of the steeply oval face." Within the "Schutzmantel Madonna" (formerly at Schloss Grafenegg, Austria, but "lost" since 1945) is a virtual replica of the man portrayed in Frankfurt (though kneeling). Fortunately a banner in the Schutzmantel identifies the kneeling "Frederick Elector of Saxony" (in Latin). Bodo Brinkmann and Stephan Kemperdick, *Deutsche Gemälde im Städel 1300–1500*, Kataloge der Gemälde im Städelschen Kunstinstitut Frankfurt am Main, vol. 4 (Mainz, 2002), 368–74, summarize well the history of interpretation since 1953 as well as the museum's own investigations of the "resolute face . . . marked by a pronounced nose and prominent brown eyes" (translated). The identity of the artist can be no more specific than a Nuremberg Master.

6. Cf. Ingetraut Ludolphy, *Friedrich der Weise: Kurfürst von Sachsen, 1463–1525* (Gottingen: Vandenhoeck & Ruprecht, 1984), 14 (translated): "This head, whose severity is underlined by a sprouting beard, expresses concentration, willpower, and strength."

7. Germans for centuries regarded the rabbit as a symbol for cowardice. The great eyes portrayed for Frederick are probably valid. No other portraits from the period show enlarged eyes, so evidently the artist did not gratuitously add them as a desired attribute of the time.

8. Eduard Heyck, *Deutsche Geschichte; Volk, Staat, Kultur und geistiges Leben*, vol. 2, (Leipzig, 1906), 368, states that Albrecht by 1487 was called "the emperor's right arm" (translated).

9. Hans-Stephan Brather, "Administrative Reforms in Electoral Saxony at the End of the Fifteenth Century" in *Pre-Reformation Germany*, ed. Gerald Strauss (New York: Harper & Row, 1972), 236, characterized Hugold von Schleinitz, high marshal (*Obermarschall*) since 1464, as virtually all-powerful in Elector Ernst's court.

10. For a superior treatment of the division of Saxony, see Ernst Hänsch, "Die wettinische Hauptteilung 1485 und die aus ihr folgenden Streitigkeiten bis 1491" (PhD diss., University Leipzig, 1909), or see the more accessible Karlheinz Blaschke, "Leipziger Teilung der wettinische Länder von 1485" in *Sächsische Heimatblätter*, (1985), 276–80.

11. Brigitte Streich, *Zwischen Reiseherrschaft und Residenzbildung der wettinische Hof im späten Mittelalter* (Cologne: Böhlau, 1989), 534, notes the Wettin princes were so adverse to designating any permanent residence, their court (*Hof*) was highly mobile; Ernst and Albrecht, nevertheless, clearly preferred Dresden and began in the 1470s a grand residence in nearby Meissen (now called the Albrechtsburg).

12. Blaschke, 277.

13. Franz Thurnhofer, "Die Romreise des Kurfürsten Ernst von Sachsen im Jahre 1480," *Neues Archiv für sächsische Geschichte* 42 (1921): 3. Ernst's trip to Rome for an appeal to Pope Sixtus IV, and considerable money well spent, secured the future archbishopric of Mainz for his son Albrecht and the diocese of Halberstadt for his son Ernst, the latter already on track to become archbishop of Magdeburg. Moreover, (Thurnhofer, 22f.) the pope awarded Ernst the prestigious Golden Rose, an honor no previous Wettiner had received.

14. This is not equivalent to Frederick later entrusting Saxony to a coalition of Johann and Frederick's trusted councillors. Johann was a lightly experienced twenty-year-old.

15. This was already in Albrecht's inheritance since 1464. Streich 1989, 22, noted that the last will of Frederick the Meek (1459), in addition to the demand for "indivisibility *with no exception*" of the territory, bequeathed Albrecht (translated) "the castle and city of Dresden, the castle and city of Torgau together with Lochau, as well as a yearly pension of fourteen thousand gulden."

16. Streich 1989, 24: Wilhelm often left Thuringia in charge of his favorite nephew, Albrecht.

17. R. Kötzschke and H. Kretzschmar, *Sächsische Geschichte* (Dresden: 1935), revised H. Schiekel (Weidlich: Frankfurt am Main, 1965), 138–38. Also Karl Czok, *Geschichte Sachsens* (Weimar: Böhlau, 1989), 165.

18. Elector Frederick II (1412–64) was dubbed "the Meek" (or "Gentle") only in comparison to his father Elector Frederick I (1370–1428) who was called—for good reason—the "Warlike" or "Belligerent." Frederick the Meek, anything but meek, ruled so strongly that he formed Saxony into a powerful territorial state at the expense of the cities. Ernst Ullmann, ed., *Deutsche Architektur und Plastik, 1470–1550*, (Gütersloh: Prisma Verlag, 1984), 61, gives one example. Frederick the Meek's 1462 territorial protection letter for the entire construction trade (*"gesamte Bauwesen"*) allowed him to enlist any craftsman at any time for his own territorial projects.

19. Margaretha had indeed mediated between her husband and Wilhelm, according to Brigitte Streich, "Politik und Freundschaft. Die Wettiner, ihre Bündnisse und ihre Territorialpolitik in der zweiten Hälfte des 15. Jahrhunderts" in *Kontinuität und Zäsur: Ernst von Wettin und Albrecht von Brandenburg*, ed. Andreas Tacke (Göttingen: Wallstein Verlag, 2005), 25.

20. Kunz von Kaufungen, beheaded in the Saxon town Freiberg just days after the crime.

21. Blaschke, 278.

22. Reiner Gross, *Geschichte Sachsens* (Berlin: Edition Leipzig, 2001), 31. Chapter 1, "Historical Survey of Saxony before 1486," in Maria Grossmann, *Humanism in Wittenberg, 1485–1517* (Nieuwkoop: B. de Graaf, 1975), 10–19, is an excellent overview in English. Paula Sutter Fichtner, *Protestantism and Primogeniture in Early Modern Germany* (Yale University Press, 1989), 8, noted for "German houses": "Partible inheritance of all private and even some public resources associated with princely titles remained the rule until the beginning of the eighteenth century . . . There were, however, serious limitations on what any territorial ruler could do with the lands attached to whatever office he held in the empire." Ernst technically did not divide the electorate defined by the Golden Bull.

23. Holborn, 27, alludes to tension caused by the Habsburg dynasty becoming more European than German, especially after 1477 when future emperor Maximilian wed Mary of Burgundy. How could the aims of a "European" emperor ever agree with those of the German princes?

24. F. A. von Langenn, *Herzog Albrecht der Beherzte* (Leipzig, 1838), 550–53, quotes Albrecht's own statement that the scheming Schleinitz caused both the alienation of his brother and the bizarre Leipzig Division. Klaus Kühnel, *Friedrich der Weise: Kurfürst von Sachsen* (Wittenberg: Drei Kastanien, 2004), 11–12, and Ernst Borkowsky, *Das Leben Friedrichs des Weisen, Kurfürst zu Sachsen* (Jena: Eugen Diedrichs, 1929) assert Frederick also vigorously objected. Neither author, however, supports assertions with sources. Bernd Stephan, "Beiträge zu einer Biographie

Kurfürst Friedrichs III. von Sachsen, des Weisen (1463–1525)," (PhD diss., University Leipzig, 1980), 299, n. 130, notes that archives show only that Frederick and his brother Johann were in Leipzig with their father from September 20 to November 17, 1485; Ernst and Albrecht officially signed the division on November 11.

25. Enno Bünz, "Die Kurfürsten von Sachsen bis zur Leipziger Teilung, 1423–85," in *Die Herrscher Sachsens*, ed. Frank-Lothar Kroll (Beck, 2004), 54–55: A territorial prince of that time who admired nation-building would have been rare; they regarded their territory a family possession, their goals dynastic. Larry Silver, *Marketing Maximilian: The Visual Ideology of a Holy Roman Emperor* (Princeton University Press, 2008), repeatedly points out the Wettiners (and the Wittelsbachs even more so) viewed the Hapsburgs not as empire-builders but as a rival dynasty.

26. Bünz, 53.

27. The name "Meissen" referred to three entities in the divided Saxony of 1486 to 1539: (1) the *bishopric* of about 150 square kilometers; (2) the *city* of Meissen southeast of the bishopric; and (3) the *territory* of Mark Meissen, built up to about 5,000 square kilometers by the early Wettiners, that enveloped the other two.

28. Streich 1989, 470–75, argued that Kreuzkirche in Dresden has the strongest claim as the church for the royal court in the time of Ernst. Kreuzkirche did seem favored, much as Dresden was the favored residence. Yet, before their rift, Ernst and Albrecht were pulling the court to Meissen, to the Wettin burial site, and one main residence with one main church.

29. James C. Cornette, *Proverbs and Proverbial Expressions in the German Works of Martin Luther*, ed. Wolfgang Mieder and Dorothee Racette (Bern: Lang, 1997), 95: a rhymed proverb, "*Wer es reücht, aus dem es kreucht,*" that does not rhyme in literal translation.

30. Max Lewy, *Schloss Hartenfels bei Torgau* (Wasmuth, 1908), 9. The Wettins were indeed fond of Hartenfels castle in Torgau. Frederick the Meek was married there in 1428 and regularly resided there from October to Ash Wednesday. Hartenfels was weakly fortified but commodious for the time. Albrecht particularly liked to stay there.

31. Albrecht had clouded the issue even more by demanding compensation for all the money Ernst had doled out to secure two prime ecclesiastical positions for his sons (Mock, 13).

32. Maximilian Moritz Tutzschmann, *Friedrich der Weise, Kurfürst von Sachsen, ein Lebensbild aus dem Zeitalter der Reformation nach den Quellen für alle Stände dargestellt* (Grimma, 1848), 48, also assessed it in terms of travel time. Both the north-south distance and east-west distance are about 250 kilometers or 155 miles, but that is misleading as to the actual area. Thomas Klein, "Politik und Verfassung von der Leipziger Teilung bis zur Teilung des ernestinischen Staates (1485–1572)," in *Geschichte Thüringens*, eds. von Patze, Hans and W. Schlesinger, vol. 3. *Das Zeitalter des Humanismus und der Reformation* (Cologne/Graz, 1967), 148, calculates an area of 21,780 square kilometers (or about 8,400 square miles).

33. Werner Rösener, *Peasants of the Middle Ages*, trans. Alexander Stützer (Cambridge: Polity Press, 1992), 231. Many Saxon countryfolk were landowners and virtually free, stemming from incentives to move them from Flanders and other lands to farm the Saxon frontier. The writer uses countryfolk in preference to "peasants" and its multitude of connotations.

34. Ludolphy, 285–89, discusses sources of electoral income.

35. Gerald Strauss, *Nuremberg in the Sixteenth Century* (New York: John Wiley & Sons, 1966), especially 205–7, reports wages in detail.

36. Numerous studies estimate populations for this time. Among several relevant to Ernestine Saxony is Edith Eschenhagen, "Beiträge zur Social- und Wirtschaftgeschichte der Stadt Wittenberg in der Reformationszeit," *Lutherjahrbuch* 9 (1927): 29–41.

37. It is revealing and suggestive of future events that secular power was concentrated in the north and east; ecclesiastical power in the south.

38. Cornette, 85 (translated).

39. Ludolphy, 45–47, describes Frederick's education and training, but she relies primarily on Spalatin, 22–23.

40. Paul Kirn, *Friedrich der Weise und die Kirche* (Leipzig/Berlin, 1926), 9. Elector Ernst received the golden rose. Kirn is an excellent source for all matters concerning Frederick's religious beliefs and practices.

41. Heiko A. Oberman, *Luther: Man Between God and the Devil* (Yale University Press, 1990), 16–17.

42. Streich 1989, 407–8.

43. Bernd Stephan, "Kulturpolitische Massnahmen des Kurfürsten Friedrich III., des Weisen, von Sachsen," *Lutherjahrbuch* 49 (1982): 53.

44. Streich 1989, 515. All the boys ate in the women's quarter (*Frauenzimmer*), even into their early teen years.

45. Also prominent in a common household must have been Uncle Albrecht's wife Sidonia (1449–1510), daughter of George Podjebrad, the king who ruled Bohemia until 1471.

46. Among them were three future rulers of the split Saxonies: Frederick, Johann, and George.

47. Streich 1989, 407–8.

48. George E. Ganss, "Changing Objectives and Procedures in Teaching Latin, 1556–1956," *The Classical Journal* 52 (1956): 15.

49. Mock, 212.

50. Spalatin, 32.

51. Cornette, 69, 149, 37 (all translated).

52. Eschenbach performed in the court of Landgrave Hermann I of Thuringia. Hermann's residence was none other than the fabled Wartburg. During his rule, Frederick possessed this great castle, which would become Luther's refuge in 1521 and 1522.

53. Maria Dobozy, ed. and trans., *The Saxon Mirror: A Sachsenspiegel of the Fourteenth Century* (University of Pennsylvania Press, 1999). Superb English version.

54. G. Ronald Murphy, S.J., *The Heliand: The Saxon Gospel* (Oxford University Press, 1992).

55. Paul Salmon. *Literature in Medieval Germany* (New York: Barnes & Noble, 1967), 17, implies that the alliterative verse in the *Heliand* is not only unpleasant to read or speak, but it is also jarring.

56. Stephan 1982, 68. Also Stephan 1980, 374, n. 484: Frederick's grandmother Margaretha wrote his uncle Albrecht (translated), "Understand well astronomy and the motion of heavenly bodies," in 1472, the very year she took charge of Frederick. By "astronomy," she meant astrology.

57. Grossmann, 43. Dr. Mellerstadt, a physician, was also known as Martin von Pollich.

58. Spalatin, 32: one of Frederick's nineteen favorite proverbs (translated).

59. David Curtis Steinmetz, *Luther in Context* (Indiana University Press, 1986), 4–5.

60. Thomas N. Tentler, *Sin and Confession on the Eve of the Reformation* (Princeton University Press, 1977), 140–43.

61. Richard van Dülmen, *Theatre of Horror: Crime and Punishment in Early Modern Germany* (Cambridge: Polity Press, 1990).

62. Strauss 1966, 230.

63. Caroline Dann, "The Language of Ravishment in Medieval England," *Speculum* 86 (2011): 79–116, discusses rape in the late Middle Ages. She notes, 115, the vague regard for a difference between knightly conquest and rape in a chivalric epic like that of Chretien de Troyes. The German epic *Parzival* is similar. Did not Parzival rape the sleeping Jeschute? Certainly the influence of these widely-admired, orally transmitted epics was no help to women.

64. Streich 1989, 500.

65. Streich 1989, 496–97. Also Fritz Stoy, "Friedrichs des Weisen Hoflager in Lochau in seinen letzten Lebensjahren," *Forschung und Leben. Heimatblätter des Schönburgbundes. Arbeitsgemeinsch. f. Heimatpflege im Regierungsbezirk Merseburg* 2 (1928): 288.

66. Albrecht der Beherzte (the Courageous) was subject (as brother Ernst never was) of many books, past and present. Recent is Andre Thieme, ed., *Herzog Albrecht der Beherzte (1443–1500) Ein sächsischer Fürst im Reich und in Europa* (Cologne: Böhlau, 2002).

67. "Albrecht der Beherzte" in *Allgemeine Deutsche Biographie*, ed. Historischen Kommission bei der Bayrischen Akademie der Wissenschaften, vol. 1 (1875), 314: "*Kaisers gewaltiger Marschall und Bannermeister.*"

68. The Brandenburg elector was also the brother-in-law of Ernst and Albrecht, having married their sister Anna in 1458, yet another example of the intertwined higher nobility.

69. "Burgundy" is somewhat misleading. Burgundy *per se* was a large territory west of Basel (Switzerland), deep within the continent. Not obvious is that Charles the Bold (and thus Mary of Burgundy, then the Habsburgs) also ruled a sprawling territory on the North Sea that included roughly what is now Luxembourg, Belgium, and the Netherlands.

70. Spalatin, 23, 52. Notably, Spalatin's spare biography describes this incident twice.

71. Spalatin, 52. Spalatin's source was Sebastian von Mistelbach, about the same age as Frederick and a member of the electoral entourage since at least 1491.

72. Ludolphy, 86, quotes a story from Luther's table talk in which grandfather Frederick the Meek crowed (translated), "He is of our blood!" after toddler Frederick gulped down wild boar meat. Source is *D. Martin Luthers Werke: Kritische Gesamtausgabe, Tischreden* 6 volumes (Weimar: Hermann Böhlaus, 1912ff) 4:224, hereafter abbreviated WA TR.

73. Bear pens exist today in the moat around Hartenfels castle in nearby Torgau. Local lore claims the pens were there in some form since 1452, the Wettiners keeping as many as thirty brown bears, with eleven of the bears being slaughtered for the feast at Johann's coronation as elector in 1525. That is plausible, because princely feasts were often on such a colossal scale that all food had to be garnered. Ludolphy, 88, documents 11,500 guests attended Johann's wedding with Sophie of Mecklenburg in Torgau in 1500.

74. Even noble ladies felt pressure to join the hunt. In 1482, Maximilian's pregnant wife, Maria, fell from her horse while hunting and died. See Hermann Wiesflecker, *Maximilian I.: Die Fundamente des habsburgischen Weltreiches* (Munich: Oldenbourg, 1991), 51. Wiesflecker distills his definitive five-volume biography of Maximilian I into this one volume, which also includes his reflections over the intervening years.

75. Erwin Panofsky, *Life and Art of Albrecht Dürer* (Princeton University Press, 1943), 93: Frederick was "more than normally afraid of those epidemics which had haunted Germany."

76. Gerhard Benecke, *Maximilian I (1459–1519): An Analytical Biography* (London: Routledge, 1982), 158–62.

77. For Nuremberg: Benecke, 158–62. For Erfurt: Erich Kleineidam, *Universitas studii Erffordensis: Überblick über die Geschichte der Universität Erfurt im Mittelalter 1329–1521* (Leipzig, 1964), 1:180.

78. Streich 1989, 493.

79. Paul Bacon, "Art Patronage and Piety in Electoral Saxony: Frederick the Wise Promotes the Veneration of His Patron, St. Bartholomew," *Sixteenth-Century Journal* (2008): 973–1001, on page 989. Elisabeth died March 5, 1484, in Leipzig.

80. Paul Bacon, "Mirror of a Christian Prince: Frederick the Wise and Art Patronage in Electoral Saxony," (PhD diss., University Wisconsin-Madison, 2004), 64.

81. Klein, 181.

82. Klein, 179–80.

83. Maximilian Buchner, "Zur Biographie des Stammvaters des sächsischen Königshauses, Herzog Albrechts des Beherzten, und seines Bruders, Kurfürsten Ernst von Sachsen," *Neues Archiv für sächsische Geschichte* 29 (1908): 155–62. Details of the Amberg trip.

84. Mock, 15.

85. Jonathan Sumption, *Pilgrimage: An Image of Mediaeval Religion* (London: Faber & Faber, 1975), 265–66.

86. Stephan 1980, 30, believed Frederick was in Aschaffenberg with Albrecht.

87. Kirn, 166.

88. Thurnhofer 1921, 29, offers the example of Ernst visiting "beautiful women" in Venice during his 1480 Rome trip.

89. Brather, many pages.

90. Burchard-Gotthelf Struve, the librarian at Jena, attributed this in 1719 to Spalatin. Implied was documentary evidence. Hänsch, 9, confirms only the favorable part (translated): "Albrecht honored in Ernst the scrupulous conscientiousness, steadiness, and moderation."

91. Ludolphy, 306.

92. Stoy, 280f.

93. Klein, 183–84, offers a succinct account of Frederick's difficulties with Bohemia and Hungary in his earliest days of rule.

94. Barbara, half-sister of Brandenburg elector Johann Cicero, had married King Vladislaus only that August in 1476. This suggests the impetus was coming from Corvinus.

95. Wiesflecker 1991, 55.

96. Brather, 268, 244. Also Stoy, 277. Weimar had been under Uncle Wilhelm until 1482.

97. Streich 1989, 534: Saxon court councillors even into the 1500s strongly advised against any permanent place. Streich, 505–6: Only the most important castles had furniture and kitchenware. For lesser residences, all necessities had to be transported or borrowed locally.

98. Chapter "The Hussites" in Hans Delbrück, *Medieval Warfare* (1923 original in German, English reprint University Nebraska Press, 1990), 483–503.

99. Johann Cicero's father had voted (like Frederick's father, Ernst) to make Maximilian king in 1486 and like Frederick's father had died that same year. Johann Cicero was as pacific as his father, Albrecht Achilles, had been prone to war. Johann Cicero was the son of Albrecht's first wife, Katherine, not the son of his second wife who was Frederick's aunt Margarethe (of Thuringia).

100. Ludolphy, 243–48, discusses relationships of Ernestine Saxony with all adjacent neighbors, including menaces to the east and south.

101. Ludolphy, 245.

102. Kirn, 29–36; Ludolphy, 375–78.

103. Frederick's advisers are assessed primarily from Uwe Schirmer, "Untersuchungen zur Herrschaftspraxis der Kurfürsten und Herzöge von Sachsen. Institutionen und Funktionseliten," in *Hochadelige Herrschaft im mitteldeutschen Raum (1200 bis 1600): Formen, Legitimation, Repräsentation*, ed. Jörg Rogge und Uwe Schirmer. (Leipzig/Stuttgart, 2003), 305–78, and Uwe Schirmer, "Die Ernestinischen Kurfürsten bis zum Verlust der Kurwürde 1485–1547," in *Die Herrscher Sachsens*, ed. Frank-Lothar Kroll (Beck, 2004), 55–71. Also Brather and Streich 1989.

104. Schirmer 2003, 368. Hugold von Schleinitz died in January, 1490. His family remained influential and the name appears often as advisers to the Wettins.

105. Brather, 236, and Ludolphy, 294. Brather notes that Doringberg may be Dörnberg.

106. From Schirmer 2003, 315–16, who attributes the information to Brather's archival work. Streich 1989, 429, noted that two important officials, Guntherode and doorkeeper Karlowitz, almost immediately had no roles at all.

107. Streich 1989, 410. The first hint of the later flood of advisers from the universities.

108. Streich 2005, 11. Prior to Ernst, many marriages occurred between Wettiners and various Braunschweig lines. Frederick's own paternal great grandfather Frederick the Warlike wed Catherina of Braunschweig-Lüneburg.

109. Klein, 184.

110. Kirn, 84 (translated): "The Franciscan order probably stood of all ecclesiastical orders closest to the Wettin princes. . . . Frederick and Johann promoted them in every manner. Also here were their aims: introduction of the devout ascetic life in every single cloister; unity within the order (of Franciscans). . . . In the following years until 1496 the following conventions were reformed: Weimar (before 1487), Wittenberg and Torgau (1488), Altenburg (1489), Saalfeld and Weida (1493), Coburg (1496). In all these cases, both princes gave the motivation."

111. Walter Zöllner, "Der Untergang der Stifter und Klöster im sächsisch-thüringischen Raum während des Reformationszeitalters," 157–69, in *450 Jahre*

Reformation, ed. Leo von Stern and Max Steinmetz (Berlin: VEB Verlag der Wissenschaften, 1967), 157.

112 Kirn, 195–97, provides a list of the reformed.

113. Ludolphy, 378. No doubt money was involved. Innocent VIII's successor in 1492 was Pope Alexander VI, even more corrupt.

114. Cornette, 111 (translated).

115. Rogge & Schirmer, 12. The medieval early-modern concept of *"Repräsentation"* means far more than its English cognate.

116. Klein, 183. Frederick's advisers had gone to Frankfurt in January that year to ask the other estates for help against Bohemia "if it came to swords" (translated).

117. Strauss 1966, is unsurpassed for a source in English that describes Nuremberg during this time.

118. Ludolphy, 140–41.

119. Ludolphy, 98–99. Nurembergers at that time crafted the finest brass instruments in the empire; they must have appreciated the famed Saxon trumpeting.

120. Excellent sources in English for politics of *Reichstags* and politics of the Holy Roman Empire are Fritz Hartung, "Imperial Reform, 1485–1495: Its Course and its Character" and Karl Siegfried Bader, "Approaches to imperial Reform at the End of the Fifteenth Century," both sources in *Pre-Reformation Germany*, ed. Gerald Strauss (New York: Harper & Row, 1972), 73–135 and 225–62. Also helpful is Wiesflecker 1991.

121. During this *Reichstag*, Frederick probably sat for the portrait by the "Nuremberg master" (see fig. 1).

122. "Chapter 1: The First Poet Laureate" in Lewis Spitz, *Conrad Celtis, the German Arch-humanist* (Cambridge: Harvard University Press, 1957), 1–10.

123. According to Spitz, 7, the physician of Frederick the Wise, Martin Pollich of Mellerstadt, had been the one who touted Celtis to the prince.

124. Patricians were wealthy urban families, arising not from nobility but merchants. In this time, the nobility accepted patricians socially more and more.

125. Ludolphy, 93.

126. Ludolphy, 94. Confirmed by records kept by Hans Hundt von Wenkheim, Frederick's keeper of the door, who managed the private purse of Frederick.

127. Ludolphy, 32: Luther many years later said the same of Frederick, that he (translated) "gathered with a shovel and gave out with a spoon."

128. Rudolf Bemmann, *Zur Geschichte des Reichstags im XV. Jahrhundert* (Leipzig, 1907), proved that the view that the curia of cities did not yet exist is incorrect.

129. Hartung, 84, noted that even by 1491 the cities as an estate still remained dependent in every way on the decisions of the two higher estates. Imperial cities

supposedly owed allegiance only to the emperor. They were concentrated in the south, the most prominent being Frankfurt, Nuremberg, Augsburg, Cologne, and Worms.

130. Another irony was that Berthold had fought hard to elect Maximilian king in 1486, deluded into thinking Maximilian was himself a reformer.

131. The old fox in his lifetime never did allow an imperial judicial court.

132. Spalatin, 36. The five electors Frederick esteemed so highly remained intact for the next twelve years. In addition, Frederick's exclusive list had only three other names, all bishops: Friedrich of Entricht, Lorenz of Würzburg, and Gabriel of Bamberg.

CHAPTER 2: VISIONS OF A MANY-EYED PRINCE

1. Johann Gottfried Schadow, *Wittenbergs Denkmäler der Bildnerei, Baukunst und Malerei mit historischen und artistischen Erläuterungen* (Wittenberg, 1825), 48, stated this motto (in Greek from Homer) was on Frederick's bedroom wall at the Lochau.

2. For political activity inside and outside Ernestine Saxony from the rest of 1487 until the end of 1489, sources are Ludolphy and Hartung and less so, Wiesflecker 1991 and Bader.

3. Hartung, 91.

4. Ludolphy, 141.

5. Wiesflecker 1991, 52–60, describes the capture, release, and revenge. The Austrian Wiesflecker has a much higher opinion of Maximilian than the Habsburg emperor's previous definitive biographer Heinrich Ulmann, *Kaiser Maximilian I. Auf urkundlicher Grundlage dargestellt*, 2 vols. (Stuttgart, 1884 and 1891). Ulmann was German. In this regard, Frederick and Berthold do not fare as well with Wiesflecker as they fared with Ulmann. Nevertheless, both Wiesflecker and Ulmann are respected scholars.

6. Wiesflecker 1991, 57.

7. Ludolphy, 141–42.

8. Brather, 230–31.

9. Streich, 602. More astonishing yet, after Blasbalg's death in 1490, his widow held the office for a while. Apollonia was from the Alnpeck banking family of Freiberg.

10. Ludolphy, 291.

11. Ludolphy, 244.

12. Mock, 22. Ernst's independence may have been due to the combination of his maturity and the deaths of his mentors, his father in 1486 and Bishop Johann of Mcissen in 1487.

13. Frederick already showed a pattern of never committing until the last possible second.

14. Corvinus was also squabbling with the papal court and the Venetians over fruits of the Ottoman civil war.

15. Hartung, 92.

16. Bader, 147, states that every proposal Maximilian advanced in imperial diets from 1486 to 1504 amounted to the same objective: to raise money from the estates so he could wage war.

17. Andre Thieme, "Herzog Albrecht der Beherzte im Dienste des Reiches" in *Herzog Albrecht der Beherzte (1443–1500) Ein sächsischer Fürst im Reich und in Europa*, ed. Andre Thieme (Cologne: Böhlau, 2002), 95: *"langwierigen und grausamen."*

18. Ludolphy, 54: based on a document in Weimar that can no longer be located.

19. Ludolphy, 55.

20. Ludolphy, 289.

21. For Frederick's strategy, see Ludolphy and Bacon 2004. Also Livia Cardenas, *Friedrich der Weise und das Wittenberger Heiltumsbuch* (Berlin, 2002). For Wittenberg see Ernest Schwiebert, *Luther and His Times* (St. Louis: Concordia, 1950), 199–253, and Grossmann.

22. Not to be inferred as *the* residence.

23. Schwiebert, 205–7: Christopher Scheurl and Philip Melanchthon, though both friends of the elector, agreed it was a dismal backward village in the early 1500s.

24. Schwiebert, 199.

25. Hans-Joachim Mrusek, "Das Stadtbild von Wittenberg zur Zeit der Reformation und der Universität" in *450 Jahre Reformation*, ed. Leo von Stern and Max Steinmetz (1967), 327 (translated): "Already by 1487, the elector had established the Elbe Bridge—a well thought-out wooden construction." Also Ludolphy, 121.

26. Robert Bruck, *Friedrich der Weise als Förderer der Kunst* (Strassburg: Heitz & Mündel, 1903), 240: In 1487, Konrad Pflüger was *"In festem Sold beim Kurfürsten"* and in 1488, *"Lebt er in Wittenberg."* Sibylle Harksen, "Schloss und Schlosskirche in Wittenberg" in *450 Jahre Reformation*, ed. Leo von Stern and Max Steinmetz (1967), 357, goes further, stating Pflüger was involved at Wittenberg since 1486. She also thinks reasonably that Pflüger helped Frederick plan the new Wittenberg castle from the outset. Pflüger's many achievements are summarized in Ernst-Heinz Lemper, *Die Thomaskirche zu Leipzig* (Leipzig, 1954), 87f.

27. The style of Arnold von Westfalen is often called "late Gothic," a term noted by many scholars as misleading. His style was more a forerunner of Renaissance architecture than a last stage of Gothic.

28. Harksen, 356, note 65: *"Er hat vielleicht in seiner trüben Wittenberge Zeit am Elbbrückenbau mitgearbeitet."*

29. Ludolphy, 121; Bacon 2004, 22; Grossmann, 114.

30. Bacon 2004, 20–21; Cardenas, 17, 127, adds as another reason that Wittenberg was a crossroad for trade routes. Stefan Laube, "Zwischen Hybris und Hybridität. Kurfürst Friedrich der Weise und seine Reliquiensammlung" in "Ich armer sundiger mensch": Heiligen- und Reliquienkult am Übergang zum konfessionellen Zeitalter, ed. Andreas Tacke (Göttingen: Wallstein Verlag, 2006), 170–207, suggests the relic collection was also a strong factor.

31. Bacon 2004, 23–36, discusses in detail the Ascanian heritage in Wittenberg.

32. Bacon 2004, 38. Meissen itself had served the House of Wettin since 1089.

33. Schwiebert, 218: The Ascanians were buried in Wittenberg but not in the memorial chapel; they were buried in the Franciscan cloister located near the north town wall. Years after Frederick's death, Johann Friedrich ordered the twenty-seven coffins moved to the basement of the Castle Church.

34. Bacon 2004, 41.

35. Mock, 188: Frederick always considered the thorn his most precious relic.

36. Laube, 174–76, notes Frederick by nature collected passionately: watches, handicrafts, coins, enameled boxes, and oddities of nature such as antlers, stones, and ivory.

37. At the 1507 Constance Reichstag, Pope Julius II appealed to the entire empire to send Frederick relics. That in no way marked the beginning of Frederick's passion. By 1507, he had already built the sanctuary for relics (as well as persuaded Julius to make the appeal).

38. Philippe Cordez, "Wallfahrt und Medienwettbewerb. Serialität und Formenwandel der Heiltumsverzeichnisse mit Reliquienbildern im Heiligen Römischen Reich (1460–1520)" in Tacke, 2006, 37–73. Among others Cardenas, 25–32, also discusses older Heiltumsbücher.

39. Ludolphy, 40, cites as the source Georg Lauterbeck's 1563 German translation of two Philip Melanchthon orations (in Latin). Melanchthon asserted the motto (in Greek) was on Frederick's bedroom wall at the Lochau. The motto was popular in Frederick's time, championed among others by Erasmus as a noble pursuit preferable to making war.

40. Laube in Tacke 2006, 183, articulates almost that same goal (translated): "Frederick of Saxony wanted to make his town of Wittenberg a center by founding a university, establishing a church foundation, and installing a sacred relic shrine."

41. Albert Jäger, "Der Übergang Tirols und der österreichischen Vorlande von dem Erzherzoge Sigmund an den Röm. König Maximilian von 1478-1490," Archiv für österreichische Geschichte 51 (1873): 399.

42. Spalatin, 45 (translated): "Oh, indeed, so polite was Emperor Maximilian, that this elector said to me, Spalatin, at Colditz after a Communion, how his Grace

thought so highly of this Roman emperor that during his entire life he would meet no man on earth more gracious."

43. Spalatin, 45 (translated), regarding the *Reichstag* in Augsburg in 1518.

44. Theodore G. Tappert, ed. and trans., *Table Talk*, vol. 54 *Luther's Works*, ed. Jaroslav Pelikan and Helmut T. Lehmann, 56 volumes (St. Louis: Concordia; Philadelphia: Fortress Press, 1955–84) 420–21, [hereafter LW]. Maximilian anecdotes in *Table Talk* probably came to Luther from Spalatin and possibly thus indirectly from Frederick himself.

45. LW 54:213.

46. Sigismund is known for little else except imprisoning, then harrying to death in 1464 one of the geniuses of the century, Bishop Nicholas of Cusa. Katharina was to have a happier fate in her second marriage in 1497 to Duke Erich I of Braunschweig-Kalenberg, who in 1504 heroically saved Maximilian's life in a battle at Regensburg.

47. Ludolphy, 143.

48. Wiesflecker 1991, 133.

49. Brittany was a 13,000-square-mile peninsula jutting from the northwest of France. For centuries Brittany struggled to remain a duchy independent of both France and Britain.

50. Ludolphy, 143. Apocryphal is the story that brother Johann earned a *Mauerkrone* (wall crown) by storming the walls of the city. No evidence supports his presence there.

51. Chapter "The Establishment of a European Infantry" in Hans Delbrück, *The Dawn of Modern Warfare* (1920 original in German, English reprint University Nebraska Press, 1990), 9.

52. Ludolphy, 302.

53. Ludolphy, 248.

54. Schirmer, 2003: short biography of Leimbach in "Part VII. Registry of the most important Wettin working officials (1485–1513)" (translated).

55. Brather, 252–53. Ludolphy, 302–3.

56. Ludolphy, 284.

57. Ludolphy, 23–24, describes early coinage with Frederick's image.

58. Ludolphy, 248.

59. Ludolphy, 303: German idioms used by Luther to praise Frederick.

60. Ludolphy, 296–99, explains in detail the nature of the *Amt* office. The *Amt* was a concept several centuries old but a useful unit especially if updated. Frederick ordered each *Amt* office beginning in 1506 to rigorously maintain *Amt* books (*Amtserbüchern*), also called "inheritance books" (*Erbbücher*). The *Amt* office recorded possessions, rights, and income of the sovereign.

61. The *Vogtei* (or less commonly the *Pflege*) was even smaller, but it was local (often one castle or one village).

62. Gerald Strauss, *Law, Resistance, and the State: The Opposition to Roman Law in Reformation Germany* (Princeton University Press, 1986), 96.

63. Ludolphy, 298, quotes Luther.

64. Ludolphy, 294.

65. Spalatin, 33. *"Man soll nicht alles glauben wie es gesagt wirdet."*

66. Cornette, 55: *"Heute from, morgen ein schalck."*

67. Siegfried Bräuer, "Wallfahrtsforschung als Defizit der reformations-geschichtlichen Arbeit" in *Spätmittelalterliche Wallfahrt im mitteldeutschen Raum*, ed. H. Kühne and others (Eisleben, 2002), 15–49, notes gaps regarding Frederick's acts of piety even in the excellent works of Reinhold Röhricht und Heinrich Meisner (1883) and Kirn (1926). C. A. H. Burkhardt, *Hand- und Adreßbuch der deutschen Archive* (1887 2nd edition), 132, characterized the Ernestine Saxony archives in Weimar as virtually inexhaustible (*unerschöpflich*). It is no wonder subsequent studies keep filling in holes in earlier "comprehensive" studies.

68. Bräuer, 24–25. The six stops were, in order: "Fourteen Saints" near Jena, Ziegenhain, Heiligenleichnam south of Altenburg, St. Wolfgang Chapel "before" Meissen, Hayn (probably Großenhain), and Eicha near Naunhof.

69. Kirn, 166, 178.

70. Ludolphy, 351.

71. Streich 1989, 482. The three were not alone but with their marksmen, falconer, and ever present jester.

72. Ludolphy, 339–42, 354, relates Frederick's relation with Paltz in 1490 and before.

73. Ludolphy, 342.

74. Robert Fischer, "Paltz und Luther," *Lutherjahrbuch* 37 (1970), 31.

75. Bernhard Lohse, *Martin Luther's Theology: Its Historical and Systematic Development* (Minneapolis: Fortress Press, 1999), 15–16.

76. Spalatin, 28.

77. C. S. Lewis, *Studies in Medieval and Renaissance Literature* (Cambridge University Press, 1966), 45, points out that the medieval mind absorbed all knowledge, contradictory or not. Given time and patience, the medieval mind believed it would find an explanation to harmonize the contradictions. Rarely was knowledge "wrong."

78. Lohse, 13.

79. Kirn, 84.

80. Ludolphy, 361. She was the daughter of Prince Heinrich I of Münsterberg and later the wife of Ernst of Anhalt.

81. Ludolphy, 361–62 (translated).

82. Characterization of the Franciscans by Ludolphy, 368.

83. Cornette, 55: "*Ist einer from, so sind sie es alle.*"

84. Benecke, 160–61.

85. Ludolphy, 343.

86. Frederick attained a reputation later in life for being withdrawn, even aloof, but in his prime, when it came to representation, he often created a sensation.

87. Hartung, 84.

88. Hartung, 96.

89. Wiesflecker 1991, 74. "*Eine solche Schande ... könne nur durch Blut abgewaschen warden.*"

90. From age 13 in 1483 until 1491, Charles VIII had been under the regency administered by his older sister Anne, who was as strong and shrewd as Charles was weak and foolish.

91. Wiesflecker 1991, 79.

92. Jan Chlibec, "A description of Guido Mazzoni's Lamentation in Venice by a Bohemian traveller in 1493" in *The Burlington Magazine* 144 (2002), 19, indicates Beatrice, a stunning beauty who may have inspired da Vinci's "Mona Lisa," gave birth in 1493 to a son "Maximilian."

93. Ducat was a coin similar in weight and gold content to the Rhine gulden.

94. Wiesflecker 1991, 47. In a letter to confidant Sigismund Prüschenk (translated). Buxom "Rosina" seems yet another love of Maximilian.

95. Wiesflecker 1991, 79.

96. Bruck, 35–46 and Ludolphy, 120–25. Of Pflüger's castle-church complex, the church itself has been so damaged, rebuilt, and modified that virtually nothing but the dimensions is the same today. Best representation of the original church is Lucas Cranach's 1509 woodcut, shown in many references, including Martin Brecht, *Martin Luther: His Road to Reformation, 1483–1521* (Minneapolis: Fortress Press, 1985), 116.

97. Ludolphy, 123. Scheurl reported the old chapel still existed in 1508, after the new church was erected.

98. Ludolphy, 127–28. Frederick's brother, Archbishop Ernst, consecrated the church in 1499. Ironically, the "*Schöne Kirche*" was completely razed after only thirty-four years.

99. Lewy, 12–13.

100. Bruck, 239, shows Vogtsberg as "Voitsbergk."

101. Grossmann, 114.

102. Bacon 2004, 2.

103. Ludolphy, 314 (translated).

104. Heiko A. Oberman, *The Roots of Anti-Semitism in the Age of Renaissance and Reformation*, trans. James I. Porter (Philadelphia: Fortress Press, 1984), 85.

105. Jeremy Cohen, "Traditional Prejudice and Religious Reform: The Theological and Historical Foundations of Luther's Anti-Judaism" in *Anti-Semitism in Times of Crisis* ed. Sander L. Gilman and Steven T. Katz (New York University Press, 1991) and also Jeremy Cohen, *Living Letters of the Law: Ideas of the Jew in Medieval Christianity* (University California Press, 1999). These two Cohen articles and Oberman (1984) were used for the discussion of Frederick's anti-Semitism.

106. Benjamin Arnold, *Medieval Germany, 500–1300: A Political Interpretation* (University Toronto Press, 1997), 154.

107. Oberman 1984, 84–85.

108. The *Pharetra* was widely read, much more so than the now infamous *Malleus Maleficarum* written against witches by the Dominicans in 1487.

109. Unless noted, the source for all details about Albrecht's pilgrimage are from Folker Reichert, "Von Dresden nach Jerusalem. Albrecht der Beherzte im Heiligen Land" in Andre Thieme, ed., *Herzog Albrecht der Beherzte (1443–1500): Ein sächsischer Fürst im Reich und in Europa* (Böhlau Verlag, 2002), 55–71.

110. Spalatin, 27–28, "*Kirchbäuden, Zierden, Heilthum und Wallfahrten.*"

111. Bacon 2004, 44. The dread of death was lessened by a popular belief of the time that any pilgrim who died on a trip to the Holy Land went straight to heaven. Bacon 2004, 40–58, provides in English an extended summary of Frederick's trip to the Holy Land.

112. Reichert, 55.

113. All details of the will from Ludolphy: 316, 352, 378, 384.

114. Ludolphy, 378.

115. Ludolphy, 351. This was four days after Columbus returned to Spain from his world-changing voyage to the "Indies." Frederick must have heard about it on his trek to Austria, possibly hearing actual details of the voyage while at the imperial court in Linz.

116. Spalatin, 27. Also Ludolphy, 352.

117. Spalatin, 90. Some, of course, were already in Frederick's court.

118. Bacon 2004, 46. Frederick's Wettin predecessors had similar chroniclers: personal physician Hunolt von Plettenberg for Wilhelm the Brave in 1461, and *Landrentmeister* Hans von Mergenthal for Uncle Albrecht in 1476.

119. Frederick's trip is preserved in two primary sources: Reinhold Röhricht and Heinrich Meisner, "Hans Hundts Rechnungsbuch (1493–1494)," *Neues Archiv für sächsische Geschichte* 4 (1883): 37–100; Spalatin, 26–27, 76–91. After thirty years, Frederick could still remember dates, locations, and activities of his itinerary. Ludolphy, 106, mentions as a lesser source of participants a letter of April 1493 from

Munich citizen Andreas Sluder to Viennese merchant Hans Weinmann. Details about other pilgrimages of the time abound.

120. Duke Christoph was also younger brother of grumpy Duke Albert (1447–1508), mentioned frequently in later chapters.

121. Heinrich Röhricht, *Deutsche Pilgerreisen nach dem Heiligen Lande* (Innsbruck, 1900), 172–93, provides a listing concentrated from Spalatin, Hans Hundt (Röhricht and Meisner), and Sluder.

122. Schaumburg had actually been on a previous pilgrimage with none other than the Dominican friar Felix Faber, who left detailed journals of his pilgrimages.

123. Röhricht and Meisner, 46, 49, 53, 60, 62, mention expenditures for Hänsel but none for Hänsel in the Holy Land. A jester was too conspicuous for a prince traveling incognito. Kirn, 15, states Frederick sent Hänsel back from Venice.

124. These names from Röhricht and Meisner, 41. Although the Johannes Maler is often speculated to be Lucas Cranach, that is improbable.

125. They traveled about six hundred miles over a crooked route of easiest travel. They averaged daily on horseback an impressive thirty miles. This speed precludes wagons (still primitive in their suspension and axles), though the wagons could have followed.

126. The long designation indicating Freiburg in Breisgau, a region between the Rhine River and the *Schwarzwald* (Black Forest). Also called simply Freiburg.

127. Wiesflecker 1991, 76.

128. His indifference was possibly also due to the rough-and-tumble jouster Maximilian's contempt for the weak French king Charles VIII.

129. Wiesflecker 1991, 77.

130. Spalatin, 27. *"Hat ihn vielleicht geahnt, er würde ihn nicht mehr sehen. "*

131. Reichert, 65.

132. Spalatin, 78.

133. Much of the description of the Venetian passenger trade is from David Hannay, *The Sea Trader* (Boston: Little, Brown & Co., 1912), 56–60. Hannay, in turn, uses much information from the writings of Felix Faber.

134. It seems likely, therefore, that Frederick contracted the entire ship.

135. Hannay, 57–58, relates a pilgrim's experience sleeping in the hold below the horses on deck.

136. Georges Duby, ed., *A History of Private Life: Vol. II - Revelations of the Medieval World*, trans. Arthur Goldhammer (Cambridge, MA: Belknap Press, 1988), 587–88. Many versions of Felix Faber's diaries exist. One online source with his Latin translated into English is The Palestine Pilgrims' Text Society of London.

137. Reichert, 64.

138. Reichert, 68–71; Ludolphy 352. Albrecht took sixty-six days from Venice to Jerusalem, Frederick 59.

139. Reichert, 54; Röhricht and Meisner, 55.

140. The Hospitallers of the Knights of St. John was one of three religious orders that arose during the crusades for the defense of the Holy Land and the protection of pilgrims. Knights of St. John, sanctioned by Pope Gelasius in 1118, were true hospitallers for the sick and needy, whereas the other two orders, the Teutonic Knights of St. Mary's Hospital and especially the Knights Templar, were warrior knights.

141. Reichert, 59.

142. Reichert, 53–54, 60. In the 1700s, Johann Böttger, famous as the inventor of European porcelain, used this trophy to demonstrate a cutting edge developed by him. He skillfully sliced the "Temple of Solomon" into thin discs.

143. Felix Faber, *The Wanderings of Felix Faber*, trans. Aubrey Stewart, The Library of The Palestine Pilgrims' Text Society of London, vol. 8 (London, 1897), 567.

144. "Then Herod, when he saw that he had been tricked by the wise men, became furious, and he sent and killed all the male children in Bethlehem and in all that region who were two years old or under, according to the time that he had ascertained from the wise men."

145. Felix Faber, PTTS, 1897, 566.

146. Paul Kalkoff, *Ablaß und Reliquienverehrung an der Schloßkirche zu Wittenberg unter Friedrich dem Weisen.* (Gotha, 1907), 7.

147. Documents show it was typical for these fiery sea captains, despite their experience, to get in trouble with authorities onshore.

148. Reichert, 66.

149. Röhricht and Meisner, 39.

150. Ludolphy, 95.

151. Bacon 2004, 42.

152. Laube, 176, from his examination of Hans Hundt's accounting book.

153. Stoy, 282.

154. Ludolphy, 354. Today the Greek liturgical book is kept in the research library at Gotha in Thuringia.

155. Andreas Meinhardi, *The Dialogus of Andreas Meinhardi: A Utopian Description of Wittenberg and its University* (1508), trans. and ed. E. C. Reinke (Ann Arbor, MI: University Microfilms International, 1976), 242.

156. Spalatin, 128.

157. Ludolphy, 354. Bacon 2004, 55, states four deaths occurred on Frederick's trip to the Holy Land and several who were severely ill were left behind to recover.

158. Röhricht and Meisner, 39.

159. Spalatin, 89.

160. Wiesflecker 1991, 77.

161. Wiesflecker 1991, 78: The emperor would be buried ceremoniously in December in Vienna's great St. Stephan cathedral.

162. Röhricht and Meisner, 67.

163. Röhricht and Meisner, 44.

CHAPTER 3: IMPERIAL BEAU TO DISENCHANTED FOE

1. Spalatin, 33. "*Es ist von mancher Sachen leichtlich zu reden, aber schwerlich zu thun.*"

2. Spalatin, 33. "*Ein itzlichs Werke lobet seinen Meister.*"

3. Ludolphy, 121. Grossmann, 114, stated construction began in 1490.

4. Harksen, 356.

5. Harksen, 355–56.

6. The word *Wehrbau* originally meant a military construction or fortress, but later came to also mean a four-sided structure.

7. Sibylle Harksen, 341–66, discusses in detail how the original structures in the complex can be visualized. The castle of today is a bland reminder of the original. Today the southwest corner tower is round and undistinguished. The west and south wings are flat-roofed, seemingly sheer walls of a mortared cobble of bricks, natural rock and rough-cut stone. Set in the walls are relatively small, undistinguished rectangular windows.

8. Steffen Delang, "Der Schloßbau" in Ernst Ullmann 1984, 210, states that among lesser elements, the vaulted ceilings and curtain-arched windows verify that Frederick's ideal for his castle was Arnold's masterpiece, the Albrechtsburg in Meissen. Frederick did not slavishly follow Arnold's design, because the Albrechtsburg offers almost no military accommodation.

9. Were the windows honeycombed small bull's-eye panes?

10. Heinrich Kühne, "Der Wittenberger Buch- und Papierhandel im 16. Jahrhundert" in *450 Jahre Reformation*, ed. Leo von Stern and Max Steinmetz (1967), fig. 82 (woodcut from about 1550 of Wittenberg from the south, possibly by Cranach the Younger) shows the rose window.

11. Harksen, 346. A much later report (1760) stated the castle cellars were "all exceptionally nice and precious."

12. Ludolphy, 123–24.

13. Dimensions are from Bruck, 36, and Harksen, figure 107. Ground plans from that time were usually scaled in "*Ellen,*" which appear to be about one-half meter.

14. Harksen, 346.

15. Mock, 75.

16. Harksen, 364 (translated).

17. Harksen, 345, notes that the most relevant sources of what the interior might have looked like are castle inventories as well as the *Dialogue of Andreas Meinhardi*. Because the oldest inventories come from 1538, the best source is Meinhardi from 1508. This will be discussed in the following chapter, which better fits that time frame.

18. Bruck, 30–32, for details of the "butter money" and engineering difficulties.

19. The River Elbe was generally three hundred or so meters across and at its deepest three or four meters.

20. In 1494 and 1495, Behaim was the master builder of Nuremberg's colossal granary (*Kornhaus*), still standing today (on Königstrasse) after five hundred years.

21. Ludolphy, 359.

22. Bruck, 54.

23. Bruck, 50–52.

24. Uwe Schirmer, 2003, 365. Sebastian von Mistelbach would become Frederick's *Hofmarshall* in 1516.

25. Wilhelm Ehmann, "Johann Walter, der erste Kantor der protestantischen Kirche" in *Musik & Kirche* 6 (1934): 188–203.

26. By 1495, Frederick had at least five singers and three boy singers.

27. Robin A. Leaver, *Luther's Liturgical Music: Principles and Implications* (Eerdmans, 2007), 33.

28. Bacon, 67, 71, 73.

29. Cohn, 14. The old emperor, father of Maximilian, had particularly despised all Wittelsbachs. Elector Philipp, though much liked by Saxon elector Frederick, was belligerent and too often overplayed his hand.

30. Ludolphy, 159. Author's note: The ambiguity of English translations of offices and officials necessitates inclusion in the text of the "exact" German term. Even the German term can be confusing because of a lack of consistency at the time. For the absurdity of a literal English translation, consider the translation of *Hofgericht* as "court court." A liberal translation might be a jarringly unsatisfying "court judicial court." A liberal translation does not prevent confusion. The term *Reichsregiment* has had several renditions. Use of the exact German term does not eliminate confusion but minimizes it. Hartung, 123, pointed out that Rudolf Smend in *Das Reichskammergericht*, vol. 1 (Weimar: H. Böhlaus Nachfolger, 1911), had shown in detail the seemingly haphazard way the "imperial chamber court" was designated in documents at the time even by the estates and the emperor. It was designated *Reichskammergericht* (literally "imperial chamber court") but also designated *kaiserliches Kammergericht* (literally "emperor's chamber court"). Smend asserted the

traditional importance formerly attached to these two different names has been lost. Smend's work is still highly regarded.

31. By terms of the Golden Bull, the king had to be crowned by the pope to become the emperor.

32. Ludolphy, 145–47.

33. Designated as two hundred "horses." Fritz Redlich, *The German Military Enterpriser and His Work Force* (VSWG Beiheft 47), 2 vols., (Wiesbaden, 1964), 9, explains "horse" at the time meant one knight with his accompaniment of several war horses, one more lightly armed helper and one servant. This contract did not even necessarily require the knight and his contingent to be at hand but only to be available. The knight was more or less on a retainer.

34. Wiesflecker 1975, 247.

35. Redlich, 96.

36. Spalatin, 23–24 (translated).

37. Spalatin, 223–34, reproduced the logbook (*Tagebuch*) that chronicled the journey and the festivities once in Mechelen. Karl von Reitzenstein, "Unvollständiges Tagebuch auf der Reise Kurfürst Friedrichs des Weisen von Sachsen in die Niederlande zum Römischen König Maximilian I. 1494." in *Zeitschrift des Vereins für Thüringische Geschichte und Altertumskunde* 4 (Jena, 1861): 127–37, also presented the *Tagebuch* in a less edited way.

38. Today called the Palace of Margaret of York (Charles the Bold's widow), of which only the great entrance hall survives. It was home both to Maximilian's son Philipp the Fair and Maximilian's grandson, future emperor Karl V.

39. This is the knight who told Spalatin (page 13 of this book) how hard Frederick fought in the joust.

40. Ludolphy, 91.

41. Ludolphy, 91.

42. Benecke, 12, on Maximilian: "A tremendously prominent hooked nose . . . prone to colds, with a jutting chin and distorted jaw that made efficient mastication difficult and slobbering easy. . . . A very slight tendency towards obesity may be seen in the formation of . . . [a double chin] . . . Maximilian was a vigorously ugly man with thick features."

43. Benecke, 13. In 1518, after Albrecht Dürer showed Margarethe his portrait of her father, the artist recorded in his diary: "She so violently disliked it, I took it away with me again."

44. Benecke, 26. The double marriage with "Spain" (Aragon and Castile) had been negotiated since 1490. Could an insider like Frederick not have known about it?

45. Wiesflecker 1991, 94–97. The marriages were carried out in 1496 for Philipp and in 1497 for Margarethe.

46. Wiesflecker 1991, 84. The Burgundians loved Philipp, whom they considered a true Burgundian. Maximilian was not sanguine about the transfer of power. He wanted Philipp as a figurehead. With Philipp he left advisers who were to report to Maximilian. Philipp, under the influence of Franz von Busleyden, the provost of Lüttich, had ideas of his own and actually resented his absentee father. This relationship never improved.

47. After the death of the all-powerful Lorenzo de Medici in 1492, the Italian states had become unstable, ripe for conquest in the eyes of some.

48. E. R. Chamberlin, *The Bad Popes* (Dial Press, 1969), 180–86, narrates the invasion and the weakness of Charles VIII.

49. Ludolphy, 147.

50. Fritz Redlich, 1964, called condottieri and similar types "military enterprisers." These enterprisers, like the later infamous Franz von Sickingen, had the skill and reputation to gather thousands of troops and manage a campaign. Frederick's uncle Albrecht, though not dubbed a "condottiero," was essentially such an enterpriser. It is possible that, for a time, Frederick's brother Johann had such an ambition.

51. Wiesflecker 1991, 98: The irony is that during the *Reichstag*, the Italian problem with France was being resolved by the Italians.

52. Narrative of the famous 1495 *Reichstag* draws from Hartung, 101–28, and Ludolphy, 140, 147–50.

53. Also translated often as "Court of Appeal" or "Superior Court of Justice." The latter seems to best catch the intended meaning. It was to be a central judicial court with jurisdiction over all judicial entities.

54. *Reichsregiment* is literally "imperial authority." As implemented by the Habsburgs, it was a regency that governed (weakly) when the emperor was absent. Hence, the various translations of the term. Most scholars use "imperial governing council" but many also use "imperial council of regency." The latter captures not the literal meaning but the historical reality.

55. Hartung, 119.

56. Ludolphy, 152.

57. Ludolphy, 140. The bulk of the narrative of the *Reichstag* at Lindau is from Ludolphy, 139, 153–55.

58. Peter Schmid, "Kurfürst Friedrich der Weise von Sachsen als Reichspolitiker," in *Fortschritte in der Geschichtswissenschaft durch Reichstagsaktenforschung: Vier Beiträge aus der Arbeit an den Reichstagsakten des 15. und 16. Jahrhunderts*, ed. Heinz Angermeier und Erich Meuthen. (Göttingen: Vandenhoeck & Ruprecht, 1988), 49. Schmid cites Ingeborg Schick, "König Maximilian I. und seine Beziehungen zu den weltlichen Reichsfürsten in den Jahren 1496–1506" (diss. Graz, 1967).

59. R. W. Seton-Watson, *Maximilian I: Holy Roman Emperor* (London, 1902), 42.

60. Benecke, 94–95.

61. Wiesflecker 1975, 98. Full text of the plan on page 602 of Hermann Wiesflecker, "Der Italienzug König Maximilians I. im Jahre 1496" in *Carinthia* I 146 (1956), 581–619.

62. Wiesflecker 1975, 138.

63. R. W. Seton-Watson, 44.

64. Bacon, 73–74.

65. Ludolphy, 102. Some speculate Jhan was the Dutch master Jan Joest. Also, records from this time show two other painters named Cuntz and Ludwig. The latter two were particularly involved later with painting murals and such in the castle at Wittenberg.

66. Hutchison, 24–25.

67. Hutchison, 25. Wolgemut also trained Dürer in woodcuts, a major source of income for Dürer later.

68. Heinrich Wölfflin, *Die Kunst Albrecht Dürers* (Munich: Bruckmann, 1908), 2nd edition, 148–49, also states (translated), "An attempt is found here to give form to human greatness, which truly does Dürer honor."

69. Erwin Panofsky, 1943, 40, recognizes the influence of Andrea Mantegna, a northern Italian artist who was a master of perspective. Dürer admired this popular contemporary.

70. Bacon, 76–77.

71. Jane Hutchison, *Albrecht Dürer: A Biography* (Princeton University Press, 1990), 66.

72. Bruck, 135. Johann (Jhan) had been in Frederick's court since 1491. The Dutch master traveled frequently for Frederick, including the trip to Cracow in 1494 and also Venice the same year. By 1495 he had departed.

73. Elisabeth would not marry until 1515 at age 32. She died at thirty-three giving birth to her only child, who also died.

74. Ludolphy, 57.

75. Story recounted by both Ludolphy, 57, and Iris Ritschel, "Friedrich der Weise und seine Gefährtin: Überlegungen und Erkenntnisse zu fünf verdächtig(t)en Kunstwerken" in *"Wir wollen der Liebe Raum geben": Konkubinate geistlicher und weltlicher Fürsten um 1500*, ed. Andreas Tacke (Göttingen: Wallstein, 2006), 330–31. The bridal quest motif recurs in the German epics as heroic endeavors. This booklet casting Frederick as the hero could have served many purposes.

76. Ludolphy, 152–55.

77. Ironically the Italians thought Germans were too backward to be "Machiavellian."

78. Often rendered "imperial council." In English, "court" is ambiguous.

79. Harksen, 351.

80. Schirmer in Rogge & Schirmer 2003, 323.

81. Ludolphy, 291.

82. Enno Bünz, "Die Heiltumssammlung des Degenhart Pfeffinger," 125–69, in Andreas Tacke, ed. *"Ich armer sundiger mensch": Heiligen- und Reliquienkult am Übergang zum konfessionellen Zeitalter.* Schriftenreihe der Stiftung Moritzburg, Kunstmuseum des Landes Sachsen-Anhalt. (Göttingen: Wallstein Verlag, 2006).

83. Brather, 228.

84. Ludolphy, 157.

85. The Swiss situation from Wiesflecker 1991, 112–15; the quote translated from page 115.

86. Frederick's activity for most of 1497 is from Brather, 242, and Wiesflecker 1975, 408.

87. Ludolphy, 161–63.

88. Wiesflecker 1975, 127. This was a popular weapon among the royalty of the time, including Frederick.

89. Frederic J. Baumgartner, *Louis XII* (Palgrave Macmillan, 1994), 52.

90. Francois is of course king years later.

91. Wiesflecker 1975, 132–33.

92. Married to three wives for a span of more than forty years, Louis remained fatherless.

93. Durant, 95.

94. Wiesflecker 1991, 417–18.

95. Wiesflecker 1975, 127.

96. George the Rich was the son of Ludwig the Rich and Amalia, the sister of Frederick's father, Ernst.

97. Ludolphy, 151.

98. Jay A. Levenson, ed., *Circa 1492* (Yale University Press, 1991), 259. Grossmann, 130, is dismissive of the Fiorentino sculpture, stating that Frederick is idealized to the point of appearing a beautiful man. Today, this sculpture is in the Green Vault Museum in Dresden.

99. This and the following discussion of northern Italy from Ludolphy, 161–63, 195. Also Wiesflecker 1975, 136.

100. Frederick began to relinquish the properties in 1506. They were completely lost by 1509 in the Venetian triumph and the total failure of Maximilian's Italian adventure.

101. Wiesflecker 1975, 408–9.

102. Benecke, 26.

103. Benecke, 7.

104. Brather, 243.

105. Wiesflecker 1975, 247–48, noted Maximilian's serious misjudgment and misuse of Berthold, treating him as an enemy rather than a friend with mutual interests. Italians in the court of Maximilian thought if he had brought Berthold into the circle he would have avoided many subsequent problems. Another glaring blunder of Maximilian's executive vision was his blindness to oceanic exploration. He had easy access to the North Sea.

106. Brather, 243.

107. Schmid, 51–52.

108. Ludolphy, 173. This in a letter to Serntein from Heinrich von Fürstenberg, who added knowingly, "I don't know what good that would do."

109. Ludolphy, 169–73, discusses Heinrich von Bünau's report dated December 5, 1498, and interpretation of its hidden contents.

110. Schmid, 51–52, from studying volume six of the *Deutsche Reichstagsakten Mittlere Reihe 1486–1518 unter Maximilian I* [Middle Series of the German *Reichstag* Activities under Maximilian I] ed. H. Gollwitzer (Göttingen: Vandenhoeck und Ruprecht, 1979).

111. Spalatin, 131. Letter (translated) of January 3, 1499.

CHAPTER 4: HASTY RETURN TO SAXONY

1. From Spalatin, 53.

2. Brather, 243–48. Discussion of 1499 order by Frederick and Johann.

3. Schirmer in Rogge & Schirmer 2003, 356, notes Heinrich von Ende is still documented as Hofmeister in 1507, and this may be the last time in that office. Schirmer adds, however, that he remained in the closest circle of advisers until his death in 1515.

4. Grossmann, 15, cited as her source C. A. H. Burkhardt, *Ernestinische Landtagsakten* (Ernestine territorial diets), vol. 1, *Die Landtage von 1487–1532* (Jena, 1902) (Thüringische Geschichtsquellen NF 5), iii.

5. Brather, 248, and Schirmer in Rogge & Schirmer 2003, 318.

6. University-trained men would so dominate by 1510 that, in addition to these "educated" court (*Hofrat*) councillors, a separate kind of councillor would be distinguished: "*Räte von Haus aus.*" This term implied men of nobility as well as a

lower status administratively. This terminology was not used only in Electoral Saxony but throughout the empire.

7. Brather, 235.

8. Ludolphy, 293.

9. Otto Behaghel, *A Short Historical Grammar of the German Language* (New York: Macmillan, 1891), 30, translated from Johann Aurifarber's cobbled together Latin and German. Ludolphy, 293, quotes this as well: WA TR 1:524–25; 2:639–40. Unsaid by Luther is the influence on the standard language at the time by his wildly popular Bible in that same Maximilian-Frederick German.

10. Johann von Staupitz was general vicar of numerous Augustinian monasteries. He was much more than that to Frederick as will be discussed below.

11. The discussion of the relationship of the three bishops and Frederick is from Ludolphy, 247–48, 377.

12. Christoph Volkmar, *Reform statt Reformation: Die Kirchenpolitik Herzog Georgs von Sachsen, 1488–1525* (Leipzig, 2008), 193–204 (section titled "*Der Machtkampf mit Johann VI von Meissen*").

13. Ludolphy, 191. It was this bishop whom Frederick ordered to expel Jews in 1493. The Schönbergs were a noble family originally in the Markgraf of Meissen that had served the Wettins in many capacities. Many were bishops in the church. Nikolaus, related to Johann III, became a cardinal in 1535.

14. Wiesflecker 1991, 119.

15. Paul Van Dyke, "The Literary Activity of the Emperor Maximilian I," *The American Historical Review* 11 (1905): 19.

16. Wilhelm Oechsli, *History of Switzerland, 1499–1914* (Cambridge University Press, 1922), 13.

17. Oechsli, 13.

18. Ludolphy, 175–76.

19. Discussion of the *Reichstag* and subsequent imperial governing council from Ludolphy, 175–86.

20. Quote (translated) from Ludolphy, 179.

21. Ludolphy, 182: Frederick seemed to be the mediator of choice in many circumstances. In March 1500, he settled a dispute between the city of Cologne and its archbishop, Hermann IV, over brewing rights. He also mediated without success the dispute between the two Hohenzollern margraves in the Nuremberg region. This would erupt into a small war in 1502.

22. Ludolphy, 180.

23. Spalatin, 139.

24. "*Sang- und klanglos*" in Ingeborg Friedhuber, "König Maximilian I., die Erbländer, das Reich und Europa im Jahre 1500" (diss., Graz, 1963), 89.

25. C. A. H. Burkhardt, "Die Vermählung des Herzogs Johann von Sachsen 1. bis 5. März 1500," *Neues Archiv für sächsische Geschichte* 15 (1894): 283–98. Exhaustive five-thousand-word account of the wedding.

26. Her sister Anna, then just fourteen, would one day (after she married Landgrave Wilhelm of Hesse) become a thorn in Frederick's side. Katharina, another sister of Sophie, married Frederick's Albertine cousin Heinrich the Pious in 1512.

27. Streich 1989, 503: Forty years earlier, 3,600 guests came to the wedding of Ernst and Elisabeth in Leipzig.

28. Burkhardt 1894, 291: Not without hard feelings. Torgau was in the diocese of the bishop of Meissen.

29. Streich, 500–504, emphasizes that all festivities for the Saxon court were open in part to burghers and countryfolk. It was yet another form of "representation," which was costly to the court and whatever *Amts* or other entities could be dragged in to contribute.

30. F. A. von Langenn, *Züge aus dem Familienleben der Herzogin Sidonie* (Dresden, 1852), 89, letter no. 6. Ensuing years reveal Frederick became irrevocably attached to this "God-given wife"; no other wife was possible. This shifted the necessity of a power marriage to brother Johann and the duke's future offspring.

31. Irmgard Höß, *Georg Spalatin. Ein Leben in der Zeit des Humanismus und der Reformation* (Weimar, 1956; 2nd edition, Weimar, 1989), 70: Frederick sent his oldest natural son, Sebastian, to Wittenberg to study during the summer semester in 1514. This suggests he was born in 1499 or 1500.

32. WA TR 4:322.2–14, n. 12. More than two hundred years later, the name "Anna Weller of Molsdorf" surfaced via Johann Gottlob Boehme, *Sächsisches Groschen Cabinet*, Fach 2 (Leipzig/Züllichau, 1769). This name from this unsubstantiated source has been cited by many scholars and persists. Most comprehensive speculation about the identity of Frederick's companion is by Iris Ritschel in Tacke, 296–341, but also by Ludolphy, 47–50.

33. Ludolphy, 49.

34. Schirmer in Rogge & Schirmer 2003, 348. "N. Watzler" is in the list of people serving the Saxon electoral court in 1518. Langenn, 522, 523, 525, 527.

35. Ritschel in Tacke 2006, 296–341, covers five objects of art fully.

36. Ritschel in Tacke 2006 does not discuss Cranach's Torgau Altarpiece of the Holy Kinship (1509) in Frankfurt or Cranach's Princes' Altarpiece (c. 1510–12) in Dessau.

37. Ludolphy, 49, asks (translated), "Who, then, shall the wife-ish companion to Friedrich be?"

38. Hans Virck, "Die Ernestiner und Herzog Georg von 1500–1508," *Neues Archiv für sächsische Geschichte* 30 (1909): 1–75. Virck, 2, points out that Albrecht was totally absorbed in his imperial ambitions. Local squabbles with nephews seemed

unrewarding. Also, in the late 1490s, both the Ernestiners were still without wives. Albrecht's son George already had his own son. There was (translated) "still reasonable hope that the Ernestine possession would fall sooner or later to the Albertiners."

39. Karlheinz Blaschke, "Herzog Albrecht der Beherzte—ein sächsischer Fürst im Reich und in Europa," 13–26, in Andre Thieme, ed., *Herzog Albrecht der Beherzte (1443–1500) Ein sächsischer Fürst im Reich und in Europa* (Cologne: Böhlau, 2002), 22–23.

40. Mock, 252: Separate heart funerals had been popular since the eleventh century.

41. Heinrich would prove too weak to rule, relinquishing Friesland to brother George in 1505. This major distraction for George must have pleased Frederick.

42. Luther translated much of the New Testament while exiled at the Wartburg.

43. Ludolphy, 121. Also Dieter Koepplin and Tilman Falk, *Lucas Cranach: Gemälde, Zeichnungen, Druckgraphik*, 2 vols. (Basel/Stuttgart, 1974/1976), 1:19.

44. Koepplin, 19: "*1500 Brand auf der Veste, Ausbesserungsarbeiten.*"

45. Bruck, 40.

46. Ludolphy, 105–6. He was one of the first since antiquity to master the technique of *trompe l'oeil* (French for "trick the eye"), a humorous three-dimensional trick within the painting or even appearing to be outside the painting.

47. Virtually no mural survives from this time with Frederick. Information is primarily from the Latin discourse "Dialogos" in 1508 by the Saxon Andreas Meinhardi. This university faculty member was well rewarded, becoming city scribe of Wittenberg in 1508, an office that he held until 1525. The report, which lauds many aspects of Wittenberg in glowing terms and Frederick as a humanist, also describes in specific terms much of the décor of the castle. "Dialogos" has been summarized by Grossmann, 56–60; Schwiebert, 243–44; Ludolphy, 122–23; and especially Harksen, 345–47.

48. Schwiebert, 243.

49. Some early scholars concluded Albrecht Dürer was actually in Wittenberg working in both the castle and the church. For example, Bruck, 289 (translated), stated, "Dürer painted in Frederick's rooms in Wittenberg in which were kept most of the portraits of the dukes and electors of Saxony" from original accounting entries such as "*Albrecht Maler von der gesnizten Stube vnd m. g. h. gemach zu malen.*" Also Grossmann, 123, stated Dürer worked on the Castle Church during one of his two stays in Wittenberg (1494–95 and 1503). Harksen, 350, and Bacon 2004, 5, reject these conclusions.

50. Grossmann, 125, believed that between 1495 and 1500, Cranach worked for the elector in Coburg and Gotha.

51. Max J. Friedlander and Jakob Rosenberg, *The Paintings of Lucas Cranach*, revised edition (Cornell University Press, 1978), 13. Few of his paintings before 1505

still exist and none before 1500. Friedlander and Rosenberg note that the discovery and analysis of Cranach's numerous woodcuts made scholars realize how skilled Cranach already was by 1505.

52. His annual salary of one hundred gulden confirms Cranach already had a considerable reputation.

53. Grossmann, 126.

54. Bacon 2004, 151: Cranach signed his first altarpiece (Martyrdom of St. Catherine triptych) and dated it 1506. Among the witnesses in the upper left corner of the center panel are two horsemen, thought (not by all scholars) to be the elector and his brother Johann.

55. Discussion of the physical Castle Church itself is from the well-documented works of Harksen, 353–54, and Bacon, 102–72, as well as Schwiebert, 239–40. The church of 1502 and the church of 2000 share little more than the same dimensions. A great loss in an eighteenth-century fire was Luther's "Theses Door." Moreover, "restoration" in the 1800s was aimed not at true restoration of the original but at honoring the Reformation.

56. Ludolphy, 123: This difficult task would drag on until 1506.

57. Harksen, 353: The Ernestiners purchased lead and six cases of "clear" Venetian glass discs in Leipzig in 1500 and 1501. The glazier Urban did not finish the bull's-eye pattern windows for the church until 1505.

58. Schwiebert, 238, calls this steeple a "roof rider"; this originates from the German "Dachreiter" for features that do not extend below the roof. A "roof rider" could be a steeple, but not all steeples are roof riders.

59. Bruck, 67.

60. Harksen, 354.

61. Schwiebert, 239–40. Note that "choir" refers in this case not to a singing group but to a structural part of the church intended for a group.

62. Bacon, 108. "Hallenkirche" was coined by Wilhelm Lübke in 1853 for a church in which the side aisles are as high as the nave itself, often united under a single roof (accentuated in Frederick's church, because the piers did not go to the ceiling). Light typically did not enter through a window in the upper part of the nave (as in "basilica-type" churches) but through side-wall windows rising to the top of the interior. Steffen Delang in Ullmann 1984, 161, suggests Frederick may have been influenced by his brother Ernst's experiences ten years earlier building the elongated, one-naved Castle Church at Wolmirstedt. Archbishop Ernst, often depicted only as an aggravation to Frederick, must have been close to Frederick in earlier days.

63. Bacon, 112. Also Ludolphy, 41.

64. Bacon 2004, 117. Various contemporaneous reports indicate sixteen altars by 1507, twenty by 1510 and twenty-six by 1519. At its maximum development, eleven altars were in the lower church and fifteen were in the upper galleries.

65. Bacon 2004, 122.

66. Discussion of the bull from Bacon 2004, 122–23.

67. Brecht 1985, 117–18. Granted by Pope Boniface IX in 1398. Rome had long recognized the relic collection in Wittenberg as significant.

68. Brecht 1985, 117.

69. Bacon, 145. All three were done by 1496 or so and stored elsewhere.

70. Not all historians agree with this assessment. All agree the two works of art—"Dresden Altarpiece" and "Seven Sorrows of the Virgin"—were completed by this time but do not agree as to their location. Relevant facts suggest it unlikely Frederick would have commissioned these works for another location. Bacon, 159–67, describes and interprets the two works of art.

71. So titled because it now resides at the Gemäldegalerie Alte Meister in Dresden.

72. The seven side panels are also at the Gemäldegalerie Alte Meister in Dresden, but the large central panel is at the Alte Pinakothek in Munich (though severely damaged by an acid attack in 1988).

73. Schwiebert, 1950. Chapters 6–8 offer details of Wittenberg. Mrusek in *450 Jahre Reformation*, ed. Leo von Stern and Max Steinmetz (1967), 322–40, is also excellent.

74. Just a few years later, the western half was to be called *Schloss Gasse* (Castle Lane) and the eastern half *Collegien Gasse* (College Lane).

75. Schwiebert, 218. The "Market Master" administered houses offering prostitutes. Married men, however, could be fined for using the services.

76. Was this a concession to the high-powered Augustinian Johann von Staupitz? Frederick had to draw him away his monastery in Munich and entrust him to mastermind the beginning of Wittenberg's university.

77. Part of the castle would also be used for the study of law. By 1509 (significantly, before Martin Luther), the popularity of Frederick's university would require a second Frederici Collegium separated from the first by a courtyard.

78. Inception and first years of the university are from Schwiebert, 221–72, and Grossmann 1975, 36–75.

79. Schwiebert, 254, and Grossmann 1975, 41.

80. Ludolphy, 123, 134.

81. He also was in charge of building the Augustinian monastery. He would later bring in high-powered Augustinians such as John Lang and Wenceslaus Link, as well as Martin Luther.

82. Grossmann, 56: Only fifty-five enrolled in 1505.

83. Bacon 2004, 127.

84. Ludolphy, 48, 252.

85. Ludolphy, 242.

86. Mock, 20.

87. Jakob von Liebenstein would succeed Berthold. Liebenstein did not come from a powerful family, but he had been an active religious in the archdiocese since 1470. There was also a new pope, Julius II. He would prove to be as ambitious and overreaching as Maximilian, but in his early reign he was not as desperate for money as he would be later.

88. Virck 1909, 1–75.

89. Kirn, 3–4. Virck, 2.

90. Grossmann, 31.

91. Virck, 6. Senftenberg was located in one small prong of Albertine territory that the Low Road had to cross.

92. Ludolphy, 244.

93. Spalatin, 35–36.

94. Virck, 9: Friesland turned out to be a disaster financially (and politically). During fifteen years, the Albertiners poured 800,000 gulden into the defiant territory (without success).

95. Ludolphy, 244.

96. Spalatin, 33.

97. Ludolphy, 183.

98. Ludolphy, 185–89, discusses the short-lived revolt of the electors.

99. The duke's mother was Amalie (of Saxony), sister of Frederick's father, Ernst.

100. Ludolphy, 190.

101. Heinrich Ulmann, *Franz von Sickingen* (Leipzig, 1872), 11–15, describes the war. Ulmann casts some blame on the ambitions of Ruprecht's wife, Margarethe.

102. Two of the most feared (and revered) knights in German history cut their teeth in this vicious war. Among the knights fighting for the Palatine was twenty-three-year-old Franz von Sickingen, who lost his father, Swicker (the Palatine electoral *Hofmeister*), in the war. On the other side, Götz von Berlichingen, at age 24, lost his right hand. Although Berlichingen would afterward become the legendary knight with the iron hand, the volatile Sickingen became truly dreaded and a major threat throughout the middle Rhine. His support of Luther cast a pall over the famous 1521 *Reichstag* in Worms.

103. The same duke who married Frederick's niece Katharina of Albertine Saxony in 1497.

104. Benecke, 17.

105. Wiesflecker 1991, 146–47.

106. This grisly scene was also preserved in a Hans Burgkmair woodcut.

107. Main points of the 1505 *Reichstag* in Cologne from Ludolphy, 191, and Wiesflecker 1991, 397.

108. Ludolphy, 191. Frederick and Johann would never pay their assessment, because Maximilian already owed them more than sixty thousand gulden.

109. Spalatin, 145–46.

110. Such early commitments were shaky at best. This one was even shakier. The mother, Anne of Brittany, approved it, but the French king, Louis XII, did not. Louis wanted his daughter Claudia to marry Francois of Angouleme. After Anne died in January 1514, Claudia married Francois before the year ended.

111. Even Spaniards themselves did not yet know about the enormous amounts of silver and gold in the New World even though corrupt Pope Alexander VI had ceded the entire New World to Spain and Portugal in 1493. Combined, Castile, Aragon, and Navarre, however, had internal wealth.

CHAPTER 5: CONSUMMATE TERRITORIAL PRINCE

1. Spalatin, 32 (translated).

2. German Proverb of the time: "*Ein Unglück kommt selten allein.*"

3. Benecke, 162, for 1506: "Good summer, ample harvest. Wormy fruit."

4. Wiesflecker 1991, 487. This action by the French could also be due to his loose cannon of a son Philipp impulsively cozying up to King Henry VII and supporting claims of England against France.

5. Hermann Wiesflecker, *Osterreich in Zeitalter Kaiser Maximilian I* (Vienna, 1999), 375–76 (translated).

6. Wiesflecker 1986, 426 (translated).

7. Wiesflecker 1999, 376.

8. Karl's younger brother Ferdinand remained in Spain, joined by his sister, Catherine, born January 1507. The boy was a great favorite of his grandfather, Ferdinand of Aragon.

9. Discussion of Heinrich von Bünau from Uwe Schirmer in Rogge und Schirmer 2003, 351, and Grossmann 1975, 38–40.

10. Grossmann 1975, 39.

11. Mock, 188–93, reports Ernst's battle with syphilis.

12. Discussion of Frederick's problems with brother Ernst beginning in 1500 is drawn from Mock's "Der Bruderzwist zwischen Erzbischof Ernst und Kurfürst Friedrich," 211–19, unless attributed otherwise.

13. The unpublished proceedings are preserved: Thüringisches Hauptstaatarchiv, Weimar, Ernestinisches Gesamtarchiv, Reg. B 518, fol. 3r–13v.

14. Grossmann 1975, 40, 48, 50, 56. Bacon 2004, 127.

15. Trebelius joined the faculty at the new university in Brandenburg. Petrus, brother of Vincentius, went to the university at Cologne.

16. Ludolphy, 318–21. Martin Brecht 1985, 98, and Manfred Schulze, *Fürsten und Reformation* (Tübingen: Mohr, 1991), 169–70. Staupitz was in Rome primarily to achieve reorganization of the Augustinians in the empire, including union of the reform congregation with the Saxon Province, with full approval of the Saxon Provincial, Gerhard Hecker. Staupitz also aimed at uniting the German reformed Augustinians with the Lombardy Augustinians, who enjoyed extensive papal privileges. Staupitz's first emissary to the pope, Nicholas Besler, was imprisoned in 1505 for circumventing the general of the Augustinian order. After the death of that general, Staupitz himself went to Rome at the end of 1506 and seems to have successfully negotiated several orders of business with the new general of the order, who was sympathetic to reform. Among them, the reform congregation would unite with the Saxon provincial order. Staupitz, as Frederick's emissary, no doubt spoke also to Pope Julius II about concerns of Frederick.

17. Staupitz was, after all, the dean of the faculty of theology.

18. Discussion of the *Reichstag* at Constance in 1507 principally from Ludolphy, 192–94, and Wiesflecker 1991, 153–56.

19. Bruck, 209. The bull from Julius II is mentioned in many sources, yet as Kalkoff, 1907, 68, notes, the original document to Frederick has never been found.

20. Many think the size of Frederick's relic collection exploded after 1507 as a direct result of the bull. That is incorrect, as shown by recent work of Laube 2006 and Herbert Immenkötter, "Albrecht von Brandenburg and Friedrich the Wise: One way to two aims," in Andreas Tacke, ed., *Cranach. Meisterwerke auf Vorrat* (München, 1994), 11–21. The explosion came later in response to competition from Albrecht of Mainz.

21. Schmid, 53.

22. Ludolphy, 58. A "German mile" was an imprecise distance, but was probably about 7.5 kilometers or 4.7 American/British miles.

23. In 1494, Frederick likely had broken his arm jousting in Mechelen. Ludolphy, 91.

24. Ludolphy, 73. Also, D. J. Smith, *Discovering Horse-drawn Vehicles* (Osprey Publishing, 1994), 14–16. Coaches for personal travel with suspensions and moveable axles did not appear until the middle of the 1500s. Wagoneers and horsemen universally hated coaches as "road hogs."

25. Frederick's personal coach, though primitive, nevertheless required representation. Ludolphy, 108, notes that none other than court artist Lucas Cranach was charged with the painting and decoration of carriages. The results must have been colorful and ornate.

26. Ludolphy, 89.

27. Ludolphy, 200.

28. Ludolphy, 180. Derisively called "*morbus diplomaticus*" by detractors.

29. Ludolphy, 273–74.

30. Benecke, 17. Maximilian failed to some extent because the territorial princes would not support him with money and soldiers; nevertheless as a commander with vision he should have factored into his efforts this predictable response from the princes.

31. Ludolphy, 38, quotes a Martin Luther sermon that claimed Frederick said, "*Ich will nicht anheben, muß ich aber kriegen, so sollst du sehen, das Aufhören soll bei mir stehen.*"

32. Virck, 75 (translated).

33. Discussion of the "Erfurt Quarrel" is based mainly on Ludolphy, 252–55. Brecht 1985, 23–26, is also helpful, though less comprehensive.

34. Roughly ten miles (or fifteen kilometers) in radius or about three hundred square miles (or seven hundred square kilometers) in area. At least five small outliers were also Erfurt territory.

35. The so-called "year" began in 1508, reached a crescendo in 1509, but continued to erupt sporadically for several years. Even in 1514, prominent citizens were murdered and executed.

36. Much of Erfurt's insolvency was due to George's father, Albrecht, who persuaded Maximilian to transfer Erfurt's fair privilege to Leipzig in 1497.

37. Ludolphy, 38, from Martin Luther's table talk on the Erfurt situation: "*Es wäre an einem zu viel.*"

38. Discussion of Hessian Regency from Richard A. Cahill, *Philipp of Hesse and the Reformation* (Mainz: von Zabern, 2001). Also Ludolphy, 242, 256–59, and H. C. Erik Midelfort, *Mad Princes of Renaissance Germany* (University Press of Virginia, 1994), 41–44.

39. Midelfort, 41–43. It is probable that Wilhelm I was mentally ill. It is also probable that his brother Wilhelm II (the Middle) prevented any form of treatment that might have helped him recover. Wilhelm I lived twenty-two years after abdicating, getting little if any treatment the first nineteen years.

40. Cahill, 22.

41. Cahill, 23.

42. Grossmann, 20–24, is excellent among sources in English for essential facts about Spalatin. Irmgard Höß (1956, revised 1989) wrote the only work approaching a definitive biography of Spalatin, but it is in German.

43. Höß, 48. Spalatin's old friend Veit Warbeck held a similar position with Frederick's brother Johann. Warbeck was as big and muscular as Spalatin was diminutive and frail-looking. The two priests dressed alike and were frequently seen together, becoming the subject of many good-natured jokes.

44. Also, the décor of Frederick's residences testify to his respect for antiquity, which humanists championed.

45. Höß, 42 (translated).

46. Höß, 42–46, discusses Spalatin's initial difficulties with his pupils and Johann's *Hofmeister*. Höß is silent about the presence of Sebastien and Fritz, who were almost certainly among the seven pupils, perhaps as well as Otto and Ernst of Braunschweig-Lüneburg (sons of Frederick's sister Margarete).

47. Höß, 61.

48. Höß, 46.

49. Höß, 48.

50. Höß, 56

51. Ludolphy, 333–35.

52. In 1511 in Wittenberg, Spalatin also tutored Otto and Ernst of Braunschweig-Lüneburg for the university. They were several years older than Johann Friedrich.

53. Discussion of Christoph Scheurl from Grossmann 1975, 60–64, and Steven Ozment, *Flesh and Spirit: Private Life in Early Modern Germany* (New York: Penguin Putnam, 2001), 53–131.

54. Grossmann, 62, 67.

55. Grossmann, 67.

56. Schwiebert, 256: Liberal arts was undergraduate study; the other three were graduate studies.

57. Schwiebert, 256.

58. One example is Christian Beyer, who in these early days switched from the faculty of the humanities to the faculty of law. Beyer eventually became chancellor of the electorate.

59. Staupitz served Frederick many ways. According to Ludolphy, 58, in 1509 while Staupitz was visiting his monasteries in the Netherlands, he assessed Maria of Jülich-Berg as a potential bride for Frederick. He did not recommend the seventeen-year-old princess for the sovereign he knew so well.

60. Preserved Smith, *The Life and Letters of Martin Luther* (New York: Houghton Mifflin Co., 1911), 21. The story is from *Table Talk* no. 3143b, WA TR 3:187–88.

61. Quote from Brecht 1985, 126. Fife, 182, agrees.

62. Ludolphy 125, 307–8.

63. Cornette, 68. Also Luther in his table talk in Preserved Smith, *Conversations with Luther* (Pilgrim Press, 1915), 53.

64. Bacon 2004, 121. Discussion of altarpieces and liturgy of the Castle Church in Wittenberg is based heavily on Paul M. Bacon 2004, chapter 3, "All Saints in

Wittenberg: The Form and Functions of the Castle Church Under Frederick the Wise," 102–41, and chapter 4, "Art and Liturgy: The Decorative Program of All Saints in Wittenberg," 142–72.

65. Bacon 2004, 154. Also Bacon 2004, 117, regarding the ultimate total of twenty-six altars: "Only five besides the All Saints' altar (i.e., the high altar) have ever been linked to a specific location." Bacon 2004, 118, speculates on the location of each altar.

66. According to Bacon 2004, 176, this panel now in the Uffizi Gallery in Florence may be the missing center panel of the controversial "Jabach altar," once part of a triptych and now in the Städelsches Kunstinstitut in Frankfurt am Main; Jabach is a family in Cologne that once owned the work.

67. Matthew 2:11: "And going into the house [the Magi] saw the child with Mary His mother, and they fell down and worshiped Him. Then, opening their treasures, they offered Him gifts, gold and frankincense and myrrh."

68. Paul M. Bacon, "Humanism in Wittenberg: Frederick the Wise, Konrad Celtis, and Albrecht Dürer's 1508 Martyrdom of the Ten Thousand Christians," Konsthistorisk Tidskrift 82 (Swedish Journal of Art History, 2013): 1–25.

69. Bacon 2004, 149: After Bavarian elector Maximilian I acquired it around 1729, it was substantially altered.

70. Bruck, 70.

71. Bruck, 79, surmised from Scheurl what the sculpture looked like.

72. Bacon 2004, 171.

73. Cranach produced another "Martyrdom of St. Catherine" the previous year (not for the Castle Church). It is a much harsher version with no recognizable contemporaries.

74. Now in Städelsches Kunstinsitut in Frankfurt am Main. Some scholars believe this was created for Torgau, not Wittenberg. This triptych was discussed in the previous chapter regarding Frederick's partner, Anna.

75. Reference to the side panels as "left" and "right" is unrewarding, because there is no universal agreement on this. Also, identity of the women in the side panels is in dispute. In truth, both princes look like Frederick; neither looks like brother Johann, whom Cranach portrayed accurately in the "Dessau Princes' Altarpiece."

76. Now in the Staatliche Galerie in Dessau.

77. This also corresponds to his first complaints about being less and less mobile.

78. Bacon 2008, 977.

79. Bacon 2004, 157.

80. Bacon 2008, 991–92.

81. Bacon 2008, 973–1001, has explored this subject exhaustively. As an example of Frederick's "traditional piety" Bacon, 993–94, notes Frederick believed the legend that each apostle wrote one of the twelve articles of the Apostles' Creed and

Bartholomew wrote the eighth article: "*Credo in Spiritum Sanctum*" (I believe in the Holy Spirit). Cranach's woodcut "The Martyrdom of St. Bartholomew," c. 1512, supports this belief of Frederick (Bacon, 982).

82. The reverse could be true. Frederick acquired particularly fine relics, because Bartholomew was his favored saint.

83. Bacon 2004, 158.

84. Ludolphy, 359. Most relics were in silver containers.

85. Ludolphy, 345, and Brecht 1985, 118.

86. Discussion of 1507 incorporation of the All Saints' Foundation into the University of Wittenberg from Bacon 2004, 127.

87. Leaver, 33.

88. See below the discussion on the special portiuncula indulgence for All Saints' Day beginning in 1510.

89. Discussion of the "Relic Catalog" (*Heiltumsbuch*) is from the definitive book on the subject by Cardenas 2002 and also from Bacon 2004, 193–204.

90. Brecht 1985, 117–18.

91. Cardenas, 7, 10, points out that, until recently, little attention was paid to this magnificent publication, because the relics and their valuable containers have scattered to the four winds. The only known preserved piece of the collection is the glass of St. Elizabeth (*Elisabethglas*), now in the art collection of the Veste Coburg.

92. Perhaps six copies in paper and five in parchment still exist.

93. Cardenas, 36.

94. All descriptions of relics, unless noted otherwise, are from Cardenas, 45–110.

95. Bernd Moeller, "Eine Reliquie Luthers" in *Die Reformation und das Mittelalter: kirchenhistorische Aufsätze*, ed. Johannes Schilling (Göttingen, 1991), 249–62. Also Stefan Laube, "Von der Reliquie zum Relikt" in *Archäologie der Reformation: Studien zu den Auswirkungen des Konfessionswechsels auf die materielle Kultur*, ed. Carola Jäggi and Jörn Staecker (Walter de Gruyter, 2007), 429–35. According to Herbert von Hintzenstern, "Kurfürst Johann von Sachsen," 98–105, in *Kaiser- König- Kardinal: deutsche Fürsten 1500–1800*, ed. Rolf Straubel and Ulman Weiß (Leipzig: Urania-Verlag, 1991), 99, Johann the Steadfast himself was responsible for melting down the reliquaries to obtain the valuable gold, silver, precious stones, and pearls. The glass itself survived only because sometime after Frederick's death either Johann or his son Johann Friedrich gave it to Martin Luther. Its fate between about 1541 and 1910 is unknown. Somehow by 1910 it ended up in the Ernestine residence in Coburg. Frederick apparently was fond of the relic, because he considered himself related to St. Elizabeth of Hungary, also Duchess of Thuringia, who lived at the Wartburg castle from about 1207 to 1227.

96. Cardenas, 71.

97. Ludolphy, 355.

98. Schwiebert, 235.

99. Schwiebert, 243.

100. Roland H. Bainton, *Here I Stand* (Abingdon-Cokesbury Press, 1950), 71. Hardcover edition.

101. Ludolphy, 200, 360.

CHAPTER 6: THE GOOD LIFE IN FREDERICK'S COURT

1. Ludolphy, 352, 383. Motto translated from Latin: "*Crux Christi Nostra Salus.*"

2. He was the last non-priest to be elected pope. *After* he was elected pope, he was ordained a priest.

3. Sidney Dark, *The Story of the Renaissance* (Doran, 1924), 149: Quote by Marino Giorgi in 1517.

4. Discussion of the three open religious positions in 1513 and 1514 from Schwiebert, 306–7; Brecht 1985, 178–79; and Ludolphy, 242.

5. Mock, 218–20, 252–54. Ernst had hectored Frederick almost to the end about his supposed inheritance. His funeral at Magdeburg was elaborate. His heart had been buried earlier in his new gem, the Mary Magdalene Chapel in the Moritzburg.

6. Albrecht of Brandenburg (1490–1545) was yet another example of how Frederick was related to all the great houses of the empire. Albrecht was the son of Elector Johann Cicero (1455–99) and Margarethe of Saxony (1441–1501), daughter of Wilhelm III the Brave (1425–82). In other words, the Frederick of our story and Albrecht of Brandenburg were "second cousins."

7. The Teutonic order gambled in 1510 that the prospering Brandenburgs would strengthen their position against Poland, just as they had gambled in 1497 that the Albertine Wettins under Frederick's fierce uncle Albrecht would strengthen it.

8. Ludolphy, 375.

9. Ludolphy, 250–52. Documentary evidence for Frederick sharing governance with Johann is poor.

10. Ernst Müller, "Die Mutschierung von 1513 in Sachsen," *Jahrbuch für Regionalgeschichte* 14 (Leipzig, 1987): 173–82. Johann resisted the Power Sharing for months, forcing a confrontation in July 1513 with Frederick and his most powerful advisers.

11. Brather, 248.

12. Müller, 179. Johann discovered to his horror that the modest wedding cost him 26,000 gulden, and it was his debt alone.

13. Ludolphy, 241, cites Johann Joachim Müller, *Annales des Chur- und Fürstlichen Hauses Sachsen von Anno 1400 bis 1700* (Weimar, 1700), 68.

14. Streich 2005, 33, cites Hans Herz, "Zu einigen Problemen der Landsteilungen in Thüringen vom 16. bis zum Beginn des 19. Jahrhunderts," *Zeitschrift des Vereins*

für Thüringische Geschichte 46, (1992): 147ff., as the basis for her assertion (translated). Müller 1987 disputes that reason. Frederick was burned out and wanted to shed half his burden. Johann stumbled in governing his half. Sharing the advisers was nominal. Johann was not only inexperienced but had only two advisers of first rank: Nickel vom Ende and Gregor Brück.

15. Adolf II of Anhalt-Zerbst was bishop of Merseburg from 1514 to 1526. Who can know to what degree the measures of this staunch foe of Luther's reforms were softened (if at all) because of Margarete?

16. Ludolphy, 302.

17. Burkhardt 1902, *Landtagsakten* 94, Nr. 157.

18. Ludolphy, 388.

19. Maria Dobozy, 82–83.

20. Ludolphy, 50, citing Luther in *Table Talk* no. 4455 (as WA TR 4:322.5f.).

21. Norman P. Tanner, ed. *Decrees of the Ecumenical Councils* (Sheed & Ward, 1990).

22. Tanner, Session 9 (May 5, 1514).

23. James Hastings, gen. ed., *Encyclopedia of Religion and Ethics*, vol. 6 (New York: C. Scribner's Sons, 1925), 818.

24. Ludolphy, 51.

25. C. A. H. Burkhardt, "Das tolle Jahr zu Erfurt und seine Folgen 1509–1523," *Archiv für sächsische Geschichte* 12 (1873/74): 414, terms it *"Schwermüthigkeit."*

26. William Walker Rockwell, *Die Doppelehe des Landgrafen Philipp von Hessen* (Marburg, 1904), 152–53.

27. Ludolphy, 203.

28. Ludolphy, 51: In both 1516 and 1520, Francois I invited Sebastian to live in the French royal court.

29. Ludolphy, 207.

30. To try to win Frederick's support, Maximilian talked to Pfeffinger in two audiences (Ludolphy, 205).

31. Discussion from Ludolphy, 202. Isabella was reasonably attractive for a Habsburg, by reason of not possessing the elongated face with pronounced underbite.

32. Christian II continued his affair with a young Norwegian mistress until she mysteriously died in 1517.

33. Discussion of Hans von der Planitz from Ludolphy, 202, and Schirmer 2003, 368.

34. Ludolphy, 255–56.

35. Göde provided a great story for Luther's table talk [no. 3769 in LW 54:269–70]. Henning was audacious enough to advise Frederick that he should not burn green wood at court. Frederick's withering reply was an old German proverb, *"Was in*

eurem Haus Rat ist, das ist in meinem Unrat," a play on words meaning "What in your house is good advice is in my house garbage."

36. Philipp I of Hesse was born November 13, 1504, in Marburg.

37. Discussion of the 1513 and 1514 events from Ludolphy, 256–59, clearly sympathetic to the Ernestiners, and Cahill, 23–30, who is just as clearly unsympathetic to the Ernestiners.

38. Cahill, 25. Philipp admitted later that it happened in an argument among playmates.

39. Because the testicles descend into the scrotum during development, there is an avenue that might later allow the bowel to descend causing a lump.

40. Cahill, 27.

41. Olivia Cardenas, "Albrecht von Brandenburg - Herrschaft und Heilige. Fürstliche Repräsentation im Medium des Heiltumsbuches" in Tacke 2006, 239–70.

42. Cristoph Volmar, "Zwischen landesherrlicher Förderung und persönlicher Distanz. Herzog Georg von Sachsen und das Annaberger Heiltum" in Tacke 2006, 100–24.

43. Ludolphy, 327, 328, 330, 348.

44. Ludolphy, 125.

45. Discussion of the construction at Hartenfels castle in Torgau and its previous history is from Bruck 1903, 14–35; Lewy 1908, 9–17; and Ludolphy, 125–28.

46. Lewy, 11. Two other features much noted in the literature are additions years after Frederick's death. Elector Johann Friedrich added the great winding staircase of wing C in 1536. He replaced an older Castle Church (*Schlosskappelle*) in wing B in 1544. Steffen Delang in Ullmann 1984, 221, noted this new Torgau Castle Church "consecrated by Martin Luther himself, became the prototype of most castle chapels of the sixteenth century in Germany" (translated).

47. Lewy, 16.

48. Scholars before Bruck 1903 designated the west wing as wing D even though it was probably the oldest wing. The others are respectively: northwest wing (A), northeast wing (B), and southeast wing (C).

49. Bruck, 23 (translated): "Under Elector Frederick begins from the year 1514 . . . new building of the wing called D as well as the eastern part of wing B."

50. Unless noted otherwise, life in Frederick's court is based on pages 76–116 of Ludolphy's section titled "Der Kurfürstliche Lebenststil" ("The Elector's Life Style").

51. An entertaining overview of most trades of the time is the classic "*Ständebuch*" of 1568, offered now as Jost Amman and Hans Sachs, *The Book of Trades* (New York: Dover, 1973).

52. Streich 1989, 507.

53. Streich 1989, 508.

54. Streich 1989, 516.

55. Ludolphy, 80: Still preserved today are documents for every year of Frederick's electoral court, detailed with patterns, fabric type, cost, and colored figures.

56. Streich 1989, 444 (translated).

57. Streich 1989, 486.

58. Ludolphy, 82.

59. Streich 1989, 513.

60. Spalatin, 31–32 (translated).

61. Ludolphy, 87. Because fish was desirable, especially for religious fasting periods, Frederick flooded areas off rivers to create ponds for fisheries. Stocked with carp and pike, these ponds were harvested every three years.

62. Ludolphy, 97.

63. Willy Andreas, *Deutschland vor der Reformation. Eine Zeitenwende*, 6th edition (Stuttgart, 1959), 579.

64. Buchner 1908, 160. Implied is that the Saxons had already convolved their trumpets, a highly sophisticated accomplishment in metalwork.

65. Beth Bullard, ed. and trans, *Musica Getutscht: A Treatise on Musical Instruments (1511) by Sebastian Virdung* (Cambridge University Press, 1993). Priest Sebastian Virdung of Amberg, a contemporary of Frederick, described the musical instruments.

66. Among the singers was Conrad Rupsch, who later led the vocal choir and is also notable because he became a friend of Martin Luther and even Luther's musical adviser.

67. One example of the contrast between Frederick and his brother Johann occurred after Frederick's death. Johann immediately released all the singers, though Martin Luther begged him to keep them. Years later, a still angry Luther groused, "Our gracious lords have saved 3,000 florins on music; in the meantime the king and princes have wasted 30,000 florins" (WA TR 2:518.8–11).

68. Discussion of the music at Maximilian's court is based on text by Philip Thorby (Senior Fellow at Trinity College of Music in London) provided for *The Triumphs of Maximilian*, a 1999 album he directed for Signum Records (SIGCD 004).

69. Ludolphy, 114 (translated). Printed in 1511 but read earlier. George Sibutus Daripinus (called Sibutus) was one of the poets crowned poet laureate by Maximilian.

70. Ernst Hildebrandt, "Die kurfürstliche Schloß- und Universitätsbibliothek zu Wittenberg 1512-1547. Beiträge zu ihrer Geschichte," *Zeitschrift für Buchkunde* 2 (1925): 109.

71. Ludolphy, 77–78. Also Tutzschmann, 12.

72. Spalatin, 52–53.

73. Streich 1989, 494. The sovereign's court never had female jesters.

74. Ludolphy, 95.

75. H. C. Erik Midelfort, *A History of Madness in Sixteenth-Century Germany* (Stanford University Press, 1999), 257. The best "contemporary" account (as well as most reliable of any accounts) of Claus Narr was written by Petrus Ackermann, the deacon and vicar of Weida, in 1536.

76. Ludolphy, 96. Staupitz knew Claus, and Luther knew of him. Claus was so sly and mean as well as clairvoyant that both thought he might be demonic.

77. Ludolphy, 96, citing Luther's *Table Talk* (WA TR 3:132.24f.)

78. Midelfort 1999, 260, from Peter Ackermann's 1536 account.

79. Midelfort 1999, 265, believes the choice of increasingly abnormal jesters was in response to the increasing sophistication of court culture: "We can see why dwarfs, cripples, and hunchbacks could also be counted along with the retarded as fools. Courtly culture was increasingly demanding a smooth behavior and appearance of just the sort that one could not expect of the fool."

80. No festivity allowed participation of all citizens as much as carnival.

81. Hubert Ermisch, "Eine Hofhaltsrechnung Markgraf Wilhelms I (1386)," *Neues Archiv für sächsische Geschichte* 18 (1897): 1–30. Detailed accounting records of 1386 show Duke Wilhelm (the Brave) stayed at eighty localities that year, yet was in Meissen for twenty continuous days during Easter and before that in Dresden for twenty-four continuous days for carnival.

82. Ludolphy, 92.

83. Ludolphy, 91: Frederick's nephew Johann Friedrich alone organized dozens of jousting tournaments between 1521 and 1534.

84. Kirn, 7.

85. Spalatin, 149.

86. Discussion of armor from Ludolphy, 92, and Grossmann, 120.

87. Lucas Cranach also preserved hunting scenes with Frederick (and later electors) with their elite guests such as Emperors Maximilian I and Karl V.

88. Streich, 496–97.

89. Described as long ago as five or more centuries before Frederick's time in *Beowulf*. An intricate ritualistic process evolved for the nobility all over Europe; it is described in detail by John Cummins, *The Hound and the Hawk: The Art of Medieval Hunting* (UK: Weidenfeld & Nicolson, 1988).

90. Discussion mainly from Ludolphy, 84–86.

91. Johann Gottfried Rüger, *Geschichte und Beschreibung des kurfürstlich Sächsischen Soldatenknaben Instituts zu Annaburg evangelischer und katholischer Religion* (Leipzig, 1787), 10 (translated).

92. According to Ludolphy, 128–36, the great mansion may no longer exist. The present town of Annaburg has a fine five-storied mansion that may originate from a later time or, as many scholars believe, may be an enhancement by the Wettins of Frederick's mansion.

93. Ludolphy, 132–33.

94. Stephan Hoppe, "Anatomy of an Early 'Villa' in Central Europe. The Schloss and Garden of the Saxon Elector Frederick the Wise in Lochau (Annaburg) according to the 1519 Report of Hans Herzheimer" in Monique Chatenet, ed., *Maisons des champs dans l'Europe de la Renaissance* (Paris: Picard, 2006), 159–70, details in English this lush complex of diversions.

95. Ludolphy, 328.

96. Preserved Smith, *Luther's Correspondence and Other Contemporary Letters,* vol. 1 (Philadelphia: Lutheran Publication Society, 1913), 33.

97. Grossmann 1975, 21, asserts Luther and Spalatin exchanged at least nine hundred letters.

98. Smith 1913, 47. Ludolphy, 389, cites WAB 1 Nr. 30 (14.12.1516).

99. Bernhard Lohse, *Martin Luther: An Introduction to His Life and Work* (Minneapolis: Fortress Press, 1986), 28–31.

100. Luther was not at this time prior of the Augustinian monastery in Wittenberg. That was Wenceslas Link (from 1511 to 1515).

101. Oberman 1990, 171.

102. Lohse 1999, 85–95.

103. Luther aired ideas with others besides Staupitz and Spalatin. According to Brecht 1985, 121–22, fellow monks Wenceslas Link and Johann Lang were valuable to Luther in shaping his thoughts. Humanistically-trained Lang especially was an original thinker. Luther often was inspired by Lang's ideas, which he then reworked independently. Notably, in a letter to Lang of May 18, 1517, in LW 48:41–42, Luther refers to "our theology." Both Link and Lang left Wittenberg in 1516 for new assignments.

104. Brecht 1985, 147. Also Höß, 80–81.

105. Letter to Spalatin in LW 48:17–18. Discussion of Luther's sermon and subsequent comments about Frederick from Ludolphy, 388–89.

106. Quotes from Bainton, 1950 (hardcover), 53–54. Also discussed by Lohse 1986, 42–45.

107. Lohse 1986, 41, believes Luther was unique among all his contemporaries in delving into the original meaning of the passages.

108. That a scholar who might be bringing new light to the world was a Saxon must have been a great source of pride for Frederick as well.

109. Ludolphy, 288, 351, 384.

110. Pope Leo X's allusion to Luther in his bull "Exsurge Domine" of June 15, 1520.

111. Lohse 1986, 30, 44, notes his theses against scholasticism were "much more radical" than the later Ninety-five Theses.

112. Harold J. Grimm, "Introduction and Translation of Disputation Against Scholastic Theology" in LW 31:5–16.

113. Much of the discussion on indulgences is from Lohse 1986, 42–45.

114. Bainton, 1950 (hardcover), 78, 87. In German from many sources: "*Sobald das Geld im Kasten klingt, Die Seele aus dem Fegefeuer springt.*"

115. Brecht 1985, 180–82.

116. Excerpts (translated) from Luther's 1541 "Against Hans Wurst" in *Hutten Müntzer Luther*, vol. 2, ed. Forschungs- und Gedenkstätten der klassischen deutschen Literatur in Weimar (Berlin: Aufbau-Verlag, 1978). Remarkably, in this same passage Luther states that Elector Frederick once intervened to save Tetzel, condemned by Maximilian to death by drowning. If true, Frederick intervened only because Tetzel was born a Saxon.

117. Preserved Smith, *The Life and Letters of Martin Luther* (Houghton Mifflin, 1913), 41–42.

118. Brecht 1985, 203.

119. Ludolphy, 60, noted Frederick began wearing eyeglasses in 1516. Spalatin and others probably read a great deal to Frederick.

120. Brecht 1985, 202–3.

CHAPTER 7: THE MARTIN LUTHER MAELSTROM

1. Spalatin, 33 (translated).

2. Brecht 1985, 204–5.

3. Kirn, 26, and Ludolphy, 361, among others. Steinlaussig is now called Muldenstein.

4. LW 48:43–49, letter to Cardinal Albrecht, archbishop of Mainz, October 31, 1517.

5. LW 48:50–52, letter to Elector Frederick, November 6, 1517.

6. Bernd Stephan 1982, 68.

7. Discussion of these early charges and countercharges are from Brecht 1985 ("Reactions to Luther's Attack on Indulgences and the Effect of the Theses" in chapter 6), 202–20, unless noted otherwise.

8. Smith 1913, 66, letter from rector and councillors of the University of Mainz to Cardinal Albrecht, archbishop of Mainz, December 17, 1517.

9. Boehmer, 202, states: "The Magdeburg councillors quite correctly concluded . . . that His Grace did not wish to be annoyed any further with the matter."

10. Account of denunciation by the Dominicans from Heinrich Boehmer, *Martin Luther: Road to Reformation* (Muhlenberg Press, 1946), 203–4.

11. Most scholars believe Tetzel's refutation of Luther was written by Wimpina (Konrad Koch), a former pupil of Mellerstadt.

12. Cahill, 41. Frederick shed few tears over Hessians, who had treated him badly during the long, turbulent regency.

13. Brecht 1985, 206. Brecht 1985, 204, also states, "Apparently it was not until February 1518 that Luther was aware of what he had touched off with his theses on indulgences."

14. Ludolphy, 398.

15. Höß, 127.

16. Boehmer, 181.

17. Smith 1913, 70–71, letter from Luther to Spalatin, February 5, 1518.

18. Oberman 1990, 192, pointed out that "Sermon on Indulgences and Grace" contained two of the three principles of the Reformation. First, the truth of any assertion must be tested and verified by Holy Scripture. Second, God's grace is unmerited. The third principle—God wants faith alone—would appear in public only four weeks later, just before Easter.

19. Brecht 1985, 209.

20. Brecht 1985, 214.

21. LW 48:60–63. Luther's account to Spalatin of the meeting.

22. LW 48:63.

23. Smith 1913, 82.

24. Smith 1913, 83.

25. LW 48:60

26. Boehmer, 211. Luther at this time was not at all plump (as he later became). Smith 1913, 261, translated a 1519 letter from Petrus Mosellanus to Julius von Pflug which describes Luther as being so thin "you can almost count his bones."

27. Brecht 1985, 211.

28. Schwiebert 1950, 336: In May 1518, Eck did seek reconciliation with both Karlstadt and Luther, indicating how scholars' hyperbole in print often went beyond their intentions.

29. LW 48:68.

30. Fife, 273. Official dogma of papal infallibility is a nineteenth-century event.

31. Smith 1913, 86.

32. Quotes from the tract in Brecht 1985, 212.

33. Boehmer, 213.

34. Events in Rome and Augsburg involving Luther and his process with Rome during the summer and the fall of 1518 are from Brecht 1985, 239–73, and Boehmer, 211–49, unless noted otherwise.

35. Ludolphy, 400, recounts the exchange of letters in July 1518 between Frederick and Cardinal Riario.

36. Demand for trial within the empire by an imperial subject was not an obscure loophole in the law. As recently as 1497, Maximilian had ceremoniously confirmed to Frederick that Saxon electoral subjects would have their day in a judicial court only before the dukes of Saxony and their *Amt* officials (Ludolphy, 157). Allowing anyone outside that privilege first granted by Emperor Sigismund in 1423 was a gracious concession by the elector.

37. Höß, 128. Also LW 48:70–73: Luther to Spalatin, August 8, 1518.

38. Ludolphy, 404.

39. Ludolphy, 329.

40. Martin H. Jung, *Philipp Melanchthon und seine Zeit* (Vandenhoeck & Ruprecht, 2010), 16. His Wittenberg colleagues were at first put off by his appearance. Only five feet tall, Melanchthon was mocked on the street by children.

41. Höß, 129. Because Spalatin's letters to Luther no longer exist, his letters must be inferred from Luther's correspondence with him and others. It is likely Spalatin was writing comforting letters to Luther, perhaps even sanguine letters about his negotiations with the imperial councillors. Höß, 129, believed Luther's letter to Spalatin (LW 48:73–76, August 28, 1518) indicated that Luther already knew by then that he would not be extradited to Rome but tried somewhere in the empire by Cardinal Cajetan. That conclusion is arguable.

42. Brecht 1985, 249.

43. Smith 1913, 105–6.

44. Smith 1913, 101–4.

45. Smith 1913, 106–8. Volta had been appointed that same year, "because Leo thought him the best man to deal with Luther."

46. Luther's August 28, 1518, letter to Spalatin, from LW 48:73–76; to Staupitz, from Smith 1913, 109–10.

47. Midelfort 1999, 61, warns *Anfechtung* is "often blandly translated as 'temptation.'" *Anfechtung* is anything but bland; it carries "the forceful idea of an attack, a miserable agony of doubt, verging on despair."

48. Wiesflecker 1991, 193.

49. Smith 1913, 98–100.

50. Ludolphy, 404.

51. Wiesflecker 1991, 194.

52. Oberman 1990, 195.

53. Spalatin, 37.

54. Wiesflecker 1991, 197.

55. Wiesflecker 1991, 288. In 1507, Maximilian had been so angry at Julius II refusing to crown him that he threatened, "I will move to Rome to become a pope and emperor at the same time."

56. Spalatin, 51.

57. Boehmer, 229.

58. Brecht 1985, 250. The following trip to Augsburg from Brecht 1985, 250–51, and Boehmer, 232–34.

59. Discussion of Luther's October 1518 meetings with Cajetan in Augsburg is based on the account in Brecht 1985, 252–64, unless otherwise noted.

60. LW 48:86. Letter to Spalatin.

61. Smith 1913, 118–20. Letter to Karlstadt.

62. Boehmer, 242: "*a papa male informato ad papam melius in formandum.*"

63. Many sources.

64. Smith 1913, 121–22.

65. Smith 1913, 129–30.

66. Reuchlin's acquittal, however, was only a temporary victory. Rome would later pursue the charges again.

67. Frederick was not passive but quietly pursued the opinion of great scholars. In spring 1519, Antwerp Erasmus wrote him (Smith 1913, 177–81): "As it is your Highness's duty to protect Christianity, you should exercise caution not to let an innocent man, under the protection of your justice, be sacrificed to the impiety of others on the pretext of piety . . . here his books are eagerly read by the best men."

68. Smith 1913, 125–27.

69. Quotes from Smith 1913, 125–27.

70. Smith 1913, 127–28.

71. Smith 1913, 127.

72. Smith 1913, 124–25. The pope provided Duke George with yet another name for Luther: "Son of Perdition."

73. Smith 1913, 143. "Drinking wine" was a proverb for letting all the troubles of the world go by.

74. Truth often has been lost under the flood of vituperative accounts about all participants in the Reformation, particularly lesser ones. Miltitz, long regarded a fool, is an exception. Heinrich Creutzberg, *Karl von Miltitz* (Freiberg im Breisgau, 1907) provides details of his behavior that were not just foolish but also irresponsible.

75. Buchner 1908, 156: Siegmund had been in the large contingent with Ernst and Albrecht to the great 1474 wedding celebration in Amberg.

76. Smith 1913, 134–35.

77. Discussion of Miltitz activity is based on the accounts in Brecht 1985, 265–273, and Boehmer, 250–59, unless otherwise noted.

78. Smith 1913, 136–37. Luther to Spalatin, December 9, 1518.

79. LW 54:55–56.

80. Schwiebert 1950, 369, citing Heinrich Boehmer, *Der junge Luther*, 3rd edition (Leipzig, 1939), 229. This 1939 Boehmer biography is not the source of the English version published in 1946, which unfortunately is a translation of the 1929 2nd edition.

81. Bainton 1950 (hardcover), 101.

82. Bainton 1950 (hardcover), 101.

83. Ludolphy, 35, notes that Luther (WA TR 2:556, 559) thought the knight Fabian von Feilitzsch had great common sense, more than any jurist.

84. Brecht 1985, 267.

85. Ludolphy, 212. Also the following discussion of Frederick's indifference to the *Vicariat*.

86. Kehrer, 234.

87. Discussion of the "Hildesheim Feud" from Ludolphy, 261–72, unless noted otherwise.

88. At one point Margarete tried to see Frederick, but he refused to see her, because he would not appear partisan as vicar.

89. At the June 1519 election meeting in Frankfurt, the electors would issue a mandate that the feud cease.

90. Discussion of imperial election from Ludolphy, 213–24, unless noted otherwise.

91. Baron John Emerich and others, ed., *The Cambridge Modern History*, vol. 2 (Macmillan, 1904), 41, estimates Karl spent 850,000 gulden on the election. Karl had also hired the Swabian League after they defeated Duke Ulrich of Württemberg to try to intimidate those gathered at Frankfurt.

92. Ludolphy, 212 (translated). It is somewhat revealing that Frederick in his German would use the French word *Aide*.

93. Ludolphy, 214.

94. Karl Brandi, *The Emperor Charles V* (New York: Knopf, 1939), 111, believed that Frederick was not "unbribable," actually accepting 70,000 gulden from Karl. Ludolphy, 219, could find no confirmation of this, suggesting reasonably that to ingratiate himself to Frederick, Karl had paid a debt left behind by Maximilian.

Spalatin, 133–34, specifically mentions a debt of 65,334 gulden that Maximilian owed Frederick.

95. Ludolphy, 216. The French must have choked when on June 25, Frederick politely refused their marriage proposals because of "another arrangement." On June 27, Frederick ordered his horses be held ready at Coburg for the return journey.

96. David Jayne Hill, *A History of Diplomacy in the International Development of Europe*, vol. 2 (Longmans, 1914), 330.

97. Spalatin, 162.

98. Ludolphy, 217.

99. Paul Kalkoff, "Friedrich der Weise und Luther," *Historische Zeitschrift* 132 (Munich, 1925, 29–42): 36. Kalkoff took this further by suggesting that the military presence of the Swabian League forced Frederick to refuse the victory. This thesis is almost universally rejected.

100. Hill, 346.

101. Yet the election satisfied Maximilian's most grandiose plan. The old warrior had not succeeded at all by war but by his much belittled over-reaching. Andrew Phillips, *War, Religion and Empire: The Transformation of International Orders* (Cambridge University Press, 2011), 85, asserts that in the fifty years from 1477 to 1527, Maximilian's seemingly haphazard marital alliances vaulted the House of Habsburg into a virtual hegemony covering central and western Europe. Habsburgs ruled nearly half the population of Europe as well as great financial centers and vast mineral wealth in the New World. The analysis of Phillips is too sanguine but captures the enormity of what ever-restless, ever-scheming Maximilian accomplished.

102. Hill, 346–47.

103. At the next *Reichstag* Karl did indeed cite Heinrich von Lüneburg and the bishop of Hildesheim. Anticipating this, Heinrich had handed his rule over to his sons and fled to France.

104. Discussion of Frederick's illness and Luther's "Fourteen Consolations" from Ludolphy, 58–59, 392–93, unless noted otherwise.

105. Spalatin, 37.

106. Ludolphy, 59: Even the following April, Frederick would write Cousin George, "I am not walking very well."

107. Christian Gottlob Lorenz, *Die Stadt Grimma im Königreiche Sachsen* (Dyk, 1856), 615.

108. Brecht 1985, 354–55.

109. LW 31:318–25, in Luther's July 20, 1519, letter to Spalatin.

110. Boehmer, 278. Duke George and his bishop of Merseburg were not always of one mind. Nevertheless, George, like Frederick, dominated his clerics.

111. Boehmer, 282–83.

112. LW 31:324.

113. Boehmer, 288–89.

114. Brecht 1985, 363: Luther had a much more sophisticated opinion on followers of Huss. He regarded radical Hussites as heretics, but he considered the moderate Utraquists only schismatics.

115. Brecht 1985, 320. Scott Hendrix, *Luther: A Very Short Introduction* (Oxford University Press, 2011), 9, noted that after the Leipzig debate, Luther actually read the writings of John Huss and shocked, he wrote Spalatin, "We are all Hussites and did not know it." He labeled his mentor Staupitz a Hussite as well.

116. Boehmer, 291.

117. Brecht 1985, 310.

118. Schwiebert, 415. Schwiebert offers, 384–437, an excellent treatment in English of the Leipzig Disputation.

119. Höß, 166.

120. Kirn, 138.

121. Brecht 1985, 342.

122. Discussion of the strengthening fury in Rome beginning in January 1520 is from Brecht 1985, 389–432, unless noted otherwise.

123. Ludolphy, 332.

124. Brecht 1985, 275–82, discusses the reform.

125. Brecht 1985, 282.

126. Brecht 1985, 282.

127. Schwiebert, 416. His literary production in the two years after the debate was enormous (Schwiebert, 438).

128. Schwiebert, 439.

129. LW 48:143–48.

130. From 1517 to 1520, Luther authored eighty percent of all the writings in German printed in the empire (whether authentic or pirated). The estimated output was 250,000 copies.

131. Oberman 1990, 42.

132. Among Sickingen's advisers were the calm Martin Bucer and the explosive, reckless Ulrich von Hutten.

133. Smith 1913, 338.

134. Discussion of "To the Christian Nobility" from Brecht 1985, 369–79.

135. Brecht 1985, 376.

136. Quotes from Hintzenstern in Straubel and Weiß 1991, 100.

137. Discussion of Frederick's journey in 1520 to the coronation and various encounters from Brecht 1985, 415–23, unless noted otherwise.

138. Brecht 1985, 416: This is known only from Erasmus.

139. Smith 1913, 421–22.

140. Boehmer, 366: Aleander despised Erasmus, whom he regarded the root cause of Luther's heresies.

141. Spalatin, 164.

142. Brecht 1985, 418.

143. The two nuncios were trying to burn Luther's books and tracts throughout the empire as they delivered the Exsurge Domine. Local clerics had frequently duped them, even in Cologne and Mainz, by burning papers other than Luther's.

144. This letter has disappeared.

145. Bainton 1950 (hardcover), 137.

146. This was not such a giant step. Parish clergy in the Roman Church in the late Middle Ages, though priests in name, were not necessarily highly qualified. Susan Karant-Nunn, "Luther's Pastors: The Reformation in the Ernestine Countryside," *Transactions of the American Philosophical Society* 69 (Philadelphia, 1979): 20, noted, "In 1471 Bishop Wedego of Havelberg had stated that men desiring a pastorate should be able to recite the Lord's Prayer and the Apostles' Creed; they had to know what the seven sacraments were and be sufficiently familiar with Latin to read the Mass. They were in any case to know more than the laity."

147. Brecht 1985, 423.

CHAPTER 8: NEW TEACHINGS AND A WORLD UPSIDE DOWN

1. Spalatin, 33 (translated).

2. Hans Küng, *Great Christian Thinkers* (New York: Continuum Publishing, 1995), 139.

3. Discussion of France's relations with the empire is from Ludolphy, 226–27.

4. As in Maximilian's case, in this narrative the title of emperor is used for Karl, though he was officially king until 1530 when Pope Clement VII crowned him Holy Roman Emperor.

5. Discussion of the non-Luther business of the 1521 *Reichstag* in Worms and subsequent activity of the imperial governing council (*Reichsregiment*) is from Ludolphy, 227–38, unless noted otherwise.

6. Ludolphy, 229: Frederick's session was the quarter from the first of July to the thirtieth of September, 1522.

7. Subsequent events would show how little interest Karl had in his German-speaking estates. According to Karlheinz Blaschke, "Kurfürst Friedrich der Weise von

Sachsen und die Luthersache" in *Der Reichstag zu Worms von 1521*, ed. Fritz Reuter (1971), 332, Karl was "an emperor who had left Germany for nine years and was fully occupied on the battlefields and campaigns of his war against France" (translated).

8. Ludolphy, 223: "*lieben Schwager.*"

9. Georg Mentz, *Johann Friedrich der Großmütige* 3 vol. (Jena, 1903/1908), 15–16, describes Johann Friedrich's activities at the Worms *Reichstag*. Fife, 615, 682: Also Johann had been at the *Reichstag* presumably for the jousting but had departed before the arrival of Luther.

10. Mentz, 16. Johann Friedrich improved over the years, although he later broke his thigh, which ached sporadically the rest of his life. Often his opponent was Philipp of Hesse. Johann Friedrich (born June 30, 1503), Philipp (born November 13, 1504) and Karl V (born February 24, 1500) were indeed contemporaries whose lives were intertwined for decades.

11. "German public grievances" (*gravamina nationis Germanicae*) were raised as early as 1456 by Archbishop Dietrich of Mainz. Humanist Jakob Wimpfeling consolidated grievances in 1510 into the form of *Gravamina* that came up again and again (revised) at *Reichstags*.

12. Discussion of the Luther business at the 1521 *Reichstag* in Worms is from Brecht 1985, 433–76, unless noted otherwise. Superb source for the *Gravamina* is Gerald Strauss, ed. and trans., *Manifestations of Discontent in Germany on the Eve of the Reformation* (Indiana University Press, 1971), 52–63 (Chapter 5: The Statement of Grievances Presented to the Diet of Worms in 1521).

13. Glapion was Franciscan. According to Karl V's biographer Brandi, 129, Glapion's eloquence was matched only by his duplicity. He lied to the Saxon chancellor, Gregory Brück, that he had long been sympathetic to Luther's proposed reforms.

14. Luther's journey to Worms is a story in itself. According to Leaver, 34, Johannes Cochlaeus, one of Luther's more vile contemporaries, reported the scandal that, "In the inns they [Luther's party] found many a toast, cheerful drinking-parties, music, and enjoyments; to such an extent that Luther drew all eyes to himself in some places by playing songs on a lute." It is no surprise Germans everywhere admired Luther and despised his self-righteous critics.

15. Brecht 1985, 450.

16. Brecht 1985, 439.

17. Adolf Wrede, ed., *Deutsche Reichstagsakten unter Kaiser Karl V.*, Jüngere Reihe II (Gotha, 1896), 844. April 8, 1521.

18. Bainton 1950 (hardcover), 184.

19. Brecht 1985, 460.

20. All quotes from Brecht 1985, 461–62.

21. Blaschke 1971, 335, considered Frederick's gushing approval of Luther's performance (to Spalatin) a turning point. Before Worms, Frederick's actions could be interpreted as the duty of a Christian sovereign to protect his subject. After that, such a neutral appraisal of Frederick's actions is not possible.

22. Spalatin, 29.

23. Quotes from Brecht 1985, 462–63.

24. Fife, 678.

25. Fife, 686.

26. LW 48:200–202.

27. Discussion of the "kidnapping" and Wartburg exile is from Martin Brecht, *Martin Luther: Shaping and Defining the Reformation* (Minneapolis: Fortress Press, 1990), 1–56, and Ludolphy, 436–52, unless noted.

28. Frederick would have been appalled to know Luther had already left a paper trail (to Cranach), even before the "kidnapping."

29. Brecht 1985, 475–76.

30. May 12, 1521, letter to Melanchthon (LW 48:215–17).

31. Ingetraut Ludolphy, afterword in Martin Luther, *Das Newe Testament Deutzsch* (Leipzig facsimile of 1522 Septembertestament: 1972) 1–7, explains in detail the development and printing of the first New Testament in the High German of the "Saxon chancellery."

32. Luther had left Worms escorted for a while by twenty knights in the service of Franz von Sickingen.

33. Albrecht was made a cardinal at the 1521 *Reichstag* in Worms.

34. Preserved Smith and Charles Jacobs, *Luther's Correspondence and other Contemporary Letters*, vol. 2 (Philadelphia: Lutheran Publication Society, 1918), 63.

35. Schwiebert, 522.

36. Brecht 1990, 29–30.

37. LW 48:350–52.

38. On January 6, 1522, the Augustinian Congregation at Wittenberg completely disbanded, but Luther had probably anticipated this.

39. Hintzenstern in Straubel and Weiß 1991, 100.

40. Bornkamm 1983, 65.

41. LW 48:381 n. 11.

42. Ludolphy, 448.

43. Bainton 1950 (hardcover), 210.

44. In Theodor Kolde, *Friedrich der Weise und die Anfänge der Reformation* (Erlangen: Deichert, 1881), Johann's letters to Frederick as early as 1520 and 1521 indicate he was more overtly receptive to Luther's reforms than was Frederick.

45. Kolde 1881, 42–44 (translated).

46. Mentz 1903, 30–31 (translated). The letter is now lost.

47. Black days pervaded Johann's residence in Weimar. In their four years of marriage, he and his second wife, Margarete, had two daughters, one stillborn son, and finally another son Johann Ernst, who was in line for rule. Margarete's health, however, failed after the birth of the baby, and she died October 7, 1521. A widower once again, Johann had four children ranging from eighteen-year-old Johann Friedrich to the five-month-old Johann Ernst.

48. Smith 1918, 2:90–92.

49. Smith 1918, 2:98.

50. Smith 1918, 2:100.

51. Ludolphy, 454.

52. Boehmer, 85.

53. Bainton 1950 (hardcover), 296: Years later, Luther mocked the practice, "And how does it happen that eighteen apostles are buried in Germany when Christ had only twelve?"

54. Bacon 2004, 158–59: the triptych in its entirety no longer exists. The center panel may reside in the Kunsthalle in Bremen.

55. These sculptures (by an unknown artist) are now at the rear of the chancel, Frederick on the north side and Johann on the south side.

56. Spalatin, 30.

57. Discussion of strife in the electorate, as well as drastic changes in Frederick's showcase Castle Church in Wittenberg, from Ludolphy, 444–80, and Brecht 1990, 25–136, unless noted otherwise.

58. Cousin George had reasons to be unhappy and angry. Unambitious brother Heinrich, little help to him in governing either Albertine Saxony or Friesland, was satisfied with an annuity and the districts of Freiberg and Wolkenstein. Friesland had been a thorn in George's side until 1515 when he sold whatever claim he still had to the Burgundians. Six of George's ten children died as infants or toddlers. One who survived was mentally unstable. All his sons would die before his own death in 1539. George's marriage alliance with Hesse became an embarrassment when his son-in-law Philipp began cheating on Christine weeks after their wedding. Philipp became a nightmare for George when he became one of the standard bearers of the Reformation.

59. Discussion on marriage of Saxon clerics draws from Marjorie Plummer, "Clerical Marriage and Territorial Reformation in Ernestine Saxony and the Diocese of Merseburg in 1522–1524," *Archive for Reformation History* 98 (2007): 45–70. Plummer notes the maddening tactics Frederick and Johann used against the bishop of Merseburg (and thus, Cousin George).

60. Discussion of Kramer is based on Marjorie Elizabeth Plummer, " 'The much married Michael Kramer': evangelical clergy and bigamy in Ernestine Saxony, 1522–1542" in *Ideas and Cultural Margins in Early Modern Germany* eds. Plummer and Robin Barnes (Ashgate, 2009), 99–115.

61. Andrew Colin Gow, *The Red Jews: Antisemitism in an Apocalyptic Age, 1200–1600* (Brill, 1995), 141–42. Kramer published a popular tract in 1523 drawing on the writings of Luther and others.

62. Among many sources, Helen Parish, *Clerical Celibacy in the West: c. 1100–1700* (Ashgate, 2010), 145. Parrish makes the point these nuns had appealed futilely to their families for help. Katherina von Bora was twenty-four years old, having been confined in the nunnery for nineteen years. Like thousands of other monks and nuns, she became "inconvenient" as a child at the age of five when her father remarried.

63. Discussion of the succession of *Reichstags* and the actions of the imperial regency council are from Ludolphy, 230–38 and 468–78, unless noted otherwise.

64. Ludolphy, 272 (translated). Letter from Planitz to Frederick, November 1521. This conveys the enormous influence Frederick had on even his fellow electors. It was more than his knowledge of protocol; it was his wisdom in avoiding conflict.

65. Planitz, a nobleman trained in law, excelled in diplomacy. He was clever, able, and utterly devoted to Frederick but never in a servile way.

66. Ludolphy, 468.

67. Ludolphy, 470: Von der Planitz was upset to learn Luther had returned to Wittenberg just as the *Reichstag* started. If Luther promoted some radical change while Frederick and his electoral officials were at the *Reichstag*, they were an arm's length from being arrested. Luther seemed oblivious to their vulnerability.

68. Höß, 250. Spalatin finished this overview of the ban in 1523. It was brief, and he ridiculed the lack of success that Roman threats carried.

69. Höß, 91: Spalatin also often served as Frederick's father confessor.

70. T. G. Tappert, *Luther: Letters of Spiritual Counsel* (Regent College Publishing, 2003), 192–94.

71. Ludolphy, 230.

72. Self-righteous Henry VIII had not yet begun murdering his wives. He had, however, been executing political enemies since 1510, one year after his inauguration.

73. H. G. Haile, *Luther: An Experiment in Biography* (London: Sheldon Press, 1980), 152–53.

74. Ludolphy, 471 (translated). Ranke, 270, quotes the count as also replying to George, "We perceive that your grace feels displeasure at insults to the pope's holiness and the emperor's majesty, and we thereupon make known to your grace, that we would not patiently endure insult or injury to the emperor's majesty, wherever we should see or hear of it."

75. That following spring, artillery of Hesse, Palatine, and Trier bombarded Sickingen in his castle Nanstein. The council forbade that action. Again it made no difference. Sickingen died from ghastly wounds in the attack. Sickingen had attempted what many powerful men in the empire were contemplating. Church property might be taken during the chaos of church reform. Philipp of Hesse had demanded four hundred knights on horse and two thousand foot soldiers from Frederick and threatened him when Frederick refused (Cahill 2001, 50, 80). Sickingen's volatile gadfly Ulrich von Hutten had earlier slipped away to Switzerland where at thirty-five he succumbed to syphilis.

76. For all his cynical ambitions and supposed worldly acumen, Clement VII made wrong decision after wrong decision. After France conquered Milan in 1524, the pope left his alliance with Karl to join other Italian forces and, of course, France. Then Karl gained a great victory over France at Pavia in February 1525, even capturing the French king, and Clement VII leaped back to Karl's side. The pope would ally himself again with France in 1526 after the French king's release, causing a split in the Roman Church hierarchy. During the sack of Rome by imperial forces in 1527, Clement VII was hiding in the castle of Sant' Angelo.

77. Both quotes from Ludolphy, 476 (translated).

78. Ferdinand also involved himself in the imperial governing council, violating the rules within its original order. For his own convenience he moved it from Nuremberg to Eßlingen. He had the audacity to try to draw Frederick back to the council in late 1524. By that time Frederick was virtually an invalid, most of the time resting at his hunting palace in Lochau.

79. Discussion of Luther's return and the subsequent three years from Brecht 1990, 25–135, and Ludolphy, 444–80.

80. Smith 1913, 102.

81. Gabriel Zwilling, as prior of the Augustinian monastery, had participated willingly with Karlstadt and the Zwickau prophets. He did recover his reputation, thanks to Luther. Certain proof of his acceptance was his appointment in 1523 as preacher in Frederick's beloved Torgau.

82. Disposition of the Zwickau prophets from Smith 1918, 2:81.

83. Ludolphy in Luther, *Das Newe Testament Deutzsch* (1972) discusses New Testament translation and printing. So does Schwiebert, 528–31.

84. Schwiebert, 527. Highly-respected Johann Bugenhagen became pastor of the Wittenberg city church in 1523.

85. Hintzenstern in Straubel and Weiß 1991, 100–101.

86. Schwiebert, 226.

87. Discussion of Christian II from Ludolphy, 274–79.

88. Seven years later, Christian II tried unsuccessfully to recover his kingdom.

89. Ludolphy, 312–13: In general, Frederick had delegated the small local areas of unrest to Johann, who in turn involved his son Johann Friedrich.

90. Brecht 1990, 150.

91. Bainton, 263.

92. Tom Scott and Bob Scribner, ed., *The German Peasants' War: A History in Documents* (New Jersey: Humanities Press, 1991), 19–24. The Peasants' War of 1524 to 1525 has a large literature. It was a colossal disruption in a time already choked with change. Discussion here, focused on Ernestine Saxony, is from Bainton, 260–84, and Brecht 1990, 137–94, but also Ludolphy.

93. Bainton, 263.

94. By March 1525, Müntzer managed to cause the citizenry of Mülhausen to vote out the old council and form a new "Eternal League of God."

95. Fritz Stoy 1928, 276–90, discusses Frederick's preference for Lochau and its details.

96. Höß, 256–60.

97. Höß, 267: Correspondence between Frederick and Dr. Pasca (or Paßka) was not suspect; it was well-known that Frederick's daughter lived with the physician.

98. Höß, 269–74: In September 1524, Spalatin tried to resign. He had become so important to Frederick in so many ways that he virtually had no private life of his own. Apparently his duty to be court chaplain and preacher was particularly irksome. Luther convinced Spalatin that he must remain.

99. Frederick's loyal friend Staupitz died that very month. The old vicar had finally found some peace, not as bishop of Chiemsee but nearby in Salzburg as abbot of St. Peter's since 1522. He had escaped the maelstrom of Luther, though he wrote his protégé in 1524, "My love for you is most constant, passing the love of women" (Smith 1918), 2:226.

100. Höß, 274.

101. Adolf Hausrath, *Luthers Leben 2* (Berlin, 1905), 13 (literally "bishops for breakfast, princes for a snack, and the knights for a nightcap").

102. Bornkamm, 365–66.

103. Karl E. Förstemann, *Neues Urkundenbuch zur Geschichte der evangelischen Kirchen Reformation* (Hamburg, 1842), 259, Letter 22 (April 14, 1525). Translation by E. Theodore Bachmann in Bornkamm, 375.

104. Förstemann, 275, Letter 47 (May 4, 1525). Translation by E. Theodore Bachmann in Bornkamm, 376.

105. Spalatin, 64 (translated).

106. Förstemann, 274, Letter 40 (April 30, 1525; translated).

107. Ludolphy, 456.

108. Details of Frederick's last two days are from Spalatin, 63–68 (translated), much of which is also in Ludolphy, 482–84.

109. Spalatin, 65; Ludolphy, 483. Also Smith 1918, 2:318: Luther knew of this too, writing, "He died in a gentle spirit, with mind and reason clear, after receiving the sacrament in both kinds, but no unction."

110. According to Spalatin, 44–45, Frederick at court in Saxony was hard on his servants, whereas "out in the empire" he treated them mildly.

111. Spalatin, 67: "*Nichts denn die Schmerzen.*"

112. Discussion of the superficial "autopsy" is from Spalatin, 68–69, and Ludolphy, 61–62, who drew on another more revealing report by Spalatin written in Latin.

113. The timing of the printing of Luther's supplement to "Admonition for Peace" titled "Against the Robbing and Murdering Hordes" was unfortunate. It justified in some ruling eyes severe punishment even after countryfolk were defeated. According to Bainton, 280, "Some of the princes were only too ready to smite, stab, and slay." Luther's loyalty to the nobility was one permanent blot on his reputation.

114. Smith 1918, 2:317–19.

115. Translated from Ludolphy, 373, who cites as her source *Table Talk* (WA TR 1:15).

116. Discussion of Frederick's funeral from Ludolphy, 484–86.

117. Leaver 2007, 149.

CHAPTER 9: THE HALF MILLENNIUM AFTER FREDERICK

1. Ludolphy, 62–63 (translated). The eulogy was composed in Latin by Melanchthon.

2. Summary of the "Peasants War" from Hajo Holborn 1959, 173–74.

3. Scott and Scribner, 201: The rebels, too, had been brutal, particularly to the unarmed religious. At Heldrungen they beheaded five priests. At Frankenhausen they coerced women into beating two priests to death with clubs.

4. Cahill 2001, 103–4.

5. Holborn, 174.

6. Scott and Scribner, 301.

7. Holborn, 174, emphasizes that *only one* German prince, Elector Frederick, had held hope of a peaceful settlement with the countryfolk.

8. Mentz, 39: Johann Friedrich, twenty-two years old and as fierce as Duke George was himself at that age, told the Albertine things that "he would rather have not heard" (translated).

9. Hintzenstern, 101.

10. Luther, who died in 1546, never referred to his protector as "Frederick the Wise."

11. Kurt Aland, 1960, "Wendepunkt der Weltgeschichte: Das Problem des Glaubenswechsels bei Konstantin dem Großen, Chlodowech und Friedrich dem Weisen" in *Kirchengeschichtliche Entwürfe* (Gütersloh, 1960), 25–26.

12. Boehmer 1946, 152–53, who himself concluded, "Thus Luther already understood Frederick quite well and formed a more exact estimate of him than any of his contemporaries."

13. LW 54:164 (1532).

14. LW 54:194–95 (1533).

15. Brecht 1985, 291.

16. Brecht 1985, 183.

17. Spalatin, 25.

18. Ludolphy, 172.

19. Likewise *"Tantum quantum possum"* ("Only as much as I can") became his supposed personal motto. Yet the only known link to Frederick is its use in *Table Talk* (WA TR 4:376) in which the phrase is noted as *symbolic* of Frederick. Joachim Camerarius, an acquaintance of Luther, used the Latin motto in his own writings (with no connection to Frederick).

20. Michael Bauman and Martin Klauber, ed., *Historians of the Christian Tradition* (Nashville: Broadman & Holman, 1995), 169. Although Ranke introduced ethical presuppositions, his new archival-based historiography nonetheless was a step forward.

21. Many sources: *"wie es eigentlich gewesen."*

22. On p. 301 of Thomas A. Brady, Jr., "Review: Imperial Destinies: A New Biography of the Emperor Maximilian I," *The Journal of Modern History* 62, No. 2 (June, 1990): 298–314.

23. Leopold von Ranke, *History of the Reformation in Germany*, trans. Sarah Austin. (London: Routledge and Sons, 1905), 168.

24. Ranke, 210.

25. Ranke, 269–70.

26. Ranke, 257.

27. One example is Marjorie Plummer 2007. Also Karant-Nunn 1979, 60, hints at Frederick's duplicity in his continual attempts to usurp the authority of the bishops but makes it clear that whatever Frederick did was overwhelmed by the magnitude of his successor Johann's overt usurpation of ecclesiastical powers. Brecht 1990, 269, stated it "was primarily during the seven years of John's reign, in fact, that the structuring of the Reformation did occur."

28. Wiesflecker 1986, 5:42. Wiesflecker at least knew the imperial activity of Frederick during the Maximilian years. Most other researchers prior to about 1980 were misled by examining the activity of Frederick only during the eight years of the "Luther Affair."

29. Wiesflecker 1991, 227.

30. Wiesflecker 1986, 5:36.

31. Wiesflecker 1986, 5:38.

32. Wiesflecker 1991, 269.

33. These scholars, nevertheless, are well aware of Frederick's agonizing deliberations and temporizing.

34. Oberman, 18. Bainton 1950, 99, foreshadowed Ludolphy and Oberman: "He differed from other princes of his time in that he never asked how to extend his boundaries nor even how to preserve his dignities. His only question was, 'What is my duty as a Christian prince?'" Ironically, according to Oberman, 20, Luther's repeated and severe attacks on Frederick for allowing old faith practices "blocked the future appreciation of the Elector as a 'Christian sovereign.'"

35. Oberman 1990, 32.

36. Schmid, 64.

37. Available in 1988 in this still unfinished "Middle Series" (1486–1518) of the *Reichstag* activity (*Reichstagsakten*) were 1488–90 and 1495–98.

38. Brecht 1985, 111–12.

39. The difficulties of Dr. Ludolphy's effort while residing in East Germany (DDR) can scarcely be imagined by western scholars. Although colleagues such as Wolfgang Ratzmann and Franz Lau encouraged her, Professor Ludolphy finally had to immigrate to West Germany to find a publisher.

40. Ludolphy, 487–88, concludes her life of Frederick.

INDEX

Indexed for persons and places in the main text only (i.e., no frontal material or endnotes). No biblical figures or saints are indexed. Also not indexed but marked as *passim* are two ubiquitous figures (Frederick the Wise and his brother Johann).

Luther's Works

American Edition, New Series

General Editor Christopher Boyd Brown

"This new series should delight scholars as well as engage laity and clergy." —Mark U. Edwards Jr., Harvard Divinity School

"Provides a tremendous service to historians, theologians, pastors, and students." —Amy Nelson Burnett, University of Nebraska—Lincoln

"Casual readers and those seeking to expand and deepen their knowledge of the Reformation will profit greatly from these carefully translated and edited volumes." —Robert Kolb, Concordia Seminary, St. Louis

Even now, amid the fifth century after his death, Luther remains an epochal figure in the history of the Christian Church, a prominent shaper of the religious and cultural history of the West and a provocative voice still heard and engaged by theologians, pastors, and laity around the world as a witness to the Gospel of Jesus Christ. The new volumes of Luther's Works in English will serve their readers with much that has proved and will prove its importance for the faith, life, and history of the Christian Church.

Concordia Publishing House is currently in the midst of an ambitious expansion of the American Edition to include an additional 28 volumes (now including Luther's postils). You can receive a 30% savings by subscribing to the series! Your subscription starts with the newest volume and you will continue to receive each new volume until the series is complete. Subscribers can purchase previously published, in-stock volumes at the same 30% discount.

For information on the newest volumes and on how to become a subscriber to Luther's Works, visit cph.org/luthersworks.

For information on digital editions of Luther's Works, visit logos.com/Concordia.

Concordia
Publishing House

www.cph.org • 1-800-325-3040

Christian Freedom

Faith Working through Love: A Reader's Edition

Martin Luther and Philip Melanchthon

In Luther's day, the message of Christian freedom was readily misunderstood by those whose focus was on worldly things rather than on Christ and the cross. Luther was not a politician; he was a pastor who found real freedom in the Gospel.

This new translation incorporates material on ceremonies not included in the text of the Weimar edition, as well as Melanchthon's summary on freedom. The book also includes a 40-day reading plan, introductory notes, illustrations, and a glossary.

(P) 272 pages. Hardback.

15-5184LBR   978-0-7586-3102-2

Martin Luther: Preacher of the Cross

A Study of Luther's Pastoral Theology

John T. Pless

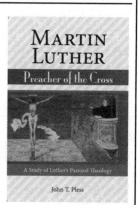

"This book is a significant contribution to pastoral theology . . . Pastors are entrusted with the task of being caretakers of people's troubled consciences and struggles in life; this book will again bring to the attention the truth and seriousness of pastoral care and ministry." —Klaus Detlev Schulz, Concordia Theological Seminary, Fort Wayne

Martin Luther was not only a theologian, but a pastor engaged in the care of souls. This new resource provides evidence for Luther's application of his evangelical theology to consciences burdened with sin, haunted by death, and afflicted by the devil.

Through the use of selected letters, *Martin Luther: Preacher of the Cross* presents compelling evidence for the reformer's application of his evangelical theology. Luther believed that above all else, the pastor offers spiritual counsel, and this is nothing less than speaking the stuff of faith.

(P) 144 pages. Paperback.

15-5090LBR   978-0-7586-1113-7

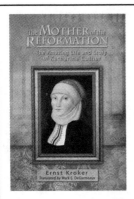

Faith and Act

The Survival of Medieval Ceremonies in the Lutheran Reformation

Ernst Walter Zeeden, Translated by Kevin Walker

"Faith and Act [is] . . . a mix of exacting research and historiographical vision that may justly be viewed as one of the foundation texts of modern Reformation history."
—C. Scott Dixon, Queen's University, Belfast

"Historians of liturgy and church discipline will welcome the reappearance of Zeeden's classic monograph, gracefully translated and with updated bibliographical references." —Ralph Keen, University of Illinois at Chicago

Prof. Dr. Zeeden's classic study of how Medieval Church practices continued and developed within Lutheran Church orders offers readers a unique perspective on how faith influences the act of worship. Historians of liturgy and theology will discover insights and important continuity between the Lutheran churches of the sixteenth century and their forebears of the late medieval period. (P) 186 pages. Paperback.

53-1182LBR   **978-0-7586-2701-8**

Divine Kingdom, Holy Order

The Political Writings of Martin Luther

Jarrett A. Carty

"Carty has wisely selected and intelligently abridged Luther's most important political writings from 1520 to 1546. His introductions to the selections are careful and insightful, written with a full awareness of the large secondary literature. . . . A highly recommended resource."
—Denis R. Janz, Loyola University New Orleans

The canon of western political theory has long misrepresented Luther's political thought, mistaking it as a forerunner of the "freedom of conscience" or the "separation of church and state," or an ancestor of modern absolutism and even German totalitarianism. These misleading interpretations neglect Luther's central point: temporal government is a gift from God, worthy of honor and respect, independent yet complementary to the purpose and mission of the Church. Spanning Luther's career as a reformer, the writings in this anthology will demonstrate his resolve to restore temporal government to its proper place of honor and divine purpose. (P) 544 pages. Hardback.

53-1183LBR   **978-0-7586-2711-7**

---

www.cph.org • 1-800-325-3040

Concordia
Publishing House